AWAKENING

NATHANIEL FRANK

AWAKENING

HOW GAYS AND LESBIANS BROUGHT

MARRIAGE EQUALITY

TO AMERICA

The Belknap Press of Harvard University Press
Cambridge, Massachusetts · London, England
2017

Library of Congress Cataloging-in-Publication Data
Names: Frank, Nathaniel, author.
Title: Awakening : how gays and lesbians brought marriage
equality to America / Nathaniel Frank.
Description: Cambridge, Massachusetts : The Belknap Press of
Harvard University Press, 2017. | Includes bibliographical references and index.
Identifiers: LCCN 2016041974 | ISBN 9780674737228 (alk. paper)
Subjects: LCSH: Same-sex marriage—United States—History. |
Gay culture—United States—History. | Gays—Legal status, laws, etc.—
United States—History. | Gay liberation movement—United States—History. |
Gay rights—United States—History.
Classification: LCC HQ1034.U5 F73 2017 | DDC 306.76/6—dc23
LC record available at https://lccn.loc.gov/2016041974

In memory of Frank Kameny, 1925–2011

―――――

For Dominick,
my husband

It's just possible that a small and despised sexual minority
will change America forever.

—Andrew Kopkind, *The Nation*, 1993

CONTENTS

Contents

Abbreviations

ACLU	American Civil Liberties Union
ACT UP	AIDS Coalition to Unleash Power
AFER	American Foundation for Equal Rights
AFM	Alliance for Marriage
APA	American Psychiatric Association
BAGL	Bay Area Gay Liberation
BLAG	Bipartisan Legal Advisory Group
CLIP	Colorado Legal Initiatives Project
CMC	Civil Marriage Collaborative
DOB	Daughters of Bilitis
DOMA	Defense of Marriage Act
FMA	Federal Marriage Amendment
FREE	Fight Repression of Erotic Expression
FTM	Freedom to Marry (the national organization)
FTMCM	Freedom to Marry Coalition of Massachusetts
GAA	Gay Activists Alliance
GLAD	Gay and Lesbian Advocates and Defenders
GLF	Gay Liberation Front
GMHC	Gay Men's Health Crisis
HRC	Human Rights Campaign (formerly Human Rights Campaign Fund)
IAV	Institute for American Values
LCR	Let California Ring (and elsewhere, Log Cabin Republicans)
LGBTQ	lesbian, gay, bisexual, transgender, and queer
MCA	Massachusetts Citizens Alliance
MFI	Massachusetts Family Institute

Abbreviations

NAACP	National Association for the Advancement of Colored People
NACHO	North American Conference of Homophile Organizations
NCLR	National Center for Lesbian Rights (formerly Lesbian Rights Project)
NOW	National Organization for Women
Task Force	National Gay Task Force (later the National Gay and Lesbian Task Force, and then the National LGBTQ Task Force)
VA	U.S. Department of Veterans Affairs
VFTMTF	Vermont Freedom to Marry Task Force

AWAKENING

PROLOGUE

MARRIAGE IS ONE OF OUR MOST PRIVATE BONDS AND MOST PUBLIC institutions. It is defined both by individual commitment and by social recognition. Getting married is a profoundly intimate act, a couple's pledge of their love to each other, but it also calls on a community to bear witness to that promise, giving the couple and their union a visibility and a sense of belonging that's difficult to achieve through other means. It is no surprise, then, that many Americans view marriage as a unique rite of passage, a key element of personal identity and community belonging, and an essential aspect of adult citizenship.

Yet if marriage can help bring lovers, families, and the community together, if it can thrust people into the center of mainstream society, it also helps define who lies outside that core, who appears as less than a full adult citizen. And as loath as we often are to admit it, we easily internalize the designations that marriage creates, allowing its marks of inclusion and exclusion to shape our very identities. The exclusionary dimensions of marriage have been especially resonant for lesbian, gay, bisexual, transgender, and queer (LGBTQ) Americans, who across the second half of the twentieth century watched as personal freedoms, including the freedom to marry, expanded for many groups while seeming to stall or even contract for them. Indeed, many LGBTQ people observed—and helped precipitate—the emergence of a dramatically new social landscape during this period, one in which their freedom to marry soon shimmered as a modern birthright.[1]

The most essential story about marriage equality—how it was won by a divided LGBTQ community, what the achievement meant to that community, and how this triumph changed America—remains untold. This book seeks to tell it. The question at the heart of the story appears simple: how did an idea that once seemed so unfathomable become, in just half a century, not only a legal right nationwide but a moral good in the eyes of a substantial majority of Americans? From a distance, the answer seems straightforward, too: gays and lesbians—and eventually their straight supporters—pushed for the freedom to marry, and won, while social and religious conservatives fought against it, and lost. Yet the real story is far more complex. In fact, battles within the gay and lesbian community were just as fierce as the fight against gay rights opponents. Perhaps surprisingly, the divisions within what we now call the LGBTQ movement shaped the quest for same-sex marriage as much as, if not more than, clashes with social conservatives. There was no monolithic movement working together to push toward a single, shared goal; rather, marriage equality resulted from a complex and contentious set of interactions among professional movement activists, gays and lesbians from outside the movement, politicians, cultural and intellectual leaders, straight allies, and the courts. Creating an effective strategy to win national marriage equality ultimately required forging a base level of unity out of a boisterous, unwieldy, multifaceted social change movement that resisted leadership by a single voice or organization.

The tensions over how to secure marriage equality mirrored an even deeper disagreement: whether marriage was worth fighting for at all. Many gays and lesbians—and most of those in the organized LGBTQ movement—were indifferent or actively opposed to fighting for marriage equality right up until the early twenty-first century. Similar clashes of thought arose from the very start of the organized gay rights movement in the 1950s, which staged often fractious debates about whether gays and lesbians should seek to join mainstream America or fight to fundamentally change it, about whether equality meant accepting the world as it was or transforming that world in ways that would liberate a wide range of people from oppressive laws, beliefs, and expectations. Inspired by the feminist, counterculture, antiwar, and black power movements in which many had cut their teeth, gay activists found their imaginations captured by the prospect of freeing themselves and their peers from outdated constraints, roles, and practices. Few sought assimilation into a broken world.

Indeed, across the first several decades of the gay rights movement, most of its members were working toward goals other than marriage: protecting gays and lesbians from violence, eliminating laws that made sodomy a crime and thus turned gay people into presumed criminals, fighting for child custody rights, and ensuring access to jobs, health care, and military service. To those working in the trenches of these harrowing social and political battles to protect the rights and very lives of gay people—most traumatically in the 1980s during the catastrophic AIDS crisis—marriage could seem like an impossibility or, at best, a distant luxury. In any event, as heirs to 1960s radicalism, many gay activists viewed marriage as bourgeois, constrictive, exclusionary, and—particularly among feminists—patriarchal. Outsiders to the mainstream, they hoped instead to advance an alternative vision of family and community. Some proposed entirely new legal arrangements that would recognize and protect relationships without replicating the privileged hierarchies of traditional marriage.

Yet dividing the LGBTQ movement into sides pitting "liberationists" against "assimilationists" would be reductive. Liberationist goals could coexist with conventional means of achieving them, while disruptive tactics could be deployed to win mainstream assimilation. Throughout its history, the gay rights movement has contained all these ingredients. Confrontational politics often helped awaken gays and lesbians to the full extent of their shame and exclusion, spurring a simple desire to be able to live like anybody else, while also forcing mainstream society to take seriously their claims to full citizenship, including—eventually—the right to marry. Conversely, the quest to eradicate stigma and discrimination by claiming equal dignity could unleash a powerful awareness of the broader suffering caused by ancient taboos, cementing a more radical commitment to achieving liberation for all Americans, not just gay ones.

The divisions among LGBTQ activists never disappeared. But over time, gay and lesbian leaders overcame them enough to build the unity necessary for their movement to win the right to marry. Achieving this end required something essential: an awakening by gays and lesbians to the full measure of their worth and to the new opportunities for belonging that a changing world held out to them. Starting fitfully after World War II, and then with increasing fervor across the social tumult of the next two decades, millions of gays and lesbians—both activists and those who never took a leaflet, carried a placard, or attended a meeting—began to identify as gay or lesbian, to come out of the shadows, and to insist on their equal worth and their right to be treated as full citizens. Throughout the last third of the twentieth century, many underwent a profound awakening that transformed their own view of the dignity and worth of their love and desires. As a handful of activists and a couple of states flirted with gay marriage, making the idea suddenly seem possible, more and more gay people began to wonder why marriage should exclude them. Throwing off the yoke of shame and stigma, they converted self-hatred into self-love and began to wrestle with what it could mean for their love to gain full recognition in both the court of public opinion and in courts of law. Having long viewed the right to marry as something impossible, unimportant, or undesirable, more and more came to see it as possible, even essential. It became both a logical and righteous end in itself and also the perfect tool to help the nation debate, ponder, and finally grasp the equal worth of same-sex love. Pushed, prodded, and exposed to a deeper understanding of what it meant to be gay or lesbian, the nation, too, experienced an awakening, with more and more of its people coming to see same-sex love as equal to any other love.

Winning marriage equality required two other essential ingredients: unflagging persistence and a coherent strategy. While the achievement may seem to have come out of nowhere, the process of awakening to, and persuading a nation of, the equal worth of same-sex relationships was actually the result of countless incremental changes that unfolded across more than a century, along with other transformations in the American understanding of family, identity, morality, and law. Just as gay people spent decades in the late twentieth century building toward a moment when access to marriage became possible, the enormous changes of those decades were themselves created by much larger historical forces, as well as the efforts of earlier social movements. Indeed, the dramatic shifts in attitudes about same-sex love by the dawn of the twenty-first century were spurred by sweeping social and economic developments that began in the nineteenth century, specifically the emergence of industrial capitalism and subsequent changes in social and family relations.

Until the nineteenth century, marriage had functioned as a system designed to control production of all kinds, including reproduction, a necessary tool for staffing the farmstead. Under these conditions, survival itself could depend on the enforcement of strict obligations to the heterosexual family unit. The migration of Americans from farms and towns to cities, along with the growth of wage labor, offered a critical mass of people, particularly women, a new measure of independence from those webs of obligation, creating the opportunity to build a life centered more around individual happiness than on traditional duties. The early women's movement took on the task of translating those changes into tangible advances for women and sustained critiques of male power over women's bodies—including repudiation of the idea that marriage meant subsuming women's identities under those of their husbands. Consequently marriage had already been transformed by these social, economic, and legal changes long before same-sex couples began pressing for inclusion. By the early twentieth century, fewer and fewer Americans sought to marry and start families with an eye toward securing a supply of farmhands and a subsistence living, or consolidating the property holdings of wealthy families. Most married for love, companionship, and support—both financial and emotional. If they married to survive, they also married to thrive, and their choices were shaped by the pursuit of happiness.

These shifts in the meaning and structure of family, and in the social and legal views surrounding it, did not make same-sex marriage inevitable. But by the second half of the twentieth century, the tectonic forces of modernity had created a new world of social and economic relations, one in which the rationale for gay marriage increasingly appeared no different from the rationale for straight marriage. Once this happened, only invented rationalizations could set them apart: that marriage is about procreation, and thus same-sex couples don't fit; that gay marriage would harm the institution because gay people would fail to take it seriously; that same-sex marriage is somehow bad for children and could even destroy civilization.

It fell to gay people to combat these myths by recognizing, and insisting, that their place in this changing world was one of belonging. These efforts often occurred organically, as ordinary gay people made themselves more visible and came to expect equal treatment in more areas of their lives. Some—perhaps thousands across the 1960s and 1970s—sought marital recognition in religious or social ceremonies, and a handful pressed their cases in court. Many others lived their lives as though they were married, referring to their same-sex partner as "husband" or "wife," sharing homes and chores, combining finances, and adopting the varied habits and social expectations of married couples. A number of them raised children together.

Still, coming out and coupling up were not enough to make same-sex marriage a reality. As more and more gays around the country awakened to the possibilities of full equality, as they came to realize that modern life seemed—logically, at least—to make room for them, a nascent equal rights movement began to make formal demands on the legal and political system, and to combat emerging, reactionary narratives of gay people as a menace to society.

Among the earliest participants in this organized gay movement were a small group of lawyers and legal scholars who reflected all the ideological tensions and conflicts of the gay and lesbian community as a whole. Starting in the 1970s, animated by the 1969 Stonewall riots against police harassment, these attorneys joined together to reimagine what their world could look like if gays and lesbians had the full protection of the law. Hardworking, fiercely dedicated, highly educated, intellectually gifted, and strategically sophisticated, the lawyers were mostly located on coastal cities, were liberal or left-wing, and were largely white. Eventually these attorneys, many of whom worked at a handful of nonprofit legal aid organizations, joined with gay legal scholars and some private attorneys working on gay rights cases to form the "Litigators' Roundtable," a close-knit group of two to three dozen legal thinkers who gathered regularly to share ideas about constitutional law and litigation strategy for advancing gay rights.

Although the Roundtable lawyers, with their unprecedented level of focus, coordination, and strategic prowess, would ultimately play the most influential role in obtaining marriage equality, almost none began their work fighting for it. Indeed, only a very few embraced marriage early on, while most came late to the marriage battle, viewing other priorities as paramount. Yet their persistent dedication to fighting for legal protections for gay people, which increasingly came to include recognition of same-sex relationships, helped over time to make marriage itself a possibility and then a reality. And so the story of winning marriage equality is a story of the unintended consequences that so often characterize how history unfolds. In seeking to transform their world to accommodate broader understandings of what family, community, and society should mean, the lawyers of the Roundtable ultimately helped reform—and arguably strengthened—existing institutions and social patterns, making mainstream assimilation—for better or for worse—dominant.

Despite the early resistance of many gay and lesbian lawyers, and the initial apathy or hostility of much of the larger gay movement toward marriage, a tiny marriage equality movement emerged by the early 1990s. It was propelled both by the awakening of gay people to new social and legal possibilities and by several developments over the previous decade:

custody struggles for lesbian mothers, the AIDS epidemic, and a surprise court victory in Hawaii in a case brought largely by movement outsiders. The new marriage movement consisted of these movement outsiders—"accidental activists"—who brought or backed or considered marriage equality lawsuits without the support or blessing of the gay rights movement, a handful of Roundtable lawyers who began to consider the value of such lawsuits, a couple of (mostly conservative) gay writers, and an unknown number of grassroots activists—who talked up, wrote about, marched for, and dreamed of a world where they could marry the person they loved. Such efforts put pressure on the larger gay rights movement, and eventually the nation, to take the matter seriously.[2]

Even this minute alliance had its divisions. Early on, the few Round-table lawyers who supported the push for marriage sometimes had to battle colleagues within their own organizations and comrades in the larger gay movement who opposed or declined to prioritize marriage. The legal organizations, due to a mix of ideological resistance and strategic caution, frequently declined to represent same-sex couples trying to win marriage rights in court, and even the pro-marriage lawyers discouraged the filing of certain lawsuits when they thought they were poorly conceived or timed, or felt the groundwork had not been adequately laid for a victory that wouldn't court reversal or a backlash. For their part, plaintiffs and would-be plaintiffs often viewed requests to respect a careful strategy of incremental change as needless snubs or inexplicable efforts to block progress. They and other grassroots activists who prized marriage as a movement priority were sometimes enraged when they encountered the cold shoulder of established movement groups with little interest or faith in advancing marriage, or at least in supporting their particular cases.

Over time, and in response to pressure from committed marriage proponents inside and outside the LGBTQ movement and to unexpected developments on the ground, the Roundtable lawyers took the lead in pushing same-sex marriage, having coalesced around a common belief: that fighting for legal recognition of same-sex relationships and for social recognition of their dignity through equal access to marriage was critical to advancing LGBTQ equality. Once united around the goal of marriage, the Roundtable lawyers set about creating a plan to win the freedom to marry nationwide through litigation, lobbying, and public education, a plan that ultimately would prove successful. Yet in the midst of combat, these highly cautious, strategic legal thinkers repeatedly found themselves losing control of the battles they sought to direct, as grassroots activists, couples seeking their day in court, and gays and lesbians who simply wanted equal rights charged ahead with their own plans to get married and—as one grassroots outfit christened its group—"get equal." Still, the remarkable ability of the Roundtable lawyers to collaborate effectively, air differences productively, respond to a changing landscape, and ultimately create the framework for a winning strategy to secure marriage equality is a key lesson in what makes for a successful social change movement. It was an incremental strategy—evolution rather than revolution—that won marriage equality, even as the goal was achieved with unprecedented speed. An edifice can be built slowly or quickly, but it must be built from the ground up, one brick on top of the next.

Marriage became a paramount priority of the LGBTQ movement, then, largely in reaction to developments outside the movement's control. But it was also a strategic choice, one made earlier by some activists than by others. That choice was a decision to advance LGBTQ equality by framing gay rights as a fight for equal dignity and for access to the most traditional ideas and institutions of American life: marriage, the military, family, and faith. The choice reflected a growing recognition that acceptance at the center of society was crucial to full equality, and that if the world could see gay people as fully belonging to the most mainstream of American institutions—if it could see them as assimilable—it would be impossible to view them as a subversive, destabilizing force in society.

That menacing view of gay people as a threat was pushed—increasingly in the last third of the twentieth century—by a conservative Christian movement that established a powerful new hold in American politics starting in the 1970s. The new visibility and demands of gay people created intense anxiety and backlash during this period, and the right wing saw any effort to gain equal treatment or to reimagine traditional norms with gay dignity in the mix as an attack on all they cherished about America. Erecting an empire known as the "religious right," religious leaders cast gay people as an acute danger to the American way of life, and helped spread a sense of moral panic about the challenges posed by new ideas about sexual freedom and equal treatment. In the 1990s, following a court victory in Hawaii that seemed to put gay marriage on a course to legalization there, anti-gay backlash widened, and the nation saw the passage of the federal Defense of Marriage Act along with dozens of state gay marriage bans. And back and forth it went, as gay demands and visibility spurred expanded efforts by social conservatives to clamp down on pleas for tolerance and liberation, part of the larger reaction to an era of social tumult and a new assertiveness by minorities and the counterculture.

If the religious right was the most vocal and active force in seeking to block gay equality, a quieter majority of Americans nevertheless looked upon gay people as unfamiliar oddities—alternately threatening and ridiculous—and viewed marriage as so obviously heterosexual as not to need explanation. As political and court battles began to question this assumption, more and more Americans began to perceive that their most cherished assumptions were under assault. Marriage felt to many Americans like an institution so central to their way of life that the effort by gays and lesbians to join it drew more starkly than ever before the battle lines for the soul of the American mainstream.

While the gay movement had not set out to make marriage central to its conception of either liberation or equality, the sense gays and lesbians had of being under attack awakened a response. The grassroots gay marriage champions and the professional legal advocates who had joined together—often uneasily—to push gay marriage to the center of the LGBTQ movement now worked to push it to the center of American life. The question of what place gays and lesbians should occupy within the American mainstream thus animated the fight for equality throughout the decades before and after the turn of the century. A handful of gay conservatives began to champion gay marriage as a natural embodiment of the conservative principles of family, stability, and responsibility. Gays on the left decried this notion—or agreed with it and hence steered clear of marriage. For many years gay marriage was considered too conservative a goal for the left-leaning gay movement. That interpretation was, of course, anathema to the religious right. Yet while the lives that gay and lesbian marriage proponents aspired to were hardly radical, and the tactics they used to achieve their goals were often conventional, marriage equality was largely indebted to America's liberal tradition of political protest. To reach their ambitious goal, the marriage movement drew on the rhetoric, strategies, philosophies, and legacies of egalitarianism, liberal jurisprudence, and left-wing social protest honed by the black civil rights, feminist, labor, antiwar, and student movements. It would take decades of social disruption, street rallies, political agitation, and civil rights activism to arrive at a point where same-sex marriage was even imaginable by a critical mass of movement activists, much less a legal reality embraced by a majority of the American people. It took sustained, relentless work to change millions of minds about who gay people were, what marriage meant and ought to mean, and how and whether gay people fit into it. It required battling entrenched religious hierarchies and social and cultural contingents that devoted every last ounce of their energy to defeating the inclusion of gay people and families in the fabric of American society.

As the following story shows, marriage equality ultimately emerged through a combination of ragtag lawsuits and uncoordinated actions by ordinary individuals and scrappy activists; incremental strategic work by gay and lesbian legal advocates; and the growing awareness—by not only straight people but gay people themselves—that same-sex love had a dignity no different from any other love and fit squarely into the contours of what modern marriage had, by the late twentieth century, become. Like so many chapters in America's long reckoning with civil rights, this is a story of progress and backlash, of carefully laid plans for cultural and legal change and improvised reactions to unexpected events. It's also the story of a contest of values among gay advocates—spurring an ongoing dialogue over the meaning and place of gay people in the American mainstream—and between those gay advocates and a variety of social conservatives who characterized demands for equality as an attack on the foundation of American society. Above all, the battle for marriage equality is a love story. Because no matter how political the battle for marriage became, no matter how pragmatic the focus on benefits and legal protections, no matter how dogmatic the arguments against including gays and lesbians in this central American institution, this was a quest by LGBTQ people to take themselves and their love seriously, and to have both recognized—unalterably, simply—as equal.

"Homosexual Marriage?"

THE STIRRINGS OF A NEW IDEA

IN 1963 A SCRAPPY LITTLE MAGAZINE CALLED *ONE* RAN A PROVOCATIVE story on its cover. In "Let's Push Homophile Marriage," a writer using the name Randy Lloyd argued that the nascent gay press was paying too much attention to the "trouble-causing, time-wasting, money-scattering, frantically promiscuous, bar-cruising, tearoom peeping, street crotch-watching, bathhouse-towel-twitching, and movie house-nervous-knee single set." Instead, he sought a little respect for marrying types. "The truth is," Lloyd wrote, "many of us married homophiles regard our way of life as much, much superior" to that of single gay men. The preferable path, he argued, invoking the term then in use for gay people, was "homophile marriage."

ONE was the first enduring gay-themed magazine in the United States, publishing monthly from 1953 to 1967. It published work by both women and men, but Lloyd's article was entering a debate focused mainly on the lives of gay men. He readily identified himself as "married" to another man; that his union was not legally recognized went without saying. It was a reflection of how common it was, even in the mid-twentieth century, for same-sex partners to identify themselves—and to live—as married couples, albeit without official recognition of their union. The point of Lloyd's article was not that the gay rights movement should lobby for access to legal marriage, but simply that living in a long-term partnership should be

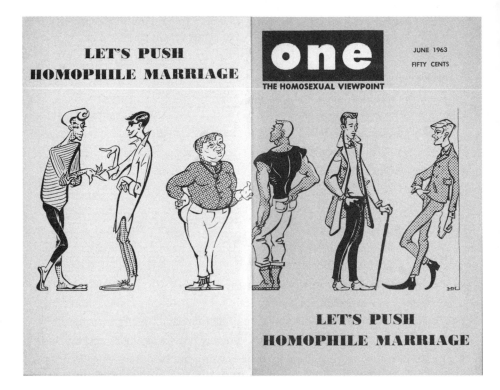

LET'S PUSH
HOMOPHILE MARRIAGE

one

THE HOMOSEXUAL VIEWPOINT

JUNE 1963
FIFTY CENTS

LET'S PUSH
HOMOPHILE MARRIAGE

The cover of ONE *Magazine in June 1963, fifty years before the Defense of Marriage Act was struck down, pushed "homophile marriage." The caricatured images of effeminate gay men reflect both the era's gay stereotypes and a self-image appropriated by elements of gay culture.*

viewed as a plausible, even preferable, option for gay people, and one that could help usher in gay equality.[1]

While Lloyd acknowledged the challenges of finding love in a homophobic world, too many gay people, he complained in a derisive tone that smacked of his own hostility toward gay culture, had "just plain given up the fight in a great big tizzy of petulance and despair," careening to one extreme or the other: celibacy or "cynical promiscuity." He saw the pursuit of married life as a path toward both self-respect and social approval.

Lloyd predicted that as social acceptance of gay people grew, the number of homophile marriages would grow. As discrimination lessened, he argued, "it is going to dawn on more and more homophiles that they can quit sneaking into bars, urinals, bathhouses, etc." and instead meet viable prospects for long-term relationships in more respectable settings. Indeed, Lloyd maintained that social acceptance and "marriage" would be mutually reinforcing. "It seems to me," he wrote, "that when society finally accepts homophiles as a valid minority with minority rights, it is going first of all to accept the married homophiles. We are, after all, the closest to their ideals."

"Let's Push Homophile Marriage" ran six years before the uprising at New York's Stonewall Inn that gave new energy to the inchoate gay rights movement, and neither the countercultural fervor nor the sexual liberationist ethos of that decade had fully taken root yet. The magazine's cover featured caricatures of elaborately dressed, swishing, flitting, effeminate men engaged in flirtatious banter, reflecting an internalization of the era's gay stereotypes. Indeed, as forward-thinking as it was, Lloyd's article pushed back against the more radical aspirations of urban gay culture, and in that regard, it struck an essentially conservative tone. It touted a conventional model of domestic life for gay people that repudiated the embrace of limitless sexual freedom and challenges to respectability that pockets of gay culture had already begun to valorize. Lloyd disapproved of sexual promiscuity and was not shy about declaring the coupled life morally superior to the single life. He believed that anti-gay stigma and exclusion from the institutional sanctions of marriage were partly to blame for gay male promiscuity. He viewed certain behaviors of gay people as immature. He believed that committed gay couples would be the easiest for the non-gay world to accept as virtual equals and seemed intent on winning such mainstream approval. Homophile marriage, he concluded, "is the most stable, sensible, and ethical way to live for homophiles."

Lloyd was a man of his time; he likely had no idea that marriage could ever become a legal option for same-sex couples. But in focusing on a certain set of gay social and sexual norms, he anticipated claims to legal marriage itself that gays and lesbians—both activists and ordinary people waking up to their full self-worth and the opportunities emerging around them in the second half of the twentieth century—would make in future decades in the course of pursuing equality.

That 1963 issue was not the first time that *ONE* had put marriage on its cover. The magazine had featured a story on the topic in 1953, a decade earlier. "Homosexual Marriage?" the magazine asked in white block letters on a green background. Written by E. B. Saunders—likely a pen name, like Lloyd's, since few would dare to publicly reveal their homosexuality in print—the story raised a prospect the author considered horrifying: that social acceptance of homosexuality would lead to homosexual marriage. If the new movement for gay and lesbian rights focused on normalizing the "deviate," he worried, it might also mean imposing on gay people the same constraints that bound heterosexuals—the very ones Lloyd would be happy to impose ten years later. "Equal rights mean equal responsibilities," wrote Saunders. "Equal freedoms mean equal limitations." And at this notion he was simply aghast. "The idea seems stuffy and hide-bound," he wrote, adding that "rebels such as we" join movements not to place limits on their liberty but to "demand freedom!" Gay men—Saunders's focus far more than lesbians—currently enjoyed unalloyed "sexual abandon." Were they—should they be—ready to trade it for respectability?[2]

Saunders's belief that marriage would stifle the freedoms that gay people enjoyed anticipated the sentiments of gay liberationist thought that would flower in the 1970s. But, having internalized a specific set of normative views common in mid-twentieth-century America, he also voiced what seemed then, and continued to seem to many people long afterward, like commonsense and even definitional objections to the idea of same-sex marriage. Those concerns contained nearly all the key ingredients of the battles over same-sex marriage that both gay and non-gay Americans would wage over the next half century. In deriding the prospect of homosexual marriage in favor of a vision of limitless freedom, Saunders laid out many of the thorny questions that heterosexual opponents of same-sex marriage would raise over the course of that debate. What about parenting? Would the state have to allow legally married same-sex couples to adopt children? What impact would it have on children to have two parents of the same sex? Would the existence of homosexual marriage mean that married gay couples would be expected to have children, much as heterosexual couples were? And what about gender roles? Would same-sex unions wind up blurring or eliminating gender expectations in opposite-sex marriages? In short, would marriage itself—and the larger gendered configuration of family—be irreversibly harmed by letting gay couples join the institution? "Heterosexual marriage," Saunders wrote, "must be protected," since no better arrangement had yet been devised for structuring the optimal family unit.

Viewing marriage as he did—as a way to structure gender roles and child-rearing—Saunders naturally considered it to be the exclusive purview of heterosexuals. And yet, almost unwittingly, he made a robust case for making marriage a top priority for the early gay rights movement. Homosexual marriage, he wrote, would need to be the "keystone" of any movement seeking mainstream approval: "One would think that in a movement demanding acceptance, legalized marriage would be one of its primary issues. What a logical and convincing means of assuring society that they are sincere in wanting respect and dignity!" Inasmuch as Saunders's logic bolstered the case for same-sex marriage, his argument, like Lloyd's, was a conservative one, anticipating the more extensive and sophisticated arguments that some gay writers would put forward more than a generation later. Saunders noted that marriage helped to foster stability, self-respect, and conformity to social norms. Even among "the most stable and respectable of homosexuals," he wrote, few couples remained committed to each other over the long run, a phenomenon exacerbated by their systematic exclusion from the expectations of marriage. Saunders was no supporter of monogamy—or marriage—for gay people. But his article ultimately made one point abundantly clear: since the public associated gay people with promiscuity and lax social norms, the best way to make homosexuality acceptable was to bring about homosexual marriage.

The very idea that marriage could apply to same-sex couples emerged in tandem with the growth of an anti-gay ideology whose zeal and reach were also new. Indeed, secrecy, stigma, shame, and invisibility may have appeared to be permanent features of gay life when they came under fire by early gay advocates and writers starting in the 1950s. But they weren't. The historian George Chauncey has uncovered the presence of surprisingly confident—occasionally even visible—subcultures of gay men and lesbians who, along with a wide range of gender-nonconforming social outlaws, thrived in pockets of early twentieth-century America. Certainly laws and attitudes in the first half of the twentieth century suppressed both gender outlaws and any expression of same-sex desire. Overt homosexuality brought with it considerable risk of social exclusion, job loss, intimidation, violence, and even jail. Yet punitive laws and customs were unevenly enforced, were in some cases less restrictive than they became later in the century, and reflected the sense that sexual minorities were more of an oddity or a nuisance than a genuine threat.[3]

In big cities especially, gay men and women had considerable opportunities to flourish. They built a culture with a coded language and a set of signs and behaviors that allowed them to identify one another and socialize in relative safety, all while remaining part of the larger mainstream society around them. In 1920s New York, bars, nightclubs, performance spots, and social networks were the locus of cross-class and often interracial same-sex liaisons, relationships, and friendships. Middle-class curiosity-seekers attended Harlem drag balls where they mingled with drag queens, nances, and other self-styled "degenerates," and watched ministers from the community preside over elaborately ritualized same-sex weddings—without, of course, the force of law.[4] Lesbian relationships were sometimes more tolerated during this period than they came to be later. The term "Boston marriages" referred to close companionships among unmarried women that may have had a romantic or sexual component. In several big cities, lesbians operated many of the best coffeehouses and tearooms in the most fashionable districts, spaces that were frequented by a mix of gay and non-gay patrons considering themselves sophisticated for being in the presence of the queer set.[5]

The relative openness of gay life in the first third of the twentieth century was shattered as the Jazz Age under Prohibition gave way to the Great Depression, the start of a massive, decades-long process of redefining same-sex desire and gender nonconformity as a threat to the American way of life. Much of the opposition to gay and lesbian freedom was rooted in a broader resistance to sexual freedom that was a response to both economic anxiety and the loosening gender roles of the early twentieth century. The economic turmoil of the Depression exacerbated these concerns in particular among men, whose role as provider suddenly became insecure. Many began to see gay and gender-nonconforming individuals, alongside working or ambitious women, as challenges to their survival. Economic fears were matched by social and psychic ones, as some came to view the Depression as a direct result of the hedonistic Jazz Age, with gay culture standing as a symbol of such decadence at its most unrepentant.[6]

The attempt to render all aspects of gay culture invisible was part of a larger effort by the government to make gayness disappear from the public sphere during the middle third of the twentieth century.[7] Ironically, World War II helped both to strengthen gay identity and community and to prompt a brutal crackdown on any expression of either.

The massive mobilization for military operations meant that millions of young men were suddenly thrown together in often intense, intimate, all-male settings. Their travels through both major U.S. port cities and foreign countries exposed them to new experiences of personal freedom, social innovation, and cultural experimentation—awakening many to the exciting new prospect of belonging to a community of like-minded men.[8]

The same was true for women. Not only did many young lesbians find themselves surrounded by other lesbians when they volunteered to join the newly created Women's Army Corps, but the military mobilization of men left millions of jobs ordinarily taken by men suddenly open to women. This development accelerated a shift in gender roles that had begun in the 1920s with the "flapper," and the realignment had profound implications. Women felt newly empowered as their demonstrated ability to step into traditionally male workplace roles furthered the demise of stereotypes and assumptions about women's limited capacities. The notion that women might not need to depend on men for their economic sustenance gave limitless new potential to the lives of women, signaling to millions that women could live truly independent lives, as either single heterosexuals, working married women, or lesbians. In this sense the growth of lesbian identity and community was bound up with broader advances in women's rights, indebted, to some extent, to the exigencies of world war.[9]

At the same time, the war also accelerated a key shift in understandings of sexuality that had begun earlier in the century. Previously seen as a fallen act to which anyone could occasionally succumb, homosexuality became an identity that defined who a person was. During the war, the military sought to screen twenty million young male draftees to determine who was suitable and who was likely to compromise the mission through immorality or disloyalty. This meant going beyond punishing isolated acts of sodomy; it required identifying the kinds of people who were too risky to induct, hence defining gay men as a class of people who must be pushed outside the bounds of American respectability. Enlisting the burgeoning psychiatric profession to help separate the good citizens from the undesirables, the military authorized "the wholesale discharge of suspected perverts" who were henceforth deemed unfit for service and, by extension, for full American citizenship.[10]

This shift in emphasis from behavior to identity made it both easier and harder for gay people to advance. The emerging "minority model" of gay identity helped many gay people envision power in numbers. The idea that gays and lesbians were members of a distinct group, like African Americans or ethnic or religious minorities, enabled a positive, more hopeful perspective on the prospects of eventual majority tolerance, especially as the early black civil rights movement was beginning to organize and make a similar case. And the ability of many gay people to see and meet other gay people helped confirm for them the righteousness of their cause. Ironically, by insisting that same-sex desire was an essential component of identity—and one that should be used to screen, mark, and exclude a whole swath of the population from civilized society—the government during and after World War II was instrumental in creating the momentum toward gay rights that authorities had hoped to quash.[11]

Yet in the decades before that momentum translated into tangible gains—much less a successful marriage equality movement—the government at the federal, state, and local levels played a major hand in driving homosexuality and gender nonconformity out of the public realm, spawning some of the most hateful, repressive, and destructive attitudes and laws regulating gay and lesbian citizens that the nation had ever witnessed. In 1950 Joseph McCarthy's name became synonymous with "witch hunts" designed to root out communists from positions of power. But the gravest damage from his attacks was visited upon gays and lesbians, whom he targeted as perhaps the most dangerous and threatening presence in the government. McCarthy's assertion of a homosexual infiltration prompted a Senate committee investigation, which found that "sex perverts" in the government had become a "corrosive influence" and security risk because they were prone to blackmail and lacked "the emotional stability of normal persons."[12]

In 1953, the year *ONE* published the Saunders article, President Dwight Eisenhower, following the Senate's recommendation, signed an executive order banning "sexual perversion" anywhere in government. Thousands of government employees lost their jobs or job prospects as a result. Congress also passed legislation requiring that immigrants and even travelers seeking to enter the United States swear an oath that they were neither communist nor gay. The measures were part of what became known as

the "lavender scare," a deliberate effort to tie homosexuality and commu-
nism together in the public imagination as an enemy mind-set, and thus
to depict gays and communists (often imagined as one and the same) as
outside the bounds of American citizenship.[13]

State laws against sodomy and certain kinds of free association
inherently criminalized gay life, but the impact of those laws went further,
forming the basis for discrimination and even purges by private employers,
which not only made every gay person vulnerable to economic ruin but
also impeded the growth of a gay social or political movement because it
raised the risks of being visibly gay. Making matters worse, after the war,
states began passing additional laws referring "sexual deviants" to psychiatrists who had the authority to institutionalize them against their will. In
1952 the American Psychiatric Association (APA), whose members had assisted the military in screening out gay men from service during World
War II, first classified homosexuality as a mental disorder, calling it a "so-
ciopathic personality" without bothering to gather evidence of any actual
symptoms.[14] With little self-awareness of how bias and a deeply moral
overlay had infected their judgment, psychiatrists touted their ability to
"cure" homosexuals with procedures that included electric shock, hor-
mone injections, lobotomy, and even castration.[15]

Urban police forces joined the federal and state governments in relentlessly quashing a gay presence in the public sphere. As early as 1923, New
York State had banned gay men from gathering in public places.[16] Over the
next forty years, more than 50,000 New York men were arrested for this
offense, far more than were prosecuted for the felony of sodomy. Swept
up in Cold War anxiety and hatred of perceived outsiders, urban police
forces not just in New York but also in Los Angeles, Chicago, Philadelphia,
Washington, D.C., St. Louis, and other big cities stepped up enforcement,
including constant raids of the gay and lesbian bars and social spots that
were proliferating at mid-century. At times vice squads hauled in more gay
men than the courts could process.[17]

The tiny gay rights movement emerging in the 1950s—as well as the
broader but still limited group of Americans who identified as gay or lesbian and attended gay bars and other social gathering places—was thus
shaped by the constant interplay of concealment and the push for visibility,
of repression and the nascent assertion of a rights-bearing gay identity.
The ubiquitous presence of the police as the face of anti-gay repression

and a constraint against these first ventures out of the closet framed the experiences of the gay rights movement in profound ways from its start. Just at the moment when an increasing number of gays and lesbians began to identify and behave as a distinct minority with a claim to all the rights of American citizenship, the Cold War "pervert" menace loomed everywhere.

Gays and lesbians sought safety from such persecution in two distinct but overlapping refuges: bars and political organizing. Gay bars and nightclubs in big cities had long offered opportunities to converse, dance, find partners, and hire hustlers. Many were owned and operated by organized-crime figures. Some catered exclusively to gays and lesbians (often one or the other), while others were known as sympathetic, or welcomed gay patrons on particular nights. Police raids were routine, with managers issuing warnings when they could by blinking on and off the lights, signaling that patrons should stop dancing, separate, or depart. Payoffs to the police were an integral part of the raids, as were the humiliation and arrest of patrons, something more likely to befall those who were nonwhite and / or gender-nonconforming.[18]

In the 1950s, gay and lesbian bars and social clubs multiplied, all the while contending with increasing crackdowns spurred by Cold War paranoia. In this climate, some activists, often conferring at bars or coffeehouses, began contemplating efforts to organize through newsletters and political societies. *ONE* was published by members of the Mattachine Society, a secret organization founded in Los Angeles in 1951 under the leadership of Harry Hay. Mattachine had to operate under the radar, with members taking oaths of secrecy. "We had to be very, very careful," Hay recalled, "because if we made a mistake and got into the papers in the wrong way, we could hurt the idea of a movement for years to come." Hay and his cofounders were highly conscious of creating a movement, as these words reveal, and took seriously the obligation to make it both safe and enduring.[19]

Hay was aware that several changes were needed for his movement to see effective results. First, homosexuals needed to change their self-image, instilling in themselves a "new pride—in belonging, and in participating in the cultural growth and the social achievements of the homosexual minority." That language contained another radical idea for the time, one that Lloyd took up when referring to gay people as "a valid minority with minority rights": that homosexuals were not simply isolated deviates but part of a naturally existing minority group deserving of the same recognition, rights, and protections as any other minority. The growing visibility of black identity and the black civil rights movement was a particular inspiration for Hay, who absorbed from his study of that struggle a third key principle of change: an understanding of the role of identity consciousness and social solidarity in the rise of social movements. And by raising consciousness among gay people as a distinct minority worthy of equal treatment, a fourth ingredient might emerge: a concrete political agenda that allowed gay people, by learning to press the right levers of power, to "renegotiate the place" of homosexuals in the larger society. "What we had to do was to find out who we were," he once said. "What we were for would follow."[20]

The Mattachine Society eventually developed a reputation among younger gay activists for being timid, conservative, and overly focused on mainstream assimilation, in part because of reactionary leadership. Yet Hay himself and the earliest incarnation of the society were pathbreaking. Hay wanted respect for homosexuals, but not at the cost of conformity, and he sought the approval of non-gay society "for our differences not for our sameness to heterosexuals."[21] Unlike many of his peers, he did little to conceal his true identity, enduring the scorn of his fellow communists, who were appalled by his relative openness.[22] His willingness to express his authentic self publicly, to synthesize the lessons of history, to organize his fellow homosexuals, and to contemplate a political role in advancing the well-being of gay people lent great staying power to his early leadership, even when his organization initially petered out.

Nineteen fifty-one also saw the publication of a book that shook the earth for gay people who read it. *The Homosexual in America* was written by Edward Sagarin under the pen name Donald Webster Cory. Like Hay, Sagarin, a sociology professor in New York City, had a wife and family. His book, which went through seven printings, was a blunt critique not just of the provincial homophobia and antisexual culture of straight America but also of the complicity and internalized shame of its gay citizens. "There is surely no group of such size, and yet with so few who acknowledge that they belong," he wrote in a call to consciousness for gay America. Prejudice, he noted, "is most demoralizing when we homosexuals realize to what extent we have accepted hostile attitudes as representing an approximation of the truth." Tying the struggle for gay equality, as Hay had, to that of African Americans and women, Sagarin argued that while the prejudices of the dominant culture were reprehensible, only the persecuted minorities could do something about it.[23]

What that required was full consciousness by gays and lesbians of their equal worth as members of a legitimate minority. The most important thing for gay people to do, he argued, was to shed their invisibility by coming out. If gays and lesbians became as recognizable as other minority members, he contended, stereotyped thinking "would collapse of its own absurdity." Imagine, he exhorted, "if only all of the inverts, the millions in all lands, could simultaneously rise up in our full strength!" That he wrote from behind a pen name was a testament to just how unlikely such an eventuality seemed at the time. Indeed, it was ironic counsel coming from a man who lived and died in the closet—married to a woman while carrying on secret affairs with other gay men.[24] Still, Sagarin's book was groundbreaking for its bold depiction of gay people as sympathetic figures who, through claims to social and political equality, might one day occupy a legitimate place in the American mainstream.

As the 1950s wore on, some activists took Sagarin's advice to heart, willing to show their faces publicly as a necessary part of claiming legal and political equality as part of their birthright. Franklin Kameny had a Ph.D. in astronomy but in 1957 was fired from his job at the U.S. Army Map Service after his employers learned he had been arrested for disorderly conduct as the result of a public restroom solicitation. So Kameny sued, in one of the earliest lawsuits that positioned the U.S. Constitution as a document that applied to gay people and ought to guarantee them equal protection of the law. His suit failed when the Supreme Court declined to take his case, and the loss of his job left him penniless and hungry.[25]

Kameny, who seemed to have a preternatural certainty that there was nothing wrong with his homosexuality, went on to start a Washington, D.C., chapter of Mattachine, one that took the name but little else from that largely defunct organization. Along with his cofounder, Jack Nichols, Kameny set about radicalizing an inchoate movement known more for being tentative than for seeking confrontation. They forged an alliance with Barbara Gittings, who had started a New York chapter of Daughters of Bilitis (DOB), the first lesbian organization in the United States, and the coalition soon grew into a larger group, the East Coast Homophile Organizations.

DOB was cofounded by the San Francisco couple Del Martin and Phyllis Lyon in 1955, and its publication *The Ladder* was the first nationally distributed lesbian magazine in the United States. When Martin and Lyon first met around 1950, while working for a construction trade journal in Seattle, Lyon had hardly ever heard the word *lesbian*. One night over drinks the subject came up, and Martin held court, impressing Lyon with her intimate knowledge. "How come you know so much about these people?" Lyon asked. "Because I am one," came Martin's reply. But it was not easy to find other lesbians. DOB was their answer.[26]

Finding other lesbians was certainly a challenge for Edie Windsor. Raised in Philadelphia as Edith Schlain, Windsor became engaged at a young age to her older brother's best friend, Saul Windsor. During the engagement, she fell in love with a woman and tried to call off the wedding, but Saul was persistent and eventually she gave in.[27] The marriage didn't last a year. "Honey," she told Saul, "you deserve more, and I need something else." She was divorced at twenty-three. The year was 1952.[28]

Shortly after her divorce, Windsor moved to New York to, as she put it, "be a lesbian." Here she could find the early stirrings of a cultural and social flowering for lesbians and gay men. One day, flipping through a short paperback about a lesbian schoolteacher who spent a summer in New York looking for love, Windsor was struck by the story's sense of promise. Dressed in her cutest outfit and primping in the mirror, the protagonist feels the palpable excitement of adventure in the big city. "You're in New York, where anything can happen," she tells herself, wondering just what might befall her. When she finally answers her own query—"I could kiss a woman!"—Windsor practically exclaimed to herself out loud, "Where!?"[29] Living in the heart of Greenwich Village, Windsor began coming out, and going out—to lesbian bars night after night to dance, read magazines, and meet women. She had taken a job at IBM as a computer systems consultant. There she had close friends, but none who knew her secret. "Everyone lived in the closet," she said of that era, and it was often lonely.

While restaurants and coffee shops catering to lesbians were sprouting up in various cities throughout the 1950s, their emergence accelerated in the 1960s. It was early in that decade, at a restaurant called Portofino in Greenwich Village, where Fridays were known as lesbian night, that a friend introduced Windsor to Thea Spyer, the well-born daughter of Dutch Jewish pickle-makers, and a clinical psychologist. With a group of women, the two then moved on to a nearby apartment where they danced the night away, stopping only when Windsor had danced a hole in her stocking. Spyer was the first lesbian, Windsor thought, who knew how to lead. Still, they didn't become a couple for two more years, after Windsor hatched a plan to show up at a house in the Hamptons, which she heard Spyer would be visiting. "Is your dance card full?" Windsor asked Spyer, remembering that she was "wild for her" from the start.[30] "It is now," was the reply. The next summer they were renting their own house together, and soon—never mind the law—they were engaged.[31]

It was, of course, a long engagement. Same-sex marriage wasn't legal anywhere in the world, and wouldn't be for thirty-four more years. And the climate for same-sex couples was deeply hostile for most of that period. Although Windsor was out to other lesbians, she was still in the closet to most of the world. Simply going to gay or lesbian bars meant a serious risk of exposure, which could mean losing a career, family, friends—everything. When Spyer proposed, Windsor opted not to wear an engagement ring, fearing inquiries at work about a husband. Spyer gave her a diamond pin instead. They would mark their commitment quietly and in private.[32]

If Windsor and Spyer had a low-key engagement, elsewhere gays and lesbians were tired of doing things quietly. In the early 1960s, the sense of possibility and change was everywhere—helping, perhaps, to explain the optimism of Lloyd's vision of "homophile marriage." Across the decade, and increasingly during its latter half, not just gay people but a whole generation of young people were awakening to the promise of securing rights and dignity long denied to many segments of the American population. Reflecting internal tensions that carried through all aspects of the era's social protest movements, activists' tactics and goals varied based on differences of class, age, race, and personality, which shaped the often divergent assumptions that different groups and individuals brought to their work. Those with little to lose might more readily translate feelings of powerlessness into a disruptive politics, while those with more privilege might focus less on basic rights and more on the wish to secure respectability.

Setting the early tone for the decade's activism was the black civil rights movement, which had won a dramatic victory in 1954 with the Supreme Court's *Brown v. Board of Education* decision outlawing school segregation, followed by the Montgomery bus boycotts that integrated public buses in that city and elsewhere. Starting in 1960 with a string of sit-ins in southern cities, that movement entered a new, more assertive phase of protest and direct action that drew in thousands of young blacks and whites suddenly willing to challenge long-standing patterns of social authority and hierarchy.

Inspired by the strategies and successes of the black civil rights movement—along with international and cultural developments including the escalation of the U.S. role in Vietnam—Americans of all stripes began turning the decade into one of consciousness-raising, organizing, and disrupting the status quo. The 1960s saw an unprecedented wave of social activism that encompassed movements for pacifism, free speech, students' rights, environmental protection, the elimination of poverty, and equality for Native Americans and a wide range of other ethnic minorities, as well as the emergence of hippies, sexual freedom, a new wave of feminism, and eventually the counterculture, black power, and queer power.

Gays and lesbians fit uneasily into this swirling mix of consciousness, idealism, and change. Many participated directly in the larger movement for social change, animated by their own quest for freedom even if, not yet identifying as gay, they were unaware of precisely how they were oppressed and why a movement for change would hold such appeal. Most felt they could not afford to identify publicly as gay, and may for this reason have gravitated to causes other than their own. Leaders of the New Left and related social protest movements were often complicit in deriding gays and lesbians and making them feel decidedly unwelcome in the larger movement. Tom Hayden, the president of Students for a Democratic Society and drafter of the student movement's influential 1963 manifesto, "The Port Huron Statement," declared homosexuality unacceptable for movement participants.[33] Betty Friedan, whose 1963 book *The Feminine Mystique* helped launch what became known as the "second wave" of feminism, viewed lesbians as a "lavender menace" that threatened to "warp the image." and derail the goals of the women's movement, which, like elements of the gay movement, traded on its leaders' middle-class, white sensibility to advance its goals.[34] Bayard Rustin, a gay African American who was a close advisor to Martin Luther King Jr. and the chief organizer of the 1963 March on Washington, was forced to remain out of the public eye because of his homosexuality.

And yet the black civil rights movement was enormously influential to leaders of the gay rights movement. Kameny and a small cadre of comrades had quietly organized a gay contingent to walk in King's march. That movement's rhetoric, tactics, and appeals to America's founding principles of equal treatment were natural models for a movement based on gay identity—once it occurred to enough people that sexual difference could be the basis not of social ridicule, moral condemnation, and legal exclusion but of a rights-bearing political and legal identity. This awakening was spurred not just by far-thinking new leaders but also by the larger context of the sixties: a new focus, largely by young people, on challenging authority, demanding equality, and holding out personal authenticity as the basis for a social and political movement.[35]

The black civil rights movement was particularly helpful in shaping gay leaders' focus on the psychic damage caused by oppression and the need to eradicate its shackles to achieve progress. In his manifesto, Sagarin had compared the internalized self-hatred of African Americans to that of gays and lesbians, a concept he learned from reading the black intellectual W. E. B. Du Bois. "The worst effect of slavery," Sagarin summarized, "was to make the Negroes doubt themselves and share in the general contempt for black folk." Nichols, too, applied the principle to gays and lesbians, particularly in urging the need to refute the psychiatric community's view of gay people as mentally ill, something too often internalized. "The mental attitude of our own people toward themselves," he held, is "responsible for untold numbers of personal tragedies and warped lives." What gays and lesbians needed more than anything was "to see themselves in a better light."

Kameny agreed. After conducting some brief research, he was stunned to learn that the psychiatric profession had spun the entire edifice of homosexuality as mental illness out of whole cloth, inserting moral judgment where they had claimed to rely on science. He became steadfast in his commitment to fighting the falsehoods and replacing the ensuing self-doubt of gay people with pride in their inherent worth. Quite simply, he insisted from then on that there was nothing wrong or "immoral" about being gay. In fact, same-sex relationships "are moral, in a positive and real sense, and are right, good and desirable, both for the individual participants and for the society in which we live." In 1964, in an address to the far more staid New York Mattachine Society, Kameny insisted that "the entire homophile movement is going to stand or fall upon the question of whether homosexuality is a sickness, and upon our taking a firm stand on it."[36]

Their work was cut out for them. That same year, the *New York Times* reacted to news that an aide to President Lyndon Johnson was gay by insisting the White House not tolerate "a person of markedly deviant behavior."[37] And until that year, even the American Civil Liberties Union (ACLU) had declined to defend gay people, taking the position that it was not the group's role "to evaluate the social validity of the laws aimed at the suppression or elimination of homosexuals," and that homosexuality was "a valid consideration in evaluating the security risk factor in sensitive positions."[38] Kameny was undeterred. With relentless pressure, he convinced the ACLU that year to change its stance and condemn the government's anti-gay purges as "discriminatory," setting up the national organization to become a consistent defender of gays and lesbians (some of its local affiliates had begun to represent gays and lesbians years earlier).

By the second half of the sixties, in tandem with an emboldened national protest movement and the birth of the counterculture, gay and lesbian leaders increased their visibility and began more directly attacking government and social persecution. While the gay rights movement remained small compared to the broader protest movement of the decade, the mass proportions of that movement had begun to infuse the quest for gay rights in irrevocable ways. And although gay rights organizing was concentrated disproportionately in New York and San Francisco, advocates were stirred to action across the country, in places such as Los Angeles, Chicago, Boston, Philadelphia, St. Louis, Washington, D.C., and many college towns.

In 1965, under Kameny and Gittings's leadership, a small group of homophiles became the first to organize a protest by visible gays and lesbians outside the White House. They led an orderly march of seven men and three women, the men in suits and the women in dresses, as Kameny always required, in a public performance of private dignity ("If you're asking for equal employment rights," he said, "look employable!").[39] The group carried signs decrying their mistreatment by the federal government. Demonstrations were also held at the Pentagon, the State Department, the Civil Service Commission, and Philadelphia's Independence Hall. In each case large placards demanded recognition, equal treatment, and first-class citizenship. In 1966, a year after the North American Conference of Homophile Organizations (NACHO) formed as the first national alliance of gay organizations, the group held a conference to plan a multicity protest. On Armed Forces Day, they held demonstrations in five coastal cities protesting their exclusion from military service. The first truly national action by the nascent gay movement, it reflected the mix of dissidence and assimilation that would characterize so much gay rights activism over the years, as it pushed the conventional limits of gay visibility while seeking access to a highly traditional American institution (one embodying the use of state power that, in the Vietnam era, many gays and leftists were coming to see as illegitimate).[40]

The black civil rights struggle, and eventually the black power movement, continued to influence the gay rights movement profoundly in the latter part of the decade. In 1968, for instance, after hearing the chant "Black is beautiful" led by black power figure Stokely Carmichael, Kameny began spreading the message "Gay is good." As a movement slogan, the phrase embodied his belief that homosexuality was not to be merely tolerated and confined to the shadows but should be celebrated as a moral good, just as casting blackness as beautiful framed racial difference as an American strength.[41] Yet if the black civil rights movement served as inspiration for early gay rights leaders, solidarity between the two groups proved far easier in theory than reality. Few of the organizers or leaders of the early gay rights groups were nonwhite, though of course black gays and lesbians were sometimes visible players in the civil rights movement and the African American literary and artistic worlds. One result of the white leadership of early gay groups was that debates over goals and tactics—which were fierce from the very start of the homophile movement—often failed

One of the first protests by visible gays and lesbians was this 1965 march in front of the White House. Frank Kameny is second in the line, with Jack Nichols at the front.

to reflect a full understanding of the uneven workings of social power. It was no coincidence that the earliest public gay leaders were largely middle-class white men and, to a lesser extent, women. They were the ones who were most able to leverage the appearance of respectability for their fight, and however despised and marginalized they were as sexual minorities, their whiteness gave them privileges and opportunities that African Americans in particular lacked. It wasn't that most white gay leaders chose to exploit their racial privilege; yet the ultimate drive to seek access to marriage—one of the central, mainstream institutions of American life—was a choice shaped by the greater access to power and respectability that their whiteness granted them.[42]

The quest for respectability was, of course, an inherent part of what would become the fight for access to marriage. In addition to the legal benefits and protections of marriage, the social recognition it confers is an inseparable part of what gives it meaning and power. And so the tension between seeking social approval and acceptance from the dominant culture, on the one hand, and demanding equal treatment in the legal, economic, and institutional realms, on the other, characterized the gay movement from its very start. In some ways, the divides lined up neatly: early homophile leaders tended to be conventional in their tactics, reserved about going public, and limited in their goals of ending governmental mistreatment. By contrast, a younger generation of activists, beginning in the 1960s, not only presented themselves in more defiant, disrespectful ways but also made more vocal, visible, and immediate demands, expressed greater anger, more strongly asserted their entitlement to equality, and often sought not to win acceptance into existing institutions but to challenge those institutions' power and existence altogether. In this context, one of the major fault lines of debate among gay advocates was between those who wanted to be treated like everyone else (equal rights for gays and lesbians) and those who sought to radically transform how everyone and everything was treated (gay liberation and liberation more generally). The goals and tactics of the gay movement would be contested along these lines throughout the twentieth century and into the twenty-first.

Yet it is easy to draw these differences as far tidier than they actually were, both among different constituencies and even within any one individual. For generations, young people in particular have insisted they care nothing for the respect of their elders or society at large, but it would be as foolish for others to believe it as it was callow for the youth to claim it. Even on their face, these concepts overlap as much as they conflict, and any attempt to evaluate them must take into account the era and context in which they appeared. For homophiles of the 1950s, identifying as gay was almost always a risky and radical act, even if their ensuing demands were "merely" to be treated like everyone else. The first gay Americans to picket the White House without hiding were bluntly challenging the status quo even if their suits and dresses marked them as conventional, as did their engagement with traditional centers of political power. Defying views of gay people as sick, immoral, criminal, and disloyal was revelatory, but it could be undertaken with the goal of replacing such views with approval by churches, doctors, politicians, and the law. Conventional tactics do not always mean limited goals, and vice versa, since an activist can adopt an incremental approach as a strategy with the ultimate goal being radical change. Liberating Americans from traditional constraints on sex and other roles had the potential not just to be transgressive, disruptive, and destabilizing but also to serve as a safety valve for social pressures, thus spurring reform instead of revolution. There was a fine line between self-respect and respectability, and the process of throwing off internalized shame was often helped along by winning the imprimatur of others. And legalizing marriage for same-sex couples, some early advocates recognized, could be transformative, even as it also reaffirmed the role of the state in both governing private relationships and neglecting the needs of single people.[43]

Such ideological and strategic tensions help explain the context for what happened on the hot summer night of Friday, June 27, 1969. A motley bunch of 200 drag queens, cross-dressing lesbians, hustlers, students, tony gay men, and what one admirer called "flaming faggot types" had gathered, as they often did, at the Stonewall Inn, a bar in New York City's West Village. That afternoon and into the night, 20,000 fans and well-wishers had lined up outside the Frank Campbell funeral home uptown to say goodbye to Judy Garland, the gay icon whose life had ended with a barbiturate overdose in London the previous week. Some at the Stonewall Inn may have been toasting her memory (more than one had used "Judy Garland" as a nom de plume when signing in at the door, a practice required because the bar branded itself a private "bottle club" instead of a public establishment that would need a liquor license) when, just after midnight, a group of police officers filed in to raid the place. Normally the authorities gave the owners, who were associated with the Mafia, a warning before their raids, but for whatever reason, that night's intrusion was a surprise. And for whatever reason—the cumulative weight of decades of derision and persecution, the inspiration of a new generation of youthful protestors, the rebellious spirit of the 1960s, the collective sadness and anger over Judy Garland's death—this time the patrons fought back.[44]

As the police began hauling off a few employees and drag queens in paddy wagons—wearing gender-atypical clothing was still illegal in New York—the crowd spontaneously erupted. The city during this period was not the well-kempt model of urban luxury it later became, and the small park across the street was littered with bottles and other debris that the throng gleefully converted into weapons. They hurled whatever they could get their hands on—including a parking meter they yanked from its socket—shattering windows and driving many of the raiding police inside for cover. When other officers turned a fire hose on the demonstrators, someone cried, "Grab it, grab his cock!" while others yelled, "Gay power!" The protestors taunted the raiders with references to the regular payoffs the corrupt police took from the mob bosses who owned the bars. Early on, a cross-dressing, biracial lesbian, Stormé DeLarverie, struck a police officer in retaliation, she said, for being hit. By the end of the night, four officers had been injured and many others had been terrorized. "There was never any time that I felt more scared than then," recalled one of the leading police officials, who said their guns had been trained on the door from inside. "You have no idea how close we came to killing somebody."[45]

No one died, but a movement was born—or reached its rebellious adolescence. It was no doubt indebted and deeply connected to the rudimentary efforts of Mattachine and Daughters of Bilitis during the previous decade, but it was newly emboldened in palpable and ultimately enduring ways. The unrest continued for several nights that summer, as hundreds of additional gay and non-gay participants and curiosity-seekers, including press, made their way to Christopher Street. One was the gay Beat poet Allen Ginsberg, who noticed right away a change in gay men's bearing and poise. "The guys there were so beautiful," he said. "They've lost that wounded look that fags all had ten years ago." Other gay observers echoed the sentiment, calling the event a "homosexual revolution" that young activists should study and carry forward into the anti-gay churches, psychiatric offices, "councils of the U.S. Government," and city and state legislatures that "make our manner of love-making a crime." Many saw Stonewall, even then, as part of something bigger, "a larger revolution sweeping through all segments of society" that carried the promise of upending long-standing forms of repression and prejudice.[46]

The coverage of Stonewall by the mainstream press reflects just how contemptuous most Americans—including liberals—felt toward sexual minorities. "Homo Nest Raided, Queen Bees Are Stinging Mad," screamed the *Daily News*. "Village Raid Stirs Melee," read the *New York Post*. Even a New Left publication, the *Village Voice,* dubbed the event the "Great Faggot Rebellion" and recounted a scene in which "wrists were limp, hair was primped," and "queers," "swishes," and "fags" were everywhere.[47]

For most of the straight world, Stonewall failed to register. The *New York Times* ran two short articles on the event, with no byline. Many straights were among the hundreds of curious onlookers who gathered at the scene over the next few days and nights to witness the continuing tensions, but they were as likely to be there to gawk as to lend support. And while in the popular imagination Stonewall has become the touchstone of the gay rights movement, at the time many gay people themselves, focused more on gaining respectability than on seeking full equality, were aghast at the prospect that violence, militancy, and drag queens might become the central images of the movement. Others were concerned about practical missteps, viewing progress as requiring a more incremental, establishment-friendly path that would gradually win over the hearts and minds of mainstream society rather than demand immediate change. In the hours after Stonewall, Mattachine members called for calm, posting a notice on the front door of the bar asking "our people to please help maintain peaceful and quiet conduct on the streets of the village." Yet a different sign likely caught more attention when it appeared nearby the next morning: "Support Gay Power."

Within days after Stonewall, a largely younger, more radical contingent of gay and lesbian activists had set out to harness the newly assertive spirit of the moment—respectability be damned. Mattachine was still the nerve center of the tiny movement, but the folks showing up at its offices were already clashing with the old guard. As Mattachine members passed out leaflets asking "Where do we go from here?" in an effort to remain relevant, a jolt of new committees, meetings, rallies, and protests broke with the reticence and patience of the older leaders and began to issue louder demands. Reflecting the more radical spirit of anger and action demonstrated by black nationalists and antiwar protesters, these younger activists wore tattered jeans and long hair, swore easily, and rarely held back their feelings or views. Over the next month, hundreds of them gathered at various spots in New York City to plot strategy, to march, and to commemorate—even then—the import of homosexual resistance. "Come out!" became a slogan and a strategy to raise consciousness, visibility, and self-esteem and to combat the oppression and persecution gays and lesbians faced on a daily basis.

The changes were dramatic. Historians estimate that in the late 1960s there were a few thousand people involved in the gay rights movement, and only a few hundred of them were publicly out. There were just a few dozen gay organizations throughout the country the night Stonewall erupted, many small social groups with little political content to their meetings. Only two organizations used the word *homosexual*, and both of those were located in San Francisco, the city with the earliest politicized gay presence. By 1974, five years later, there were nearly a thousand such groups.[48] Some of them, such as the Gay Liberation Front (GLF), fervently embraced the sexual revolution and advanced a broad attack against existing American institutions. Its leaders identified with the New Left, black power, and socialist critiques of Western capitalism and imperialism. And they were fairly unique among gay leaders in speaking openly about the need to confront racial, gender, and class biases within the movement.[49]

Yet almost as swiftly as the climate had radicalized in the late 1960s, the revolutionary spirit seemed to peak and deflate. Members of NACHO and the newly founded Gay Activists Alliance (GAA) balked at calls for a "total transformation of society." They mocked "the argot of the extremists on the left" and its "very tired 1960s rhetoric" and warned against driving away both gay and straight Americans whose support they would need to achieve reform and respect. Critics of the GLF also found that the more militant group was so antagonistic to the exercise of power that it could barely run a meeting, let alone an organization, and that its commitment to solidarity with minorities everywhere, some of whose members were stridently anti-gay, made it impossible to maintain a focus on advancing gay equality. Instead, the GAA adopted more conventional modes of seeking power through political organizing and the building of institutional alliances. Its members sought not to smash the existing power structure but to force it to operate fairly by ending sodomy bans, police harassment, and government-authorized job discrimination. Still, even the more moderate gay groups in the years after Stonewall understood the need for disruptive politics. GAA members invented the "zap," a theatrical, nonviolent confrontation with a political or other authority figure that maximized the elements of surprise, campy cleverness, and public visibility, and projected an air of condescending sophistication that added to its punch. Arthur Evans, a GAA founder who had left GLF, viewed the name and tactics of his new organization, with its focus on activism, as evidence that simply being militant didn't necessarily mean achieving anything. GAA was an effort to capture Stonewall's spirit of protest while charting an effective path for advocacy between the more timid homophile movement and the already marginalized radical left. The GAA's approach became a model for gay rights organizations for decades to come.[50]

Of course, the spirit of protest did not touch everyone. Edie Windsor reacted coolly to Stonewall. Not unlike other educated gay and lesbian professionals who viewed themselves as distinct from the hustlers, drag queens, and largely working-class gays and lesbians who fought back that weekend, Windsor distanced herself from the uprising. Living just blocks from where it occurred, she and Spyer literally passed the mayhem on their way back into town from vacationing in Italy, and it didn't much register.[51] "When Stonewall happened," Windsor said years afterward, "I was really this ignorant middle-class lady who said, 'I don't see why I have to be identified with those queens.'" Only later did she come to realize how "those queens changed my life." In her eighties, she recalled that era as the beginning of her "sense of community" after she came to genuinely appreciate the queers and misfits who spurred a new assertiveness among gays and lesbians in America. "I saw them and loved what I saw," she said, using almost biblical prose.[52]

Like so many gays and lesbians who grew up in mid-twentieth-century America, Windsor had conflicting feelings about her sexuality as she made her way in a hostile world. "I certainly did not want to be queer," she said, having viewed gay and lesbian life as a "denigrated," "underground" existence. "I could not imagine a life that way. I wanted to be like everybody else." Yet for a woman at that time, the respectability she sought meant being married to a man who would support her and the children she would bear. "Never for a minute did I feel that there was something wrong with me," she insisted. But she was all too aware that others, if they knew her secret, would think there was, surely viewing her as "queer, okay? Sadly queer."

What had the early gay rights movement achieved by 1970, and what if any connection did it have to marriage equality? Before Stonewall, most—but not all—gays and lesbians lacked the sense of conscious identity or the confidence to assert their rights publicly. Most assumed that they were fundamentally flawed, that one of the deepest parts of their emotional core made them sinners, criminals, lunatics, perverts. Contributing to their psychological wounds was the fact that they had few ways to view themselves positively. There was, of course, no Internet to click on for information about what it meant to be gay or lesbian, and precious few sympathetic books on the topic. Most popular culture that portrayed gay people at all did so in derisive, exaggerated, or threatening ways, depicting gay men as prancing sideshows and lesbians as psychotic and sometimes deadly man-haters. The prospect of getting married and having a family—of having a normal, respectable future—seemed definitionally closed to them.[53]

Yet throughout the 1950s and 1960s, two decades that were very different but featured important continuity in gay rights, first a small cadre and then a larger swath of gay advocates began to awaken to the promise of their own power and dignity. The goals and tactics of these men and women were diverse and often conflicted. But most shared agreement on one principle: gay people must eliminate the shame that all too many of them had internalized as a result of living in a world that was hostile to their very being. Only then would they be able to taste true equality and true freedom. While their demands can seem tepid in comparison to the more assertive, outer-directed brand of activism that emerged in the 1970s, these early gay activists captured something that was critical to the development of marriage equality as a viable concept: that those who loved members of the same sex had every bit as much humanity, dignity, and worth as anybody else, and that it would take a new kind of certainty about that truth among gay people themselves to convince the nation to recognize it.

2

"What Was Important Was That We Were a Household"

GAY MARRIAGES AND THE

DOMESTIC PARTNERSHIP ALTERNATIVE

THE 1970S WERE A HEADY TIME FOR AMERICAN GAYS AND LESBIANS, especially those who inhabited the proliferating gay enclaves of big cities such as New York and San Francisco. After decades of hostility so fierce that few dared to admit their sexual orientation, let alone express it publicly and demand equal treatment, a grudging tolerance was emerging in the dominant culture, and gay lives became more visible. Cities and towns were beginning to offer legal protections to their gay and lesbian residents. Twenty-two states ended their sodomy bans during the decade—Illinois had been the first of the fifty states to do so, in 1961—while dozens of cities and towns, along with private companies, adopted antidiscrimination protections. In 1973 the American Psychiatric Association removed homosexuality from its list of mental illnesses after gay agitators, including Frank Kameny, demonstrated that the creation of the diagnosis two decades prior had been based on bias rather than scientific evidence. First storming APA conferences to accuse the doctors of torture, they soon earned a place at the table, culminating in a dramatic 1972 session in which the gay psychiatrist John Fryer appeared as "Dr. H. Anonymous," wearing a wig and a mask. "I am a homosexual. I am a psychiatrist," he bellowed, with his voice disguised. In 1975, a decade after homophile demonstrations began, the U.S. Civil Service Commission ended its ban on hiring gays and lesbians.[1]

Gay advocacy organizations also began to sprout during this period, ones that, unlike earlier groups, would prove sustainable. In 1973, with the help of members of the Gay Activists Alliance, including Gittings and Kameny, activists created the National Gay Task Force (which later became the National Gay and Lesbian Task Force, and eventually the National LGBTQ Task Force). Its purpose was to fill the need for a professional, national political organization that could help unify and thus strengthen the movement. The organization also chose early on to provide advice and guidance to local gay groups, an effort to balance its structure as a top-down advocacy organization with its commitment to broad grassroots input. But in a phrase that captures a central tension about the gay left, one early participant described the objective of the Task Force as bringing "gay liberation into the mainstream of American civil rights"—something of an oxymoron if gay liberation is regarded as an effort to free people from the norms and expectations of the mainstream.[2]

In the same year, 1973, the Lambda Legal Defense and Education Fund was created to provide pro bono legal aid to gays and lesbians. Modeled after the similarly named legal arms of the National Association for the Advancement of Colored People (NAACP) and the National Organization for Women (NOW) and, more recently, the Native American and the Puerto Rican Legal Defense and Education Funds, Lambda was founded by attorney Bill Thom, a GAA member, who operated the group out of his Manhattan living room. He scrawled the name on a Band-Aid, affixed it to his mailbox, and opened a bank account with $25. Lambda's bid to incorporate was turned down at first, for lack of a "benevolent or charitable purpose," and so Thom had to take the state to court simply to win the group's right to exist. Committed from the start to public education as well as litigation, it focused on securing equal treatment for gays and lesbians by pursuing cases involving child custody, immigration, sexual assault, and military service, as well as freedom of the press for gay publications. With a nearly nonexistent budget, Lambda relied on pro bono representation to press its cases, which was considerably hard to come by because even the perception that an attorney was gay, inferred by many by participation in such a case, could end a career.[3]

The Task Force and Lambda, which worked with each other and with the American Civil Liberties Union on litigation, represented the start of a permanent organizational framework within the gay movement that was national in scope, professional in operation, and fully committed to a reformist approach—not revolutionary change but conventional liberal

politics. The strategy was to lobby, litigate, march, and educate, to hold
the government, businesses, and the media accountable for unfair treatment, and eventually to join the political system by getting openly gay individuals elected to public office. Such incremental change would require
patience and the sometimes quiet, unglamorous work of pushing an unknown minority from the shadows into the light.

Socially, gay life was flowering, and the varied ways that gay and lesbian individuals expressed themselves in the communities and lives they
built for themselves cut across the diverse political philosophies those
same individuals might adopt (including having no political philosophy at
all). For gay men in particular, social opportunities seemed limitless. Emboldened by the free love and liberationist ideologies of a counterculture
that many of them had helped create, gay men living in big cities founded
community centers and activist organizations.[4] Lesbians drew inspiration
from both the sexual liberation and feminist movements—often reacting
against the exclusion of lesbians from the women's movement—to create
distinctive social networks, coffeehouses, and protest ideologies of their
own. "Smash Monogamy" and "Smash the Nuclear Family" were popular
slogans among both gay men and lesbians who embraced gay liberation.[5]

In this milieu, many of the gays and lesbians who were active in gay
politics and socializing shared a version of E. B. Saunders's view that marriage was not for them—or for their movement. There were numerous reasons for this view. Many dismissed marriage as a bourgeois, exclusionary
institution, an ill-advised shackling of their hard-won sexual freedoms.
For them, the wish to be able to marry signaled conformity to a heterosexual culture that had spurned them and seemed to offer them little. For
many lesbians specifically, marriage was seen as patriarchal and oppressive
to women; they saw little reason to embrace an institution that not long
before had rendered women the property of men. For still other gays and
lesbians, marriage meant an abandonment of the push for an alternative
social vision that broadened the definition of family beyond the conjugal
pair, an alternative that had sustained many in the face of societal exclusion.

Some same-sex couples felt emboldened by the 1960s fervor to
seek out precisely the institution that other gays and lesbians eschewed.
Jack Baker and Michael McConnell met in 1966 at a barn party; a year later,
Baker asked McConnell to move in with him. McConnell said yes but told
Baker that, to make an honest man of him, he would have to figure out

Jack Baker and Michael McConnell in 1970 applying for a marriage license in Minneapolis.

how the two men could marry. In 1969 Baker began law school, in part to research marriage law, and joined "Fight Repression of Erotic Expression" (FREE), a gay student group. Finding that Minnesota state law nowhere stipulated that only opposite-sex couples could wed, Baker felt he could keep his promise to McConnell, and the pair applied for a license at the Hennepin County courthouse. Claiming the law prohibited "the marriage of two male persons," the clerk rejected the application. Undeterred, Baker changed his legal name to the gender-amorphous "Pat Lyn McConnell" and, having "outfoxed" the system, the two secured a marriage license the next year in a different county. Roger Lynn, a Methodist pastor, presided as the couple recited their vows in front of a handful of friends. Attendees enjoyed a wedding cake topped with two grooms, jerry-rigged from a pair of plastic bride-and-groom toppers.[6]

Baker and McConnell also sued, explaining their decision to challenge Minnesota's law with reference to both the symbolic and pragmatic benefits of marriage. For two men to get married would be "a political act with political implications." It would make their love "as valid and deep as any heterosexual love" in the eyes of the state and their community, and would offer them "a new dignity and self-respect." It would also, not incidentally, allow them to participate in an institution that had become "a distribution mechanism for many rights and privileges." Access to that mechanism would be particularly helpful, as the homophobic world they inhabited had compromised their livelihood. Baker had been thrown out of the Air Force after expressing an interest in another airman. And McConnell had had a job offer rescinded after the employer learned of his effort to marry another man. In a losing lawsuit over that incident, the court rebuked him for seeking to "foist tacit approval of this socially repugnant concept upon his employer."[7]

The men's marriage lawsuit worked its way up, first to the Minnesota Supreme Court, where one justice turned his chair around to protest having to address such a matter in his courtroom.[8] The court rejected the suit, asserting that restricting marriage to the union of a man and a woman was a practice as old as the Bible. The local ACLU agreed to represent the men in appealing the case all the way up to the Supreme Court, which, in its 1972 *Baker v. Nelson* decision, dismissed the suit "for want of a substantial federal question."

Baker and McConnell weren't alone in seeking to get married. America, declared the gay magazine the *Advocate* in August 1970, was seeing a "gay marriage boom." Months after Baker and McConnell showed up at the courthouse looking for a marriage license, Tracy Knight and Marjorie Jones requested a license in Louisville, Kentucky. Refused, they too sued and lost; Knight was sent home by a judge angry that she was wearing a pantsuit. In 1971 Richard Adams met Anthony Sullivan, an Australian facing deportation, at a Los Angeles bar. Four years later, the couple was one of six that found a sympathetic county clerk, Clela Rorex, in Boulder, Colorado, who agreed to grant licenses to the same-sex couples, noting that Colorado's statute, like Minnesota's, did not specify gender requirements. But when Adams wrote immigration officials after their wedding, seeking a spousal visa for Sullivan to stay in the United States, the couple received an official letter denying the request. "You have failed to establish," said the letter, "that a bona fide marital relationship can exist between two faggots." After word got out that Rorex was issuing licenses to same-sex couples, the Colorado attorney general ordered her to stop, and she faced hate mail, death threats, and mockery from the public. Trudging up to her office with a horse trailer and coterie of journalists in tow, one man theatrically requested a license to marry his horse. "If a man can marry a man and a woman can marry a woman," he asked, "why can't a tired old cowboy marry his best friend?" (Rorex denied the request, noting that the eight-year-old horse was underage.)[9]

More than a dozen other same-sex couples sought licenses during the early 1970s, and a handful filed suits. All of them lost. But the law was no deterrent. Throughout the 1970s and 1980s, hundreds and maybe thousands of same-sex couples solemnized their unions, often finding religious leaders to officiate. Less than two years after Stonewall, GAA activists staged a sit-in at the New York City marriage bureau to protest the opposition of the city clerk to weddings performed at a gay-friendly church. An organizer was careful to point out that the group was seeking not legal marriage but only the right to have religious ceremonies go forward without interference or denigration by public officials.[10] Throughout this period, the Metropolitan Community Church, a predominantly gay denomination founded in 1968 by Rev. Troy Perry after he was kicked out of his own church for being gay, performed same-sex marriage ceremonies routinely, marrying (in the eyes of the community) tens of thousands of couples across the last third of the twentieth century. Countless other couples—including Del Martin and Phyllis Lyon, as well as Edie Windsor and Thea Spyer—continued to live their lives as married, regardless of their states' refusal to grant legal recognition.[11]

By 1974, the idea of gay marriage had taken sufficient root in some circles that public television held a debate on the subject. Arguing in favor was Frank Kameny, who previewed all the major arguments that most of the nation would not otherwise consider for another generation. The moderator said the marriage question could be "the ultimate test of our society's willingness to accept homosexuals as simply another minority group." For Kameny, "the issue at hand is whether the alleged harmful effects of homosexual marriages justify denying civil rights, imposing second-class citizenship and doing psychological damage to some fifteen million American citizens of all ages. The answer is a resounding no because no such harmful effects at all have been shown." Kameny deftly parried attacks by his opponents, who included Charles Socarides, a founding father of the psychoanalytic theory that homosexuality was a disorder that could be cured through talk therapy. Socarides proclaimed that marriage for gay people could cause them "considerable anxiety" because most gay men continually sought out multiple partners in a narcissistic need to find "replicas of themselves." Trying to "normalize" homosexuality by elevating their unions to marriage, he worried, would be "an extreme form of social recklessness" and a "psychiatric disaster." Unfazed, Kameny cited the APA's decision, influenced by his own activism, to remove homosexuality from its list of mental disorders the previous year, and he cast Socarides's views as those of an ideologically motivated outlier. "Exercise by homosexual couples of the right to marry detracts not one iota from the rights of heterosexual couples to marry," Kameny said. "Homosexual marriages interfere with no one individually, and such marriages impair or interfere with no societal interest." Echoing Randy Lloyd's conservative argument for gay marriage, Kameny said that same-sex relationships would be "stabilized" by marriage and the institution of the family "strengthened."[12]

Of course, many of the gays and lesbians who did embrace marriage in the 1970s had no interest in advancing its conservative principles. For some, seeking access to marriage—or living as though already married—could feel like a deeply radical step, a thumb in the eye of a social establishment that had long sought to quash same-sex love and keep gay people invisible, marginal, and ashamed. For them, pushing to include gay unions under the rubric of marriage was wholly consistent with gay liberation, as it meant bringing a despised minority from the margins of society to its very core by staking a claim to one of its most central, mainstream institutions. At the heart of this claim was the insistence that gay people and their love were equally deserving of the status, dignity, and government protections that heterosexual people and relationships enjoyed. Thus some supported the cause of gay marriage precisely because they viewed it as a path to reconfiguring both marriage and the established social structure, particularly gender relations. Gay marriage promised to finally dislodge the notion that marriage, sexuality, and pleasure must be pegged to—indeed, justified by—procreation. What could be more radical than that?[13]

Yet the marriage push of the 1970s failed to take root. Baker soured on the gay rights movement, believing that its leaders dismissed as "crazies" those who, like him, viewed the right to marry as paramount. He rejected alternatives and compromises as a "cop-out."[14] But Baker and the other advocates actively pushing for the freedom to marry were in the minority. In the big cities and university communities where the bulk of gay politicking and organizing was occurring, consciousness *was* rising, and gay and lesbian advocates were challenging both heterosexual persecution and homosexual shame. These were also places where the sort of male sexual freedom that Saunders valued was available as never before, where fealty to norms of long-term coupling and monogamy were increasingly rejected as outmoded, and where feminist critiques of marriage as patriarchal were at their height. Gays and lesbians were no doubt awakening from shame and repression, and asserting their dignity and worth. But most did not appear to be putting their hopes into marriage. As the decade wore on, the combination of the failure of the early marriage lawsuits, the emergence of different priorities for a new battery of national gay rights organizations, and the embrace of gay liberation in numerous pockets of urban gay life had conspired to move same-sex marriage off the agenda entirely.

At the same time as gays and lesbians were debating among themselves whether to reject or remake existing social institutions, a powerful new force was gathering steam in the nation's churches, living rooms, and statehouses. Christian conservatives, known collectively as the religious right, began to build a movement in the 1970s that parlayed anxieties over changing social and cultural norms into a potent political force. The religious right viewed the nation as besieged by moral and spiritual decline at the hands of abortionists, feminists, gays, and other groups who seemed to be steering the country down a dangerous road toward secularism, liberalism, and general malaise. Voices of the gay left that castigated marriage and questioned the patriarchal and moralistic aspects of the nuclear family proved the perfect foil for the religious right, which began to target homosexuality as perhaps the single gravest threat to the American way of life. The insistence by gay people that they and their relationships mattered and deserved equal worth simply drew louder expressions of repugnance and disgust by conservative religious leaders.

Christian leaders such as Jerry Falwell, Pat Robertson, and James Dobson established a powerful empire of churches, radio and television programs, and, increasingly, political pundits and candidates—all dedicated to spreading the gospel with a new level of political engagement

aimed at organizing true believers into an effective voting bloc. Scapegoating homosexuality, abortion, and feminism, along with making thinly
veiled appeals to racist and anti-Semitic sentiment, proved effective at galvanizing voters, raising money, and keeping the national media focused on
an alleged threat to traditional values.

The 1970s, then, became an era marked by multiple philosophical and
strategic debates simultaneously playing out within the gay and lesbian
community. The first was over the extent to which gay advocates, generally
situated within a broader left-wing movement that was newly questioning
established social norms, ought to push for alternatives to traditional marriage and family structures. The second was how to address the challenge
of an increasingly powerful religious right that was beginning to weaponize
that internal debate to scapegoat gay people and lives as a vile danger to
the republic. And a third was just how important it was to make inroads
into the great American mainstream. This last question raised a subset of
both tactical questions (whether the movement should deploy the conventional tools of electoral politics, lobbying, and the justice system to
achieve equality) and questions about ultimate goals (whether the movement should be one of equal rights, seeking the ability to assimilate into all
aspects of American life, or essentially a liberationist movement, seeking
the more radical end of changing social roles, cultural norms, and hierarchies and inequalities of all kinds, even beyond those that targeted sexual
orientation). What kind of movement, that is, would best serve the needs
and desires of gay and lesbian Americans? The movement's eventual embrace of marriage equality as a unifying goal is best understood in the context of these questions and concerns, and in the face of a rising opposition
that explicitly attacked gay dignity.

In the late summer of 1974, Matt Coles arrived at Hastings Law School in
San Francisco. A Connecticut native, Coles had made his way west after
four years at Yale to live at the epicenter of California's gay scene. Like
Edie Windsor, he picked a city where he felt he could come out and be
part of something larger than himself. Coles sought an environment that
would be personally liberating and would allow him to make a difference.

He found it in the city's Castro district. Coles became a gay activist when a cat he knew took ill. "A friend had a sick cat and I had a car," Coles recalled of his first year at law school. He drove his friend to the vet, located on Castro Street. Someone pressed a flier into his hand, and Coles folded it up and put it into his jacket pocket. The next day he read it. It announced a meeting for a group called Bay Area Gay Liberation, or BAGL. The group worked to forge coalitions with housing, labor, prisoner, Native American, and Puerto Rican advocacy organizations. Its members—essentially anyone who attended meetings—viewed oppression of gays and any other minority group as a divide-and-conquer strategy, intended to keep the powerless fighting against each other instead of targeting the "ruling class."[15] It was one of the first organizations to use the word "gay" in its name, a sign of the new assertiveness of the burgeoning post-Stonewall gay rights movement.

At BAGL meetings, members noted that dozens of cities now had ordinances protecting gay residents from discrimination (although sometimes only in one area of law or another, such as hiring, housing, or public accommodations); why not San Francisco?[16] Coles wrote to officials in all the cities with gay rights laws asking for copies. Then, as the only law student in the group, he wrote a draft law of his own. The group sent out a hundred copies, including one to every person serving on or running for the Board of Supervisors, San Francisco's city council. To their surprise, one member introduced a bill based on that draft. They were disappointed, however, to find it drastically watered down.[17]

Recognizing he had lost control of the bill, Coles wandered into the Castro Street camera shop owned by Harvey Milk, who was then making a run for the board in hopes of becoming one of the first openly gay Americans to be newly elected to office, and plunked himself down for a chat. "We're in a horrible mess," Coles said, explaining that there was no one his group could rely on to move a good bill forward. "Is the bill the way you want it?" Milk asked. Coles said no, and Milk told him to write the one he wanted. If he got elected, Milk said, he'd help pass it.[18]

Milk was a funny, flirtatious, charismatic leader who spoke loudly but warmly about the rights of gay people and the need for young gays and lesbians to have hope. He helped popularize the dictum that would become central to the gay rights movement: every gay and lesbian person must come out. That was the only way, Milk counseled, to combat the lies and myths and distortions that people circulated about gay people. When he first ran for the Board of Supervisors in 1973, he was told by the head of the main gay rights groups in the city that "it's not time yet for a gay supervisor."[19] He lost, but made a strong showing despite being an out gay man and a newcomer to the city and its politics. Milk cut his hair, began wearing a coat and tie, and ran again two years later on a platform that was fiscally conservative but socially liberal. He lost again, but with an even stronger showing. On his third attempt, in 1977, Milk became one of the first openly gay elected officials in America.[20]

The first thing Milk did was to introduce Coles's bill. It passed in a nearly unanimous vote. A similar ordinance, also written by Coles, passed in Berkeley. These successes elated California's gay community and buoyed hopes that the momentum could spread elsewhere. In banning discrimination based on sexual orientation in hiring, housing, public accommodations, and schools, the Bay Area bills were the most comprehensive in the nation, as the others covered limited areas of law or applied only to municipal employers.

There was one member of the San Francisco Board of Supervisors who voted against the antidiscrimination bill. Dan White was a conservative Irish Catholic former cop who often seemed ill at ease holding office and who responded poorly to the rise of the relatively pro-gay, liberal, and minority coalition that was sweeping San Francisco politics that decade. He repeatedly clashed with Milk and other members of the board, and eventually resigned his seat. After changing his mind, he failed to persuade Mayor George Moscone to reappoint him. Milk had spoken out against White's reappointment. On November 27, 1978, White entered Moscone's office claiming he wanted to chat and shot him to death, then strode down the hall and assassinated Milk. A jury convicted White on the meager charge of manslaughter due to "diminished capacity" (in what came to be called the "Twinkie defense," his legal team argued that consuming excessive junk food while depressed had further hampered his judgment) and he served just over five years in prison.[21]

The verdict enraged the gay community, who took to the streets, streaming along the Castro to city hall, attacking police cars, breaking store windows, and throwing rocks along the way. The "White Night" riots further inflamed tensions between the gay community and the police, already exacerbated by White's past career as a cop. The uprising marked a dramatic contrast to the peaceful candlelight march by tens of thousands that had taken place on the night of the assassinations, when Joan Baez sang folk songs and mourners laid flowers at city hall.

Yet it was hardly surprising. The Castro had become the go-to spot in the country for expressing the hopes and agony of gays and lesbians in the 1970s, a decade of promise and possibility for gay liberation. But just as they were beginning to see progress in terms of social empathy and equal treatment, an organized force of enormous scope and strength was arraying itself against them. In 1977 a new icon of the religious right, Anita Bryant, had burst onto the scene in Florida, portraying gays and lesbians as an insidious threat to America's children. Bryant was a former Miss Oklahoma, a mother of four, a popular singer, and the face and voice of the orange juice industry. She parlayed her popularity into a campaign to repeal a Dade County, Florida, gay rights law that had passed early in the year. The name of her coalition, Save Our Children, reflected an anti-gay stereotype then gaining traction: the belief that homosexuals recruited children in schools and on playgrounds through seduction and molestation. Bryant warned that while gay activists said they were simply seeking human rights, "no one has a human right to corrupt our children. Prostitutes, pimps and drug pushers, like homosexuals, have civil rights too, but they do not have the right to influence our children to choose their way of life." After early polls seemed to show an uphill battle for Bryant in her effort to repeal Dade County's antidiscrimination ordinance, her campaign won a lopsided victory in June. She vowed to export her campaign to other states to block gay rights, promising a "crusade" against "a lifestyle that is both perverse and dangerous to the sanctity of the family, dangerous to our children, dangerous to our freedom of religion and freedom of choice, dangerous to our survival as one nation, under God."[22] Bryant kept her promise, lending her support to the successful repeal of gay rights laws in St. Paul, Wichita, and Eugene the next year.

After each of those votes, gay advocates gathered in the Castro and held demonstrations. And in California gay rights supporters defeated the Briggs initiative, a 1978 California bill sponsored by State Senator John Briggs, that would have banned gay people from teaching. But Bryant and a growing army of conservative religious foot soldiers continued their attacks, vilifying the quest for equality as a threat to everything the nation held dear. Again and again, activists in gay enclaves such as New York and

San Francisco vented their frustration. By the time White's sentence was announced, the gay community was reeling from a string of reversals, spurring the mayhem of the White Night riots.[23]

Gay advocates took two powerful lessons from the roller-coaster years of the late 1970s. The first was that popular participation in marches, rallies, and the electoral process could function as an effective means of political mobilization and, in some cases, tangible achievements. In 1979 grassroots activists led by the lesbian performer Robin Tyler organized the first national march on Washington, D.C., something most established gay organizations opposed either because they doubted the organizers' planning abilities or because they saw no compelling reason to put their resources behind it. Initially Milk had opposed the march, too, but he came to support it before he died, and it took on new momentum after his murder. An estimated 100,000 people gathered in Washington that fall, making the march a stunning show of support for gay equality and a catalyst in nationalizing the movement. Whatever later lessons would have to be learned about the need to capture the American center to achieve deep and lasting equality, now what mattered was enlisting the foot soldiers for battle with confrontational but ultimately conventional political tactics.[24]

The second lesson was more defensive: that when gays and lesbians took their case to the public, they could expect to lose. Time would prove this a valid concern. Between 1977 and 1993, nearly forty anti-gay measures were put to a popular vote, and 79 percent of those succeeded. Dozens of states would later amend their constitutions to block gay marriage. Not only could gay advocates suffer harrowing losses at the polls, but they could face harmful, demeaning political campaigns that spread hurtful messages about gay people and emboldened opponents to create more anti-gay policies. The lesson was the first of several that would create a sense of profound cautiousness among many gay rights advocates.[25]

Yet the rise of the religious right, the inspiration and martyrdom of Harvey Milk, and the 1979 march on Washington only energized and swelled the ranks of gay activists dedicated to pushing gay equality forward. So did the election of Ronald Reagan in 1980, which signaled the triumph of a rejuvenated conservative movement and, within it, the power of the new religious right. After that election, the Human Rights Campaign Fund (later Human Rights Campaign, or HRC) was set up as a political action committee to establish a sustained gay political presence in Washington, D.C. Its founding director was Steve Endean, a Minnesota activist who came out after reading Donald Webster Cory's *The Homosexual in America,* and belonged to FREE, the University of Minnesota gay group that Jack Baker had joined. From its earliest years, HRC, which would later broaden its mandate to include advocacy and education beyond the narrowly political, was focused on building up support for gay rights among lawmakers, deploying the conventional, time-consuming political tactics of supporting candidates, building relationships, and familiarizing lawmakers with who gay people were. HRC was bipartisan from the start, with one of three founding donors a Republican, and another a former Republican—the gay meat-packing heir, James Hormel. (And in a sign of things to come, the group relied on celebrity connections from the get-go, with its very first fund-raising letter signed by Tennessee Williams after HRC dispatched a handsome young emissary to the playwright's hotel suite to flirt his way to a signature.) After the Bryant-era defeats in Dade County, St. Paul, Wichita, and Eugene, some began to think that progress was more likely to come through Congress than state by state. HRC was their answer, part of a longer-term strategy that involved making gay lives visible and familiar, laying the groundwork of understanding and approval that would ensure future wins in due time. Endean considered himself a "committed incrementalist," fully grasping how long it could take to build gay support in Congress. "I'm prepared to be here for as long as it takes," he said when he first arrived in Washington.[26]

By the 1980s a multitrack approach had been born. It involved applying conventional political pressure on several fronts to advance gay equality, defined more as a liberal civil rights mission than as anything resembling a battle for gay liberation writ large. Both political and legal groups played a role.[27] As HRC worked on Congress, the Task Force lent further support to exert pressure on the federal government, while also working to nationalize a strategy of empowering local and state advocacy groups. On the legal side, Lambda, joined in 1977 and 1978 by the Lesbian Rights Project in San Francisco and by Gay and Lesbian Advocates and Defenders in Boston, worked on litigation and public education in their respective regions and nationally. All these organizations were committed to a form of incremental change. And all were animated by an awakening among gays and lesbians to the central importance of visibility and public acceptance. Still, none made access to marriage a priority.

———

This national organizational muscle was concentrated mostly in East Coast cities. Meanwhile activists out west and elsewhere began to push local-level reforms that included legal recognition for same-sex relationships, something that would have the largely inadvertent consequence of advancing same-sex marriage. Relationship recognition was not a goal shared by everyone in the era of gay liberation. But as more and more gay people began living openly as couples, the pragmatic began to shape their objectives as much as the ideological did. And the early successes they had seen in working within the political system to obtain legal protections for gay people inspired visions of what else could be achieved by working incrementally within traditional channels of power.

In 1979 Tom Brougham, who had been involved with the Gay Liberation Front, sent a letter to his employer, the city of Berkeley, seeking to enroll his partner in the city's group health plan that was available to all its workers' legal spouses. Inspired by the passage of the Berkeley and San Francisco gay rights bills, Brougham was nevertheless frustrated that, although he now enjoyed legal protections in employment and housing, his relationship of ten years earned his partner no health benefits through his job.[28] The letter declared that Brougham was submitting an application "to enroll my domestic partner" in the employer health plan. Brougham chose the phrase "domestic partner," he later explained, because it was "quasi-legal sounding," was nonsexual, and used commonly understood words. "We wanted to emphasize the everyday living and sharing of people," he said years later in an interview. "What was important was that we were a household." Berkeley denied his request.[29]

Matt Coles's work on the gay rights bill with Milk had earned him a reputation as the go-to gay legal mind in the Castro. When Berkeley said no to Brougham, Coles was enlisted to draft a domestic partnership bill.[30] In 1982 Coles's bill was introduced in San Francisco by Harry Britt, Milk's openly gay successor on the Board of Supervisors. Although the bill applied to different-sex couples as well as same-sex ones, it was designed by gay people to solve a gay problem. "We are denied the right to be married," Britt said, and were thus "cheated out of benefits" that marriage grants to heterosexuals.[31] The *San Francisco Examiner* opposed the bill, writing that treating an unmarried union as "the equivalent of marriage is an attack on social norms."[32] The bill passed, only to be vetoed by Mayor Dianne Feinstein, until then a strong ally of the gay community and beneficiary of its support, who had sprung from city supervisor to mayor upon Moscone's death. But in 1984, with Brougham's help, Berkeley enacted the first domestic partnership law extending insurance coverage to partners of municipal employees. Several other California municipalities (and a handful of cities in other states) followed suit, expanding the concept over the next few years from a city employment policy to a "registry" that couples could sign up for. It would take until 1990 for Coles's bill to become law in San Francisco, after a version that passed in 1989 was briefly repealed by the city's voters, a reminder of the widespread anti-gay animus even in the most progressive of cities.[33]

In developing the concept of domestic partnerships, gay activists such as Coles began to realize that agitating for gay relationship recognition carried an importance and promise that transcended its immediate practical benefits. In the gay and straight worlds alike, gays and lesbians were often seen as damaged, incomplete people, incapable of having mature relationships or even adult emotions. Advocating for recognition of committed relationships was a way not only to secure needed protections for couples who lacked access to marriage but also to bring visibility and familiarity to the very concept of loving, committed same-sex relationships. The political work would help humanize gay people. And by starting with the somewhat easier task of passing laws that applied to municipal employers, activists would create a mechanism for the much wider world of private employers and individuals to recognize gay employees and their relationships. Invisibility, it turned out, was not just a by-product of anti-gay stigma and discrimination but a tool the dominant society used to prevent even a debate about gay equality. Making gays and their relationships visible would help to undermine the very basis of discrimination.

The story of California's early gay rights bills reveals how allowing room for risk and defeat would eventually lead to long-term victories. "I started my work by losing my first case," said Coles, referring to a lawsuit on behalf of an activist named Larry Brinkin, who sought bereavement leave from his employer after his partner took his own life. It became a common refrain among gay rights lawyers, who understood as well as anyone the methodical, often plodding, and sometimes agonizingly slow pace of social change. Coles served as a cooperating attorney with the ACLU, and although Brinkin lost, the case introduced Brougham's new concept, "domestic partnership," as a legal term for a committed relationship that didn't qualify as a marriage. The story of that concept is also the story of how a handful of dedicated activists reacted to their particular circumstances in ways that ultimately transformed, often in unintended ways, the social, legal, and political landscape.

Within the gay and lesbian activist community, sharply different views emerged about the role of domestic partnerships in the larger gay rights movement. Britt had cast the domestic partnership bill as a way to demand equal treatment for gay couples who were denied the right to marry. But other activists took up the cause of domestic partnerships as a way to broaden the definition of family altogether. Although Coles would come to embrace the notion that marriage ought to be available to same-sex couples, back in the 1980s he "thought it was also quite possible that the gay rights movement might be able to spearhead an alternative legal institution" that would "give people a lot more flexibility."[34]

That goal was a particular focus of lesbian activists whose worldview was shaped by the radical fervor of the 1960s and the feminist movement that grew out of it. These women, many of them lawyers and legal scholars, often excluded from the male-dominated leadership of the protest movements, felt their struggles and experiences could be used to help change the world instead of to adapt to a broken system that was patriarchal, that penalized individuals who were not married, and that neglected the needs of anyone who lacked access to employer-provided health benefits. They viewed domestic partnerships not as a remedy for gay couples who were excluded from marriage but as an improvement over marriage that ought to be available to society as a whole. And they held up the gay and lesbian community as an alternative model for a liberated future in which human relationships were cemented through love, sex, friendship, and attunement to social and community needs rather than primarily through legal ties sanctioned by the state.

When she came out in the 1970s, explained lesbian law professor Nancy Polikoff in a 1993 article, "my lesbian identity was intertwined with a radical feminist perspective." She pointed out that many straight feminists declined to marry in order to make a statement that the institution was fundamentally oppressive to women. "I believe that the desire to marry in the lesbian and gay community," she wrote, "is an attempt to mimic the worst of mainstream society, an effort to fit into an inherently problematic institution that betrays the promise of both lesbian and gay liberation and radical feminism."[35] Apart from the feminist angle, they were words that could have been written forty years earlier by E. B. Saunders in *ONE*.

Polikoff became one of the most prominent champions of an alternative, broader view of family structure, later crystalized under the rubric "Beyond Marriage." In the view of these advocates, the narrow privileging of traditional families was a problem that feminists, gays and lesbians, and other leftists should oppose in solidarity. Domestic partnerships, which began as something available to both straight and gay people, represented a promising path in the early 1980s. "Although heterosexuals *could* marry," Polikoff has written of that era, "domestic partnership recognition was consistent with the proposition that they should not have to. Recognition of those who *could not* and those who *chose not to* marry was two sides of the same coin."[36]

In a reflection of changing social mores and the realities of how Americans lived their lives, the legal trend of the 1970s and early 1980s was to make marriage less important, not more, as Polikoff pointed out. The Supreme Court ruled during this period that birth control could not be restricted to married women, and that governments could not deny public assistance to unmarried women or to children born outside of marriage. For many lesbian feminists, such liberal jurisprudence was helping move society in ways consistent with their 1960s idealism, in which the government did not intrude in the bedroom, force people to live in needlessly restrictive ways, or make them conform to norms that served no purpose beyond perpetuating tradition.[37]

In 1984 Paula Ettelbrick graduated from law school and went to work for the United Auto Workers. She soon landed in New York, as the first paid lawyer at Lambda.[38] Ettelbrick and Polikoff were kindred spirits—lesbian feminists who advocated passionately for the interests of women, gays and lesbians, and anyone else they felt was historically excluded from power. Rather than have marginalized groups participate in flawed institutions such as marriage, Ettelbrick wanted the institutions to be replaced or reformed in ways that better served the needs of a broad and diverse populace. For her, the problem that had to be addressed "is not so much that lesbian and gay couples cannot marry. Rather, it is that all of the legal and social benefits and privileges constructed for families are available only to those families joined by marriage or biology." She believed that the "singular pursuit of same-sex marriage serves to reinforce the primacy of marriage in family definitions," rather than further opening the door to benefits for those who functioned as a family but had not legally formalized their relationships.[39] Ettelbrick worked with Mayor Ed Koch to extend New York City's bereavement leave policy to same-sex partners, and later helped pass a major domestic partnership law under the Giuliani administration.

But if in the 1980s domestic partnership was the primary framework within which gay legal advocates sought relationship recognition, the intellectual foundations were simultaneously being laid for the revival of the pursuit of marriage itself as a legal strategy. In 1983 a precocious gay law student named Evan Wolfson turned in his third-year paper at Harvard Law School. The topic was marriage for what he called "samesex" couples. Wolfson's sharp gaze and strong opinions belied the good nature lurking just under his surface. All three had gotten him through his studies at Yale and Harvard and a stint in the late 1970s as a Peace Corps volunteer in Togo. Wolfson came from a tight-knit Jewish family. His parents were happily married. He always felt like one of the lucky ones, not particularly weighed down by his sexual orientation. "I never thought there was anything wrong with being gay," he said, "and I had a healthy sense of entitlement" to the same treatment anyone else would get. When it came time for him to choose a paper topic, gay legal equality was a natural choice, but when he proposed writing about same-sex marriage, he nearly failed to find an advisor willing to take him on. Even liberal law professors demurred. Some thought the prospect of gay marriage was too unlikely to be worth exploring, while others thought it was unimportant or unserious. With persistence, he found willing readers and set to work.[40]

As he researched his paper, a central conclusion hardened in his mind: there was no good reason to deny gays and lesbians the right to marry, and many good reasons to fight for that right. He argued that marriage ought to be a paramount goal of the gay rights movement, suggesting—as others did of domestic partnerships—that it would both produce tangible benefits and help pave a path to full gay equality.[41] Winning marriage would not

Evan Wolfson at his desk in the mid-1980s.

just be about marriage, he reasoned. Simply talking about it would entail "claiming a vocabulary of love and commitment and equality and fairness," and such conversations would change understandings—not just in the straight world but in the gay community as well—of who gay people are. Wolfson's philosophy echoed that of Coles and his San Francisco comrades, who began to grasp the critical importance of activism to spurring a national conversation about gay lives and the dignity they deserved. Yet for Wolfson, more than for almost anyone else in the movement, access to marriage became *the* key to gay equality. Paraphrasing Martin Luther King Jr., he believed that activists could not expect to achieve their full goals by "asking for half a loaf."[42]

Wolfson's 141-page paper, "Samesex Marriage and Morality: The Human Rights Vision of the Constitution," made a legal and moral case for the full loaf, marriage equality. First and foremost, it addressed straight America. Seeking the freedom for gay people to marry, he argued, was not an effort to change marriage but reflected the fact that marriage had already changed. The idea that marriage was primarily concerned with procreation was "increasingly anachronistic and hollow," a point already acknowledged in Supreme Court decisions uncoupling the right to marry from procreation. Not only was marriage no longer expected to always result in child-bearing; it was not always permanent, it was not confined to unions within a single race, and it did not result in stripping women of property rights or even in creating strictly gender-defined roles in the household. Indeed, largely as the result of several waves of feminist agitation, marriage had undergone a revolution in the past century, with particular acceleration of its changing shape in the 1960s and 1970s. All of this turned appeals to "traditional definitions of marriage and the family" into wholly "inaccurate depictions of the ways people share their lives."[43] Drawing the line at gay marriage would increasingly reveal the prejudice that lay at the root of opposition to gay equality.

Wolfson then took on the link between morality and the law. Whatever one's views about the morality of homosexuality, he maintained, the promotion of morality was not an acceptable role for the courts. Using morality as a basis for opposing gay marriage "assumes both the immorality of gay citizens and samesex marriages, and the power of the state to define and enforce its own parochial vision of morality." Notably, even as Wolfson insisted that barring gay marriage was not within the appropriate purview of the state, he refused to cede the moral ground of the debate. Same-sex love, he believed, adopting Kameny's philosophy of "gay is good," was not something that society should begrudgingly tolerate. Instead, he laid out a very different moral foundation for constitutional law, one in which morality no longer served as a stand-in for Puritan religious strictures. Law is moral, he argued, when it broadly guarantees diversity of opinion in the universal pursuit of happiness. "The Constitution morally respects the freedom of individuals to create, live, and love in the happiness they can make for themselves in the world, consonant with the rights of others," he wrote. Marriage for gay people, he asserted, is a human right, and "the Constitution and real morality demand its recognition."[44]

Finally, Wolfson laid out an argument that would become crucial in making the marriage equality case not only to the straight world but to gay people as well: the right to marry is critical to gay dignity. "The reason samesex marriage is particularly essential to gay individuals," he wrote, "is perhaps precisely the reason it continues to be withheld: the importance it has as an expression of their equal worth *as they are*." His concluding remarks on this point constituted the preeminent early statement on the importance of marriage to the gay rights struggle. "Refusing people samesex marriage denies them the opportunity to develop their loving selves, and contributes to negative perceptions and feelings about gay people," he wrote, continuing to push the crucial insight of the early Mattachine leaders about the importance of gay consciousness. "Gay individuals, like society as a whole, lose faith in their ability to develop personal relationships and in their capacity to love. The resulting alienation often takes on a political cast as well, as gay citizens on some levels reject the society which rejects them." Barring same-sex marriage, he concluded, "is not merely the withholding of one final blessing, but a global and sometimes devastating blow to people striving to build lives for themselves in society."[45]

To Wolfson, viewing marriage as unimportant or as an appendage to the larger gay rights struggle missed the point of what was central to gay identity: same-sex love, and the fact—too often misunderstood—that being gay was about much more than sex, desire, or carefree living, a stereotype that social conservatives latched onto and exploited every chance they could. Wolfson made an alternative case for the moral nature of same-sex marriage—embodied in law, and asserted as a political act—and its defining role in advancing gay identity, dignity, and equality.

Wolfson's paper was powerful and prescient, containing the bulk of key arguments both moral and legal that advocates would use to advance marriage equality over the next generation. But at the time, Wolfson and his ideas remained eccentric and, in focusing on same-sex marriage as a paramount goal for the movement, largely isolated. Young and not yet influential in that movement, Wolfson had alighted on something big. But it was the domestic partnership effort that had the stronger backing of gay leaders and was making an impact in the real world. With an ascendant religious right and a still-tiny movement of largely despised and divided gay activists, no one could have known at that time what path the quest for an alternative definition of family—or the larger gay rights movement, let alone the push for access to marriage itself—would take.

— 3 —

"We Are Criminals in the Eyes of the Law"

SODOMY, AIDS, AND NEW ALLIANCES

THE 1980s WOULD CHALLENGE AND GALVANIZE THE GAY POPULATION like no other period before or since. And although debates over whether change should come incrementally or suddenly, whether gays and lesbians should assimilate or try to remake America, had never been merely academic, they suddenly became less abstract and far more urgent as a mysterious and deadly illness seized the gay world in cities across the country. As gay men by the hundreds, then by the thousands, received the death sentence of AIDS, systemic affronts to their self-worth became complicit in wrecking and even ending gay lives. The widespread suffering and death awakened gay people to the necessity of visibility, recognition, and action. Grassroots activists took to the streets to force action by the government and drug companies, while legal activists considered how the courts could help protect against the vulnerabilities of inequality. In both cases, a new form of gay activism was born, one that recognized the need not just to end government intrusion into gay lives but to compel government attention. Access to marriage was never central to these activists' demands, but because of the concrete protections and the presumption of dignity that marriage could confer, neither was it fully absent.

Across all gay advocacy work during this period lay also the pall of crimi-nalization. At the start of the decade, sodomy was still illegal in a majority of states. This simple fact created numerous barriers to the legal, political, and cultural battles gay people were beginning to wage. Although such laws often went unenforced, by criminalizing a fundamental aspect of ho-mosexual identity and behavior they were both an affront to gay people and a pretext for policy makers, prosecutors, and judges to deny them equal treatment. Gay people themselves—living in a legal gray area where they were always at risk of arrest and the unwanted publicity that might accompany it—had to police themselves and restrain their activism, often remaining silent, closeted, and invisible.[1]

In this context, most gay legal advocates were focused on the tangible and immediate needs of their constituents: preventing police raids, win-ning fair child custody arrangements, achieving freedom of speech and association, and dismantling barriers to employment, including access to military service. Indeed, gay rights lawyers had long believed that sodomy bans, more than the lack of legal relationship recognition, were the biggest obstacles to full legal equality.

In 1982, in the midst of ongoing discussions among gay legal advo-cates about how to take on the challenge of sodomy bans, lawyers at the American Civil Liberties Union, which had been seeking a test case to chal-lenge sodomy bans, learned of Michael Hardwick, a gay Atlanta man who was arrested in his home for performing consensual oral sex, a violation of Georgia law. The ACLU agreed to represent him in a lawsuit. The chal-lenge failed at the district court level, but the ACLU appealed the next year, and the criminal status of gay people remained in a holding pattern.

That fall Abby Rubenfeld, who was serving as legal director of Lambda, organized a meeting of key players involved in gay rights litigation. The idea was to develop a strategy for the several gay legal groups to work together in an effort to dismantle state sodomy bans across the country.[2] Out of that meeting emerged a new group, the Ad-Hoc Task Force to Challenge Sodomy Laws, which became a formal Lambda project in 1985. In addition to Lambda and the ACLU, which would create a dedicated gay rights project in 1986, participants included Gay and Lesbian Advocates and Defenders (GLAD), the Lesbian Rights Project (later renamed the Na-tional Center for Lesbian Rights, or NCLR), some law professors, and a few gay rights lawyers from other groups and private firms. The loose coalition focused most of its energy on devising ways to eliminate sodomy bans, but it also functioned as a legal debating society for gay rights litigation strategy. Participants discussed a wide range of ideas to advance equality, picking apart the constitutional landscape, both federally and in individual states, as well as how the political and social environments in different states and regions made lawsuits potentially more or less productive in various jurisdictions. Collegiality was enhanced by the group's history and geography: many of the lawyers had known each other since the 1970s, primarily in New York and San Francisco. And in 1979 Lambda's growth had occasioned a move from a room in founding attorney Bill Thom's Manhattan apartment to office space at the ACLU's building in midtown. Although sodomy bans and not relationship recognition were the Ad-Hoc Task Force's preoccupation, the creation of a structure for collaboration and cooperation among gay legal advocates would prove to be crucial in the ultimate push for same-sex marriage.[3]

Another topic the lawyers discussed was especially important to lesbians: parenting. As divorce became more widespread and as gay people—including parents—came out in rising numbers, the gay community saw harrowing cases of laws and judges awarding custody of children to a straight parent under the presumption the gay parent was immoral, criminal, or otherwise unfit to have children. Even as acceptance of gays and lesbians began to grow across the 1970s and 1980s, gay parents and children suffered because of unfounded assumptions that they did not belong together. While the standard of a child's "best interest" was supposed to prevail, that standard was not always defined well, and in certain states and courts, those in authority considered homosexuality as inherently harmful to children. In some cases judges preferred to destroy a healthy parent-child relationship rather than award custody to a gay parent. Or judges might impose as a condition of custody that a gay parent end a current same-sex relationship, even if a child had grown up with the parent's partner, viewing her as essentially another parent. In cases of a biological parent's death, grandparents or distant relatives who hardly knew the child could win custody instead of the nonbiological parent just because she was a lesbian. Often the courts were simply reflecting American opinion on the matter. As late as 1989 a national poll found that only 17 percent of the public believed gay couples should be allowed to adopt, with 75 percent opposed. The animus of judges, legislators, and the public had a searing and tangible impact on gay parents and the lawyers who sought to help them, making family recognition law a paramount concern among leading gay advocates.[4]

Yet it was neither sodomy nor relationship recognition nor parental rights that seized the attention of the gay and lesbian population in the early 1980s. In 1981 the *New York Times* published an article with the headline "Rare Cancer Seen in 41 Homosexuals." Concentrated in New York City and San Francisco, the mysterious and deadly illness seemed to strike a subset of gay men who lived or socialized in urban enclaves and frequently had multiple sex partners.[5] By 1982, 505 cases of the disease had been recorded in twenty-seven states, with two new diagnoses appearing every day. Some 40 percent of those with the disease, or 202 people, had died of what was first labeled GRID (gay-related immune deficiency), then AIDS (acquired immune deficiency syndrome).[6]

Gay people with the disease lost their jobs, and with those jobs their health care coverage, just at the moment they needed them most; with no income, many lost their homes, too. The disease disproportionately affected young people in modern urban American communities, places unused to such concentrated, inexplicable suffering. And on top of the harrowing physical anguish and uncertainty, those who had or feared having the disease faced intense emotional pain: self-blame, fear from within their own community, and immense levels of public scorn, derision, and ostracization.

By 1983 there were 1,450 cases, with half in New York City. The exponential spread of AIDS was terrifying: just two years later, more than 15,000 cases had been reported, a tenfold increase. Deaths from AIDS stood at 12,529. Because in the early years it was not yet known how the malady was spread, victims had to worry not only about infecting partners but also about whether friends and family might contract the disease from them; as with any plague, these fears could easily drive loved ones apart. This alienation only compounded the sense of isolation experienced by people whose ties to family members had often been severed by disapproval and abandonment. The emotional toll was intense, with psychiatrists, long seen by gay people as the enemy, struggling to respond to the perfect storm of illness, ignorance, and shame. And the looming insecurity was heightened by the broad array of physical ailments that could emerge from an immune deficiency. "It just hangs over your head," said a forty-one-year-old patient in New York. "There is always the overriding uncertainty that on any day you'll come down with something new that your suppressed immune system can't repel."[7]

Under the Reagan administration, the disease was ridiculed and neglected. Asked in 1982 whether the president had a response to the announcement that the disease had reached epidemic proportions, a White House spokesman asked, "What's AIDS?" and said, amid laughter, "I don't have it. Do you?" In 1985 the president was asked whether, if he had school-age children, he would send them to a school with a child who had AIDS. "I'm glad I'm not faced with that problem today," he answered, adding that he had "compassion" and could see both sides of the issue. By then, medical experts were aware that the human immunodeficiency virus (HIV), which causes AIDS, could not be spread through casual contact. President Reagan did not make a major speech about the subject until 1987, when a staggering 59,572 cases had been reported, resulting in 27,909 deaths from the virus. Throughout his presidency, Reagan refused to prioritize funding for AIDS research. During a year when 2,000 AIDS cases resulted in the death of 1,000 Americans, the Centers for Disease Control could secure less than $1 million to fight the disease, while it spent $9 million on Legionnaire's disease, which resulted in just fifty deaths. When Tylenol laced with cyanide killed seven people, the government spent $10 million investigating, but after a thousand had died from AIDS, it had yet to fund one study of the disease.[8]

AIDS created profound new challenges for legal advocates, who were among the first to comprehend and respond to the enormity of the problem. Under the direction of Tim Sweeney, who had cut his teeth in the 1970s fighting anti-gay legislation in California, Lambda was besieged in the early 1980s with calls for help from gay men who faced discrimination because they had become infected or because of public fears that all gay men carried the deadly virus.[9] The law did little to protect them from fear, hatred, and ignorance about the rapidly spreading new illness, which had come to be known as the "gay disease." Antidiscrimination protections covered only a sliver of the gay population, and now some conservatives planned voter initiatives that would quarantine people with AIDS. The father of modern conservatism, William F. Buckley, proposed that everyone with AIDS should be forcibly tattooed on the arm and buttocks.[10]

Although tiny and poorly funded, the gay legal community threw itself into the task of addressing the acute legal needs of AIDS patients. In 1983 Lambda joined the state of New York to successfully sue a Greenwich Village apartment building for trying to evict a doctor who treated AIDS patients in a ground-floor office. The state charged that the building had violated state laws barring discrimination against people with physical disabilities. That same year GLAD created its AIDS Law Project, and it successfully defended the right of a surviving partner to respect the deceased's dying wishes about what to do with his ashes after blood relatives had seized them. In a suit brought by Lambda and the ACLU, a federal court ruled that discrimination against HIV-positive applicants to government rehabilitation programs violated federal disability law. By the end of the decade, AIDS had spurred more litigation than any other disease in U.S. history.[11]

It is impossible to overstate the impact of the AIDS epidemic on gay life and activism across the course of the 1980s and beyond. While for some in the larger population the spread of the disease confirmed the perception that gay people were a vile, dangerous threat to national well-being, for many others the enormous suffering among gay Americans exposed and humanized their plight as victims of contempt, neglect, and unfair blame. Contracting HIV and battling the effects of AIDS—both its physical effects and its emotional and political fallout—outed thousands of gay men who had previously opted for the relative safety of secrecy. This was a mixed blessing, in that visibility was a crucial force in advancing understanding of gay lives and the suffering of AIDS patients. Thousands of personal encounters and increasing media attention began to change the derisive attitudes that many held toward gay people. In 1988 Gallup conducted a poll that showed a significant drop in the number of Americans who thought same-sex sexual activity should be illegal, from 57 percent to 36 percent in just a year.[12]

As the plague wore on, the dire medical needs of sick and dying patients exposed the insidious unfairness of denying equal treatment to same-sex relationships. The failure of both the law and a couple's community to recognize the reality of the couple's intertwined lives and commitments had devastating consequences. Partners of ill or dying patients were frequently denied the right to visit them in the hospital. Surviving partners could lose all rights to their beloved's estate or even the right to make funeral arrangements as blood relatives swept in and took over, not knowing or caring that their son or brother had a long-term partner who had been providing heroic care for years. On top of it all, many AIDS patients lacked health insurance because they had lost jobs or did not qualify for coverage under their partner's plan.

If AIDS spurred greater familiarity, sympathy, and understanding of the gay community by the straight world, it had an equally profound impact on gay people and activism. After a decade during which many gays and lesbians enjoyed the opportunities that gay liberation afforded in major American cities—social and sexual possibilities that seemed endless and unbounded by traditional forms of restraint—the emergence of AIDS sent waves of fear through the gay population. In the early years of the epidemic, and especially before doctors knew how it was transmitted, AIDS ignited a debate among gay men, in particular, about the risks and rewards of the philosophy of radical sexual freedom embraced by some adherents of gay liberation in the decade since Stonewall.[13] Even when the HIV virus was identified and knowledge spread about how it was contracted, some bristled at the idea that constraints on their hard-won sexual freedom could be an acceptable solution to the threat of the disease.

Yet whatever one thought about the proper limits of sexual freedom, a growing number of gays and lesbians agreed that things had to change in the gay community in order to save lives. The movement's energies had to turn to the immediate needs of a desperate population, one facing an extraordinary degree of suffering and death. Those changes began with a new form of activism that sharpened its focus on political engagement and shifted its approach from a concern with pushing government out of gay lives to demanding, in the vein of traditional twentieth-century liberalism, that government recognize and help resolve the problems this community faced.

In 1982 the Gay Men's Health Crisis (GMHC), a call center and informational group, was born in the living room of the irrepressible writer and activist Larry Kramer, with the goal of raising money for research and providing education and support to those afflicted. That same year, on the other side of the country, AIDS Project LA was founded with the support of Hollywood stars who helped bring money and visibility to the cause. These and similar organizations that sprang up during the 1980s did the work that local and state governments did not. In 1987 the AIDS Memorial

Quilt—the world's largest quilt, consisting of thousands of three-by-six-foot patches—was displayed on the National Mall in the capital as part of the second march on Washington for gay rights. Cleve Jones, a Harvey Milk protégé, had conceived of the quilt to honor the memories of those AIDS had killed, seeing it as an effort to transcend divisions over culpability and instead bring visibility to the love and beauty of gay life.

By that time Larry Kramer had split from GMHC and founded the AIDS Coalition to Unleash Power (ACT UP), a direct-action group that urged faster action on AIDS research and treatment with disruptive tactics that were designed for maximum media impact, including shouting down officials and blocking traffic. And while tactics had become more radical during the second half of the 1980s, the gay movement's goals had also changed. When police raids and government firings were the main threat to the freedom of gays and lesbians, activism focused on the right to privacy, a negative conception of liberty that demanded simply that the government leave gay people alone. In the age of AIDS, more was required. If gay activists of the 1970s had forced psychiatrists to stop diagnosing them with a made-up disease, here was a real one crying out for attention. People ravaged by a new and mysterious disease needed the government's recognition and assistance: they needed research and treatment for their illness, and they needed it quickly; they needed the government and their communities to acknowledge the contributions that partners made to each other; and they needed society to grant them the same benefits and protections that straight couples enjoyed as a result of their partnerships and families being legally recognized.

That urgent need for relationship recognition did not translate, for most gay movement leaders, to a demand for marriage equality, something that remained far below most people's radar throughout the 1980s. But the needs, visibility, anger, desperation, and innovation in tactics and goals spurred by the epidemic transformed the movement. The crisis made it suddenly urgent to ensure that the law protected same-sex relationships. And in so doing, it prepared the way for a new attitude among gay people themselves about where to focus their activism, what the roles of community and government should be in their lives, and what true liberation looked like. In years to come, the response to AIDS would play a significant role in laying the groundwork for what would become the marriage equality movement.

As in war, the loss of men to sickness and death from AIDS brought women into new positions of leadership and visibility. Lesbians increasingly began to participate in and run what had been disproportionately male-led activist organizations, started food banks, volunteered in hospitals, and became de facto nurses to thousands of sick and grieving gay men. The epidemic thus brought lesbians and gay men together after a decade of pronounced animosity that resulted from the widespread perception among lesbians that gay activism was tainted by male chauvinism and neglect of women's needs. In 1970 Del Martin had told gay men in the movement that she was "pregnant with rage at your blindness and your deafness" to the needs and concerns of lesbian activists.[14] Across the 1970s tensions between the sexes hardened, as lesbians and gay men kept their distance in activist circles, tended to their distinct agendas, and expressed grave disappointment amid hopes that liberation would involve transcending sexism and sexual difference. But the middle of a catastrophe was no time to dwell on past divisions, and many lesbians (along with some straight women) jumped into the fray with heroic levels of support— delivering meals, walking dogs, taking patients to the hospital and back home, helping where they could with financial and legal matters as the disease laid waste to so many thousands of lives.

In 1986 Michael Hardwick's case, pushed forward by the ACLU, reached the Supreme Court. That April, in oral arguments for the case, now known as *Bowers v. Hardwick,* the state of Georgia contended that the federal Constitution did not make same-sex relations a fundamental right and that "our legal history and our social traditions have condemned this conduct uniformly for hundreds and hundreds of years." But the state also went further. Perhaps in an effort to avoid appearing to target only gay people, the state condemned "any other sexual conduct outside the bonds of marriage." Georgia's strategy made the case into one with far broader privacy implications than just whether gay sex could be deemed criminal. A ruling that found a constitutional right to sexual intimacy of any kind outside of marriage, argued Michael E. Hobbs, an assistant attorney general for the state of Georgia, would undermine the state's interest in maintaining a "decent and moral society." While the Constitution protects the right to liberty, Hobbs said, "liberty is not unrestrained; it is ordered liberty, not licentiousness." Beyond that, protecting nonmarital sexual intimacy could open a "Pandora's Box" that also shielded polygamy, adultery, incest, prostitution, and drug use. It could also, he warned, lead to same-sex marriage.[15]

Though Hobbs's slippery-slope argument served as rhetorical hyperbole, it was true that the stakes were higher than just criminalization of gay sex. Gay legal advocates had brought the suit in the first place because they believed laws against sodomy were a tip-of-the-spear issue for gay legal equality and hoped for a decision that would be a game-changer. Representing Hardwick in collaboration with the ACLU, Harvard Law School's Laurence Tribe rejected the idea that majority moral sentiment was a sound basis for a sweeping law that intruded into the most intimate private conduct. Besides, he pointed out, twenty-six states had eliminated laws banning same-sex sodomy (the remaining states still had them on the books, but only five of those punished gay sodomy alone, with the rest, including Georgia, also banning heterosexual sodomy). A belief that same-sex intimacy ought to be punished, he argued, was no longer a majority sentiment.[16]

On June 30, 1986, the court announced its decision, a 5–4 ruling that was a stinging defeat for gay advocates. "It is obvious to us," wrote Justice Byron White for the majority, that the Constitution did not "extend a fundamental right to homosexuals to engage in acts of consensual sodomy." To the contrary, "proscriptions against that conduct have ancient roots." White explained that sodomy had been made criminal by each of the original thirteen states, that all fifty states had continued to ban it until 1961, and that twenty-four still did. "Against this background, to claim that a right to engage in such conduct is 'deeply rooted in this Nation's history and tradition' or 'implicit in the concept of ordered liberty' is, at best, facetious," he declared.[17]

Chief Justice Warren Burger wrote a concurring opinion emphasizing just how execrable homosexual sex was. "I write separately to underscore my view that in constitutional terms there is no such thing as a fundamental right to commit homosexual sodomy," he wrote. "Condemnation of those practices is firmly rooted in Judeo-Christian moral and ethical standards." It was a capital offense in ancient Rome, its criminal status imported into English common law and eventually into the American colonies. It was castigated by eighteenth-century English society as a "deeper malignity" than rape, "a disgrace to human nature," and "a crime not fit to be named." Burger concluded, "To hold that the act of homosexual sodomy is somehow protected as a fundamental right would be to cast aside millennia of moral teaching."[18]

Justice Harry Blackmun issued a stern dissent. He insisted the case was not about the right to engage in "homosexual sodomy"—after all, the Georgia statute criminalized sodomy for both heterosexuals and homosexuals. It was the majority justices who chose to frame the case around *homosexual* sodomy. Blackmun argued that the case was really about "the right to be let alone," the enjoyment of privacy, which he called "the right most valued by civilized men." He accused the majority of having "distorted the question this case presents" with its "almost obsessive focus on homosexual activity."[19] But only four justices agreed with this framing of the question.

The *Bowers* decision crushed morale among gays and lesbians, especially among legal advocates, who were left still trying to convince the world that their very existence should not be criminalized. Rubenfeld called the ruling "a devastating defeat and a terrible blow to our movement." Within weeks of the decision, a court in Missouri upheld that state's sodomy ban. In the following years, state and federal courts throughout the country would rely on *Bowers* in ruling against gay rights—upholding bans on adoption and fostering of children by gays and lesbians, allowing the Pentagon to continue ousting gay members of the military, and awarding children to the straight parent in child custody battles—just as Jack Baker's court loss would be repeatedly cited in anti-gay-marriage rulings more than thirty years after *Baker v. Nelson*. It is impossible to overstate how harmful such Supreme Court decisions were to the cause of advancing gay and lesbian equality, and the harrowing impact they had on legal advocates, who saw firsthand how a federal court loss could halt progress for generations to come. "We are criminals in the eyes of the law, and that is used against us," Rubenfeld told an audience of law students just after the *Bowers* decision came down. And now the federal courts seemed to be closed to gay rights advocates for the foreseeable future.[20] "One bad loss can mean wiping out a generation of rights," Paula Ettelbrick said in 2009, reflecting the scars of the *Bowers* ruling more than twenty years later. The lawyers felt a strong sense of responsibility to think of the long-term effects of their litigation work. "We didn't want to screw the whole thing up for generations to come," said Ettelbrick, echoing Harry Hay in founding the Mattachine Society, "and we took very seriously our responsibilities as lawyers to be prudent and thoughtful when messing with the constitutional rights of millions."[21]

Gay legal advocates thus returned to the lessons that Coles and other activists had taken from battles over local and state protections beginning in the 1970s: litigation and the accompanying public education around a range of issues—job discrimination, adoption rights, child custody, the need for relationship recognition—would spur both small victories and an ongoing national conversation about the equal worth of gay people. Federal court wins might be off the table for now, but local and state advances could help bring awareness, respect, and real protections to gay people, which would in turn prime the public and the courts to support additional gay-friendly laws and rulings.

The lesson of *Bowers* was that movement wins would require leaders to be cautious, strategic, and patient, and to devote their energy to laying the groundwork for public approval of homosexuality before filing further lawsuits, especially in federal court. "There is a scramble now to read articles about and learn how to use state constitutions and state courts," Rubenfeld said that fall, noting how ironic it was to "have basically written off the federal [court] system," which had proven the most promising venue for minority rights claims in the black civil rights struggle.[22]

Yet like the AIDS epidemic, the *Bowers* decision produced new passion, new commitment, and a fresh dose of financial and intellectual energy devoted to finding a new way forward. Evan Wolfson, who had written Lambda's *Bowers* amicus brief (before joining the group full-time in 1989), described the court decision and the AIDS epidemic as "the two towering paradigm shifters of the '80s," saying the court case "energized a grass-roots movement and tapped into a deeper anger and politicized people."[23] It also gave a jolt of support to gay organizations. Lambda and other gay groups grew in stature, visibility, and budget.[24] The National Gay and Lesbian Task Force created a Privacy Project designed to help repeal sodomy laws in a state-by-state effort.[25] The lawyers' Task Force changed its name to the Gay Rights Litigators' Roundtable, and while it continued to prioritize ending sodomy bans, it began to work more on public education,

Attorney Abby Rubenfeld calls to order a meeting of the Gay Rights Litigators'
Roundtable at the New York City Bar Association in 1987.

delivering testimony before government bodies, debating constitutional
theory, and forging alliances.[26]

The new urgency and new opportunities meant renewed debates
about strategy. While some began to speak of the importance of relationship recognition, others wanted to maintain the focus on sodomy. "In my
view," Rubenfeld argued months after the *Bowers* decision came down,
"we cannot concentrate on things like spousal benefits until we put considerable resources into ridding ourselves of sodomy laws."[27] But Rubenfeld
also wanted to broaden the base of gay activism. She noted that the public
reaction to *Bowers* had been uniformly negative, creating an opportunity
to build coalitions, educate the public, and enlist both mainstream and
grassroots support. Even from her perch at Lambda, where lawsuits were
the mainstay of activity, she viewed *Bowers* as instructing the movement
that a broader and more incremental approach was needed. "Litigation will
not be enough," she concluded. "We need to do grassroots organizing.
We need to have people register to vote. We need to change the political

system." She called for the movement to "shift our focus" and concentrate on long-term public education, political engagement, and grassroots organizing, with litigation as just one piece of the puzzle.[28]

Of course, it didn't require calls from professional gay leaders to unleash anger and energy among grassroots gay activists in the aftermath of *Bowers,* as popular protests sprang up in cities around the country. Along with despair and frustration over AIDS, the court ruling helped inspire a march on Washington in 1987 that drew more than half a million participants. Six hundred people were arrested on the steps of the Supreme Court building in a protest of the decision, marking it as the largest instance of civil disobedience since the Vietnam era. Rallied by the National Gay and Lesbian Task Force, participants returned from the march to create more than forty new grassroots organizations.[29]

Although the 1987 march was focused on the twin challenges of sodomy bans and AIDS, activists included relationship recognition among their demands. Grassroots organizers went further. Ignoring objections from the march's executive committee, Robin Tyler, who had helped organize the 1979 march, held a mass wedding in front of the Internal Revenue Service building, with hundreds of same-sex couples exchanging vows. Indeed, even as the organized gay rights movement grew and became more professional in the years after *Bowers* and the onset of AIDS, marriage was seldom a priority within their ranks. Yet the broader gay and lesbian population had become newly politicized by the wreckage, denigration, and neglect of the 1980s. ACT UP showed that if the nation's political and medical leaders were unwilling to take the mass death of gay people seriously, the community would take care of itself. This went for grassroots gay activists, too, who increasingly took matters into their own hands when they felt gay organizations were not adequately representing them. As the mass wedding in Washington showed, many of these folks thought having their relationships recognized, and specifically having legal access to marriage, was critically important. The event—and its backdrop of gay deaths and the loss in *Bowers*—captured their awakening to the urgency of legal equality, government awareness, and social empathy, all of which the concept of gay dignity and gay marriage itself increasingly seemed to encompass.[30]

By the end of the decade, notwithstanding Wolfson's pioneering 1983 paper or the 1987 wedding demonstration, there was hardly a consensus in the gay community on the importance of marriage. Still, the extraordi-

Two brides embrace at a mass wedding held by grassroots activists at the 1987 March on Washington. © Sara Jorde

nary strategic cooperation among gay legal groups that took root during this period, along with the burst of grassroots energy and incipient mainstream engagement spurred by the decade's developments, would ultimately prove essential in securing marriage equality in America.

———

The year that *Bowers* was decided was a wretched one for Miguel Braschi, a native of San Juan, Puerto Rico, who had settled down in New York City with the love of his life, Leslie Blanchard. The two men lived in a rent-controlled apartment on East 54th Street that became a spot for legendary dinner parties with the couple's friends and celebrity clients from their hair salon. The two traveled extensively, won the support of their parents, whom they visited frequently, and built a life together as partners for more than a decade. In May of that year Blanchard developed flulike symptoms, and he was quickly diagnosed with AIDS. He died in September, as Braschi held him tightly in his hospital bed.[31]

Although the two men had been living in the apartment as partners for eleven years, only Blanchard's name was on the lease. Within weeks of his death, the building owner notified Braschi that he had one month to vacate or he would face eviction. Because Braschi was not "family," the landlord argued, he did not have the right to take over the lease with the preferential rent.[32]

Braschi decided to sue. Owen Wincig, a private attorney, agreed to take his case. Soon members of the Litigators' Roundtable heard about the case and contributed amicus briefs. Ettelbrick authored one for Lambda and Bill Rubenstein wrote one for the ACLU, which had just started its new Lesbian and Gay Rights Project, for which he served as director. When an appellate court rejected Braschi's claim, the ACLU took over the case.[33]

In 1989 New York's highest court ruled in *Braschi v. Stahl* that the ability to inherit rent-control privileges, which Braschi would have enjoyed if he had been married to Blanchard, "should not rest on fictitious legal distinctions or genetic history, but instead should find its foundation in the reality of family life." It was a rousing victory, which Rubenstein called "the most important single step forward in American law toward legal recognition of lesbian and gay relationships."[34]

In allowing Braschi to inherit the apartment lease, New York's highest court helped broaden understandings of what "family" meant—at least for the moment. In his opinion, Judge Vito Titone repudiated the family model based narrowly on legal and blood ties, making the case for a much more modern definition of family. "A more realistic, and certainly equally valid, view of a family," wrote Titone, "includes two adult lifetime partners whose relationship is long-term and characterized by an emotional and financial commitment and interdependence." He even emphasized an understanding of family that went beyond coupledom, quoting dictionary definitions of the word as "a group of people united by certain convictions or common affiliation" and "the collective body of persons who live in one house."[35]

The law's embrace of this more flexible definition of family was exactly what most of the gay lawyers who argued or supported the case had hoped for. Rubenstein, after input from the Roundtable, had deliberately built his case around it. And it was an approach that was applauded not just by gay rights groups but by a broad liberal coalition that included advocates for low-income, minority, ethnic, immigrant, and elderly communities, many of whom had long sought a more expansive definition of the family unit. Ettelbrick's brief for Lambda explained that the court's interpretation of "family" would have a bearing not just on same-sex partners but on thousands of other nontraditional households such as cohabiting straight couples, as well as low-income people and racial and ethnic minorities whose households were more likely to include extended-family members, unmarried adults, or nonrelatives.[36] Advocates for the poor submitted their own briefs in Braschi's case, arguing that a narrow, normative definition of family would punish their constituents, whose diverse households often consisted of relationships never formalized by law because adoption or marriage or divorce proceedings were financially burdensome or culturally alien. All these advocates—gay and non-gay alike—hoped to nudge society's definition of "family" in a broader direction, and to support laws and legal precedents that reflected the actual realities of modern American life.

To these advocates, Judge Titone's opinion was an especially sweet victory because it was based not on casting Braschi and Blanchard's relationship as analogous to a marriage but on recalibrating how the law viewed the meaning of family. And yet, in a reminder that history often produces unintended consequences, the language of the decision would ultimately prove essential in galvanizing a movement not toward alternative notions of family but toward including same-sex couples in the existing institution of marriage. For supporters of alternative families, Titone's conclusion that the law saw a family as simply an emotional and financial support network meant that a procreative, opposite-sex marriage was not necessary to create a family. But for the few gay advocates who were beginning to press the idea that gay couples fit squarely into the modern meaning of marriage, the impact of the decision was dramatically different. For them, the point was not that marriage was unnecessary or unimportant but that gay couples were entitled to it just like everyone else.

At the same time, the acute medical and legal needs of those afflicted with AIDS were inspiring thousands of new foot soldiers—ordinary gay men, lesbians, and allies who did not necessarily share the alternative-family ideology—to join the push for relationship recognition. And gay and lesbian parents—many of whom also did not come out of the alternative-families movement—were increasingly aware of the impact of continued bias in laws and court decisions around gay parenting. After an initial wave of legal fights involving lesbian parents in the 1970s, the next couple of decades saw what was dubbed by the media a "gayby boom," hastened by advances in reproductive technology and changing social mores. The result was a new level of interest among gay and lesbian parents in laws and activism that could help secure their legal ties to their children.[37] Access to marriage, many increasingly felt, seemed like the simplest path to that reality. By the end of the 1980s, what had started out as a countercultural movement to alter the meaning of family was poised to be repurposed as a movement for same-sex marriage.

= 4 =

"A Tectonic Shift"

EARTHQUAKE IN HAWAII

By 1989 the world looked dramatically different for gays and lesbians than it had on the eve of Stonewall. In the aftermath of that uprising, gays and lesbians were more apt to structure their lives around their often newfound sexual identity than to take their place in a heterosexual marriage just because it was expected of them. As more gays and lesbians created lives anchored by their connections to other gay people, the refusal of the law to respect and protect those relationships became not only an indignity but a genuine hole in a legal system that was constitutionally required to provide equal protection to all its citizens. The glaring gap could be filled, it seemed, either by creating new legal structures or by insisting that gay people's lives fit into existing ones.

Andrew Sullivan, for his part, was not in the business of radically reenvisioning society. Sullivan arrived at Harvard in 1984 from his native England as an openly gay supporter of British prime minister Margaret Thatcher and American president Ronald Reagan. His family leaned conservative, but his politics turned further rightward after experiencing 1970s Britain as overtaken by government and unions, with little capacity to make things work. He attended a school for high-IQ students, and when the Labour government chose to shut it down for being elitist, he said, "that's when I started to hate the left." While at Harvard, he began writing as an intern for the *New Republic,* a prestigious political magazine with a storied liberal past but a penchant for pushing provocative ideas, and he

Andrew Sullivan in 1991, the year he became editor of the New Republic.

later joined its staff in Washington. The spread of domestic partnerships in various cities throughout the 1980s caught the attention of the magazine's staff, who began discussing the idea at editorial meetings. As the publication's only openly gay writer, Sullivan was solicited for his opinion on the matter. "First of all, it's a horrible name," he said of domestic partnerships. "It sounds like a legal contract." But he also couldn't help but wonder, "We already have an institution that deals with these questions—why don't we just have the right to marry?" Sullivan was convinced that should be the conservative position: to make the existing bundle of rights and responsibilities—civil marriage—available to same-sex couples.[1]

Editor Michael Kinsley, who delighted in riling up the right wing, saw in Sullivan's far-out idea the perfect story. It would be a wonderful way of showing that so-called family-values conservatives weren't really out to protect family and tradition but simply wanted to stigmatize gay people.

"The whole idea was a provocation," Sullivan recounted years later, "a thought experiment; it was not a proposal for reform."

The story idea languished for a while. But when the *Braschi* ruling was reported in the media, Kinsley called up Sullivan: "You know that piece you never wrote on the conservative case for gay marriage? Now's the time." Sullivan obliged, and the piece ran as the cover story in August 1989.

Although neither liberals nor conservatives seemed to notice, Sullivan argued in "Here Comes the Groom: A (Conservative) Case for Gay Marriage" that both ends of the political spectrum should support going even further than the judge in the *Braschi* case had. Rather than declaring a gay partner to be amorphously part of the family, he wrote, the better alternative "is the legalization of civil gay marriage." Sullivan framed his argument as a conservative proposal in that marriage was a traditional institution, with certain domesticating objectives and effects. But he also cast the proposal as conservative in two other ways: as a preferable alternative to the emergence of domestic partnerships, which he believed "chip[ped] away at the prestige" of marriage itself, and, in the vein of Randy Lloyd, as the better direction for the gay rights movement than where it currently seemed headed.[2]

Domestic partnerships, Sullivan complained, invited couples "to qualify at little personal cost for a vast array of entitlements otherwise kept crudely under control." Marriage was not simply a basket of rights and benefits granted by the law. It was also a social custom purposely designed to make entry and exit difficult so as to cement a couple's commitment to each other and to their community. Any lighter, less serious arrangement, such as domestic partnerships, threatened to undercut this stabilizing power of marriage. This was why full marriage for gay couples was actually the more conservative, less threatening alternative, Sullivan argued. "Legalizing gay marriage," he wrote, would offer gay people "the same deal society now offers heterosexuals: general social approval and specific legal advantages in exchange for a deeper and harder-to-extract-yourself-from commitment to another human being." It would encourage greater responsibility and "foster social cohesion, emotional security, and economic prudence" in gay couples, just as it did for straight couples. And it would help nurture healthy children in gay households, since research showed that stable adult unions helped minimize stress in children's lives.

Above all, legalizing gay marriage could remove the devastating stigma that attached to gay people, help them assert their dignity and bring them into the mainstream in the deepest way possible. Letting gays wed would "help bridge the gulf often found between gays and their parents. It could bring the essence of gay life—a gay couple—into the heart of the traditional straight family in a way the family can most understand and the gay offspring can most easily acknowledge. It could do as much," he wrote, "to heal the gay-straight rift as any amount of gay rights legislation."

The response to Sullivan's piece was far more powerful than he had anticipated. "Mike didn't tell me he put it on the bloody cover!" Sullivan remembered. "I just expected it to be a regular little piece." Conservatives ridiculed the idea of gay marriage as bizarre, ludicrous—an oxymoron. But some on the gay left reacted to Sullivan with downright anger. In his article, he had provoked not just conservatives but the gay movement itself, accusing it of having "ducked" the issue of marriage equality in deference to an "outsider, anti-bourgeois, radical" self-image. Yet in the age of AIDS, Sullivan argued, "to be gay and to be responsible has become a necessity." He viewed the dominant gay thinking of the time as overly focused on subverting heterosexuality, deconstructing the family, and provoking people at every turn, and he sought to reframe the national conversation around what he believed was the quiet majority of ordinary gays and lesbians, especially crucial at a time when the community was being ravaged by AIDS. Most in the "fast-maturing" gay world, he believed, were now ready to take their place as upstanding members of bourgeois society. "A desire to rebel has quietly ceded to a desire to belong," he wrote. To some this assertion (like Kramer's urging that gay men rein in sexual excess in the face of HIV) looked like an effort to equate gay liberation with perpetual adolescence, which seemed to evoke the old psychiatric view that gay people suffered from arrested development.[3]

Having published his article to some buzz, he now had to defend as a genuine policy proposal what had begun as essentially a lark. Sullivan's essay and growing visibility won him invitations to speak at college campuses and other venues across the nation, but he was occasionally picketed and heckled by gay activists who decried his "assimilationist" position. He was undeterred, however. The more he thought about and spoke about gay marriage, the more he realized, just as Wolfson had, how critical it could be to showing the world "who we really are."

Unlike Wolfson, however, who came from and embraced liberal values, Sullivan's understanding of who gay people were had a decidedly conservative hue, which would color his approach to framing the issue for years to come. "We should have a PR campaign to present normal-looking gays," he thought, in an echo of Frank Kameny's concern with the tactical value of mainstream appearances. But for Sullivan, such a focus also came naturally. Living in Washington, he was drawn to what he saw as burly, "heartland" gay men, many of whom served secretly in the military. He was appalled at how they were treated under military policy, which could send them to jail and even end their careers if they were found out. And getting to know them was also an education in just how different— indeed, how much more conservative—many ordinary gay people were compared to more visible members of the gay movement.

To Sullivan, all this was a welcome surprise. While he wrote that he sought to combine liberal and conservative approaches to gay equality, he had a true conservative's view of the issue, seeing marriage as a path to personal responsibility, social cohesion, and economic prudence. He considered access to marriage and military service—highly traditional institutions revered by conservative Americans—as the two critical items needed to establish gay equality, both as ends in themselves and as tactics to familiarize the nation with gays and lesbians as ordinary people who wanted to live regular lives and serve their country. In his piece, and in a series of longer follow-up pieces, including his controversial 1995 book, *Virtually Normal,* he cast marriage as "an essentially civilizing activity" that would help give gay people the benefit of a "formal, moral stricture" to curb the excesses of personal freedom, the same role it played for straight people. It wasn't that Sullivan sought to disparage all other forms of coupling, or the choice not to couple at all, but his conservative sensibility borrowed from Edmund Burke and John Adams a fundamental distrust of the human capacity to do right without structural constraints. "Not to promote marriage," he wrote, "would be to ask too much of human virtue." It was a worldview largely lost on most of those who led the gay movement, whether they came out of the liberationist or alternative-families movement or simply adhered to the tenets of mainstream liberalism, with its belief in government neutrality about personal freedom and moral virtue.[4]

Although—or perhaps because—he was an outsider to that movement, Sullivan's voice quickly rocketed to the top of the airwaves on gay
issues. He took the reins of the *New Republic* in 1991, becoming one of
its youngest ever editors, and began writing regularly for the *New York
Times*. His prominence as the go-to voice on gay issues in the mainstream
press, along with the assimilationist, often conservative stance he took on
issues, irked many in the gay movement. But Sullivan confidently asserted
that his was the broader, more accurate view of who gay America was
and what it wanted, and he declared that marriage was "the only reform
that truly matters."[5] Sullivan and Wolfson became pragmatic allies in their
common quest to elevate marriage to a top priority among gay advocates.
But Sullivan's sharp focus on marriage and his insistence that it was "more
important than any other institution" put him a world away from the likes
of Ettelbrick, Polikoff, and the liberationists, who sought to bring about a
society quite different from the one they knew.[6]

<hr />

While Sullivan traveled the country making a conservative case for gay
marriage, the staff at Lambda was facing a deepening split over the issue.
Evan Wolfson, naturally, trumpeted the centrality of marriage to the gay
movement, as he had been doing for a decade. Wolfson also had the support
of Tom Stoddard, Lambda's director. Well-spoken and attractive, Stoddard
was a charismatic leader—some called him Kennedyesque (all the more
so in hindsight, as he would die young, lost to AIDS in 1997 at the age of
forty-eight).[7] According to those who worked with him, he could also be
glib, self-absorbed, difficult to work with, and, in the words of one activist,
"a total egomaniac."[8] But he was a smart and strategic lawyer, capable of
seeing many sides of an issue. Personally, he was ambivalent about whether
marriage was a worthy movement priority. But ultimately Stoddard threw
his support behind it, both as an end in itself and as a critical strategic step
toward furthering understanding and acceptance of gay people and their
relationships.

Reflecting the views of lesbian feminists and many gay liberationists,
Paula Ettelbrick considered that path a mistake and an abandonment of
the alternative-families ideal. When, in 1989, the newly installed (straight)

president of the influential California Bar Association endorsed same-sex marriage in a speech, Ettelbrick dismissed the statement as misguided do-gooderism. "It was well-meaning straight people who took the debate away from us," she told a reporter at the time. "Nobody was even pushing that issue in the gay community."[9] Said Stoddard the same year, "As far as I can tell, no gay organization of any size, local or national, has yet declared the right to marry as one of its goals."[10] Speaking in 2009, Matt Coles observed that "the marriage movement inside the community is a classic example of a situation in which a motivated minority trumps an apathetic majority."[11]

That may have been true inside the movement itself. But the evidence suggests that marriage as an issue resonated among ordinary gays and lesbians as far back as the 1980s (not to mention those mavericks who pushed the idea in decades prior to that). Indeed, movement leaders, who tended to skew left, were not wholly representative of their constituents on this matter. In addition to the thousands of couples who exchanged vows despite their lack of legal status and those who showed up to participate during the mass wedding at the 1987 march on Washington, one survey undertaken in 1988 found that 83 percent of lesbians and gay men would marry if they were allowed to do so. The survey had its flaws—respondents consisted of those who were already part of a couple, and the people surveyed were drawn from a convenience sample rather than a randomized pool—but it gives some indication of the popularity of marriage. A poll conducted in 1994 by the *Advocate* found a similar result: almost two-thirds of those surveyed said they would marry a same-sex partner if allowed, with a total of 85 percent saying they either would or might get married. Eighty-two percent of another nonrandom call-in survey of nearly 90,000 gay respondents said they "would like to" legally marry someone of the same sex.[12]

Of course, support for the idea of marriage in the abstract does not necessarily translate into what pollsters call "salience"—how strongly people feel about their support rather than simply which side of an issue they are on. There is also research suggesting that people often don't do in reality what they say on surveys they will do. Despite the limitations of such survey data, the polls undercut the claim—made often during this period and since by gay activists and academics (not to mention anti-gay activists who doubted that gays and lesbians would take marriage rights seriously)—that most gay people did not wish to wed.

Some within the gay community seemed more attuned to the diversity of opinion about marriage than others. In 1989 the magazine *Out / Look*
approached leaders at Lambda asking them to write articles representing
opposing views on the issue. "We had heard rumblings in the community"
about marriage, remembered Debra Chasnoff, who was the magazine's
editor at the time and was aware of growing tensions among gay advocates about the role of marriage in the movement—powerful feelings that
marriage either should or should not become a priority. Chasnoff and her
colleagues at the magazine thought that hearing from two legal minds
on the matter could be important in helping the community consider the
issue thoughtfully.[13]

The Lambda staff welcomed the opportunity, and in the fall of 1989
Ettelbrick and Stoddard published opposing takes on the same-sex marriage debate, perhaps the first time these positions had been put so clearly
into print. They then took their debate on the road to a dozen cities with
gay and lesbian communities to hear what members of those communities had to say about whether marriage was the right priority for the
movement.

In Stoddard's piece, "Why Gay People Should Seek the Right to
Marry," he wrote that he was "no fan" of the way marriage was currently
practiced, as it too often "appears to petrify rather than satisfy and enrich."
Nevertheless, he felt that marriage should "rise to the top of the agenda
of every gay organization" for two reasons. First, gay people quite simply
deserved the very same rights as straight people. And second, marriage
was a strategic path to gay equality. Marriage was "the political issue that
most fully tests the dedication of people who are *not* gay to full equality
for gay people," he wrote. That is, as Wolfson had come to believe while
writing his law school paper, marriage could serve as a strategic proxy for
support of gay equality, both a marker of a straight person's level of support
and a spur to that support. The question of whether to allow gay marriage
forced non-gay people to clearly see same-sex love, often for the first time,
and to think through what true equality should entail. Declining to push
for marriage, Stoddard felt, would mean embracing implications about
gayness that he was loath to accept: that homosexual love was somehow
inferior to heterosexual love; that it was unworthy of the same respect,
value, and protections; that two men or two women were simply incapable of achieving the same kind of "exalted domestic state" as a man

and a woman.[14] For Stoddard, marriage itself—whether for straight or gay couples—was hardly the pinnacle of dignity, but fighting for equal access to marriage was a useful tool to advance the larger society's understanding, approval, and equal treatment of gay people.

In Ettelbrick's essay, "Since When Is Marriage a Path to Liberation?," she argued that focusing on marriage would undercut the broader goals of the movement. Marriage would "constrain us, make us more invisible, force our assimilation into the mainstream and undermine the goals of gay liberation." For Ettelbrick, being queer meant more than "setting up house, sleeping with a person of the same gender, and seeking state approval for doing so." It should also mean, she believed, "pushing the parameters of sex, sexuality, and family, and in the process transforming the very fabric of society." Ettelbrick knew of Harry Hay, who had insisted on respect "for our differences not for our sameness to heterosexuals." She saw little need to give the state the power to regulate intimate relationships, and, like Hay, she argued that justice for gay men and lesbians would be achieved "only when we are accepted and supported in this society *despite* our differences from the dominant culture." As a passionate humanist who knew all too well what exclusion felt like, Ettelbrick also abhorred the idea of perpetuating inequality among the gay and lesbian community, something that an exclusionary institution such as marriage would perpetrate against singles. Marriage would mean "gaining rights for a few, but would do nothing to correct the power imbalances between those who are married (whether gay or straight) and those who are not. Thus, justice would not be gained."[15]

The two Lambda lawyers aired their differences in a context of respect and friendship, but the marriage issue had opened within the organization a rift that mirrored the gulf in the gay and lesbian community. The debate over marriage perfectly crystalized the philosophical disagreement running through gay activism since the 1950s: whether the goal of the gay and lesbian movement ought to be to change society or to assimilate, to smash existing norms or to show the world that gays and lesbians actually conformed to them, to expand and celebrate personal freedom and cultural differences or to present gay people as no different from anyone else. How gays and lesbians answered these questions would shape, in large part, individuals' views about the role of marriage in the larger movement.

In the aftermath of the Ettelbrick-Stoddard debate, Roundtable participants—as committed as ever to maintaining the collegiality and solidarity of their collaborative tradition—decided to hammer out a document expressing their common ground. It was written by Evan Wolfson. "All families have a right to secure formal recognition of their relationships," said the Family Bill of Rights. Where a benefit is "conditioned upon such recognition, it should not depend on marital relation, genetic history, or other arbitrary distinctions, but rather should reflect the defining family values" outlined in the document's preamble: the varied living arrangements that real families found themselves in, the diversity of cultures and variety of individual choices that made up American family units, and the range of ethical values that different families adopted. While the document said that same-sex couples should have equal access to marriage, its emphasis was on the assertion that no one should have to marry to enjoy the legal benefits and protections of family life.[16]

The document never progressed beyond draft form. But it stands as a telling reminder of three important historical points: that thoughtful gay and lesbian lawyers with a wide range of beliefs continued to work together cohesively despite profound disagreements; that the gay legal community throughout the 1980s was largely focused on supporting alternatives to traditional family arrangements; and that even Evan Wolfson in the year 1989 supported on paper—indeed, personally drafted—a document that minimized the importance of marriage, equated its legal recognition with "arbitrary distinctions," and emphasized alternatives to marriage instead.

Mary Bonauto showed up for her first day of work at the Boston office of Gay and Lesbian Advocates and Defenders in March 1990. She was just shy of thirty and a few years out of law school.[17] At GLAD, Bonauto would quickly become Evan Wolfson's sister-in-arms, methodically making the case for the importance of marriage to any of her colleagues who would listen. In 1987 she had attended the march on Washington, with its mass wedding organized by marriage supporters. A protest of that event by gay opponents of prioritizing marriage was also planned, and Bonauto's two lesbian roommates were among the protestors. "They thought the whole idea of marriage for same-sex couples was ridiculous," she remembered years later. Bonauto understood their perspective—that marriage was synonymous with the oppression of women, bourgeois assimilation, exclusion of singles—but did not share the view that the institution was impervious to reform, and she did not join in the anti-marriage protest at the march.[18]

At the time, Bonauto had never dated anyone she thought she'd like to marry. But by the time she arrived at GLAD, she had met someone she couldn't see living without. She and her partner discussed whether to hold an event celebrating their commitment but decided they didn't want to do so until it was legal. For Bonauto, the inability to marry was a personal deprivation, but it also represented the wider injustice of being branded inferior. She became hooked on the idea that she must do all she could to help win the freedom to marry.

Still, it would be years before she would push a marriage lawsuit. In her first week at GLAD she turned down a marriage case, much as the NAACP's Thurgood Marshall had spent a decade turning down requests for help challenging school segregation in the 1940s. "What was I supposed to do," Bonauto explained, "waltz up to a judge and say, 'Can't you read the equal protection clause of our Constitution? It says no person shall be denied equal protection of the laws. That means marriage, and we win!' We'd be laughed out of court." Instead, GLAD, which was established in 1978 in response to complaints of police entrapment of gay men, focused its resources on basic safety, access to the legal system, and the ability to contact the police without being harassed or humiliated. Until around the time she began at GLAD, Bonauto recalled, "We felt under siege by the police." She recalled an epidemic of anti-gay violence and a "pervasive sense of unsafety and vulnerability." Facing threats and abuse, gay people frequently had nowhere to turn without risking further harm or being outed to hostile friends or families. "People were having their skulls smashed in with baseball bats," said Bonauto, and more often than not, the perpetrators suffered no consequences.

One of Bonauto's jobs at GLAD was to speak to every person who phoned in for help, which gave her a front-row seat to the sufferings of gay New Englanders. She remembered the case of a lesbian couple who entered a car dealership to buy a used car; when the dealer realized they were a couple, he ripped off the antenna of a nearby car and attacked them with it. A patron at a Dunkin' Donuts, suspected of being gay, was beaten as management stood by, unwilling to lift a finger. A fourteen-year-old attacked several gay men with a baseball bat right in the middle of Boston Common, but it was left to GLAD to ensure that charges were filed. Bonauto had to go to court fourteen times just to make sure a criminal complaint was issued.[19]

Local police could be not only unhelpful but a chief part of the problem. Two decades after Stonewall, raids in bars and restaurants had become far less common, and relations with the police were improving, in part thanks to the efforts of GLAD. But stings persisted in parks and public bathrooms, and the sense of vulnerability lingered. "It was about putting a whole community under siege," said Bonauto. The AIDS epidemic intensified this fear, as illness and death from the disease compounded the toll of anti-gay violence and government neglect. Meanwhile, cities and states continued to attack the legal and expressive rights of gay citizens, with some towns even in relatively liberal New England passing measures that banned discussion of homosexuality in schools. As GLAD fought these measures, guidance counselors complained that the laws forced them to refer questioning youth to anti-gay literature and groups that urged them to seek sexual orientation conversion therapy, which could include electrical shocks to punish same-sex desire.[20]

These were the realities that dictated the focus of GLAD's work in the 1990s: ensuring that battered youth saw their abusers punished, securing health care and partner recognition for those dying of AIDS, and fighting laws that would prohibit the very discussion of homosexuality in public schools. Mindful of what these challenges said about the dim prospects of winning something like the right to marry, GLAD saw little room on its agenda for what seemed like an impossible luxury. So Bonauto had to repeatedly turn down callers wanting to sue for marriage. "I understand, I agree, you're right," she would tell them, "and it's the wrong time." As sympathetic as she was, she felt the nation would not be ready for same-sex marriage until activists spent years building public approval. "I'm sort of amazed that I had that amount of strategic sense at that time," she says.[21]

Bonauto regarded this approach as a "brick by brick" strategy for building a legal edifice to protect gay people and their families. She fully understood that getting to marriage would be a long road, and that an incremental approach that built protections along the way was the most strategic and humane way to get there. Like Wolfson and Coles, Bonauto grasped the importance of spurring conversations across the country about gay people and their relationships through advocacy work and the public education that accompanied it. "As Rev. Dr. Martin Luther King, Jr. explained," she would later write, "no minority can succeed without the assistance of the majority." But Bonauto also saw that it wasn't only straight obstructionists who needed to be persuaded on marriage equality. Many gays and lesbians, she noticed, had "cut off" whole aspects of themselves, a kind of coping mechanism given the limits of what they felt they could achieve. "They didn't even dare to think about" marriage, she said. While there were certainly those who opposed fighting for marriage on principle, others could barely bring themselves to contemplate the possibility. "Some people just shut down the conversation and did not want to hear about it if it was not doable. It's just the kind of thing where you don't even bother thinking about things you can't have." Others were simply unaware of all that came with marriage rights. "Part of the job of people like Evan and myself and other advocates was to talk about what's at stake in marriage" when speaking with the gay community. This included the tangible benefits and protections it provided—things like tax savings, health insurance through a partner's employer, and social security or pension payments. Still, to Bonauto, as to Wolfson, such rights paled in comparison to the significance of marriage as "a badge of citizenship." She encouraged other gay people to ponder all the categories of people who could marry, while they themselves were barred from the institution, an exclusion she regarded as a "massive statement of disrespect" by the government toward its gay and lesbian citizens.[22]

Not all gays and lesbians in the early 1990s put marriage out of their minds, as Bonauto knew from the phone requests she fielded from all kinds of gay New Englanders wanting to wed. Among those who very much had marriage on their minds were several couples and a handful of activists in Hawaii, about as far away from Boston as one could get while still on U.S. soil. For Ninia Baehr and Genora Dancel, the road to marriage equality started with an ear infection. Not that there wasn't romance: the

Ninia Baehr and Genora Dancel at the Hawaii State Supreme Court in 1993, moments after the positive ruling.

two women had fallen in love in the spring of 1990, and they routinely talked about getting married. "At the time, it was just something you'd say," recalled Baehr, "because it didn't seem possible." But when the pain in Baehr's ear worsened and she realized she had no health insurance, the two women looked in the yellow pages and called up Honolulu's gay and lesbian community center. They wanted to know if there was a domestic partnership law that could allow Baehr to obtain coverage through Dancel's employer.[23]

At the center, they reached Bill Woods, an ornery but dedicated area activist, who explained to the pair that if Dancel's employer did not offer health benefits voluntarily, they were out of luck. Woods told them something else: some activists he had been consulting believed that the Hawaii state constitution might require allowing same-sex marriage. For a while now, Woods had been talking to same-sex couples about testing that interpretation by showing up at the offices of the Health Department and demanding marriage licenses. "Would you want to go for marriage?" he asked the women.[24]

Although Baehr and Dancel had discussed the prospect of getting married, it had never risen to a serious consideration. Contemplating Woods's idea, and with her ear now throbbing, Baehr felt a growing anger compound her physical pain. How could her health be held hostage to an arbitrary rule that punished her just because she was the "wrong" sex? What began as a starkly pragmatic concern—access to health care—quickly became a quest for equal dignity as well. "For me it's an emotional decision," Baehr told a reporter in 1995. She did not view their quest as part of a long-term strategy. For much of her life she had simply wanted a relationship that would last, and "when it finally happened, I wanted recognition of that." Much like heterosexual couples, the women contemplated marriage with a mix of practical and emotional concerns—but buttressed by a sense that equal justice demanded access to marriage. They could find no reason why they shouldn't be allowed to wed, and many reasons why they needed and deserved the same privileges, protections, and responsibilities as married straight people.[25]

Woods found two other couples willing to participate in a challenge to Hawaii's marriage laws, Pat Lagon and Joseph Melillo and Tammy Rodrigues and Antoinette Pregil.[26] Lagon and Melillo had met in 1978 at a disco lesson. "We weren't looking for the marriage on paper—that's not what we were fighting for," recalled Lagon in 2006, after Melillo's death from throat cancer. Rather, the two saw the benefits that came with marriage as the main impetus for joining the suit. Pregil and Rodrigues had met in 1981 and soon began living together, eventually having a child. They joined the suit hopeful that being married would grant their family all the legal protections that so many other families took for granted.[27]

The night before the group planned to show up at the Hawaii Health Department, Dancel was still not sure if she wanted to go forward. She wasn't fully out to her family, even though she and Baehr often stayed together at the family's home, and she was by nature more private than her partner. She had a mortgage to pay and didn't know how her employers would respond to hearing she was gay and had begun agitating for equality. She was also less tuned in to gay rights battles than Baehr, who had lived in New York City for years. "Ninia was more politically inclined than I was," remembered Dancel later. "I was just following along." Eventually Woods phoned Dancel and told her, "You have thirty minutes to decide if you're going to show up tomorrow," explaining that he was trying to arrange media coverage for the next morning and needed to know if they planned to join.[28]

Woods's plan was to show up at the Health Department with the three couples asking for marriage licenses and, if they were rejected, to march to the local American Civil Liberties Union office to formally ask for representation in a lawsuit, seeing this as a way to force the issue with the civil liberties group. Woods had previously contacted the ACLU to discuss a lawsuit, but to his consternation, no one at the local chapter expressed support. The staff were not unsympathetic, but they did not take seriously the viability of a same-sex marriage suit or feel that it was a reasonable use of limited resources. Discouraged, Woods had vowed to press the issue in the media spotlight.[29]

As Dancel thought about it all, she said to herself, "I'm tired of being treated differently, and I have as much right as anyone else to get married and enter that union." Although she still had reservations, she had always believed that important things required sacrifice. "This is what I need to do," she thought. She told Woods that she and Baehr would be there the next day.[30] The two women were not active in the gay rights community and, as they recalled it, did not fully understand that the ultimate plan was to file a lawsuit. They thought they might very well be granted the marriage license they were after.

That morning the couples assembled at the Health Department, where they were met by a slew of cameras and reporters. When they asked the clerk for a marriage license, it seemed initially as though she were ready to give them one. But suddenly she paused and said she had to speak to a supervisor. When she returned to the window, she apologetically told the couples—one after another—that she was advised she could not give licenses to same-sex couples. With cameras trailing them, Woods and the couples marched to the ACLU office, whose staff told them that they had to confer before answering their request for representation. The day ended with the parties in a holding pattern.[31]

With the stakes raised, the ACLU staff phoned the organization's national headquarters and reached Nan Hunter at the group's Lesbian and Gay Rights Project. Trained to be cautious about the risks of impact litigation, Hunter, who taught law and later served as a lawyer in the U.S. Department of Health and Human Services, counseled the local ACLU chapter to be sensitive to the wishes of the area's gay and lesbian population. Her suggestion was to gauge the sentiment of local leaders and to talk through what the community wanted. "Anyone could bring a marriage case anywhere at any time," Hunter later recalled. "The question is how you strategize to not just act on the request of one group."[32]

Taking Hunter's advice, the Hawaii ACLU reached out to leaders of the local gay and lesbian community to assess the population's support for pursuing same-sex marriage. The step provoked anger among some activists, who complained that the ACLU was hedging rather than taking a leadership role on something the activists viewed as a fundamental right. Hunter found it ironic that people were criticizing the ACLU for hesitating to take on the case or being insufficiently pro-gay. "The ACLU was just trying to respect the community," she said. "It was a great example of no good deed going unpunished."[33] Finding little support from the gay community, scarred by the *Bowers* outcome and the consequent lesson that lawsuits brought with insufficient groundwork risked devastating setbacks, and with few people on staff who were passionate about pushing marriage, the ACLU declined the case.[34]

When the ACLU said no, Ninia Baehr got in touch with Evan Wolfson, whom she had met some years earlier when she was living in New York City. Wolfson had been a full-time staff member at Lambda for just over a year, and he was eager for Lambda to take the case. But given the concerns held by some members of the Roundtable, persuading Lambda to back Woods's lawsuit would not be easy. For starters, Lambda was still a small organization with limited resources. Even if it won this lawsuit, the group would have to defend against efforts to reverse it through a constitutional amendment. (Like most states, Hawaii permitted voters to approve constitutional amendments through a ballot referendum, a step that could override a ruling by the state's highest court.) If Lambda and the other groups lacked the capacity to make a court win durable, a loss by public referendum could devastate momentum. A related concern was the long list of immediate threats to the safety, job security, and health of gays and lesbians. Could Lambda really afford to fight for something like marriage amid all these other pressing needs?

The greatest reservations, however, were ideological. Baehr's appeal to Lambda set off a new round of deliberations in the organization, suddenly shifting the Roundtable's long-standing debate over marriage from the academic into the concrete. Ettelbrick, who at the time was Wolfson's boss, remembered the period as "probably the tensest moment within Lambda. Evan was chomping at the bit to do it and almost threatened mutiny." Ettelbrick said the "conventional wisdom among the national groups was that we didn't want to push marriage at that point. The feeling was it was just too soon." Consistent with the alternative-families perspective held by most leaders of the legal groups, Ettelbrick and others at Lambda sought instead to strategize other ways to raise the visibility of same-sex couples.[35] Coles echoed the point: "We felt at the time that neither the legal nor the political groundwork had really been laid." Although Ettelbrick emphasized the question of timing, for her and others at that moment, marriage was simply not something to fight for. Even though Stoddard, Lambda's director, had supported marriage in the published debates with Ettelbrick, he ultimately deferred to Ettelbrick, the group's legal director—and to the larger consensus of the Roundtable lawyers—in deciding whether Lambda would join Woods's suit. After a string of contentious discussions at Lambda, Wolfson was told he could not take the case.

In the months after Lambda's decision, the personality clashes inside the office grew alongside ideological and strategic ones, and by late 1991 they were so pronounced that Evan Wolfson was fired. Yet Wolfson never cleared out his desk. When members of Lambda's board, along with other area activists who had the clout to oppose the decision, heard that the strongest voice for marriage within Lambda was about to lose his job there, some spoke out. Ultimately the board reversed the decision over the objection of Tom Stoddard, who consequently resigned as director. Lambda would eventually recover, and relations would be patched up between Wolfson and Ettelbrick (and the departed Stoddard, who continued to press for marriage—and held his own wedding ceremony in 1993, four years before he died). But the divisions present at the time reflected just how strongly many gay leaders felt about marriage. They also echoed the disagreements felt within the wider gay and lesbian community over the issue, where loyalty to liberationist ideals often clashed with the practical, the personal, and the emotional in the contest over whether and where marriage belonged on the community's agenda.

With both the ACLU and Lambda out of the picture, Woods and the three couples turned to Dan Foley, a straight lawyer who had worked at the Hawaii ACLU in the 1980s. Foley's first instinct had been that "it would be arrogant to deny" gay people the same rights he enjoyed. His uncle had opened one of the earliest gay bars outside San Francisco in the 1950s, and in the 1960s Foley wrote a college thesis on the treatment of gays and lesbians. He didn't hesitate to take on the marriage lawsuit, and with Lambda's blessing, he accepted Wolfson as a behind-the-scenes advisor on the case.[36] Because the movement groups had declined to support the suit, Baehr and Dancel had to raise money on their own to pay Foley. They asked local businesses to donate door prizes for parties at lesbian bars, and enlisted other activists to host events at their houses, taking small donations at the door. Foley invoiced for only half his time and in the end accepted only half that amount, which the women paid in small increments.[37]

The suit was filed on May 1, 1991. *Baehr v. Lewin* claimed that blocking the freedom to marry violated gay people's rights to privacy, equal protection of the law, and due process, as guaranteed by the Hawaii constitution.[38] Initially Foley was not hopeful that they could win: at the time, the Hawaii Supreme Court consisted of five (presumably straight) men in their sixties. But as the case made its way through the lower courts, several younger judges, including a woman, replaced the old guard, and Foley's estimate of the chances of victory grew slightly.[39]

In the circuit court, the state of Hawaii defended its refusal to let gays wed by arguing both that marriage was essential to straight families and that denying it to gay couples was no serious burden. The "basic family unit," said the state, meaning straight parents and their children, "provides status and a nurturing environment to children born to married persons." Excluding gay couples does not interfere with their "private relationships" and is therefore not penalizing. Marriage, the state argued, is "obviously designed to promote the general welfare interests of the community by sanctioning traditional man-woman family units and procreation." The state's marriage laws also "constitute a statement of the moral values of the community."[40]

The state's defense had all the essential ingredients of the broad legal and cultural argument against same-sex marriage for a generation afterward: marriage was definitionally heterosexual, as anyone could see by looking at existing law; the state did not, and should not have to, approve of same-sex unions, which would be the result of legalizing gay marriage; banning gay marriage was an expression of the community's moral values; heterosexual-only marriage strengthened and protected society and particularly the family, defined so as to exclude gay people; marriage existed to encourage and nurture childbearing and child rearing, and thus gay marriage was unnecessary and might even threaten marriage; and finally, restricting marriage to heterosexual couples imposed no real burden or harm on gay people.

Hawaii's defense of its marriage laws avoided the worst excesses of anti-gay rhetoric, instead featuring what could seem like a reasonable statement of self-evident facts about what marriage was for and why gay couples didn't qualify. In October 1991 the lower court concluded that the director of the state Health Department, John Lewin, was "entitled to judgment in his favor as a matter of law," and dismissed the case.[41] Foley appealed.

Over the next couple years, few in the gay and lesbian community paid much attention to the renegade case working its way through the Hawaii courts. In 1992 the Republican Party chose to make gay rights a wedge issue, throwing the gay community further on the defensive. In a fiery convention speech, the conservative commentator Pat Buchanan declared "a religious war . . . for the soul of America" and decried "militant" homosexuals as a threat to the family. As a wedge, the tactic succeeded, pushing the young, charismatic Democratic presidential candidate, Bill Clinton, to assure voters that he opposed "special rights" for gay people, as well as gay marriage—an issue that was otherwise seldom mentioned in that year's campaign. But in an unprecedented effort to engage and include gays and lesbians in his effort to win the presidency, Clinton campaigned on a promise to end the military's exclusion of gay troops, to oppose anti-gay discrimination, and to step up the fight against AIDS.

That November Clinton took the White House with the crucial help of gay dollars and votes. On election night gays and lesbians danced euphorically in the streets, feeling that they finally had an advocate in the White House—but marriage did not come up at all. Instead, they pushed him to fulfill his campaign promises.[42] After a bitter and protracted fight, Congress blocked Clinton's efforts to let gays serve openly in the military, writing into federal law a version of the existing policy barring open gays and lesbians from service. The end results were the "don't ask, don't tell" policy, a weakened Clinton, and a demonstration of the strength of the religious right. Still, despite the defeat, the Clinton White House had embraced gay people and the major priorities of the organized gay movement like no other administration in history. That—along with growing acceptance of gay people in the culture at large—inspired a change in gay political activism, marked by a greater willingness to work within the political process to effect change—a departure from the ACT UP years of direct action. "Press conferences, vs. coming out to get arrested, should make more gay men and lesbians comfortable about being involved in politics," said Michael Petrelis a year after Bill Clinton took office. Petrelis had been active in ACT UP but left the group to help form a new, more moderate organization called Gay and Lesbian Americans. Fellow member Jon Carl Lewis, preparing a series of Valentine's Day press conferences, said, "We need to create a community from a base of wanting to see good happen, and not just rebel against the system."[43]

The push by some activists for marriage equality, with its focus on mainstreaming gay life, certainly reflected that shift. Yet within the gay movement, marriage remained a fringe issue. That's why many were shocked when the news broke in May 1993 that the Hawaii Supreme Court had handed down a ruling favoring the three same-sex couples. The court found the state's defense of straight-only marriage hollow. The lower court, said Judge Steven Levinson's majority opinion, had "erroneously dismissed the plaintiffs' complaint."

Levinson's opinion relied on the plaintiffs' gender, rather than their sexual orientation, to establish a high bar for the state to meet. Historically, courts have applied one of three levels of scrutiny to constitutional challenges involving equal protection claims. The lowest bar, called "rational basis review," deems a law constitutional if it has a rational relationship to a "legitimate government interest," even if that means limiting an individual's constitutional rights. The next level, "intermediate scrutiny," requires that courts give added weight to a group's constitutional claims, and that the challenged law be "substantially related to an important government objective." The highest level of review is called "strict scrutiny" and requires the state to show a "compelling governmental interest" in any law that infringes on a constitutional right and to assure the court that no narrower course of action could achieve the same purpose. It is applied in cases involving a "suspect class" deserving of extra scrutiny when laws threaten their constitutional rights. Courts routinely apply strict scrutiny in cases involving race-based classifications, and frequently use intermediate scrutiny in cases involving gender.[44]

The Hawaii Supreme Court found that the plaintiffs were being denied the right to marry because of their sex, and that the case must be reheard, this time subject to strict scrutiny. Unlike the federal Constitution, the Hawaii constitution had an equal rights amendment, with explicit nondiscrimination language based on sex. Because Hawaii's marriage law improperly "establishes a sex-based classification," said the court, the law "is presumed to be unconstitutional unless it can be shown that the statute's sex-based classification is justified by compelling state interests." That burden would rest on the state in a new hearing.[45] The Hawaii Supreme Court was the first court to tell the world that opposition to gay marriage could not stand when defended simply through assertions rather than legal arguments and evidence.

Wolfson called the Hawaii decision a "tectonic shift" and announced that the quest for access to marriage was "on the verge of victory." Yet much stood in the way of achieving that goal. For one thing, the gay movement remained divided. For many ordinary gays and lesbians—Bill Woods and the Hawaii plaintiffs, the thousands registering their support in polls, the New England couples phoning in to GLAD and other hotlines—it was practical and personal reasons, including the simple wish to express their love, that spurred them to support marriage. Yet only a smattering of movement leaders prioritized marriage: Wolfson, Bonauto, and Stoddard, for instance, along with Andrew Sullivan with his lofty appeals to the common humanity of gay people. Movement groups on the whole, including Lambda, the ACLU, the Human Rights Campaign, and the National Gay and Lesbian Task Force, either opposed or overlooked the idea that marriage was, or ought to be, a priority. The lawsuit that had catapulted marriage equality to center stage was filed without the support of the gay movement's largest groups and leaders, and against the wishes of some of them. After Hawaii, their leaders were forced to take stock of a landscape that had been remade overnight.[46]

If accidental activists such as Ninia Baehr and Genora Dancel helped push the gay movement to take marriage seriously, Wolfson and the small cadre of marriage champions inside the movement seized the opportunity to shape the next phase of work. Recognizing the unstoppable momentum of the battle to come—gay advocates would quickly come to grasp the magnitude of right-wing opposition to gay marriage—Wolfson spearheaded a new Marriage Project at Lambda, launched the National

Freedom to Marry Coalition, and circulated a document known as the Marriage Resolution, a tool to build broad national backing for marriage equality. In a series of memos designed to enlist and coordinate movement support, Wolfson laid out the challenges and opportunities created by the Hawaii ruling. "We must begin the hard work of public education and political organizing now—nationwide and state by state," he wrote. "This landmark civil rights battle cannot be left just to lawyers." Wolfson was keenly aware that although the gay movement had not chosen the marriage battle, a war was on; the movement's foot soldiers must deploy their power to win a victory for the dignity of their relationships and defend that dignity against certain attack from the right wing. The battles, he explained, would be "cultural, political and legal." He then outlined a battery of strategic activities that gay advocates and their allies should begin to engage in to ensure victory over time: prepare public education campaigns by reaching out to community organizations, opinion leaders, lawmakers, and other potential allies; develop effective messages working with pollsters and public relations consultants; host conferences, public forums, and political briefings; develop lists of media targets, talking points, and spokespeople, and identify community leaders, religious groups, and others willing to publicly endorse marriage equality; and write memos, op-eds, fact sheets, and organizing manuals in an effort to "mainstream [the] idea of equal marriage rights." In that vein, Wolfson saw the post-Hawaii battle as "a chance to show who we are, frame the battle as we want, address our issues, and present our lives and love affirmatively." As nasty as the fight would likely become, he saw the value of keeping the engagement positive, particularly with audiences who had not yet been reached but seemed reachable. He counseled people to "tap into more comfortable, genuine rhetoric for mainstream [audiences]" and to "marshal evocative stories of how being denied the right to marry affects real people."[47]

Although Wolfson and the Lambda staff were always careful to note the political and cultural battles that must accompany legal ones, organizations such as Lambda had a specific idea of what a litigation approach should entail. It meant being highly strategic about where to pursue litigation. Despite pleas from grassroots activists tired of waiting for equality and from ordinary couples simply hoping to marry, legal advocates insisted that lawsuits should go forward only in the few states with a ripe climate: strong existing nondiscrimination law, positive public opinion, open-minded judges, and constitutions that could not be amended at the drop of a hat. People must not seek a "quick fix," Wolfson wrote shortly after the Hawaii decision, but should patiently lay the groundwork for a durable win in the courts. First, the focus should be on achieving a "final victory in Hawaii while temporarily holding back on marriage litigation" if the prospects for victory couldn't be ensured. "Impact litigation and test-cases are not the be-all and end-all of social change, and wanting equal choice regarding marriage does not in itself validate every couple's rushing out today to file a lawsuit heedless of the realities where they live," he wrote. "The wrong case, wrong judge, or wrong forum could literally set us all back years, if not decades."[48]

Although he took the long view, Wolfson predicted a win in Hawaii by 1997, calling it "highly unlikely" that voters would overturn a pro-gay court decision with a state constitutional amendment. Meanwhile, he argued, the next step for advocates was to lay the groundwork for the spread of marriage throughout the nation. The question of whether other states would have to recognize same-sex marriages performed in Hawaii was as yet unanswered. Most legal experts believed they wouldn't. Although the federal Constitution requires states to grant "full faith and credit" to the laws of other states, historically a "public policy" exception prevented states from being forced to honor public acts that clearly contradict their own laws. At a minimum, the two dozen states with sodomy bans on the books were likely to claim that gay marriage was a clear violation of their public policy. Wolfson, of course, was aware of the contested legal terrain. But, hoping to create a sense of momentum, he pushed an optimistic interpretation of the Constitution's full faith and credit clause, which presumed that states would have to honor other states' gay marriages. Gay activists must "create a non-defeatist sense of entitlement and expectation, and a climate of receptivity and inevitability," Wolfson urged, "tempered with a commitment to the long haul." It was also crucial, he argued, to awaken the gay and lesbian population itself to the importance of fighting for marriage. Gays and lesbians must "send wake-up calls to our national and local community organizations," he counseled, and tap into marriage's power as a priority "even for those less politicized people in our communities."[49]

As part of the lawyers' efforts to reach out and prepare for the marriage battle, Lambda oversaw an ambitious project to assess the climate for marriage and relationship recognition litigation in all fifty states. A committee of the American Bar Association signed on to help, as did law professor Barbara Cox. GLAD coordinated the work in the New England states. Wolfson sought extra help and broad involvement by urging the development of networks of lawyers, legal scholars, and law students across the country who could exhaustively study their own states' statutes, precedents, case law, application of public policies—anything and everything that could help prepare gay advocates to press for marriage recognition throughout the country once they had a foothold in a single state, and to gird for the mammoth backlash foreseen at both the state and national levels.[50]

By the mid-1990s gay legal advocates had developed a rough consensus that, however one felt about the merits of marriage, solidarity was needed in fighting for the equal worth of same-sex relationships. This unity was partly a response to the opportunity to build on the Hawaii win. But it was also a response to seeing their relationships directly attacked. After Hawaii, Paula Ettelbrick remembered, "we were immediately launched into a battle that made it very odd for people like myself because, obviously, in no way was I ever going to defend the attacks on the Hawaii decision."[51] Wolfson called on the leaders of the gay movement—particularly the legal groups—to put aside their philosophical differences now that the Hawaii ruling had indelibly put marriage on the map. "For the first time in living memory, we can realistically hope to see lesbian and gay couples happily joined on an equal footing with our non-gay brothers and sisters," he wrote in 1994, "if those who favor equality can put aside their divisions and unite to secure ultimate victory. For this reason, I have urged that we end, or at least suspend, the intra-community debate over whether to seek marriage. The ship has sailed." Wolfson cited the arguments of the lawyers defending the state of Hawaii against claims to equal marriage rights, who were warning that gay marriage would signal social approval of gay and lesbian life and love. Surely, he pleaded, gay advocates could unit in defense of that very goal.[52]

And so, as religious and political conservatives awakened to what they saw as a dire threat to their "traditional values" agenda, gays and lesbians awoke to the need to defend the dignity of their relationships from frontal assault. To anyone paying attention, it was increasingly clear that marriage equality had gone in a few short years from an outlandish thought experiment to a serious matter of constitutional law. Whatever one thought of that reality, there was work to be done.

"The Very Foundations of Our Society Are in Danger"

THE DEFENSE OF MARRIAGE

SOCIAL CONSERVATIVES WERE ENRAGED BY THE HAWAII COURT RULING. What they feared was exactly what Wolfson hoped: that a single court ruling in America's fiftieth state could be used as a tool to spread marriage equality nationwide, as couples married in Hawaii, then traveled or returned home expecting the other forty-nine states to recognize their legal unions. In their effort to block that possibility, they would find willing partners in national Republicans who saw in anti-gay initiatives an irresistible opportunity to increase support from the religious right and put Democrats on the defensive by painting them as cultural outcasts who were in the pocket of special interests and appallingly focused on social issues instead of Americans' economic woes.

The first order of business for marriage equality opponents was to deal with Hawaii itself. Given the state supreme court's application of strict scrutiny in its provisional decision, conservatives were not optimistic that the new hearing would give them a victory. Gay marriage would become a reality in Hawaii unless they could convince the voters to amend the state's constitution to override any such ruling. As they scoured their legal textbooks and studied the laws of Hawaii, they began to build public support for a state constitutional amendment. While the Hawaii court ruling made it a pressing concern to block marriage in that state, the focus on the state level also reflected the fact that conservatives recognized, sooner than gay advocates, the power of local political action—lessons the religious right had been applying since the 1970s, with efforts such as Anita Bryant's Save Our Children coalition and the Briggs initiative in California. In a series of preemptive strikes against the possibility of seeing gay marriage recognized at the state level, conservative activists gathered with lawyers and political consultants to draft legislation that could be introduced by state legislators. In March 1995, Utah became the first state to pass a law prohibiting the recognition of same-sex marriages, and similar campaigns followed in dozens of other states. While several bills failed, by 2000 thirty states had adopted such laws, with more pending.[1]

Simultaneously, social conservatives had to take stock of the national climate and figure out how to ensure that, even if some state did legalize same-sex marriage, the public and federal law would not come to associate marriage with gay unions. By 1994 political conservatives were enjoying a resurgence of power as the Clinton administration stumbled. Weakened by his failure to pass universal health care and lift the ban on gays in the military, Clinton watched as the GOP House minority whip, Rep. Newt Gingrich of Georgia, staged what became known as the "Republican Revolution," seizing control of the House from Democrats for the first time in four decades. Republicans also took the Senate. GOP victories both in Congress and in statehouses across the nation emboldened social conservatives, and a right wing made apoplectic over the prospect of same-sex marriage quickly found that great opportunity lay in opposing it. In the 1990s the religious right came to see fighting homosexuality as a crucial ticket to power, finding the topic more effective even than abortion in whipping up outrage, dollars, and votes. "It's great to have an enemy," said one conservative consultant working to block gays from being allowed to serve in the military. While some anti-gay activists, especially those motivated by religious zeal, continued to make their case in the unapologetic terms of religious faith and moral certitude, others were professionalizing their tactics and polishing their messages so they would appear less hateful and dogmatic and more rooted in secular concerns about research on social stability and child well-being, which they cast as imperiled by gay marriage.[2]

Beginning in 1995 conservatives at national and religious think tanks huddled to plot strategy both to contain the spread of same-sex marriage and to drive a wedge between Democratic leaders and their gay and liberal constituents, generating a backlash that could help advance conservative political interests. In January 1996 conservative Christian leaders met in a Memphis church basement to discuss ways to head off the spread of same-sex marriage. The groups represented included the Family Research Council, Focus on the Family, the Christian Coalition, and the American Family Association, among others. The coalition formed a new group, called the National Pro-Family Forum, which was dedicated to opposing gay equality, with a particular focus on same-sex marriage. With public opinion showing that two-thirds of Americans opposed gay marriage, and with Congress having handily passed "don't ask, don't tell," conservatives knew that a federal effort to block recognition of same-sex marriage would find plenty of support. If Utah could pass a law denying recognition of same-sex marriages, the group reasoned, why couldn't the United States Congress do something similar? The idea that emerged was a law that would both ensure that states could decline to recognize such marriages and, in an unprecedented step, create a federal definition of marriage as confined to a male-female union. The result would be to deny federal recognition to same-sex marriage, ensuring that gay couples would not enjoy the same federal spousal benefits as straight couples even if their state allowed them to wed. It would also give a national imprimatur to the determination that same-sex unions could not be real marriages. Finally, it would put President Clinton in a bind as he sought reelection: Clinton had already said he opposed same-sex marriage, but forcing him to take a public stand on a bill that was clearly intended to repudiate gay equality was a way to throw him on the defensive during an election year.

The next month was the Republican caucus in Des Moines, Iowa. The National Pro-Family Forum set up shop in a nearby church, invited the press, and asked the candidates to publicly endorse a "marriage protection" resolution indicating that they would support laws denying recognition of same-sex marriage. Several candidates signed the resolution, aware how popular it was with rank-and-file conservatives. In May the Defense of Marriage Act (DOMA) was introduced in both the House and the Senate

by Republican lawmakers, with Bob Dole, the presumptive GOP presidential candidate and Senate majority leader, signing on as a cosponsor.[3]

DOMA included a provision that no state would have to recognize
same-sex marriages performed in another state. This provision was largely
redundant, since most legal scholars believed the states already had the authority to determine how a marriage was defined.[4] But the most far-reaching
provision read: "In determining the meaning of any Act of Congress, or of
any ruling, regulation, or interpretation of the various administrative bureaus and agencies of the United States, the word 'marriage' means only a
legal union between one man and one woman as husband and wife, and the
word 'spouse' refers only to a person of the opposite sex who is a husband
or a wife."[5] For the United States government to establish a federal definition of marriage at all—let alone one that distinguished between worthy
and unworthy unions—marked an unprecedented incursion of federal
power into a realm that historically had been reserved to the states: the
power to determine what was a valid marriage.

Throughout 1996, lawmakers laid out the parameters of the national
debate on same-sex marriage in congressional hearings, with Republicans
scrambling to outdo one another in slamming gay marriage as a threat to
the country. Rep. Bob Barr, who sponsored the bill in the House, spoke
darkly of the existential threat that gay marriage posed to America. "As
Rome burned, Nero fiddled," he warned, explaining that a similar fate
would befall the United States if its leaders allowed themselves to become
complacent in the face of gay incursions into the mainstream. "The very
foundations of our society are in danger of being burned," he went on.
"The flames of hedonism, the flames of narcissism, the flames of self-
centered morality are licking at the very foundation of our society: the
family unit." He implored his colleagues to "wake up and see" that gay
extremists were "bent on forcing a tortured view of morality on the rest
of the country." They had to be stopped, and the best line of defense was
to ensure the maintenance of "a moral foundation" for America's families,
which meant denying any government blessing of approval or legitimacy
for homosexuality.[6]

Sen. Jesse Helms of North Carolina, a notorious enemy of civil rights,
said DOMA was needed "to safeguard the sacred institution of marriage
and the family from those who seek to destroy them and who are willing

to tear apart America's moral fabric in the process." Rep. Steve Largent of Oklahoma called same-sex marriage "a frontal assault on the institution of marriage" that would "demolish the institution" if successful. No culture that had endorsed homosexuality, he noted, had ever endured. Rep. Thomas Coburn, also of Oklahoma, cited discredited statistics claiming that nearly half of gay people have more than five hundred sexual partners. His constituents, he said, believed "that homosexuality is immoral, that it is based on perversion, that it is based on lust." As a result, "it is time to say that homosexuality should not be sanctioned on an equal level with heterosexuality."[7]

The belief that homosexuality was a choice—and a harmful one at that—imbued much of the rhetoric with a moral and religious dimension. Largent insisted that "homosexuals have the same rights as I do," since they were indeed allowed to marry—they just had to marry members of the opposite sex, like anyone else. Rep. Charles Canady of Florida complained that allowing gay marriage would mean making the law "indifferent" to whether young people "choose a partner of the opposite sex or a partner of the same sex." Rep. Stephen Buyer of Indiana called gay marriage "an attack upon God's principles" that threatened to lead the nation into chaos.[8]

A congressional report written by House Republicans asserted that DOMA was necessary to advance several "important legitimate governmental purposes," including "upholding traditional morality, encouraging procreation in the context of families, encouraging heterosexuality," and others. The report, which mocked the idea of same-sex marriage by placing scare quotes around the term "marriage" every time it referred to gay unions, claimed that laws restricting marriage to heterosexuals "reflect and honor a collective moral judgment about human sexuality" that expresses "both moral disapproval of homosexuality and a moral conviction that heterosexuality better comports with traditional (especially Judeo-Christian) morality."[9] While some conservative thinkers were beginning to urge a softer line of attack so as to obscure the rank hostility and moral judgment that undergirded so much resistance to same-sex marriage, clearly others had failed to get the memo, or had made a calculation that expressing rather than concealing such sentiment played well with constituents.

Although DOMA was a Republican initiative, its supporters were hardly confined to the GOP. Sen. Robert Byrd, a former member of the Ku Klux Klan and a stalwart of the Democratic Party, explained his fervent opposition to gay marriage by blending didactic tales from ancient history, anti-gay stereotypes, and extended quotes from his boyhood Bible, which he waved triumphantly on the Senate floor. Gay marriage, Byrd intoned, "is more than unwise; it is patently absurd. Out of such relationships children do not result. . . . Out of such relationships emotional bonding oftentimes does not take place, and many such relationships do not result in the establishment of 'families.'" History showed, he continued, that cultures that "waxed casual about the uniqueness and sanctity of the marriage commitment" inexorably declined. Then followed an extended lecture on the gender-bending behaviors of Greek aristocrats, Roman emperors, and ancient warriors—all of whom enjoyed a brief period of wealth and power enabled by their exploits and indulgences but ultimately overstepped by flouting norms and sowing the seeds of their own destruction.[10]

Unsubtly contrasting the decadence of the ancients to the Christian virtue of Byrd's own religious tradition, the senator called attention to how the Bible instructed God's servants to be fruitful and multiply, to respect the separate sexes just as God created them, and to marry someone of the opposite sex. "Woe betide that society," Byrd concluded, invoking his best preacher's cadence, "that fails to honor that heritage and begins to blur that tradition which was laid down by the Creator."[11]

For many religious conservatives, the idea that violating God's wishes would wreak havoc on earth was not merely an abstract religious precept but a daily fear: as seen in the stories of Sodom and Gomorrah, God punished earthly communities that tolerated sin. Their tradition taught that they must not only heed God's will but also take responsibility for seeing it followed wherever they could. This particular blend of Christian theology and psychology took an increasingly robust political shape with the rise of the religious right in the 1980s and into the 1990s. Looking at the underpinning theological beliefs helps explain the fervor of the opposition to gay equality among conservative Christians and allows observers to take seriously what can often seem like rhetorical excess about the perilous foundation of American civilization.[12]

There was, of course, an element of rank political expediency to DOMA. Sen. Ted Kennedy said the bill ought to be called the "Endangered Republican Candidates Act" since it was clearly a political stunt designed to put pressure on Bill Clinton and score points for flailing GOP politicians. "I regard it as a thinly disguised example of intolerance" that was also, said

Kennedy, "a flatly unconstitutional exercise of congressional authority." What the bill amounted to, he insisted, was "a mean-spirited form of legislative gay-bashing designed to inflame the public four months before the November election." Sen. Barbara Boxer called the bill "ugly politics" that was "about dividing us instead of bringing us together." In her view, Republicans were scapegoating gay people and distracting the country from attending to truly pressing needs. Rep. Barney Frank, one of three openly gay members of Congress at the time, saw "a desperate search for a political issue" that sought to divide Clinton from his base and mobilize Republican voters.[13]

Yet there were also clearly sincere feelings behind support for the marriage ban, and some lawmakers were refreshingly candid about them. Rep. Henry Hyde said he wished he had never heard of same-sex marriage, calling it a "miserable, uncomfortable, queasy issue" and adding that "the institution of marriage is trivialized by same-sex marriage."[14] Rep. Sonny Bono, the thrice-divorced former pop star and father of Chastity, who then identified as a lesbian (and later as transgender), was undeterred in voting to decline recognition of gay marriages. Bono spoke from the heart about why he could not embrace gay equality: "I like Barney [Frank], and I love my daughter," the California Republican said, but "I think we have hit feelings, and we've hit what people can handle and what they can't handle, and it's that simple. . . . I can't go as far as you deserve even, but—and I'm sorry, but I think that's the whole situation here." Frank responded that no one was seeking a "stamp of approval" or asking anything beyond that people "leave us alone." He even said if gay marriage was so disturbing, "turn your head, but don't inflict legal disabilities that carry out that feeling." It was a sign of where pro-gay demands stood in 1996: still adhering to a philosophy of seeking tolerance rather than insisting on the sort of moral embrace that advocates such as Kameny and Wolfson hoped to promote.[15]

Under persistent assault by conservatives who declared gay inclusion a threat to the dignity of marriage itself, gay advocates would eventually awaken to the need to defend the dignity of same-sex love. While some continued to oppose the push for access to marriage and others touted marriage primarily as a tool for achieving equal rights, still others saw access to marriage as inseparable from the idea that gay was, indeed, good. At its core, wrote Andrew Sullivan in a 1996 article that linked the humanity of gay people to their freedom to marry, homosexuality "is about the emotional connection between two adult human beings." Nothing is more central to that connection than marriage, he argued, and as a consequence, denying that possibility "is the most profound statement our society can make that homosexual love is simply not as good as heterosexual love; that gay lives and commitments and hopes are simply worth less." Sullivan predicted that, soon enough, those pushing gay marriage would be seen less as marginal troublemakers and more as having glimpsed "the possibility of a larger human dignity" in the embrace of gay inclusion.[16]

It was often outsiders to the gay movement who most forcefully articulated this positive message about gay relationships. Some lawmakers—nearly all of them Democrats—spoke poignantly about why they would vote against DOMA. "These couples are not hurting us with their actions," said Sen. Bob Kerrey of Nebraska. "In fact they may be helping us by showing us that love can indeed conquer prejudice and hatred." Sen. Carol Moseley-Braun, the nation's first black female senator, said the judgment of history in fifty years would not look kindly on this "mean-spirited" legislation. Others used humor to impugn the hypocrisy of the bill. Rep. Neil Abercrombie of Hawaii said: "I understand some of the people who are sponsoring this bill are on their second or third marriages. I wonder which one they are defending." Rep. Steve Gunderson of Wisconsin, the sole Republican to vote against DOMA, was also the only openly gay GOP House member. "Why shouldn't my partner of 13 years be entitled to the same health insurance and survivor's benefits that individuals around here, my colleagues with second and third wives are able to give to them?" he wanted to know.

Perhaps the most passionate speech in favor of same-sex marriage came from Rep. John Lewis of Georgia, the eminent black civil rights leader who had been beaten and jailed for his participation in anti-segregation protests. Lewis framed the debate as akin to the fight over racial justice, reminding his colleagues that earlier in the century most southerners had believed blacks should be barred from public accommodations, forced to use separate facilities, and denied the right to vote because they were considered inferior. "Many people felt that was right but that was wrong," he said simply. "I have known racism. I have known bigotry. This bill stinks of the same fear, hatred and intolerance." Why, Lewis demanded to know, "do you not want your fellow men and women, your fellow Americans to be happy? Why do you attack them? Why do you want to destroy the love they hold in their hearts?" Lewis said that gay people are "human be-ings, people like you, people who want to get married, buy a house, and spend their lives with the one they love. They have done no wrong." He concluded with a statement that reflected the love, empathy, and solidarity crystalized by the black civil rights movement: "I will not turn my back on another American. I will not oppress my fellow human being. I have fought too hard and too long against discrimination based on race and color not to stand up against discrimination based on sexual orientation."[17] For Lewis, who had seen bigotry up close as a young man and since, the thread between racial hatred and anti-gay prejudice was too clear to ignore.

Yet it was increasingly clear that there would not be the votes in Con-gress to stave off DOMA. Matters were not helped when the Clinton Jus-tice Department released a letter saying that it had determined the law was constitutional, giving lawmakers of both parties cover to vote for it. In the White House, discussion had begun immediately that spring about how President Clinton should handle the challenge of DOMA. If he opposed the bill, his staff worried, the Dole camp could use that to paint the presi-dent as being in the pocket of minority interests and cultural extremists. He had been burned by the fight over gays in the military and had resolved not to suffer that way again. Given the likely margin in Congress, vetoing the bill would fail to stop it anyway, and it could simply make him look weaker. But if he backed the bill, he would alienate gay and liberal voters who had looked to him as a youthful, progressive leader with an inclusive vision of America.

The Human Rights Campaign, by then the largest gay rights group in the nation, seemed caught in the middle of the DOMA fight. HRC's executive director, Elizabeth Birch, said in June that gay marriage was an issue "whose time has not yet come." Its communications director, David Smith, vowed to fight the bill "tooth and nail" but he simultaneously called the battle virtually unwinnable, an "out-of-control freight train" that was "darn near impossible to stop." Marriage champions including Wolfson were furious, viewing Smith's public remarks as essentially a surrender. Reports later surfaced that the group had blessed a deal worked out by Senator Kennedy with Republicans to allow a vote on employment nondiscrim-ination—a higher priority for HRC than marriage—if Democrats would allow a vote on DOMA. Yet if HRC angered marriage advocates for inad-equately attacking DOMA, it turned off other gay activists just for trying.

Citing community division over priorities and inadequate public support for marriage, Keith Boykin of the National Black Lesbian and Gay Leadership Forum complained that, in fighting for marriage, the movement's leadership was "marching down the wrong path and running a disastrous course." Boykin's lament was both ideological and strategic. "We've got to get to A and B before we can get to E," he said.[18]

About that, Boykin was right. Despite the divisions and strategic disagreements across the movement, nearly all the major players working to advance gay equality were pushing an incremental strategy that acknowledged the need to build public support over time; it was just that advocates had different views about the proper role for marriage in that strategy. HRC's political director, Daniel Zingale, defended the group's decision to focus on nondiscrimination law rather than marriage. "For us to succeed in the long term around marriage," he said, looking back from 2011, "Americans had to be made aware of the fact that it was still legal to fire lesbian and gay people from their jobs in most parts of the country." Nondiscrimination law was a vehicle for raising that awareness while also serving a diverse population, some of whom lived "in states where marriage was a pretty far-off dream." For Zingale, emphasizing discrimination over marriage "was a strategic thing to do—but also the right thing to do." Urvashi Vaid, a lesbian lawyer and activist who had led the Task Force until 1992, sought in subsequent years to shift the movement's focus away from national goals toward local and state efforts. "What we needed to learn from the military fight," she said in 1996, "is that we have to build more political power before we win any gay issue on a national level."[19]

Wolfson, for his part, was counseling a two-track strategy: build public support and state-by-state legal wins over time—the incremental component—while beating back DOMA in hopes of nationalizing the early wins by spreading marriage equality from state to state. For Barney Frank, those pushing the latter approach were being too ambitious, courting a backlash. "I was critical of them for instantly announcing that this would be nationalized," Frank recalled years later. "I was supportive of doing it locally." Frank called the national tack a "serious strategic error" that spurred the passage of DOMA. "It just created this firestorm," he said. While he spent 1996 speaking out forcefully against the bill and in favor of marriage equality as a principle, Frank said it should remain up to each state to decide if it would recognize same-sex marriage. He argued for gay marriage on the merits, but said he wanted it to be done at the right pace and "with some political wisdom that allowed it to survive."[20]

The momentum for DOMA was not lost on the White House. Although the president had called the bill "unnecessary" and "divisive" and his press secretary, Mike McCurry, had called it "gay-baiting, pure and simple," Clinton's top advisors, noting that he was already on record opposing gay marriage, ultimately recommended that he sign DOMA to avoid giving Republicans leverage against him.[21] Gay advocates were crestfallen at the news. And McCurry further infuriated them by saying that the president supported DOMA because this was "a time when we need to do things to strengthen the American family," appearing to endorse the conservative assertion that gay equality somehow threatened it.[22]

On July 12, the day after House hearings ended, the House voted to pass DOMA by a lopsided 342 to 67. While nearly twice as many Republicans backed DOMA as Democrats, the latter still turned out 118 votes, bowing, as had many more Republicans, to political expediency. The sole Republican to oppose the bill was the openly gay Gunderson. On September 10 the Senate followed suit, passing DOMA 85 to 14, with all fourteen opponents Democrats.[23] (The nondiscrimination bill failed by one vote when Sen. David Pryor, who supported the bill, had to miss the vote because of his son's emergency cancer surgery.) Bill Clinton signed DOMA into law in the dark of night on September 21. Backing nondiscrimination legislation instead of gay marriage, and as if seeking penance for his support of DOMA, Clinton released a statement saying that the law should never be used as "an excuse for discrimination, violence or intimidation against any person on the basis of sexual orientation."[24]

Despite hope among gays and lesbians at the end of 1992 that Bill Clinton's presidency might finally signal a period of inclusion in national politics, that faith was slipping away as the failure to end the military's gay ban, the Republican Revolution, and the passage of DOMA all made progress at the federal level seem distant. Throughout Clinton's first term, gay advocates were repeatedly slapped with developments that drove home the lessons of *Bowers*: broad national change was unlikely without laying the groundwork at the local and state levels. Yet disagreement persisted over how to apply these lessons. A focus on local- and state-level change would be a return to the earliest roots of gay activism, when members of the Mattachine Society, the Gay Activists Alliance, and other groups in Los

Angeles, the Bay Area, and New York pressed for improvements in areas such as police harassment, municipal employment, and limited partnership registries. But where did that leave marriage as a movement priority? With national political groups still uncommitted to the issue and legal groups more motivated but still divided, the hopes of advocates such as Wolfson returned to the states, despite this approach now looking like an even tougher climb. Wolfson was frustrated that some leaders had taken their foot off the gas pedal in fighting against DOMA. Yet his own approach was incremental as well; it was just that for him, marriage was its top priority. The passage of DOMA meant redoubling his commitment to the long haul.

On the same September day that the Senate voted to enact DOMA, Hawaii held the first-ever trial on same-sex marriage, three years after the state's high court had remanded the case to the circuit court with a requirement that the state show a compelling reason to bar gay couples from marrying. The state tried to do this with an argument centered around the threat gay marriage allegedly posed to children, who, the state contended, needed a mother and a father to thrive. "All things being equal," argued the state, "it is best for a child that it be raised in a single home by its parents, or at least by a married male and female." In a tactic the religious right would resort to repeatedly, the defense invoked research about children raised by single, unwed, or divorced parents to suggest that lacking a mother and a father put children at risk.[25]

At trial, the state also argued that barring same-sex marriage was needed to save the state money and to prevent a slippery slope from gay marriage to legalized prostitution, incest, and polygamy. It called four expert witnesses: a child psychiatrist, a sociologist, and two psychologists, one of whom denied the science of evolution and even rejected the idea that his own field had any legitimacy.[26] While the state's witnesses offered warnings that allowing same-sex marriage could undermine the family, the institution of marriage, and society itself, under cross-examination several conceded that the evidence for their warnings was thin, and that children with gay or lesbian parents would be better off if their parents had access to the legal, financial, and social benefits of marriage.

Foley and Wolfson represented the plaintiffs, now enjoying the support of Lambda, which had agreed to let Wolfson become cocounsel in the wake of the positive 1993 court ruling.[27] They called four expert witnesses, too.[28] The group, consisting of psychologists, sociologists, and physicians, reviewed the research on gay and lesbian parenting and testified that there was no evidence showing that children faced any disadvantages as a result of having gay parents. They also recounted profound changes in family structure since the 1950s that made such families seem less like outliers and more like one among many family configurations in modern life.[29]

By the trial's end, Judge Kevin Chang was thoroughly convinced that the facts of the case favored the plaintiffs. "The evidence presented by Defendant does not establish or prove that same-sex marriage will result in prejudice or harm to an important public or governmental interest," said the decision. "Defendant has not demonstrated a basis for his claim of the existence of compelling state interests sufficient to justify withholding the legal status of marriage from Plaintiffs."

Chang considered the suggestion by the state that same-sex marriage might weaken marriage itself because gays and lesbians could treat it lightly, thus trivializing the institution for others. But, drawing on testimony by the plaintiffs' experts, he noted a more conservative turn within both gay and non-gay culture since the heady years of gay liberation. "There is now a trend in which people contemplate and want to be more serious, to make families and to engage in long-term committed relationships," wrote the judge. "This is a large change from the attitudes of the late '70s and early '80s."[30]

The judge found the plaintiff's four witnesses "especially credible," calling them highly qualified and their testimony "well-founded, based on their significant research and analysis," in contrast to the "meager evidence" the defense had offered about the adverse impact of same-sex marriage. Upon reading the decision, Rick Eichor, the deputy state attorney general who had argued for Hawaii, quipped, "If I had known the judge wanted us to engage in gay-bashing, we would have done the case differently." With the state announcing its appeal of the decision, however, Chang stayed his ruling, putting the fate of marriage equality in Hawaii—and the country—back into limbo.[31]

The *Baehr* ruling was not the only major gay rights case of 1996. That same year, another pro-gay court ruling came down that would have a profound impact on the national debate over gay equality. In *Romer v. Evans,* the court weighed the constitutionality of Amendment 2, a state measure passed by Colorado's voters in 1992 (as the state backed Bill Clinton for president) that prevented cities or the state government from protecting gays and lesbians from discrimination. A few of the more liberal cities and towns—Denver, Boulder, and Aspen—had passed laws creating such protections, and right-wing religious groups, spearheaded by a local Colorado outfit backed by Focus on the Family and the Family Research Council, pushed the amendment through in response.[32]

When Amendment 2 first passed, gay and lesbian lawyers convened at conferences and by phone to debate how to fight it, as they had done so often before. A local gay rights group, Colorado Legal Initiatives Project (CLIP), had committed to bringing a lawsuit against the measure, and it brought together local lawyers—gay and straight—along with Suzanne Goldberg of Lambda and Matt Coles and William Rubenstein of the ACLU to get their input. Lawyers for the cities whose gay rights laws had been overturned by the state's voters were also involved, committed to defending their laws and anxious about threatened travel boycotts by gay rights supporters in response to Amendment 2. CLIP had secured the commitment of a prominent heterosexual lawyer, Jean Dubofsky, to take the case, but immediately questions arose about the wisdom of her taking the lead. A former state supreme court justice, Dubofsky was aware of the high stakes for gays and lesbians and the potential impact on future cases that would affect them. CLIP members liked that she was straight, a Colorado local, and a former high court judge, thinking that all this would help their case given the conservative hue of much of the state. Some gay lawyers, however, bristled at the idea of handing over key strategy decisions to someone who was not gay and who could saunter off from the case unscathed whatever the outcome, while the gay legal groups could be stuck cleaning up the damage for years, as had happened with the *Bowers* case. Eventually, after robust debate, the lawyers—gay and straight, local and out-of-state, from both private firms and movement groups—reached enough consensus to move forward. Although none of the national legal groups piloted the case, Lambda's Goldberg and ACLU's Coles took leading advisory roles. After several strategy sessions, the coalition gathered plaintiffs, including the lesbian tennis star Martina Navratilova and schools and municipalities affected by the measure, and filed suit in state court.[33]

The central legal question of the case was whether it was constitutional to single out one particular, disfavored group and deny that group the right to obtain legal protections against discrimination. In an extraordinary trial in 1993, a parade of academic witnesses debated not just the case at hand but the meaning and origins of homosexuality, whether sexual orientation could be changed, the history of attitudes toward gays and lesbians as a minority, and even the connection of modern understandings about sexuality to those of the ancient Greeks. After lower court victories, the case wound its way up to the U.S. Supreme Court, which heard arguments in the fall of 1995.

The court's ruling was handed down the following spring, and was authored by Justice Anthony Kennedy. Amendment 2, he wrote, did not even meet the rational-basis test. The measure "withdraws from homosexuals, but no others, specific legal protection from the injuries caused by discrimination," a violation of the Constitution's equal protection clause. "If the constitutional conception of 'equal protection of the laws' means anything," said the decision, citing a 1973 case, "it must at the very least mean that a bare . . . desire to harm a politically unpopular group cannot constitute a *legitimate* governmental interest." And Kennedy went further, stating that the law raised "the inevitable inference that the disadvantage imposed is born of animosity toward the class of persons affected." This, he concluded, was constitutionally impermissible.[34]

The enormous import of the ruling was evident in Justice Antonin Scalia's angry dissent. Coloradans were "*entitled* to be hostile toward homosexual conduct," he wrote. Amendment 2 was a valid expression of that view and an entirely "reasonable effort to preserve traditional American moral values." Scalia complained that, until now, it had always been considered perfectly reasonable for individuals to deem "certain conduct reprehensible—murder, for example, or polygamy, or cruelty to animals"—and to express "animus" toward it as a result. The "moral disapproval" of homosexuality being expressed by Colorado voters was of the same sort that undergirded the sodomy bans upheld by *Bowers*. "If it is rational to criminalize the conduct, surely it is rational to deny special favor and protection to those with a self-avowed tendency or desire to engage in the conduct."

Yet the *Romer* decision cast serious doubt on the idea that moral disapproval could serve as the sole basis for discrimination. "By requiring that the classification bear a rational relationship to an independent and legitimate legislative end," Kennedy wrote for the majority, "we ensure that classifications are not drawn for the purpose of disadvantaging" any particular group of people. And the ruling had an impact on gay lives for reasons that went beyond just the legal or constitutional context: homosexuality had long been regarded as immoral by large swaths of the American public, but few could ever explain exactly why it was so morally bad (apart from citing some religious or other tradition or authority) or what it even meant to call something "moral" or "immoral." Why was the simple fact of loving or partnering with someone of the same sex such a profound and dangerous transgression? Now that the Supreme Court had called imposing an anti-gay moral judgment "inexplicable by anything but animus," it raised new questions about the entire edifice of moral judgment against gays and lesbians and their relationships. To Scalia, Amendment 2 was "designed to prevent piecemeal deterioration of the sexual morality favored by a majority of Coloradans," and in his view that was an entirely legitimate use of government authority. To an increasing number of Americans, however, imposing morality by government fiat was coming to seem distasteful at best, and with *Romer,* its constitutionality was in question as well. As Scalia wrung his hands over such social changes, many others were looking anew at what it meant to arbitrarily deem some people's love inferior to that of others, marking significant changes in Americans' views about sexual norms and sexual minorities.

The *Romer* ruling not only laid the groundwork for a more deliberate national discussion of the nature and role of morality but began Justice Kennedy's ascent as a trailblazer in gay rights jurisprudence. Kennedy was a moderate conservative who had been appointed by President Ronald Reagan the year after the *Bowers* ruling. He was Reagan's third nominee for the slot, after a Democratic Senate had rejected the nomination of the outspoken conservative Robert Bork, and a second nominee withdrew after revealing he had occasionally smoked marijuana. Kennedy was seen as a "consensus nominee," angering the far right as insufficiently conservative, worrying some on the left, as any Reagan appointee would, but ultimately respected by the middle and palatable to the Democratic senators who governed his fate.[35] Appointed by a conservative icon, Kennedy nevertheless began to chart a modern course on gay rights law that took a decidedly liberal position on the need for constitutional interpretations to incorporate ever-changing social understandings of how people thought, behaved, and lived. Equally important was that his legal reasoning reflected a modern understanding of liberty as encompassing the freedom to love. Kennedy had drawn on a new capacity for empathy to enlarge the nation's understanding of moral autonomy to include the dignity of same-sex love.

Just two years after *Romer* overruled the voters of Colorado, and on the heels of the passage of DOMA, the voters of Hawaii had a decision to make: should they amend their state constitution to allow for the prohibition of same-sex marriage? The easiest way to accomplish this was to use a constitutional amendment not to ban gay marriage directly but to grant that authority to the legislature, which had repeatedly voted to ban it. With the *Baehr* case working its way through the courts, a constitutional amendment was the key to circumventing any decision that might otherwise compel Hawaii to allow same-sex marriage. In 1998, with the case still not settled, social conservatives persuaded voters to back the amendment, rendering any further action by the courts moot.[36] Marriage equality in Hawaii was dead.[37]

That year saw other gains for anti-gay conservatives as well. In addition to the constitutional amendment in Hawaii, voters passed a similar measure in Alaska, where plaintiffs represented by private lawyers had also been moving a lawsuit forward. The Alaska amendment went further than Hawaii's: rather than throw the issue to the legislature, voters in Alaska made it the first state to put an explicit gay marriage ban into its constitution. And Christian conservatives showed their muscle when enough voters braved a debilitating ice storm in Maine to vote to reverse that state's one-year-old Human Rights Act, which had protected gays and lesbians from discrimination in employment, housing, and public accommodations.[38]

The success of efforts to block same-sex marriage and other gay rights measures had an energizing effect on conservatives and a sobering effect on the strategic thinking of gay advocates. Developments in California illustrate both well. A 1977 measure there had restricted marriage to different-sex couples. But in the 1990s, as the battle for same-sex marriage gained traction in states around the country, anti-gay activists in California worried that a clause in the state's Family Code created a loophole that could force the state to recognize out-of-state same-sex marriages. The solution, they decided, was to pass a state law that, echoing the federal DOMA, would stipulate that "only marriage between a man and a woman is valid or recognized in California."

A conservative state assemblyman named William Knight took up the charge. A former career Air Force colonel who set a world record for speed in flying test planes, Knight decided to run for the state senate in 1996, seeking to represent the conservative Seventeenth District. His task was essentially to win the Republican primary, whose victor was virtually guaranteed the seat. Hence, as an editor of the local newspaper put it, Knight and his opponent, Assemblyman Phil Wyman, were trying to "out-conservative" each other. Along with his support for a bill allowing concealed weapons, Knight expressed conservative values, speaking of the need to defend traditional marriage, something he had also taken up as an assemblyman.[39] Upon winning the state senate seat, Knight pushed a bill banning recognition of out-of-state same-sex marriages, but it failed two years in a row. So, noting the successful ballot initiatives in Hawaii and Alaska, he decided to take the issue directly to the voters by launching a similar initiative.[40]

Knight insisted that his goal was not to promote anti-gay sentiment; rather, he simply didn't want to see the definition of marriage change.[41] "I'm not prejudiced against anybody," he said, "never have been." In his view, marriage was "sacred," and to allow anyone but a man and a woman to wed was "not according to natural law." A male-female union, he further argued, was the best environment for kids (he also sponsored a law to ban adoptions by gay or other unmarried couples).[42] Changing the nation's understanding of marriage to encompass same-sex unions, he believed, meant shaking it loose from any firm meaning at all, and could lead to an anything-goes definition that would include polygamy.[43] Yet despite his assertions that he was not anti-gay, in less guarded moments his language could be more forceful; at one point he even charged that the institution of marriage was "being deliberately trashed" by efforts to let gays wed.[44]

If Knight's opposition to gay marriage and parenting was political and ideological, some also suspected it might be personal. In 1995 his son

David, who had idolized his dad as a kid and followed him into the Air Force, told him he was gay, and the pair's relationship crumbled. The elder Knight denied that anything personal shaped his position on gay marriage, but the disappointment of having a gay son was not the only personal experience with homosexuality that may have played a role: he also had a gay brother who died of complications related to AIDS in 1996. Knight's view of the matter reflected what was a common approach to homosexuality during this era: don't ask, don't tell. "My brother and I never discussed it," he said some years after his brother's death. "Why would we want to discuss his sexual activities? John and I got along fine." His brother might have felt differently. Certainly David found his father's anti-gay leadership painful, especially now that his own last name was attached to an initiative that threw open to the state the question of whether his relationship had equal worth.[45]

In 1999, on the heels of anti-gay-marriage victories in Hawaii and Alaska, Knight's initiative gained steam, earning the support of church groups including Mormons, Catholics, and Southern Baptists. While a coalition of seventy progressive California churches wrote a letter imploring Mormon leaders not to support discrimination, the plea achieved little. In June 1999 the Mormon Church sent 740,000 letters to members in California urging them to vote for the anti-gay measure, and the church organized numerous fund-raising and canvassing events throughout the campaign. In November the California Southern Baptist Convention voted to ask its members to support the Knight initiative, now formally called Proposition 22. The California dioceses of the Roman Catholic Church raised more than $300,000 to donate to the campaign.[46]

Echoing Knight's claim that anti-gay sentiment did not drive his position, Robert Glazier, a spokesman for the Protection of Marriage campaign, insisted that Proposition 22 was not about discrimination but was simply about preserving traditional marriage and respecting states' self-determination. He boasted that his group had carried on their campaign "in a respectful and tolerant manner without being judgmental of anyone's lifestyle or relationship." But for gay and lesbian Californians, the 500,000 PROTECT MARRIAGE lawn signs that blanketed their state could communicate only one message: they and their families were regarded as a threat to marriage, a menacing force against which the institution itself must be fiercely protected. It hardly felt respectful or tolerant.[47]

Indeed, gay advocates, who had not asked for this battle, were keenly aware of the limitations of public support. They knew they would be hard-pressed to squeeze out a victory. Polls before the vote had consistently shown them down by double-digit margins, and many movement leaders felt that public opinion was not yet with them. Reflecting the defensive posture of their campaign against Proposition 22, gay advocates downplayed marriage itself, casting the issue as one of civil rights more generally, rather than marriage per se. It was "not about gay marriage," said one gay advocate. "It's about discrimination against gays and lesbians."[48]

On March 7, 2000, California voters decisively rejected gay marriage. The Limit on Marriages initiative passed with 61.4 percent of the vote.[49]

In the wake of defeat, some grassroots gay activists complained that the gay leadership was deploying a failed strategy. Impatient for progress, and frustrated with the failure or unwillingness of established groups to advance marriage equality, John and Tom Henning, gay brothers living in Los Angeles and San Francisco, respectively, had spearheaded a proactive initiative to legalize same-sex marriage. But getting that question on the ballot would have required gathering 670,816 voter signatures, and without the support of major gay groups or donors, this was a nearly impossible feat.[50] The Hennings thought that movement leaders were ignoring a real thirst for marriage among rank-and-file gays and lesbians. "The larger organizations are not really positioned to respond to something that really comes out of the blue," said Tom Henning, to a push "that comes straight from individuals and is not part of their strategy or their process." Tom was disheartened when, according to his recollection, Evan Wolfson asked him to stop his efforts, fearing they would invite further organizing by the state's anti-gay conservatives. "Good luck, Tom and John," wrote a sympathetic San Francisco journalist. "You'll fail but you'll go down in the history books as pioneers" for making people think about gay marriage—just what Wolfson urged people to do everywhere. "You'll help pave the way for that glorious day when gays who love each other can formalize and sanctify their bond, just like straights. You're beautiful dreamers, and that's not a bad thing to be."[51]

As the election results had made clear, the Hennings' hope to legalize gay marriage by ballot was no more than a dream. The people of California simply were not ready for it, at least not without the massive, coordinated effort by major gay groups that would have been required just to give it a chance. With dozens of states passing laws against gay marriage and some even amending their constitutions to block it, gay legal advocates were more certain than ever that an incremental approach to advancing gay equality was needed. But disagreement remained—between professional advocates and grassroots activists such as the Hennings, and within the ranks of movement leaders themselves—over what gay equality should look like, and particularly what role marriage should play in it. Not only would gay advocates have to work hard to defeat their anti-gay opponents, but they had to organize their own community better in hopes that a more coordinated strategy could avoid making the post-*Baehr* backlash worse.

Among movement lawyers, however, there *was* broad agreement that incremental change was essential to making progress, especially after the passage of DOMA. Domestic partnerships hence took center stage once again at Roundtable meetings. In 1997 the Hawaii legislature, hoping to stave off gay marriage while showing it was not driven by homophobia, passed the country's first statewide domestic partnership law, the Reciprocal Beneficiaries Act. Although legal challenges and public uncertainty about its requirements limited its impact, the bill in theory granted scores of protections to same-sex partners who registered, ensuring, for instance, that a gay man could visit his dying partner in the hospital, or that a lesbian could take leave from work to care for a sick partner. Ironically, Hawaii's law applied to both same-sex and opposite-sex couples in an effort to appease conservatives who opposed the granting of rights for gay couples, but the step also pleased alternative-family advocates in the gay community, who had long pushed for a broader array of legal relationship options for everyone, part of their vision of deemphasizing marriage in favor of widening the nation's understanding of family.[52]

Two years later, advocates finally persuaded Democratic lawmakers in California to pass a statewide domestic partnership law. Alternative-family proponents had hoped that this bill, too, would include different-sex couples. But Gov. Gray Davis feared the very thing these advocates sought: the possibility that marriage would come to seem less important if alternatives were widely available. It was an argument Andrew Sullivan had made in his 1989 article on gay marriage: that the court victory in the New York *Braschi* case threatened the primacy of marriage precisely by broadening the definition of family to include unmarried partners. Under pressure from Governor Davis, the California bill's backers narrowed the language further so that straight couples under sixty-two were not eligible for domestic partnerships. Making real the gradualist promise of the domestic partnership strategy, however, the legislature expanded its relationship recognition law repeatedly over the next four years, and in 2003 it created the nation's most sweeping law of this type, granting same-sex couples virtually all the same rights and benefits as marriage, but without the name.

The end of the twentieth century was a dizzying time to be a gay rights advocate. A Democratic president who had promised gays and lesbians that they were an integral part of his vision for a better America had signed an odious bill damning their relationships as inferior, after lawmakers used the august floor of Congress to denounce gay people as selfish hedonists who threatened the republic's very existence. DOMA's passage followed that of the military's "don't ask, don't tell" policy, and the anti-gay legislative climate put politicians across the nation—including Democrats, who some hoped would be natural allies to gays and lesbians—on notice that gay rights was the third rail of politics. Legal progress seen during the fifteen years after Stonewall, such as the repeal of state sodomy laws and the spread of antidiscrimination protections, had started slowing in the Reagan era, even as the suffering from AIDS devastated the gay community and the political energy devoted to fighting its toll tested the strength of the movement. Similar trials resulted from the further consolidation of the religious right, whose political power to thwart gay rights progress had become formidable by the early 1990s.[53]

Yet in the courts of law and public opinion, nearly two decades after the victory of Anita Bryant's anti-gay Save Our Children campaign and a decade after *Bowers,* the gay rights movement was clearly making enormous strides in visibility, respectability, public acceptance, and political power. Across the 1990s, greater attention in the news media, more and fairer representations of gay life in popular culture, and political and institutional inroads resulting from a greater number of out gays claiming a place at the tables of power were giving judges and the public a fuller sense of what it meant to be gay or lesbian.[54]

Key to the growing gay visibility and political power was a commitment to working within the established political system. In 1991 gay advocates formed the Gay and Lesbian Victory Fund, a political action committee that raised money for out gay and lesbian candidates. The network raised more than a quarter million dollars for a dozen candidates during its first election, helping launch the careers of hundreds of gay officeholders including state legislators, big-city mayors, ambassadors, and members of the U.S. House and Senate. Over time these political leaders would use their personal experience, expertise, relationships, and visibility with colleagues to help pass pro-gay laws in cities and states across the country.

Visibility in popular culture also pushed gay acceptance forward. Gay characters began to appear on highly rated television shows, where, instead of being portrayed as mincing sidekicks, they were often in healthy same-sex relationships. The most famous of these was the show *Ellen,* in which the title character came out as gay in 1997, at the same time as Ellen DeGeneres, the show's lesbian creator and star, simultaneously appeared on the cover of *Time* under the headline "Yep, I'm Gay." While social conservatives fumed and Hollywood executives fretted, *Ellen's* ratings remained strong, and amid much hoopla a whopping 36 million Americans tuned in to the coming-out episode. The next year, *Will and Grace* premiered, a sitcom about a handsome, ordinary gay lawyer and his female best friend. The show went on to top ratings and critical acclaim, and "Will and Grace" became a household phrase connoting the coming age of "normalcy" in how gay people were depicted.[55]

"Who knew how it was all going to turn out?" Paula Ettelbrick recalled thinking after DOMA passed. "It looked like the whole world was going up in flames over our relationships."[56] In the wake of those hopes, however, was a deepened commitment by gay advocates to the long road of incremental change. While disagreements remained about whether domestic partnerships, such as those now allowed in Hawaii and California, ought to be viewed as a stepping-stone to marriage or as an end in themselves, there was rising awareness by many that the national debate would hinge on the dignity of same-sex love. Often it was straight people—Sen. Bob Kerrey, Rep. John Lewis, the lawyers and judges who helped push for equality in Hawaii and Colorado, including Justice Kennedy in his *Romer* opinion—who most forcefully put that dignity front and center, with gays and lesbians debating the value of public recognition, including marriage, in advancing equality. Some participants in that debate felt that social acknowledgment of gays and lesbians' equal worth was attainable without the public recognition that came with marriage. Yet for more and more legal advocates, legal recognition of gay relationships was fundamental to their needs and desires as gay people. Together, they answered the "defense of marriage" crowd by pushing steadily toward full equality. Their next step would be to lay an immovable cornerstone for marriage.

6

"Here Come the Brides"

LAYING THE CORNERSTONE

IN MASSACHUSETTS

LIKE MANY GAY ADVOCATES, MARY BONAUTO WAS CAUGHT OFF GUARD by the 1993 court win in Hawaii. She was thrilled by the decision but knew there was an enormous amount of work to do before further Hawaii-style lawsuits were filed. She encouraged the increasing number of grassroots activists and groups that began to advocate for marriage in the decision's wake to join together and work in their communities to raise awareness about gay lives and relationships. But, fearing that additional litigation this soon could fail, she told activists to capitalize on their enthusiasm for marriage by channeling it in a way that's constructive—"other than through lawsuits."[1]

Wolfson agreed. "Anyone can file a lawsuit," he explained. "The challenge is the other work that has to go along with it." Wolfson noted that he applied the "same strategic stringency to my own efforts as to others'." Viewing the political and social groundwork as not yet robust enough, Wolfson had pleaded with activists in Alaska to hold off on filing suit. "He had screaming arguments with those guys," Ettelbrick remembered. "He'd spend most of the day telling people in Alaska and other places, 'don't bring cases.'" Wolfson (and Ettelbrick) also tried to dissuade a couple from filing a suit in Ithaca, New York, concerned that it was too soon for success. The couple, Phillip Storrs and Toshav Greene, rebuffed the movement lawyers and registered irritation "that these groups are thinking about timetables" when Martin Luther King Jr. knew it was "always the right time to do right." The challenge was dismissed, giving fodder to judges who cited it in later cases when ruling against marriage equality.[2]

At every turn, it seemed, the few movement lawyers who favored marriage in theory but counseled taking action only under carefully controlled circumstances met with resistance to their plans. The right wing found same-sex relationships morally repugnant and unworthy of legal recognition; other gay activists called marriage the wrong priority or unrealistic; and some gays and lesbians, finding movement lawyers overly cautious, wanted to press ahead even in states or courts that might be hostile, regardless of the prospects for success and the costs of failure.

In 1996 the tiny marriage equality movement got a jolt of energy when Beth Robinson and Susan Murray, lesbian lawyers who were friends of Mary Bonauto's, established the Vermont Freedom to Marry Task Force. With the outcome of the Hawaii case still unknown, both Wolfson and Bonauto remained optimistic about its success, but Bonauto was beginning to want insurance in the form of a plan B. She was pleased to find that her friends in Vermont were of like mind, especially amid ongoing disagreement in the movement about the best path forward. "The collective wisdom among the national advocates was that it didn't make sense to have any more state cases go forward," explained Robinson, referring to both legal and political groups in the gay movement. But as gay leaders were learning, the marriage battle was hardly something any one person or group could control. "There were always a couple places where advocates and litigants were pursuing state cases," she said, "notwithstanding the conventional wisdom, and they were viewed as a little bit renegade." If rogue activists striking out on their own presented one kind of threat to the overall strategy, another was pushback from national movement leaders who feared a backlash. "The political groups would come in and they would basically caution us about doing things that would trigger a federal marriage amendment," said Bonauto, adding that some seemed to think "that the legal groups were crazy" for considering new lawsuits. And even among the lawyers, disagreements loomed large. "There was a lot of reluctance for a long time to have a second state," remembered Bonauto. (Among movement lawyers, the Alaska suit hardly registered.) "There were some people who wanted to stay focused on Hawaii." One of these was Wolfson, who initially counseled movement lawyers against filing another suit, preferring to concentrate resources on the case already moving forward in the Aloha State. Bonauto, for her part, was anxious about "putting all our eggs into the Hawaii basket."[3]

The passage of the Defense of Marriage Act (DOMA) changed the calculus. Even if the lawsuit in Hawaii were successful, it was now increasingly clear that that win could not be nationalized by expecting recognition of Hawaii marriages in other states. In any event, while the lawsuit there dragged on, its prospects for success were dimming as voter support for a state constitutional amendment seemed to grow. Marriage equality proponents would need a plan B.

That plan involved opening up a litigation front in another state—but one carefully chosen and exquisitely executed by a coalition of strategic actors with a clear idea of how not only to win but to defend a victory. The three lesbian lawyers from New England had been eyeing Vermont for some time. In 1997 their plan started to take shape as Bonauto discussed the idea of a lawsuit with GLAD's supportive new executive director, Gary Buseck. Having carefully assessed the composition of the courts, the electoral and constitutional amendment cycles, the state's demographics, and the status of grassroots organizing, the lawyers noted several ingredients that made both the state and that moment auspicious. A coalition of gay rights organizations now had many years of outreach, organizing, and public education under their belts. Vermont's Supreme Court had issued a positive ruling in favor of adoptions by gay people in 1994, suggesting it might be open-minded in other gay rights cases. And it was far more difficult to amend Vermont's constitution than it was Hawaii's, so a court win would be harder to overturn. The women reached out to colleagues and other organizations in hopes of getting broad support for opening the next front. Although Wolfson was now onboard, they had become confident that this was the right move regardless of whose endorsement they had. "We didn't feel we had to get somebody's permission to go forward," Robinson said, "but we were committed to trying to move forward in a way that included some national buy-in, and I think that happened."[4]

On July 22 Bonauto, Robinson, and Murray enacted their plan B, filing suit on behalf of three same-sex couples seeking to marry in Vermont. The suit relied on the state constitution's "common benefits" clause, which was akin to a broad version of the equal protection guarantee in the U.S. Constitution. Losing at the trial level, they appealed to the state's high court in 1999. In December, the Vermont Supreme Court ruled unanimously in

Baker v. Vermont that gay couples were entitled to the same benefits and protections as married straight ones. Gay couples, said the court, "seek nothing more, nor less, than legal protection and security for their avowed commitment to an intimate and lasting relationship." Recognizing this reality "is simply, when all is said and done, a recognition of our common humanity."[5]

As in Hawaii, the Vermont court did not compel the state to let gay couples wed. Instead, it instructed the legislature to rectify the inequality without dictating whether such a step required legalizing marriage itself. In Vermont, the alternative to granting gays and lesbians full access to marriage was coming to be known as "civil unions," a new legal structure akin to the statewide domestic partnerships created in Hawaii and California. That civil unions were designed precisely to avoid granting full equality to gays and lesbians would make it an immediate legal target and eventually an object of complaint by activists demanding full equality. And yet, ironically, while many in America's middle saw them as a concession to a restive interest group, civil unions were something close to the very goal of the gay legal advocates who had pushed twenty years earlier for a broader way to recognize relationships.

A raucous debate ensued among citizens and lawmakers of a state normally known for its New England reserve and a sense of tolerance for how people lived their lives. "Take Back Vermont" signs emerged on front lawns and barns in several counties, and an ad appeared in a newspaper darkly suggesting that tolerance of homosexuality was the cause of recent turmoil in the financial markets. The ad condemned "the insufferable hubris of the narcissistic gay lobby that would place personal pleasures before public order."[6]

In two wrenching winter days cannibalized by the national media, the Vermont legislature, which had a single openly gay member, William Lippert, held hearings with an intensity that some likened to the Revolutionary War. Lippert made an emotional speech that to many involved in Vermont politics was one of the most memorable. "Who are we?" he asked. "We are committed, caring, loving individuals in a time when a desire for greater commitment, love, and fidelity [are] needed in our society." Democratic governor Howard Dean had promised to veto same-sex marriage legislation. Notwithstanding that the state's high court had ordered the legislature to essentially choose marriage or civil unions, lawmakers feared that simply carrying out the court's mandate would render them jobless.[7] Ultimately, the legislature chose to create a civil unions law. Sixteen incumbents lost their seats in an orchestrated effort to punish supporters of same-sex unions, throwing the state house to Republicans.[8]

Bonauto and her legal colleagues had mixed feelings about the outcome of their suit. Unlike the holdouts of the alternative-families movement, they joined Wolfson in viewing civil unions not as an end in itself but as a half step never acceptable in its own right, and they spent months lobbying against this being the end of the road. Yet they ultimately threw their support to civil unions when it became clear that they were not going to win marriage. They had worked closely with allies in the state legislature, and recognized that they must now stand with those allies as they faced a difficult vote that could threaten their political lives. Civil unions, in any event, brought real and positive change to the lives of gay Vermonters, giving them protections and benefits that others took for granted. "For a lot of people," said Robinson, "that's where the rubber meets the road."[9] Indeed, many in the gay and lesbian community embraced civil unions as a unique institution of their own, offering many aspects of what liberationists and alternative-families proponents had long sought, without the baggage of mainstream assimilation.

The women viewed their victory as having tremendous practical and symbolic importance in the fight for marriage equality nationally. Although the Vermont suit had not resulted in marriage, its tangible impact was greater than that of the Hawaii suit because the New England litigators had chosen a state whose constitution would be hard to modify, and had secured commitments from the Democratic legislature not to support a constitutional amendment in the event of a win in court.[10] When the legislature voted in 2000 to create a civil unions bill, Vermont sailed past California, with its still modest domestic partnership law, to become the first state in the union to offer gay couples all the same marital rights as straight ones.

The GLAD staff whose strategy had secured equal benefits—but not full marriage—for gay couples in Vermont lost no time in plotting their next steps in New England. The positive if highly imperfect decision in Vermont, they believed, was partly indebted to the preliminary legal victories in Hawaii and Alaska, which had shown that constitutional claims for the equality of same-sex relationships could be taken seriously in court. Vermont offered further momentum. The next question was where, when, and how to secure marriage itself.

The most promising answer was Massachusetts. The state had shown support for gay equality with its 1989 non-discrimination law. Its high court had proven itself open-minded, with several pro-gay decisions around adoption, parenting, privacy, and sexual harassment. The state's constitution had strong equality clauses and required a more laborious process for amendments than places like Hawaii and California. And GLAD and other gay groups and grassroots activists had been laying the groundwork for pro-gay policies and a sympathetic climate there for years. In fact, GLAD contemplated the viability of securing marriage via the state's legislature, where victory would indicate broad public support for same-sex marriage. But the advocates knew the legislature well, and despite years of outreach and organizing, they could not envision a legislative path to victory there. "Frankly, we didn't see any other way to do it" but by lawsuit, explained Bonauto.[11]

On April 11, 2001, a week after the state's first female governor, Jane Swift, promised to veto a gay marriage bill if one was passed by the legislature, GLAD sued the state of Massachusetts on behalf of seven same-sex couples.[12] The named plaintiffs in *Goodridge v. Department of Public Health* were Julie and Hillary Goodridge, Boston women in their mid-forties who had been partners for thirteen years. GLAD's brief carefully explained the couple's stellar "girl-next-door" credentials, reflecting how crucial strategists believed it was to put forward the most exemplary, mainstream stories of gay life. The couple had taken the same last name to signify their commitment to each other. They had a daughter together who was "happy and well-adjusted," had many friends, and studied ballet and piano. The mothers volunteered on school committees and limited their work hours to spend time with their family. And so it went, with the brief detailing similar stories for all seven couples: they were committed partners for life, mostly professionals or executives, supported by their friends and extended families, involved in their churches, communities, and, for some, their children's schools.[13]

The plaintiffs argued that "the right to marry the person of one's choice is protected under the liberty and due process protections of the Massachusetts Constitution," and they cited the Supreme Judicial Court's precedent of respecting personal decisions around intimate associations. Drawing on the favorable ruling from the Hawaii court in 1993, GLAD's brief also cast the state's existing gay marriage ban as an instance of sex discrimination and compared the ban to laws barring interracial marriage, which had been struck down in 1967 in *Loving v. Virginia*. "Just as barring all individuals from interracial marriage constituted racial discrimination, barring all individuals from marrying a person of the same sex constitutes sex discrimination," said the brief.[14] An amicus brief signed by twenty-six historians and legal scholars pointed out that the institution of marriage had been in flux for centuries, that it had dramatically shifted—long before gay couples sought to join it—toward a greater focus on the freedom of personal choice, and that the twentieth-century emphasis on equal rights and gender neutrality made it logical to include same-sex unions in the institution, and irrational to exclude them.[15]

For the defense, the Massachusetts attorney general argued that denying marriage licenses to same-sex couples was constitutional because the legislature *"could rationally* believe" that limiting marriage to heterosexuals "serves the Commonwealth's legitimate interest in fostering and protecting the link between marriage and procreation," in "fostering a favorable setting for child-rearing," and in "conserving limited financial resources."[16]

Throughout the second half of the twentieth century, it had become increasingly difficult to argue that marriage was something granted to people for the purpose of legitimizing procreation or child-rearing, since it was also granted to people with no children and no commitment or ability to have any—so long as they were straight. In 1987, the U.S. Supreme Court ruled in *Turner v. Safley* that prisoners have the right to marry, even if their incarceration prevents them from creating or nurturing children. The reason, said the Court, is that "many important attributes of marriage remain" even when procreation is not an option. Inmate marriages, explained the justices, "are expressions of support and public commitment" and can be "an exercise of religious faith as well as an expression of personal dedication," just like other marriages—again, so long as the couples were straight. GLAD's lawyers pointed out precisely these glaring holes in the arguments of the anti-gay-marriage forces. "None of the defendants' asserted interests to date of procreation, childrearing and conserving resources," said their plaintiffs' brief, "can be given any weight because they bear no relationship at all to the plaintiffs' exclusion from marriage." If men could marry while locked behind bars—as an expression of commitment even while they had little prospect of rearing children—it was tough to argue that loving gay couples (who increasingly were having children) should not have the same right.[17]

Judge Thomas Connolly of the Superior Court of Suffolk County, Massachusetts, did not see things that way. In May 2002 he ruled against the GLAD plaintiffs. Arguing that "procreation is marriage's central purpose" and that "same-sex couples are less likely to have children or, at least, to have as many children as opposite-sex couples" because gays must rely on "more cumbersome means of having children," the court concluded that it was rational to limit marriage to heterosexual pairs, "who, theoretically, are capable of procreation." Taking a judicially conservative approach, he asserted in his ruling that the "liberty" provision of the state constitution referred simply to "freedom from physical constraint" rather than to the opportunity to pursue personal happiness embodied by the freedom to marry. Nodding to the *Bowers* decision, the court noted that same-sex marriage was not "deeply rooted" in the history and tradition of the state and nation. The court also pointed out that no other state had chosen to legalize same-sex marriage, by either legislative or court action, and that even Massachusetts, when it created one of the nation's earliest anti-discrimination laws in 1989, had indicated within the law that it should not be construed to permit recognition of gay marriages or even the provision of partner benefits. In a dry gesture toward empathizing with the plaintiffs' plight, the decision ended with a terse reference to the political process as the appropriate means for gays and lesbians to press their case: "While this court understands the plaintiffs['] efforts to be married, they should pursue their quest on Beacon Hill."[18] GLAD appealed the ruling, and all eyes turned to the Massachusetts Supreme Judicial Court.

It was the U.S. Supreme Court, however, not the high court in Massachusetts, that took the next step. In June 2003 the justices issued an earth-shattering decision in the case of *Lawrence v. Texas*, a challenge to the Texas law that criminalized gay—but not straight—sodomy. The suit had been brought by Lambda in cooperation with local gay attorneys in Houston.

When John Lawrence and Tyron Garner were arrested there in 1998 for consensual sodomy, word of the outrage quickly spread to local gay activists, some of whom were eager to use the incident as a test case to reverse *Bowers* at the Supreme Court. The activists made their way to Suzanne Goldberg at Lambda to ask her advice. With its *Romer* victory two years behind it, Lambda too, along with the ACLU, had been hoping to find the perfect sodomy case to take back to the courts, this time seeking a gay-only law to challenge (some states penalized any form of sodomy, while others prohibited only same-sex sodomy). Now that the Supreme Court in *Romer* had struck down anti-gay laws, the legal climate seemed much more ripe for a reversal of *Bowers*.[19]

Goldberg immediately recognized the promise of the case, as did the senior staff at Lambda: Ruth Harlow, who had started her legal work at ACLU, Beatrice Dohrn, the group's legal director, and its executive director, Kevin Cathcart. Harlow and Goldberg had concerns about the case: Was the climate right? Would the plaintiffs stick with it? Would the state suddenly drop its prosecution? But in discussions between the national legal groups and the Houston activists, it was the local Texas activists who were most hesitant to press the case, fearing that the legal climate remained too conservative. "We just have to make sure we don't mess anything up," said Annise Parker, who would later become Houston's first openly gay mayor, in an echo of Paula Ettelbrick's expression of restraint in describing the Roundtable's caution on litigation.[20]

There was also the matter of the messy facts and optics of the arrest and of the pair charged, Lawrence and Garner, a working-class, interracial duo who both had unpredictable personalities and criminal records (and who, despite their arrest for sodomy, may never even have had intercourse). While it was a delicate subject that few in the movement liked to discuss, impact litigation usually involved the careful choice of plaintiffs who were thought to be most likely to win over both the public and the courts, and race, class, and biography could enter such calculations in ways that challenged the gay left's commitment to diversity and authenticity. Given the difficulty of finding ideal plaintiffs—compounded by the rare or uneven enforcement of sodomy laws in most states—Lambda had struggled to find the best avenue to challenge the law. When the Lawrence and Garner affair fell into their laps, it was difficult to resist. Lambda met with the would-be plaintiffs and the Houston lawyers and activists, where all discussed their concerns along with the risks and promise of the case. After some inspirational words meant to convince the plaintiffs themselves (who were reluctant to become the public face of sodomy), the group decided to move forward.[21]

As the suit wound its way through the U.S. Supreme Court—a Texas appeals court first sided with Lawrence and Garner and later with the state—Lambda brought on lawyers from the firm Jenner and Block to give the legal team top talent with Supreme Court experience and establishment credentials. Paul Smith, a partner there, had clerked for Justice Lewis Powell, who had cast the deciding vote against the gay plaintiffs in *Bowers*. Smith joined the cause eagerly, and when the Supreme Court agreed to hear the case, he accepted the honor of being chosen to argue before the justices. Susan Sommer, a straight Lambda lawyer who, along with Goldberg, had fought to end several state sodomy laws, coordinated over a dozen amicus briefs signed by the American Psychological Association, the American Bar Association, and other powerhouses of the American establishment, the better to demonstrate that gay rights had become a mainstream cause. Even the libertarian Cato Institute submitted a brief, lending the imprimatur of its center-right sensibility to the attack on gay-specific sodomy laws. A brief authored by ten prominent historians including George Chauncey and John D'Emilio pointed out how recent such laws were, explaining that, while sodomy itself had long been banned in American law, targeting gay people as a distinct minority was relatively new, and thus the *Bowers* Court had been mistaken in its reading of history when it claimed that "homosexual sodomy" bans were rooted in "millennia of moral teaching."[22]

Against the state's tepid and largely incompetent defense of the Texas sodomy law as a legitimate safeguard for public morality, the Lambda team mounted a thoughtful, laser-focused constitutional assault that incorporated this crucial notion that society evolves, and the law with it. The country's understanding of and familiarity with gay people and relationships had been transformed since *Bowers*. Incremental progress in ending state sodomy bans—Lambda's Sommer had led the latest victory, when the Arkansas Supreme Court struck down that state's law—furthered and reflected such change, and Texas was now one of only four states with a gay-only sodomy ban. Not only had the psychiatric profession, pushed by activists such as Kameny and Gittings, removed homosexuality from its

list of mental disorders, but many medical and psychological groups had
endorsed gay parenting. The American family had changed, with many
fewer children being raised by two married biological parents. Indeed, many
of the laws that the *Bowers* Court believed had "ancient roots" were in fact
late twentieth-century reactions to these very changes. Rather than asking
the Court to get ahead of the nation, the Lambda team was telling the
justices that it was simply time for it to catch up.[23]

The plaintiff's brief argued that punishing gay but not straight people
for the same conduct violated the Constitution's equal protection clause
and that criminalizing consensual sex improperly burdened the liberty and
privacy protected by the due process clause. But the team chose not to
emphasize wider arguments based on nondiscrimination principles, which
was tempting to some. Smith reasoned that this case presented a unique
opportunity to eradicate insidious anti-gay laws in a still-conservative climate, and they needed to focus on the practical. "We weren't worried
about establishing a precedent for the eleven other things" that might
follow with the end of sodomy bans, he recounted to the legal scholar
Dale Carpenter. "You have to take these things one day at a time."[24] The
theory embodied an incremental view of legal change, which dovetailed
with the broader theme of evolutionary social change emphasized in the
historians' brief and Lambda's overall legal strategy.

The lawyers chose not to cast sex and sexuality either as the territory
of nihilistic libertines or as a necessary evil to be tolerated though never
celebrated. A generation earlier, many gay advocates had gravitated to one
extreme or the other to advance their vision of progress: gay liberationists viewed sex as a realm of unrestrained pleasure and the right to enjoy
virtually all forms of it as the embodiment of modern freedom, while
those seeking political equality and respectability—whether for pragmatic
or ideological reasons—endorsed a more restrained view of gay life. As
recently as 1996, Barney Frank had told his colleagues on the floor of Congress that if gay marriage bothered them, "turn your head"—a pragmatic
concession to the era, no doubt, but an argument for tolerance rather than
respectability.

By the time of *Lawrence*, gay legal advocates were increasingly embracing an argument that framed same-sex desire as a positive foundation for gay relationships, even a source of dignified love, just as it was
for straight ones. Frank Kameny had insisted from the outset that "gay is

good," and now Paul Smith and the Lambda lawyers argued that gay sex is good, at least for gay people—an innate part of intimate relationships, and often the cement that helped relationships and families to endure. Casting gay sex this way was both a tactical consideration and the outgrowth of what the legal team genuinely believed. "We were trying to communicate something about what the real importance of sexuality is in people's lives," Smith explained. It was quite a balancing act: while pushing boundaries, on the one hand, by claiming that gay sex was worthy of respect, not concealment, the lawyers advanced, on the other hand, what Carpenter dubbed "the most conservative argument possible for a constitutional right to sex." They framed the end of sodomy bans not as a challenge to but as a "vindication of traditional American values," propelling same-sex desire into the American mainstream.[25]

The strategy worked. In its ruling, handed down on June 26, 2003, the Court swept aside a precedent it had affirmed just seventeen years earlier. The shrinking number of states that still had anti-sodomy laws on the books, Justice Kennedy wrote in his majority opinion, revealed "an emerging awareness that liberty gives substantial protection to adult persons in deciding how to conduct their private lives in matters pertaining to sex." The *Bowers* decision, the Court now said, "demean[ed]" gay people's privacy claims by treating them as "simply the right to engage in certain sexual conduct." The Texas sodomy law "furthers no legitimate state interest which can justify its intrusion into the individual's personal and private life." Although the decision nodded to *Romer,* particularly to its weakening of *Bowers* and its prohibition of laws "born of animosity" toward a specific group, Kennedy grounded his ruling not in equal protection arguments but in an evolving understanding of both gay people and of the meaning of liberty. Intimate decisions by consenting individuals, he concluded, are an essential component of liberty protected by the Constitution. "That analysis should have controlled *Bowers,* and it controls here. *Bowers* was not correct when it was decided, is not correct today, and is hereby overruled."[26]

It is notable that Kennedy, who authored the Court's majority opinion, had filled the seat of Lewis Powell, who four years after casting the deciding vote in *Bowers* said publicly that he had "probably made a mistake in that one." While weighing his decision before the vote, he told a closeted gay clerk that he had never met a homosexual, and then sealed the fate of millions of gay people for seventeen more years. If his clerk—and he had several gay clerks during his tenure, all closeted—had been out, perhaps Powell would have caught his mistake before the vote. Seventeen years later, it seemed likely that Kennedy's pro-gay vote and opinion—his second after *Romer,* and equally sweeping—had in part been made possible by the great strides in gay visibility of the intervening years.[27]

The *Lawrence* decision, like the Hawaii decision, changed everything. The Supreme Court declared it had made a mistake in dismissing the liberty claims of gays and lesbians. The ruling was an acknowledgment that gays and lesbians were entitled to the same rights and respect as other citizens. "*Bowers* had essentially taken away, as a legal matter, the dignity of same-sex couples in the most derisive of terms," said Sommer. "*Lawrence* gave that back to lesbian and gay Americans." The decision meant that people around the country woke up the next morning to banner headlines about the battle for gay dignity, including the dignity of gay sex. Many must have thought about the issue for the very first time. Some, viewing the Court's decision as a powerful endorsement of the moral equality of homosexuality, began to challenge lifelong assumptions that their own heterosexuality had ever been morally superior to begin with.[28]

For gays and lesbians themselves, and for the legal strategists who favored the pursuit of marriage rights, *Lawrence* was a green light to march forward. Evan Wolfson declared *Lawrence* a "tipping point, in which fair-minded people now support equality and inclusion for gay people and most Americans are ready to accept marriage."[29] Wolfson was speaking wishfully, as polls showed that a clear majority of Americans still opposed same-sex marriage, with just over a third supporting the idea in mid-2003.[30] But there was no question that *Lawrence* had radically altered the landscape. "It was a transformative case, particularly for those of us doing legal work," recalled Kate Kendell, director of the National Center for Lesbian Rights (NCLR, formerly the Lesbian Rights Project). "It marked an enormous opportunity for a huge cultural shift, because if the sexual expression of our love could no longer be considered criminal, we all knew that cleared a path for moving all sorts of other cultural signifiers of inclusion and equality and acceptance forward."[31]

In an angry dissent from the *Lawrence* majority, Justice Antonin Scalia grimly agreed. The decision, he noted, "leaves on pretty shaky grounds state laws limiting marriage to opposite-sex couples." Revealingly, Scalia even acknowledged that the way courts and legislatures historically had defended the restriction of marriage to heterosexuals was simply a way to denigrate homosexuality as inferior, and act accordingly. The phrase "preserving the traditional institution of marriage," he argued, "is just a kinder way of describing the State's *moral disapproval* of same-sex couples." Scalia was dismayed, as he had been in *Romer,* that the court "signed on to the so-called homosexual agenda," which he defined as an effort to eliminate the "moral opprobrium that has traditionally attached to homosexual conduct." He lamented that the Court was discarding the principles that underlay countless laws and court rulings that "relied on the ancient proposition that a governing majority's belief that certain sexual behavior is 'immoral and unacceptable' constitutes a rational basis for regulation." And he fretted that with the removal of moral judgment as a legitimate basis for lawmaking, laws against bigamy, incest, prostitution, masturbation, adultery, fornication, and obscenity—as well as same-sex marriage—could no longer withstand judicial scrutiny. "Every single one of these laws is called into question by today's decision," he wrote. For social conservatives like Scalia, the rising assertion by gay advocates that they were due not just tolerance but respectability spurred louder repudiations of the dignity of same-sex love and, in many cases, explicit assertions that gay people and relationships were morally repugnant.

That was an uphill battle for conservatives, who were fighting not only in courts and statehouses but also in the arena of popular culture. In 2003, five unthreatening gay men swept into Americans' living rooms via cable television to help rescue the hapless style of heterosexual men in *Queer Eye for the Straight Guy.* While criticized by some for casting gays as "minstrels," the makeover show helped familiarize Americans with gay culture and made gay-straight relations seem playful and mutually beneficial rather than perilous or fraught. This spread of approving attitudes in popular culture was nearly as important—and as threatening to anti-gay forces—as the spread of pro-gay laws and court rulings, all elements of a changing set of beliefs with little respect for state lines.

The *Lawrence* decision sent a jolt of electricity through the religious right, which stepped up its mobilization efforts. "These are the first shots in the largest battle in the culture wars since *Roe v. Wade,*" said Brian Brown, executive director of the Family Institute of Connecticut, where the legislature was considering a bill to legalize same-sex marriage. As lawmakers there and elsewhere weighed in on what marriage would mean, Brown warned that politicians would have to "choose a side" and would have "nowhere to hide." And it was not only Christian conservatives who were fired up. Mainstream Republicans, including Senate majority leader Bill Frist, began to talk more seriously of pushing a federal constitutional amendment to bar gay marriage in the wake of *Lawrence* and other developments— including news that a court ruling in May was poised to make Canada the third country, after the Netherlands and Belgium, to legalize same-sex marriage.[32] Top advisors to President George W. Bush, including Karl Rove and Ken Mehlman, took note of how angry and motivated their base of religious conservatives was by the prospect of same-sex marriage spreading across the nation and the world. How, they began to wonder, should the president respond as he faced reelection the next year?

That fall, bearing out Scalia's fretful prediction in his *Lawrence* dissent, the Massachusetts Supreme Judicial Court became the first state court in America to strike down the exclusion of gays and lesbians from the institution of marriage. In GLAD's appeal of the lower court ruling in the *Goodridge* case, the state's high court declared that the state's constitution "forbids the creation of second-class citizens." Chief Justice Margaret Marshall, joined by three Republican-appointed judges, cited the *Lawrence* decision repeatedly, as well as *Romer* before it, in her majority opinion. She wrote that the state had "failed to identify any constitutionally adequate reason for denying civil marriage to same-sex couples," including the argument that marriage could be restricted to straights since gay couples were unable to contribute to its main purpose: procreation. Even if the court were to accept that marriage was designed for child-rearing, that would hardly be a logical reason to deny it to gays and lesbians, who, after all, rear children too. Depriving their parents of access to marriage would simply penalize children "because the state disapproves of their parents' sexual orientation." Such exclusion, she wrote, "works a deep and scarring hardship" on families that include gay parents, and "it cannot be rational under our laws."[33]

The ruling was a decisive victory for same-sex marriage, appearing to promise the first legal same-sex marriages in the country. Yet, as in Vermont, the court left open the question of whether its ruling actually required the legalization of marriage for gay couples. It gave the legislature six months to rectify the unequal status of gay unions, but without stating exactly how to achieve that in a way that would satisfy the court. That uncertainty meant that enormous obstacles remained before same-sex marriage could actually come to the state. Advocates of full marriage rights had to lobby against an interpretation of the ruling that would allow civil unions legislation to pass muster. They had to ward off a series of likely legal maneuvers by opponents that could slow, weaken, or block full marriage rights based on other laws and legal precedents. And if all those efforts by conservatives failed, they still faced the prospect of the citizens of Massachusetts choosing to amend the state constitution to override the court's ruling.

Indeed, defending the Massachusetts court win was essential to the marriage equality effort well beyond the state. If the Massachusetts ruling was somehow reversed, or even if same-sex marriage survived but the politicians or judges who had supported it suffered retribution at the polls, as many had in Vermont, it could send chills across the nation, frightening officials everywhere from making pro-gay decisions in the future. Notwithstanding the positive ruling and its strong language, gay marriage advocates had their work cut out for them.[34]

The bulk of this work fell to a group of largely grassroots volunteers organized into a loose coalition that frequently resisted being named, let alone pulled together into a single organization. The "group of groups," they initially called themselves, not wanting to step on the toes of existing organizations or broadcast too loudly their ambitions and risk a backlash. Several new groups had formed in the years after the Hawaii ruling, when Evan Wolfson and a handful of marriage advocates were pushing the creation of state and local groups. "He was a bit of a prophet," remembered activist Josh Friedes, "and many of us significantly bought into his vision." Friedes went on to co-lead, with Valerie Fein-Zachary and Robert DeBenedictis, the Freedom to Marry Coalition of Massachusetts (FTMCM). Other groups had sprouted with no formal relationship to Wolfson's National Freedom to Marry Coalition, or had shifted shape from their post-Stonewall incarnations with a broad focus on gay rights to prioritizing relationship recognition or marriage itself. In the years before and after Congress passed DOMA, these groups, armed with much passion but little money, had worked to build their coalition of marriage equality supporters around the country. Their outreach earned them endorsements from forces in the labor, women's, and black civil rights movements, bisexual activists, progressive religious leaders, and singular American figures such as Coretta Scott King.[35]

In conjunction with filing both the *Baker* and *Goodridge* suits, GLAD had drawn on the talent and organizing prowess of these grassroots activists to build a climate of receptivity and durability for court wins in New England. Sue Hyde, for instance, a veteran organizer for the Task Force who lived in Cambridge, Massachusetts, and Arlene Isaacson, the lobbyist and co-chair of the Massachusetts Gay and Lesbian Political Caucus, both understood the need to mobilize marriage equality supporters and to persuade state lawmakers to side with them in legislative battles. But ultimately the political fight to win and keep marriage in New England would require a level of coordination that the loose alliance model was unable to provide. Before filing *Goodridge,* Bonauto and her colleagues reached out to a handful of activists, including Friedes at FTMCM, to discuss ways to professionalize the coalition. With a minuscule budget, Friedes agreed to be the first paid staff member of his group. Around the same time, a thirty-three-year-old conservative named Marc Solomon moved to Boston just as he was coming to terms with being gay. "I recognized that my fight was against oppression," he remembered, rather than against himself. This awakening occasioned a liberal turn as he learned of the array of advocacy groups working for gay rights in New England. Solomon began volunteering with FTMCM as a way to channel his new outlook into effective action. He soon became the group's legislative director. Robyn Maguire joined as field organizer. They were able to wrangle small grants from gay foundations and larger groups such as the Human Rights Campaign, though Friedes often felt it was "take this and go away" money, rather than a serious effort to achieve results.[36]

All that changed after the *Goodridge* victory. Suddenly, marriage seemed like a winning issue. HRC stepped up to fund the Massachusetts groups at brisk new levels, and the Task Force put up money as well. The "group of groups" had finally found a name, MassEquality, and a new structure with a mandate to protect the court win and become a permanent gay rights organization for the state. With new rounds of funding, the group hired its first director, the politically savvy Marty Rouse, who had recently deployed to Vermont to help defend Democratic lawmakers who voted for civil unions there. The effort to protect same-sex marriage in Massachusetts, which had begun even before the ruling was handed down, now kicked into high gear.[37]

The work was daunting, and mixed promise with peril. Statewide polls taken in the wake of the *Goodridge* ruling showed majority support for the court's decision. In one poll, nearly 60 percent of state residents supported the decision, while only 37 percent opposed it. Yet when asked directly about a constitutional amendment to supersede the court's ruling, nearly as many respondents were in favor as opposed. Editorial pages of large and small newspapers alike generally expressed support, but others sounded the alarm. Views on marriage seemed totally unsettled, and daily small victories in the battle were up for grabs.[38]

The Massachusetts ground game was a combination of mobilizing the public and engaging state lawmakers. Riding the wave of the Internet and new methods of viral email marketing that DeBenedictis had helped pioneer, MassEquality was able to bombard the legislature with messages of support, get activists out to events, and raise money in ways few thought possible just five years earlier. In turn, people showed up at pro-gay-marriage rallies and wedding celebrations at gay pride parades in numbers that surprised even organizers. There, supporters would line up to sign and send postcards to the state house. When the wedding floats passed by, the crowds would roar. "I hadn't seen anything like it," recalled Friedes. Not only did it reveal an unforeseen level of interest in marriage by members of the gay and lesbian community, but it made victory seem possible. "It was kind of this dawning realization," he said, "that we could really do this." On the political organizing side, the work was just as dizzying. One by one, advocates would open files on what made each lawmaker tick, what they and their families cared about, which sports teams they liked, what contacts they might have in common—anything that could be used to engage with them in ways that could ultimately bring them to support gay marriage.[39]

Although the *Goodridge* decision was local to Massachusetts, the stakes meant that the debate was immediately nationalized. Conservative reaction was fierce. Tony Perkins of the Family Research Council denounced activist courts for falling in line with the "homosexual agenda" and vowed to push a federal constitutional amendment as necessary "to stop a tyrannical judiciary from redefining marriage to the point of extinction."[40] Roberta Combs, head of the Christian Coalition, vowed, "This is not going to stop here—this is going to be in the forefront for a long time to come."[41] Republican politicians expressed identical sentiments. President George W. Bush immediately released a statement condemning the decision and vowing undefined action. "Marriage is a sacred institution between a man and a woman," it said. "Today's decision of the Massachusetts Supreme Judicial Court violates this important principle. I will work with Congressional leaders and others to do what is legally necessary to defend the sanctity of marriage."[42] Rep. Tom DeLay, the Republican leader of the House, complained of a "runaway judiciary" and endorsed a federal constitutional amendment banning gay marriage.[43] Massachusetts governor Mitt Romney, perhaps already eyeing a White House run some years away, also condemned the decision and pledged to back a state constitutional amendment. Romney indicated his support for limited partner benefits as an alternative to marriage, but in doing so he made the inequality inherent in that proposition starkly clear: "We must provide basic civil rights and appropriate benefits to nontraditional couples, but marriage is a special institution that should be reserved for a man and a woman."[44]

Reactions from local and national Democrats were scarcely more promising to gay advocates than those of Republicans. A month after the decision, the new Democratic president of the state senate, Robert Travaglini, offered up a civil unions bill in hopes that this, rather than a full marriage bill, would be enough to satisfy the court. State representative Philip Travis, a Democrat, announced he would push a constitutional amendment to ban same-sex marriage, cooperating with conservative Christian groups such as the Massachusetts Family Institute (MFI), the leading group in that effort.[45] National Democrats, long terrified of the electoral damage they associated with endorsing gay equality, closed ranks in opposition to the court ruling. Sen. Tom Daschle of South Dakota, the Senate's minority leader, who faced a tough reelection bid in 2004, said that the heterosexual essence of marriage "is as clear as can be," and touted his vote in favor of DOMA to showcase his bona fides.[46] Rep. Dick Gephardt, former Speaker of the House and then a candidate for the Democratic presidential nomination, criticized the ruling even as his daughter came out publicly as a lesbian. Sen. John Kerry of Massachusetts, who would become the Democratic nominee for president in the 2004 election, had been one of only fourteen U.S. senators to oppose DOMA in 1996, yet he used the occasion of the Massachusetts court ruling to remind voters that he "continue[d] to oppose gay marriage" itself, and supported civil unions instead.[47] Hoping to burnish his appeal to socially conservative voters, he soon announced that he supported amending his state's constitution to ban same-sex marriage, so long as civil unions were offered in its place. "If the Massachusetts legislature crafts an appropriate amendment that provides for partnership and civil unions," he told reporters, "then I would support it, and it would advance the goal of equal protection."[48] Once Kerry secured the Democratic nomination, former president Bill Clinton reportedly advised him to endorse an amendment to the federal Constitution to help strengthen his prospects with swing voters (though Clinton disputed the claim).[49]

Over the six months between the court's ruling and the deadline it had imposed on the legislature to achieve a remedy, conservative and religious groups fought hard to prevent the ruling from even taking effect. At one point, five separate lawsuits sought to block same-sex marriage.[50] The most threatening was brought by the conservative group Liberty Counsel on behalf of the Catholic Action League and nearly a dozen Massachusetts lawmakers charging that the state's high court lacked the authority to rule as it did and should have deferred to the legislature instead. The effort ultimately failed, and the group was later refused a hearing by the U.S. Supreme Court. Gay marriage opponents also readied legal challenges to same-sex marriages by out-of-state couples, and Gov. Romney invoked a 1913 law designed in part to thwart interracial marriages in order to argue that the state did not have to marry gay couples whose home state did not permit gay marriage.[51] As his options ran out, Romney took the extraordinary step of seeking special authority from the legislature to stay the court's decision. His request was denied.[52] In his opposition to the ruling, Representative Travis even went so far as to file legislation to impeach the chief justice, which went nowhere.[53]

Meanwhile, the leadership of the Massachusetts legislature determined that it needed to know, rather than to guess, what the court would ultimately accept as a remedy. In December 2003 Senator Travaglini sought a formal clarification from the court of whether civil unions would conform to the mandate of its ruling. In a blunt advisory opinion issued in February, the court answered no: the very language of the proposed civil unions bill demonstrated that its entire purpose was to continue to exclude gay people from the status of marriage. As Bonauto and Wolfson had long argued, having access to the word "marriage" is no mere matter of semantics; as the court put it, "The dissimilitude between the terms 'civil marriage' and 'civil union' is hardly innocuous." The civil unions option was a deliberate effort to give same-sex love a "second-class status," said the court, and American history had already shown that "separate is seldom, if ever, equal."[54]

Once the court had thus spoken, few doubted that same-sex marriage would come to Massachusetts that May. The court's strong advisory opinion left few options for those hoping to block same-sex marriages from taking effect. Still, many conservatives remained optimistic that even if the state began allowing such marriages, a federal or state constitutional amendment might actually win enough support to eventually override the court's ruling. Amending the federal Constitution would be a tough sell. But given public opposition to gay marriage in so many states and Republican control of Congress, it felt to some like a real threat. "The politics were very intense on this issue at the time," remembered Hilary Rosen, a political strategist who worked with HRC to defeat a federal amendment. "In the moment, it looked pretty scary." The more immediate threat, however, and the easier lift, was a series of constitutional amendments by individual states, and Massachusetts was now ground zero. Conservative organizations such as MFI and a group called Massachusetts Citizens Alliance (MCA) had been working for some time to push an amendment in the state. In July 2001, three months after *Goodridge* was first filed, MCA had announced plans to put a constitutional amendment on the ballot. "Our intention is to codify marriage to make sure it remains a special and unique relationship," announced Bryan Rudnick, the group's head. And he made no bones about the normative basis of the effort: "We're saying men should marry women and women should marry men."[55]

There were two ways to amend the Massachusetts constitution: either the state legislature could introduce an amendment and pass it with a majority vote in two consecutive sessions, after which the question would be put to the state's voters in a referendum; or a citizen initiative could introduce an amendment by collecting a certain number of signatures (in this case around 65,000), after which the measure would require approval of only 25 percent of the legislature and then a majority of voters in a referendum. The multiyear process meant that same-sex marriages could very well begin before a final referendum could be scheduled on the amendment. And that meant that social conservatives would have to convince the people of Massachusetts to yank away same-sex marriage rights after already seeing neighbors, friends, and family members marry. Gay advocates hoped this would be a far taller order than voting to block a right in the abstract. Indeed, Bonauto and her colleagues had chosen to file a suit in Massachusetts in part because its constitution was difficult to amend. Yet opposition to the court's ruling by social conservatives was so fierce—not just in Massachusetts but nationally—that a reversal was a clear danger.[56]

In the years leading up to the *Goodridge* ruling, gay marriage opponents in Massachusetts had continued to organize, raise money, collect signatures, and promote the idea that gay marriage threatened to destroy the institution of marriage, the family, even the nation. The ruling in 2003 only added new urgency to the cause. By 2004 the popular energy devoted to the battle from both sides was substantial and growing. Thousands of pro-gay supporters had showed up at the statehouse and the courts for a string of rallies throughout February and March, mobilized largely by MassEquality and FTMCM. Each pro-gay rally was met with counter-demonstrators led largely by religious conservatives and national and international religious bodies including the Catholic Church. Demonstrators traded chants: "Jesus!" "Equal rights!" "Jesus!" "Equal rights!" Finally, in March 2004, the conservative plan lurched forward when the Massachusetts legislature took the first step in reversing the court ruling. With the vocal support of Gov. Romney, the state's Catholic hierarchy, and phone calls and letters that poured into the state house from across the nation, the legislature voted 105 to 92 to amend the constitution to ban gay marriage and provide civil unions instead, an effort to soften the appearance of anti-gay sentiment. The vote was a huge disappointment for gay advocates. Yet the legislature would still need to pass the measure again the following year, and the voters would then have to endorse it at the polls, before the amendment could take effect.[57]

In May, however, the gay movement was finally able to deploy its strongest weapon yet. All the years of rhetorical sparring, politicking, and abstract debates about the worth and validity of same-sex relationships were suddenly overshadowed by emotionally irresistible imagery as the world watched the country's first state-sanctioned same-sex weddings take place in joyous ceremonies held across the state before adoring crowds and the glow of national media. The date, May 17, 2004, was the fiftieth anniversary of the Supreme Court's *Brown v. Board* ruling that forbade racial segregation. On this day, all seven plaintiffs in the *Goodridge* case got married. Guests of Julie and Hillary Goodridge sang, "Here come the brides, so gay with pride, isn't it a wonder that they somehow survived!" Across the state, crowds gathered to witness and celebrate the weddings, some passing out pink roses, others cheering and blowing bubbles. Officials estimated a crowd of ten thousand just outside Cambridge's city hall, where 250 couples showed up to get licenses, some having waited decades for the chance. Judges across the state waived the normal three-day waiting period between applying for and receiving a license, allowing weddings to begin immediately. That first day alone, nearly one thousand couples applied for licenses, several times the average number for a day in May.[58]

Social conservatives were devastated on the day of the nation's first same-sex weddings but also subdued, many expressing disappointment that more of their comrades had not shown up to register their protest. "Where is the president of the United States?" asked an Orthodox rabbi, in from Brooklyn. "There should be 1,000 religious leaders standing here today." Instead there was a smattering in each of the main towns and cities where crowds gathered for licenses. In Boston, religious opponents prayed with banners reading "Jesus, Mary and Joseph, we hope you keep the family holy." The Family Research Council showed up with cameras rolling to gather footage to use in their future campaigns against same-sex marriage. James Dobson of Focus on the Family lamented, "The documents being issued all across Massachusetts may say 'marriage license' at the top but they are really death certificates for the institution of marriage."[59] Dismissing comparisons of gay rights to civil rights—since gay people "never had to drink at different water fountains or ride in the back of the bus"— Traditional Values Coalition chairman Rev. Lou Sheldon predicted, "I think this is going to awaken people."[60]

And it had—on both sides of the debate. Social conservatives sought to consolidate their recent gains: build on the vote in the Massachusetts legislature for a state constitutional amendment, put additional state amendments on ballots in many more states, expand support for a federal constitutional amendment to ban gay marriage, and continue to cast gay people and families as a threat to the republic. Indeed, social conservatives were often the first to characterize this fight as, essentially, about reserving the dignity of sex, love, parenting, and marriage exclusively for heterosexuals. On the other side, gay people and their legal advocates came to view the defense of the freedom to marry as the most viable, direct way to assert gay dignity and approach full equality.

While the Hawaii court win had resulted from the efforts of local activists and lawyers and ordinary same-sex couples—and had soon given way to defeat—the Massachusetts win, still not safe from reversal, was the result of a meticulous seven-year strategy carried out by professional gay rights lawyers with the support of advocacy groups on the ground. Gay advocates now had to fortify what they had achieved, and, with that cornerstone in place, build a national edifice.

7

"Power to the People"

ROGUE WEDDINGS

AND BALLOT INITIATIVES

THE ECSTATIC THRONGS THAT GATHERED IN MAY 2004 TO HOLD OR witness same-sex weddings in Massachusetts were not the first to create national headlines with stirring images of gay nuptials. The year had begun with a handful of local officials on each coast striding ahead of the laws of their state and country by officiating same-sex weddings as an act of either civil disobedience or constitutional obedience, depending on one's viewpoint. These scenes from San Francisco, upstate New York, Oregon, and elsewhere gave practical expression to an awakening by gay couples across the nation that their love deserved public recognition and legal protection. Throughout the year, events on the ground—unpredictable, often spontaneous, and frequently difficult for either gay leaders or social conservatives to control—gave momentum to both the advance of gay marriage and a powerful backlash against it.

As the tremendous impact of the November 2003 *Goodridge* decision— on the heels of *Lawrence* in June—sank in for conservatives, President George W. Bush faced a balancing act. Scarred by his father's fate in 1992, when fiery culture war rhetoric at the Republican convention had been blamed for helping seal his reelection defeat, Bush wanted to avoid alienating the moderates he had courted with his image as a "compassionate conservative." Yet he also knew how important the loyalty of evangelicals was to his own reelection chances, and the president's top advisors had begun plotting ways to court the religious right.

Drawing out socially conservative voters to oppose gay marriage in state ballot initiatives could have the added benefit of amassing additional votes for Bush that November. So his advisors began working with conservative activists at the state level, while Bush tried to figure out where to come down on the specific question of whether to amend the federal constitution to ban gay marriage. His initial statement on the *Goodridge* ruling had shied away from even mentioning a federal constitutional amendment. But in the months after the ruling came down, as the election campaign kicked into high gear, Bush was pressed by his base to ramp up his support for a federal amendment. In his January 2004 State of the Union address, he inched closer to endorsing the idea. He criticized the Massachusetts decision for its role in "redefining marriage by court order without regard for the will of the people." Not yet endorsing the federal amendment, he said that "if judges insist on forcing their arbitrary will upon the people, the only alternative left to the people would be the constitutional process."[1]

That night in attendance at the president's speech was the ambitious and charismatic young mayor of San Francisco, Gavin Newsom. In Washington for his first visit there as mayor, Newsom visited with California senator Dianne Feinstein—whose political career had taken her from San Francisco mayor to California's first female U.S. senator—and Rep. Nancy Pelosi, leader of the House Democrats, who asked him if he'd be willing to stay another night to attend the president's speech. Newsom was appalled when, toward the end, the president took time in a speech focused largely on urgent international challenges—the nation had recently invaded Iraq and was now fighting two wars simultaneously—to condemn gay marriage. "I thought, 'Boy, this is an interesting speech,'" he recalled of that night at the Capitol, incredulous that a wartime president was focusing on the alleged threat to the nation of same-sex love. But in a rude awakening for Newsom and other liberal observers, it now became clear that Bush planned to exploit social issues, including abstinence, drug use, and gay marriage, as part of his reelection campaign. Afterward the mayor overheard adoring fans of the president praise the speech, declaring how glad they were that the president would finally be doing something about activist judges in Massachusetts and elsewhere, and speaking derisively of gays and lesbians. "I remember feeling I was living in a parallel universe," he said years later. That was the moment he decided he had to do something himself—to act based on both moral urgency and the possibility, risky though it also was, of political gain.[2]

That night he called his office and started a conversation with his staff about what could be done to put a human face on gay marriage and move the issue forward. Newsom spoke with Joyce Newstat, his policy director, and Steve Kawa, his chief of staff—both gay—about what to do. Newsom and Newstat coalesced around the idea of issuing marriage licenses to gay couples in the city. Their thinking was that a proper reading of the California constitution's provisions banning discrimination and guaranteeing equal protection required letting gay couples marry, notwithstanding the statutory ban created by William Knight's Proposition 22. That a state court found as much in Massachusetts gave Newsom increased confidence. But Kawa was unconvinced, seeing the idea as unnecessary and politically risky. Generally these were matters for courts to decide, not for executives to take into their own hands. Many national Democratic politicians, including Rep. Barney Frank, agreed, worrying that Newsom's plan could harm the party's fortunes in an election year. Kawa talked it over with his partner and warmed to the mayor's idea, soon embracing the strategy.[3]

Newstat and Kawa suggested reaching out to Kate Kendell at the National Center for Lesbian Rights, as well as others in the local gay community, including leaders at Equality California, the state's largest gay rights advocacy group. On Friday afternoon of the following week, Kendell was picking up her daughter from preschool. As she got out of the car, her cell phone rang; Kawa was on the other end. After exchanging pleasantries, Kawa explained he was calling to give her a heads-up that on Monday the mayor's office would begin issuing marriage licenses to same-sex couples. "I was flabbergasted and scared," said Kendell, though both feelings were quickly replaced by elation. Kendell praised the mayor for standing up and doing the right thing. "But I also threw a big caution forward, saying that after what had just happened in Massachusetts, I wasn't sure this was the right strategic move, that we needed to think about this first." Kendell also wanted to consult with her legal colleagues across the country. She asked if the actions could be put off at least long enough for a sit-down meeting between her staff and theirs. Kawa agreed, but reiterated that his call was a courtesy and that the mayor's decision was ultimately not up for debate.[4]

Kendell fetched her daughter and returned home to a weekend of phone calls with her staff and colleagues. NCLR had participated in Litigators' Roundtable conversations for years, joining the ongoing dialogue about whether, when, and where to press a marriage lawsuit. Early in 2003 their lawyers had joined other legal scholars, strategists, and activists at a Los Angeles meeting to discuss whether to file a suit in California. Neither the *Lawrence* nor the *Goodridge* ruling had been handed down yet. The usual reservations carried the day, and the participants concluded that more legislative and grassroots work needed to be done, especially considering how easy it was to amend the California constitution.[5] But by early 2004, after the U.S. Supreme Court and Massachusetts decisions had thoroughly rattled the playing field, Kendell and her staff began discussing what the changed landscape might mean for next steps in California.

Kendell herself had come to the marriage battle slowly. A decade earlier she had attended her first Roundtable meeting, at the Boston offices of GLAD, and argued, like several of her lesbian lawyer colleagues, that the movement's focus on marriage was undercutting the gay liberation struggle. Evan Wolfson did not receive her remarks well. "I thought for a minute Evan was going to jump across the table," she said. Instead, he patiently explained the reasons he believed marriage ought to be a preeminent focus for the movement. Although Kendell never lost her sympathy for the liberationist critique of the role of marriage in gay life, Wolfson's evangelizing started a process of reflection that led her to recognize how the legal and cultural denial of marriage reflected and perpetuated anti-gay sentiment and that it would be far harder to sustain that bias if same-sex couples could wed.[6] "What has been made unmistakably clear to me by the lesbians and gay men that we work with and represent," she said in 2001, "is that the denial of our right to marry exacerbates our marginalization; winning that right is the cornerstone of full justice."[7]

The events of 2004—the assaults on her community's relationships and the acts of support by allies such as Newsom—would only augment her belief in the power of marriage. In a series of conversations that January, before she was approached by Kawa, Kendell and her staff at NCLR had brainstormed about what might still be needed in order to create the right legal and political climate for a defendable, winning case in California. They wondered how they might team up with other groups, lawmakers, or political officials to move the issue forward. Recently they had heard that officials in Portland, Oregon, were considering issuing marriage licenses to same-sex couples. "What do you think?" Kendell had asked the group, contemplating whether a San Francisco version might fly. "This might not go anywhere but it would certainly ignite a dialogue." Shannon Minter, NCLR's legal director, had taken a moment to think, then said, "It's an interesting idea, but we should probably wait and see how it plays out in Oregon."

By the end of January, the NCLR staff had made no decision to move forward. They were united with other gay legal advocates who had chosen to hold off on marriage litigation in California, and they knew that issuing marriage licenses could provoke a lawsuit. "We didn't think a lawsuit in California was appropriate or timely quite yet," remembered Kendell. With no knowledge of the parallel discussion going on in Newsom's office, the NCLR folks figured it would be another year or two before the climate would be ready for litigation.[8] And they wanted to wait for the right catalyst, something that could prompt dialogue, attention, and consideration by the public before going to the courts.

So when Kawa called the following month, Kendell was caught off guard. Yet, having discussed ways to push forward on the marriage front, she and her staff were primed for action. "Some things happen by surprise and accident and some gains you plan for," she says. "We were definitely in a 'what can you plan for?' mode of thinking."

Faced with the prospect of seeing a real plan put into effect, Shannon Minter was so concerned about the risk of setbacks that he tried to persuade Newsom's office to abort the plan. As other leaders in the gay legal movement heard about the idea, some were highly concerned. Matt Coles supported the spirit of the plan but opposed it as a strategic decision, fearing that images of rogue same-sex weddings flashing across television screens might not garner public support. Jon Davidson of Lambda was livid that the Newsom camp had not sought adequate input from the gay community before deciding to go forward. "How the hell could he do this?" he thought. His concern was less that it was the wrong step than that the collaborative process of the Roundtable should be respected.[9]

Kendell next spoke to the staff at GLAD to discuss whether marriage action in San Francisco could interfere with efforts to ensure that the *Goodridge* ruling would take effect without a hitch that spring. GLAD attorneys expressed support, viewing the idea of "a western front" as a good way to show that the Massachusetts ruling was not an outlier, a quirk of liberal New England. After a few days of deliberations, Kendell and her staff became convinced that Newsom was the right catalyst. Despite continued caution, they recognized this step as both a reflection and engine of public engagement with marriage equality, at least in California, and they viewed it as a potentially "game-changing moment." Kendell came to feel that NCLR should not stand in the way of momentum coming from beyond the movement. "Who are we to do that?" she reasoned. In a meeting with Newsom's staff, Kendell, feeling increasingly giddy over the plan, looked over at Newstat and said, "Well, you know who the first couple has to be." Newstat looked back at her with a knowing smile and declared, "Del and Phyllis."[10]

Del Martin and Phyllis Lyon, who had founded the Daughters of Bilitis fifty years earlier, were friends of Kendell's, and after she met with the mayor's staff, she phoned Lyon to ask if they would be the first couple married by Newsom. The pair talked it over for fifteen seconds and then agreed. On Thursday morning, February 12, Kendell drove to the couple's house, picked them up, and brought them to City Hall to be married. Newsom opened his offices an hour early that day so there would be time to perform the marriages before the courts began work. At eleven o'clock that morning, Martin and Lyon, together for more than half a century, were married by Assessor-Recorder Mabel Teng. Issuing marriage licenses to same-sex couples was explicitly forbidden by Proposition 22, so the expectation was that the courts would order the weddings stopped. But the court order didn't come immediately—in fact, it would be weeks before it did—and soon gay couples were lined up around the block to wed.[11]

Between February 12 and March 11, when the California Supreme Court finally ordered a stop to the marriages, nearly four thousand gay couples wed in San Francisco, including State Sen. William Knight's son, David, who married his partner of ten years, Joseph Lazzaro. Some of the weddings were spontaneous, as were many of the trips downtown by supportive onlookers who'd come to witness history. Although no one could predict the ultimate legal status of these marriages, their impact at the time was immense. City Hall was ringed on all four sides by long lines of couples waiting for their turn to marry. On one of San Francisco's frequent cold, wet days, a woman pulled up to the lines in a station wagon with a giant bag of warm socks and began handing them out; others supplied hot drinks. City employees volunteered their time, even over the holiday weekend, to keep the marriages going in the race against certain intervention from the courts. "There's no way to capture what city hall was like during that period," said Kendell of the opening of the floodgates. "You could not walk into city hall as an LGBT person committed to justice, or a person who just had a heart, and not burst into tears."

Newsom's actions, in conjunction with the Massachusetts court win, transformed the marriage equality issue from a set of dry discussions about legal strategy to a vivid expression of how the matter impacted people's real lives. In the weeks after San Francisco issued its first licenses, the idea caught fire around the country. More than 150 same-sex couples lined up in Portland, Oregon, when officials there declared that the state's constitution required they be granted marriage licenses. Mayor Jason West of New Paltz, New York, was charged by prosecutors with nineteen criminal counts for performing same-sex marriages there, but vowed to continue. The twenty-six-year-old mayor said that 1,200 couples were waiting for licenses. Outside the courthouse where he pleaded not guilty, 200 supporters stood waving signs and singing "The Battle Hymn of the Republic." In counties and towns in New Mexico and elsewhere, officials announced plans to issue licenses as well.[12] Nearly thirty years after Colorado clerk Clela Rorex had issued licenses to gay couples, eliciting anti-gay slurs from the federal government and a visit from a mischievous cowboy seeking to marry a horse, marriage equality had evolved from a fringe idea even within the small and scrappy gay rights movement to an issue of national importance that engaged the attention of a broad public in unprecedented ways.

For the gay legal groups, Newsom's actions dramatically altered the calculus on litigation strategy. Now, even those who had been scrupulously counseling patience year after year were ready to jump. "The Newsom thing made everybody feel the battle was on," said Bonauto, ever more optimistic but still wondering, during moments of angst, if she'd have to wait "until those people who are now 10 years old are 55" before seeing marriage equality nationwide.[13] Now, it seemed, was indeed a time for optimism, for riding momentum. "The dams were bursting," said Lambda's Susan Sommer. The Newsom marriages brought "a surge of attention" to the issue of marriage equality, she noted, creating "much more pressure coming both from the gay community and from events over which we frankly had no control." The sense was that people were going to state challenges one way or another, so whatever reluctance some gay rights leaders felt about pressing forward with litigation began falling away.[14] Jennifer Pizer, then the director of Lambda's Marriage Project, noted some years later that, even at the time, California was "a state with a great many lawyers and LGBT people who wanted marriage." If the professional groups did not litigate, others would. At that point, "there was too much public engagement and community expectation" to slow down. Kendell agreed. "Our community would have demanded it," she said, referring to the eagerness among the gay and lesbian grassroots for a constitutional challenge to California's marriage ban.[15]

Evan Wolfson encouraged the LGBTQ movement to seize control of the Newsom moment and use it to push marriage forward.[16] Yet while the San Francisco developments had energized and emboldened gay marriage proponents, concerns and differences lingered among the legal thinkers who had worked so hard and methodically to plot a strategic path to marriage equality. The group was finding itself in a more reactive position than it had hoped to occupy, raising questions about how best to harness and control enthusiasm for gay marriage, even debating what aspects of its strategy it could "salvage" from events beyond its control. The consensus from recent Roundtable meetings was not to litigate a right-to-marry case in California. "Smart people had thought about it," Pizer recalled. "We had a plan."[17] Some worried that pushing marriage by issuing licenses without state approval could spark a backlash or create obstacles for Democratic politicians who might be important allies.[18] And while the gay lawyers were increasingly supportive of state-level lawsuits, they feared the consequences of a marriage challenge in federal court. Just as she had spent years in the 1990s discouraging couples from challenging state marriage bans, Bonauto now devoted energy to "avoiding the federal piece" and urging movement outsiders not to challenge DOMA before states had had adequate time to "wrestle" with the issue—much less to bring a full-on right-to-marry suit in federal court. She was especially concerned that a wealthy plaintiff might be the one to challenge the federal marriage ban over complaints about a high tax burden: "I can't think of a less sympathetic prospect," she said in 2004.[19]

For the moment, however, the gay groups had important decisions to make about how to react to legal developments that resulted from the Newsom weddings. Two conservative groups that grew out of the Proposition 22 organizing effort immediately filed suit to block further same-sex marriages and annul the ones that had already been authorized by the mayor. Defending the marriages was the job of San Francisco's Office of the City Attorney. But NCLR, along with Lambda and the ACLU, succeeded at "intervening" in the case, a process where additional parties petition the judge to join a suit because they share an interest in the outcome. The claims of the conservative groups trying to stop the marriages initially rested not on whether same-sex marriage should be permitted per se but on whether the city of San Francisco had exceeded its authority by issuing the licenses. Yet the case also implicated the substantive question of whether California's gay marriage ban was constitutional, and both the City of San Francisco and the gay legal groups included in their filings the argument that it was not.

Suddenly a defensive case (albeit one provoked by the actions of a pro-gay mayor) had become a proactive case challenging the constitutionality of California's gay marriage ban. An affirmative constitutional challenge was something the gay legal groups had been increasingly contemplating; the NCLR staff had expected to bring such a suit within a couple of years. But until their hand was forced by Newsom's move, the consensus among the legal groups had remained the one reached in the wake of the ballot losses in Hawaii, Alaska, and—in particular—in California with Proposition 22: don't litigate in the Golden State, where a sustainable win was far from certain, and a loss could devastate momentum and set bad precedent.

With the Newsom weddings, all that changed virtually overnight. The ability to control the timing of a proactive marriage lawsuit was slipping away, and the gay lawyers recognized the need to be on the right side of the momentum. Adding to that momentum, the week after Newsom authorized his first same-sex wedding, in Los Angeles famed lawyer Gloria Allred filed a challenge to the constitutionality of California's marriage ban. Allred was representing two same-sex couples, including Metropolitan Community Church founder Troy Perry and his partner, as well as Robin Tyler, who had helped organize the mass wedding at the 1987 march on Washington

When the California Supreme Court halted same-sex marriages in 2004, marriage equality supporters took to the streets of San Francisco.

(Tyler was seeking to marry her partner, Diane Olson, granddaughter of former California governor Culbert Olson). Representing the state's main gay rights group, Equality California, the legal groups—NCLR, Lambda, and the ACLU—also moved to intervene in that lawsuit.[20]

On March 11, the state's Supreme Court handed down its ruling halting the San Francisco marriages, sending hundreds of gay supporters into the streets to rally for marriage. The court concluded that the city had exceeded its authority in granting the four thousand licenses, a point that sidestepped the question of whether the same-sex marriage ban was constitutional. In fact, in issuing its ruling on the limits of city authority, the court seemed to invite a direct legal challenge to the marriage ban itself, stating that nothing about its present ruling would "preclude the filing of a separate action in superior court raising a substantive constitutional challenge to the current marriage statutes."

While the court's reference to a challenge on the merits did not necessarily indicate how it would rule, it appeared to both the legal groups and the city of San Francisco as a signal that the court was ready to take the idea seriously. The same day, Therese Stewart, the lesbian lawyer who led the city's legal team as chief deputy, filed suit on behalf of San Francisco challenging the state's marriage ban, and the legal groups, along with a private firm, joined together to file a second lawsuit the next day. Stewart's office and the gay legal groups collaborated on various pieces of the lawsuits, though Stewart commented that she often felt the movement lawyers wished she had been "off in the corner." All the suits were soon consolidated under the name *In Re Marriage Cases.*[21]

The heady days of late winter 2004, quickly dubbed the "Winter of Love," were tempered by the concerns of cautious gay advocates about how the country would react to the spread of gay weddings of questionable legality. As expected, social conservatives howled in protest, citing the actions of Newsom and other officials as evidence of the need for a constitutional amendment barring same-sex marriage. Two weeks after the weddings began in San Francisco, under pressure from his conservative, religious base, President Bush finally announced he supported an amendment to the U.S. Constitution that would define marriage as being between a man and a woman. Pointing to the ruling in Massachusetts and the same-sex marriage licenses granted in San Francisco and elsewhere, Bush denounced "activist judges" and officials who sought the "redefinition of one of our most basic social institutions." The developments, he said, had left as the only option a constitutional amendment. We must "protect marriage," he said from the Roosevelt Room of the White House, or face "serious consequences throughout the country."[22]

The proposed amendment was the work of a group of social conservatives who had been working together since the start of the Bush administration to diversify their coalition and expand their sway. The group included Judge Robert Bork, the conservative legal scholar whose nomination to the Supreme Court had been derailed because he was considered too extreme; Harvard Law School's Mary Ann Glendon, a consultant to the U.S. Conference of Catholic Bishops, a member of President Bush's Council on Bioethics, and former U.S. ambassador to the Vatican;

and Princeton professor Robert George, a Catholic intellectual who would lend his Ivy League credentials to the fight against same-sex marriage with writings, speeches, and think tank work that raised the profile of anti-gay-marriage organizing. George had testified for Colorado in the *Romer* case, asserting that homosexuality shared "a crucial element of masturbatory sex," and arguing that landlords should be allowed to discriminate against gay people and even straight couples who use contraception.[23]

The group also included Matt Daniels, a born-again lawyer with a Ph.D. from Brandeis University. Since 1996 Daniels had run the Massachusetts Family Institute (MFI), the group that later led the fight to amend that state's constitution in the lead-up to the *Goodridge* ruling. MFI had ties to Focus on the Family, the giant conservative Christian empire founded by James Dobson. Despite evidence of the links, Daniels tried to minimize the connections, claiming that the media was seeking to portray his group as a front for religious zealots.[24] To sharpen the separation, he left MFI in 1999 to found his own organization, Alliance for Marriage (AFM).[25] At the helm of AFM, Daniels continued to try to broaden the anti-gay-marriage coalition beyond the confines of the religious right. He reached out effectively to African American clergy, non-Christian religious leaders, and legal scholars such as Princeton's George. His plan worked. The conservative scholar Stanley Kurtz, noting that AFM had the backing of "legal experts from academia," including George and Amherst College's Hadley Arkes, along with African American and Latino ministers, wrote, "Obviously, AFM is a religiously and politically diverse coalition."[26] With the appearance of some distance from the evangelical groups that had first proposed amending the U.S. Constitution in the 1990s, Daniels drafted the language for what became known as the Federal Marriage Amendment (FMA).[27]

The FMA was introduced in Congress beginning in 2002 but failed to advance. In April 2003 a group of leading scholars and activists concerned about the future of marriage gathered at the Osprey Point conference center in Maryland for a "marriage leaders summit" hosted by the Institute for American Values (IAV). The organization had been founded in 1987 by the self-identified liberal David Blankenhorn as a place for public intellectuals to study and push for a renewed commitment to the nuclear family. It was a mission shaped by Blankenhorn's postcollege work with VISTA, the Johnson-era antipoverty program, advocating for poor, often fatherless youth. At the April meeting Blankenhorn gathered people such as

Wade Horn, an abstinence-education champion, onetime president (as was Blankenhorn) of the National Fatherhood Initiative, and a Bush appointee responsible for promoting marriage within the government; David Popenoe, a sociologist at Rutgers University and founder of the university-based National Marriage Project, established in 1997; and Maggie Gallagher, the cofounder, with Robert George and Brian Brown, of National Organization for Marriage.[28]

Gallagher had joined Blankenhorn's staff at IAV to focus on the costs to society and families of divorce, single motherhood, and feminism generally; her concern was not initially about same-sex marriage.[29] In 1996 she published *The Abolition of Marriage: How We Destroy Lasting Love,* a book which functioned as an indictment of the 1960s cultural revolution. The *Weekly Standard* called it an "obituary" of the "old, deeply internalized belief in marriage as a union until death."[30] Yet as she sat down with her colleagues at Osprey that spring of 2003, it suddenly became clear to Gallagher that same-sex marriage was coming, and that people in the marriage promotion movement would need to decide what to do about it. Blankenhorn was, at the time, reluctant to drag IAV into this particular culture war battle. Gallagher, whose opposition to same-sex marriage was stronger, left IAV and founded her own group, the Institute for Marriage and Public Policy.[31] From that perch she took to writing a barrage of alarmist articles inveighing against same-sex marriage. Citing "a consensus across ideological lines, based on 20 years' worth of social science research," that children do better with a married mother and father, she pleaded "for every American who cares about the future of American civilization" to help stop the gay marriage madness. "Losing this battle means losing the idea that children need mothers and fathers"; it meant losing "the core idea any civilization needs to perpetuate itself and to protect its children"; indeed, winning same-sex marriage meant "losing American civilization."[32] In the wake of *Lawrence, Goodridge,* and the Newsom weddings, Gallagher insisted that the only solution to the threat of same-sex marriage was to amend the U.S. Constitution.

Social conservatives were finely attuned to the nature of the threat they perceived in the spread of gay marriage. Despite the protests of gay leaders such as the pragmatic Barney Frank, who insisted that the government could allow marriage equality without equating gay and straight love, most advocates on both sides now recognized the battle for what it was: a fight to determine whether same-sex love had equal dignity. Once gay love was deemed dignified, something marriage equality would, in fact, help confer, social conservatives would lose crucial ground, and so they sought to cast gay marriage not as a matter of equal rights but as something that would undermine civilization itself. Having perhaps convinced themselves, they needed to convince their fellow citizens that the very survival of the United States was bound up with preserving the moral superiority of heterosexuality.

To that end, Daniels, Blankenhorn, and Gallagher would become smart, strategic, and pragmatic public faces of the anti-gay-marriage crusade. But even they were too liberal for the likes of Focus on the Family's James Dobson, Gary Bauer of American Values, William Bennett of Empower America, Tony Perkins of the Family Research Council, Sandy Rios of Concerned Women for America, and Paul Weyrich of the Free Congress Foundation. In July 2003 these stalwarts of the religious right had gathered in Arlington, Virginia, to push for a more pure version of a constitutional amendment that, unlike Daniels's language, would bar even civil unions. "Neither the federal government nor any state," they wanted the provision to say, "shall predicate benefits, privileges, rights or immunities on the existence, recognition or presumption of non-marital sexual relationships." It wasn't that Daniels approved of civil unions; he was simply pragmatic enough to argue for something he perceived as winnable. To some conservatives, Daniels was "a disaster," and as a result, the so-called Arlington Group excluded him from their meetings for months.[33]

But it was Daniels's comparatively more moderate version of the constitutional amendment that President Bush chose to support. The endorsement of a sitting president, which was followed by congressional hearings on the matter in early March, was a huge victory for advocates of a constitutional amendment. It also gave the green light to a parade of more strident voices linking same-sex marriage to national peril. Some even likened same-sex marriage to terrorism. Radio talk show host Dennis Prager wrote that the fight against both enemies represents "two fronts in the same war—a war for the preservation of the unique American creation known as Judeo-Christian civilization."[34] Focus on the Family's Dobson suggested that the "judicial tyranny" legalizing gay marriage was a greater threat than terrorism because it has the power to "destroy us from within."[35]

While religious and social conservatives were the most vocal and bitter in their opposition to same-sex marriage, national polls suggest that the events of 2003 and 2004 sent overall public opinion of marriage equality dramatically downward: after peaking at roughly 39 percent the month the *Lawrence* decision came down, approval of same-sex marriage sunk to around 30 percent by the end of 2003. Over the next two years, national support fluctuated but remained generally below one-third until the spring of 2005, when approval began rising again and briefly recovered the lost support.[36] Since 1996, the year DOMA was passed, when 27 percent of Americans supported same-sex marriage, that figure had been rising slowly but steadily, with a slight dip in the early Bush years. The drop beginning in 2003 makes clear that the court rulings and the subsequent outcry by social conservatives, which often vilified gay people and their relationships, eroded national support for marriage equality, reflecting and perpetuating a public backlash, just as some gay advocates had worried. Polls also showed a stark drop in those supporting civil unions or even the very legality of same-sex relations—a direct rebuke to the *Lawrence* court.[37]

Perhaps most consequential, the *Goodridge* ruling and the Newsom weddings mobilized state legislatures, particularly across the Midwest and South, where lawmakers worked with conservative activists to ban same-sex marriage and civil unions and to place anti-gay ballot initiatives before voters that fall.[38] As 2004 wore on, the backlash seemed to be taking a toll, tipping the balance during this dramatic battle year toward opponents of marriage equality. In August, the California Supreme Court, having ordered a stop to the San Francisco same-sex weddings that winter, declared them null and void. The ruling broke the hearts of many of the four thousand couples who had wed during that one-month window, even though they had reason to suspect from the outset that their legal status was questionable. That fall, state-level conservative activists, working in tandem with the Bush reelection campaign, succeeded in placing anti-gay-marriage constitutional amendment ballot initiatives before voters in eleven states (along with statutory initiatives in two more states).

The 2004 elections would now stand as an electoral test of the current political climate around same-sex marriage. In November, the forces that had been working tirelessly to block same-sex marriage won big. Bush's reelection seemed to vindicate Karl Rove's strategy of wooing conservatives by putting anti-gay initiatives on state ballots.[39] And voters in all thirteen states that considered whether to ban gay marriage (eleven in November and two earlier that year) chose to do so. It was an anti-gay-marriage sweep.

The only significant exception to the 2004 rout was in Massachusetts. Here, gay advocates succeeded at protecting the seat of every legislator who had supported marriage equality, a major victory for MassEquality and its coalition.[40] The Massachusetts victories sent a strong message that lawmakers could support gay marriage and survive. But the damage done nationally in that election was severe. In an exit poll, more voters cited "moral values" than any other issue as the most important factor shaping their vote, and the vast majority of those voters preferred Bush. The media and much of the public interpreted "moral values" as code for opposition to gay rights and abortion, and because one of the successful ballot initiatives took place in Ohio, the swing state whose capture by Bush ultimately threw him the election, many blamed Kerry's loss on the push for same-sex marriage. Senator Feinstein, who had accompanied Mayor Newsom to the Bush speech that had first inspired his actions in February, told reporters that those actions had "energize[d]" the conservative vote and that same-sex marriage had been pushed "too much, too fast, too soon." Leaders of Christian conservative groups boasted about how they had mobilized what they called "values voters" in response to the threat of same-sex marriage. The issue had "galvanized millions of Christians to turn out and vote, and George Bush and the GOP got the lion's share of that vote."[41]

Later analyses discredited claims that marriage equality was responsible for Bush's victory. In Ohio, the share of conservative Christians who voted in 2004 declined from 2000, and the president's margin over his 2000 results increased more in states without gay marriage ballot initiatives than in states with them, suggesting the initiatives did not tip the election to Bush. Moreover, when follow-up polls asked voters what they actually meant by "moral values," many more cited the war in Iraq than abortion or gay rights.[42] The conclusion that large numbers of Americans cared deeply about preventing gay marriage turned out to be a media creation, but also something of a self-fulfilling prophecy. Polls still showed majority opposition to gay marriage, but most failed to measure what pollsters call "salience"—how deeply people care about an issue rather than just what their position is. In retrospect, politicians and institutions that cited popular resistance to gay marriage as sound reasons to reject it themselves were likely exaggerating—and thus perpetuating—opposition to marriage equality.

Yet the bottom line was clear: gay marriage was not a winning electoral issue, and for conservative politicians it was in fact a mobilizing tool,
thus encouraging many to inflame opponents with anti-gay rhetoric and
policy initiatives. The margin of victory in most of the states that banned
same-sex marriage was huge. In Mississippi it was 86 percent to 14 percent;
in North Dakota, 73 percent to 27 percent. In all but two states, the opposition won more than 60 percent of the vote. In South Dakota, Senate
minority leader Tom Daschle, who was knocked on the defensive by his
evangelical challenger for not supporting the Federal Marriage Amendment, lost his election, the first time in half a century that a Senate party
leader lost his seat.[43]

As the *Bowers* ruling had done in the 1980s and as Hawaii's constitutional amendment had done in the 1990s, the 2004 election devastated
the morale of gay rights advocates, even leading some to question the push
for marriage. The Human Rights Campaign, which had worked to help defeat the Federal Marriage Amendment, signaled it would pull back from the
marriage equality fight in the wake of the November losses. HRC leaders,
like some of the gay legal advocates debating marriage equality, argued that
confrontational approaches that pushed too quickly could lead to backlash.
"When you put a face to our issues, that's when we get support," said HRC's
communications director, Steven Fisher, defending what he described as
the more gradualist approach HRC would take in the wake of the election.
"We're not going to win at the ballot box until we start winning at the water
cooler and in the church pews."[44] Hilary Rosen, the group's interim director,
took from the election the same lesson the temperamentally moderate Dianne Feinstein had. In the *Advocate,* Rosen suggested the defeats "may have
shown us that the change agents for gay marriage are looking too much like
a noisy red Ferrari speeding down quiet Main Street."[45]

HRC acknowledged that its current approach was falling short, with
a board member calling the 2004 elections "a wake-up call." Simply "continuing to do what we were doing would not be productive." A December 2004
fund-raising plea announced that their strategies would be "completely new,"
involving "different approaches, different tactics and different conversations."
Rather than push something like marriage, HRC would focus on "telling the
stories" of ordinary gay people. In particular, it would reach out to religious
groups and straight people—an effort to capture the hearts of the nation's
"moveable middle." Nowhere was marriage mentioned. Indeed, the

Advocate reported that HRC would be "downplaying marriage" and when it interviewed Rosen, she touted "incremental work" and did not include marriage in a list of priorities.[46]

To many in the gay community, demoralized by the 2004 losses and impatient with small steps, downplaying marriage felt like surrender. Critics of HRC said it was "entirely characteristic" of the group "to believe that what is required is a sort of retrenchment and a return to a more moderate message."[47] Gays and lesbians had cheered in the streets of San Francisco and Boston as same-sex couples obtained marriage licenses and took their vows, and many felt this was no time to retreat. Some state-level advocates felt that it was like pulling teeth to get the well-funded HRC to push for marriage at all (the group raised roughly $30 million in 2005, dwarfing the budgets of all other gay advocacy groups). Complaints surfaced in some of the states facing marriage referendums in 2004 that HRC had been "AWOL" in those battles.[48] Marc Solomon, now leading Mass-Equality, which worked with HRC and benefited from its funding assistance, felt "horrified at the prospect that we'd retreat in any way."[49] Larry Kramer joined dozens of other protesters at an HRC fundraiser in New York while holding a sign that read: HRC—WHAT THE FUCK ARE YOU DOING WITH ALL THAT MONEY?[50] To many, HRC and the Task Force, the two dominant national political groups, did not seem to have a winning strategy in place despite having invested considerable funds, staff, and expertise in fighting anti-gay-marriage measures.

The reality was more complex. It is true that HRC's leadership believed, particularly in the wake of the 2004 ballot losses, that more groundwork was needed in order to make tangible legal and political gains. Its staff determined, with the help of both opinion polls and membership surveys, that neither gay nor straight support for marriage equality was where it needed to be in order to justify devoting the kind of resources to it that some advocates hoped to see. And like most of the gay legal strategists of the Roundtable, they believed that progress on gay rights would come over time, through telling the stories of gay lives using a moderate, accessible message. Familiarity would breed acceptance and make resoundingly clear that conferring equal dignity on gay lives and relationships was no threat to civilization but in fact marked a triumph of its greatest promise. In the meantime, HRC's lobbyists and strategists continued to do what they had done effectively but gradually for years: introduce gay lives and issues to the public and to members of Congress—often one individual at a time. In other words, they believed in incremental change, just as Rosen had told the *Advocate*. The main difference between the staff of HRC and of the gay legal groups was that the former focused on issues other than marriage in its effort to advance gay equality, while many more of the latter had come to believe that marriage was the ideal vehicle to spur such change.

In any event, as is so often the case, there was an upside to the 2004 defeats and the decision by national gay political groups to focus on issues other than marriage. The developments presented an opportunity to expand efforts already under way to empower and organize state-based gay organizations to advance the cause of marriage equality. Gay legal advocates, of course, had been arguing for years that the path to national equality ran through the states—at least when it came to marriage. And they had long had a certain amount of company in that belief. In the 1990s, between the initial Hawaii court win and the passage of DOMA, Wolfson and a smattering of other marriage proponents had convened with HRC and the Task Force to press them to prioritize marriage, and part of this work entailed pushing a state-focused strategy that would build on what they hoped would be the legalization of same-sex marriage in Hawaii. As it became clear that the conservative opposition would be working through the states—passing dozens of "mini-DOMAs," including in Hawaii—the state-by-state approach had become more compelling to some leaders within the gay rights movement as well. Wolfson and other gay marriage proponents had begged HRC to put financial resources directly into the marriage fight in Hawaii, and to do so early on. The public education campaign required to ward off a constitutional amendment would be expensive, and so would the effort to support and protect state lawmakers who stuck their necks out for marriage. But Wolfson was bitterly disappointed with the results. While HRC remained largely focused on its federal-level work, Urvashi Vaid, who had earlier led the Task Force for six years and returned to direct its policy research institute in 1997, had recognized the importance of local and grassroots activism, and increasingly pushed to direct resources to state-based gay rights groups. After the passage of DOMA, the Task Force had continued this strategy, creating in 1997 an alliance of statewide political and advocacy groups that focused on grassroots activism (in 2004 this became the Equality Federation). None of these developments entailed a push by the big political groups—HRC and the Task Force—to make marriage a priority during the 1990s. But in the wake of Hawaii and DOMA, the gay movement was finding itself forced to innovate, and legal advocates, in particular, used the period to create the beginnings of an effective marriage equality strategy, as laid out by Wolfson and Lambda in their strategy memos of 1994 and 1995. Throughout the decade leading up to 2004, then, the marriage battle inspired activists who had enthusiasm but little structure—often working at scrappy, poorly funded organizations or volunteering entirely—to create stronger, more professional state-based organizations.[51]

Toward the end of this period, a key development injected a rather sudden infusion of new energy to those efforts. In 2003, with a multimillion-dollar, multiyear grant from the Evelyn and Walter Haas Jr. Fund, Wolfson launched a new umbrella organization called Freedom to Marry (FTM; the group was unconnected to earlier organizations with similar names, although Wolfson had also been the force behind the loosely organized National Freedom to Marry Coalition). Having left Lambda in 2001 seeking greater independence to advocate for marriage equality and a sharper tool for coordinating disparate efforts across the movement, Wolfson worked closely with Tim Sweeney, the onetime Lambda director and AIDS activist who had become a program officer at the Haas Fund. Haas was not a gay foundation. Walter Haas Jr. was heir to the Levi Strauss fortune, and the foundation, created in 1953, was known for its largesse to California institutions and liberal causes. But until then no donor, gay or non-gay, had ever given that amount of money to focus exclusively on marriage equality. With Sweeney in his corner, Wolfson made a dazzling presentation to the folks at Haas, casting marriage as a "gateway" to hundreds of rights and benefits that straight people took for granted. "You should do something nobody else is doing," Wolfson told them, "something much of the gay leadership doesn't even think about it. You should go national."[52]

By this, Wolfson did not mean bypassing the state-focused path to marriage; rather, he was saying simply that funders should think big enough to support a national-scale victory. The time was right, Wolfson thought, recognizing that his own evangelizing, together with larger developments, had helped bring a critical mass of people into his camp. Matt Foreman, then the Task Force's executive director and later a program officer at Haas, said early in 2004 that many movement leaders had spent years telling Wolfson,

"We're not ready. The country's not ready. And, by the way, you're crazy."[53] That year a board member of the gay Republican group, Log Cabin Republicans, debated Wolfson in an effort to persuade him to back civil unions. "He won," recalled the board member.[54] Wolfson was used to these sentiments, but they were quickly ceasing to become the movement's default position. While some gay leaders still felt that something less than marriage was the path forward, convincing a major foundation to fund gay marriage with a significant sum signaled the arrival of a new, mainstream understanding—both within and outside the movement—of the importance and viability of marriage itself. Wolfson and his argument had crossed a threshold. FTM quickly became the central umbrella organization funding and supporting groups in states across the country working for marriage equality, and it helped coordinate the litigation and public education aspects of moving marriage forward.[55]

The year that FTM launched, Haas also joined together with other foundations to start the Civil Marriage Collaborative (CMC), a low-profile philanthropic alliance laser-focused on funding state-based advocacy for marriage equality. CMC was created to channel major grants from gay philanthropists into strategically chosen states where marriage equality was considered most likely to succeed.[56] One of its major funding partners was the Gill Foundation, started in 1994 by Tim Gill, the Colorado software mogul who had founded the company Quark, Inc. in his apartment in 1981. Gill, who had been moved to create a gay rights foundation after the passage of Amendment 2, used the period leading up to the 2004 elections to expand and further professionalize his operations, pressing his fellow donors to make marriage equality a priority, as Wolfson had been doing for years, and to make more strategic and efficient decisions in their giving. Frustration with the unsatisfying results of the traditional approach to change—supporting established national groups such as HRC to lobby lawmakers and support public education campaigns—called for a new strategy, and the events of 2003 and 2004 created a unique window to implement one.

With the creation of FTM and the concerted decision by major funders to partner with the group in giving serious new support to state-based work, the stage was set for a critical new phase of marriage advocacy. In its first four years, CMC would hand out more than $5 million to marriage advocates in seventeen states, leaving its fingerprints on every significant effort to persuade the public and lobby legislatures to legalize same-sex marriage. The ability of MassEquality to fight off a constitutional amendment to reverse the *Goodridge* ruling was partly indebted to an infusion of funding by donors focused on giving through specific states, demonstrating what effective state-based advocacy work could do even in a negative national climate. Starting in the year before the demoralizing ballot losses of 2004, and accelerating in their aftermath, dozens of small groups increased their coordination and the gay rights movement began to dramatically enhance its efficiency in learning and deploying lessons about messaging, research, organizing, lobbying, and other tactics. The growth of smaller, state-based groups, along with the targeted giving and strategic thinking of deep-pocketed gay donors, meant dollars could bypass the national groups and go right to the states. The MassEquality coalition had trouble getting even four-figure checks from wealthy funders before the *Goodridge* ruling came down. But the combination of the *Goodridge* win and the backlash the next year had the effect of opening wallets wide. After the 2004 election, said Andrew Lane, director of the Johnson Family Foundation and a key strategist on movement financing, "funders were saying, 'the national work is broken, we can't move anything through Congress, Bush has been reelected and our legislative priorities are dead. Where it's at is in the states.'"[57] Others agreed. "Gill was instrumental in putting the state groups at the center" of the gay rights movement, said Chris Neff, the former director of Outright Vermont, Vermont's largest gay advocacy group. After the 2004 elections, he said, "it was a whole different universe. Funders were giving to Equality Federation groups in a way that had never been done before." In addition to Gill and Haas, substantial money began pouring in from the Arcus Foundation, endowed by Jon Stryker, the billionaire heir to a medical supply company fortune; the Bohnett Foundation set up by David Bohnett, who founded the Web company GeoCities; James Hormel, who had helped create HRC; the Ford Foundation; and George Soros's Open Society Foundations.[58]

The events of 2003 and 2004 drew people into both sides of the marriage equality battle in ways not previously seen. Leaders in each camp had been hard at work for years plotting strategies to expand popular involvement, and with same-sex weddings in California and Massachusetts and anti-marriage ballots pending or passing in states across the nation, the people had joined in earnest.

Despite the devastating ballot results and a dip in public approval, momentum would turn out to be on the side of the LGBTQ movement. By the end of this period, a new, leaner, and more agile state-based movement for marriage equality had been born. The new focus reflected a synergy between major donors and ordinary gays and lesbians, many of whom were not longtime activists but simply wanted to get married, perhaps awakened to a belief in that right by seeing it attacked and suffering personal denigration by social and political conservatives. "I only came around on marriage when President Bush used it as an issue for his election purposes," recalled John O'Brien, an organizer of the 1987 march on Washington who had opposed Robin Tyler's mass wedding ceremony at that event. "It was Bush promoting an official government discrimination against gays and lesbians that changed me—and many others."[59] It was this same sense of provocation that had softened Paula Ettelbrick's critique of marriage following the conservative assaults on the Hawaii win, that had motivated the Henning brothers to press for marriage in response to the Knight Initiative, drawn Gavin Newsom into the fight after hearing Bush's speech, and motivated Kendell and other legal advocates to embrace new court challenges that year. While some gay activists continued to view marriage primarily as a vehicle to help make other equality gains, it is impossible to escape the conclusion that marriage resonated with ordinary gay people in new ways as a result of seeing their humanity attacked. "Marriage energized queers on the street in a way that other LGBT issues did not," said Lane. What had taken root in the minds of both professional advocates and ordinary gay and lesbian people was a belief not always shared by an earlier generation of pioneering gay advocates, whose world looked very different: that whatever you might think about tying the knot yourself, marriage could be a transformative issue in the struggle to achieve visibility and dignity for what was once regarded as the love that dare not speak its name.[60]

8

"A Political Awakening"

CALIFORNIA'S PROPOSITION 8
CHANGES THE GAME

THE STRATEGIC ADVANCES OF MAJOR GAY DONORS WERE NOT LIMITED to the philanthropic world. In addition to funding state-based gay rights organizations, Tim Gill and several other wealthy gay philanthropists who gathered annually at the Political OutGiving conference began giving substantial donations in individual state political races. The idea was to target states where flipping the legislature to Democratic control could make the difference in either winning gay marriage legislatively or preventing a court win from being overturned.[1] Gill called it "punishing the wicked," referring to the high costs that would now be incurred by politicians who trampled gay rights for their own gain.[2] Although many factors contributed to a wave of Democratic victories in 2006, money from major gay donors helped Democrats take control of legislatures in states such as Iowa and New Hampshire, takeovers that would be critical in winning—and keeping—the freedom to marry in those states three years later. The gay donors also helped back state attorney general candidates, who would play an important role in future same-sex marriage lawsuits: attorneys general had the power to decline to defend gay marriage bans, which many would do as these lawsuits began to spread across the country.[3]

Elsewhere marriage equality momentum moved slowly forward. In 2005 the California legislature became the first to pass marriage equality through a state legislative body. Equality California had worked with a broad coalition of liberal groups, including the NAACP and the United

Farm Workers, along with openly gay assemblyman Mark Leno, to pass the bill. Leno himself had only recently come to view marriage as a crucial goal distinct from civil unions; until the *Goodridge* ruling "struck a chord" in him, he "wasn't convinced we needed to fight a war over a word." The result in the Assembly came down to how three Democrats, who had abstained on a similar measure just three months earlier, would vote. Leno had lobbied hard for the bill, eliciting promises from colleagues that they would not let him down. Dolores Huerta, co-founder of United Farm Workers, lobbied fellow Latinos in the Assembly, citing gay marriage as a "human right." In a nail-biter, with the measure one vote shy of passage, Assemblyman Simon Salinas paused for what felt like an eternity before casting a yes vote, pushing the bill over the edge. Several other Democrats who had changed their minds to support the bill cited intense cajoling from friends, colleagues, and their children. "The constituency I'm concerned about is a very small one," remarked Assemblyman Tom Umberg of Anaheim, "and that's the constituency of my three children" when they look back and consider "where I was when we could make a difference." Leno's presence as an out gay lawmaker clearly made a difference. Unfortunately, Gov. Arnold Schwarzenegger vetoed the bill (and did so again in 2007), saying that the 2000 voter approval of Proposition 22 had expressed the will of the people and could not be reversed through legislation. Besides, he said, the issue was working its way through the courts—let it be decided there.[4]

There were other bright spots during this period. Gay groups in Arizona beat back a constitutional amendment in 2006, breaking an undefeated streak for anti-gay-marriage activists that stretched to over two dozen states. (Just two years later Arizona voters would pass a narrower version of a constitutional amendment, one that was easier for moderates to support because it allowed for domestic partnerships.)[5] The margins of the anti-gay amendment wins in 2006 were significantly smaller than in 2004, showing that the trends were heading in a positive direction. And South Africa became the fifth nation, and the first in Africa, to legalize same-sex marriage.[6] In Massachusetts, gay advocates led by MassEquality again protected the state lawmakers who had supported marriage equality, and also defeated what would turn out to be the last serious attempts to amend the state constitution to trump the 2003 *Goodridge* ruling, ensuring the safety of marriage equality for the foreseeable future.

Yet there were also setbacks. In 2006 state high courts in Washington, New York, and New Jersey all ruled against marriage equality plaintiffs, although in New Jersey the closely divided court, as in Vermont, compelled the legislature to create a civil unions law so that same-sex partners would be guaranteed all the same legal protections and benefits as their straight counterparts but without being able to use the word "marriage."[7] In November voters in seven additional states chose to amend their constitutions to ban same-sex marriage.[8]

In 2006 and 2007 the lawsuits that had grown out of the Newsom marriages and related developments in 2004 made their way back to the California Supreme Court.[9] Despite the 2006 setbacks, there was reason to believe the climate was ripe for a positive ruling—one that could be defended over time. In addition to the legislature's pro-gay votes on marriage, which seemed to spur little outcry except from the far right, public support of same-sex marriage in California had been steadily climbing. Gay legal advocates, who had been cautious about embarking on the legal route in California, remained uncertain about the prospects of staving off a constitutional amendment. But having taken the litigation plunge in the wake of the Newsom developments, they focused on signals that the high court would vote their way, and hoped for the best.[10]

In March 2008, arguing for the National Center for Lesbian Rights, Shannon Minter told the state's high court that there was "absolutely nothing about a person's gender or sexual orientation" that was relevant to the "legitimate state purposes" served by marriage. "The state," he eloquently argued, "has now awakened to the reality that lesbian and gay people are entitled to all the same fundamental rights as heterosexual couples, including the fundamental right to marry." Just as when the Supreme Court overturned sodomy bans in its *Lawrence* ruling, "the court had awakened to the full humanity of gay people and to a fuller notion of what liberty and equality requires." San Francisco city attorney Theresa Stewart also argued before the court that domestic partnerships were not adequate substitutes for marriage, that there was no rational basis for excluding gays and lesbians from marriage, and that tradition alone was not an acceptable basis for passing discriminatory laws.[11]

On May 15, California's high court ruled in a 4–3 decision that the state's two laws reserving marriage for heterosexual couples violated the California constitution. Calling marriage a "basic civil right," Chief

Justice Ronald George wrote that the "fundamental constitutional right to form a family relationship" could not be denied to same-sex couples. The decision cited California's history as the first state to end bans on interracial marriage, back in 1948. The ruling also marked the first time a state court applied strict scrutiny to sexual orientation.

In his dissent, Justice Marvin Baxter echoed the popular conservative refrain that a small number of judges were substituting their own personal views "by judicial fiat" for those expressed democratically by the people of the state. Baxter's was a lament whose familiarity and simplistic logic—it was always argued that judges were arbitrary and undemocratic when the arguer didn't approve of their ruling; and by this reasoning, courts should have little power indeed—had rendered it largely devoid of credibility. But in her dissent, Justice Carol Corrigan illustrated why supporters of same-sex marriage might prefer to let popular opinion evolve in good time, without courts accelerating the process. Stating that she supported the plaintiff's right to marry, she nevertheless wrote, "We should allow the significant achievements embodied in the domestic partnership statutes to continue to take root. If there is to be a new understanding of the meaning of marriage in California, it should develop among the people of our state and find its expression at the ballot box." Virtually the same had been said by the Massachusetts lower court in ruling against the *Goodridge* plaintiffs when it had rebuffed gay couples by telling them to pursue their quest with the lawmakers of Beacon Hill.

Indeed, even at the very moment that more Americans, more legislative bodies, and more state courts were awakening to the logic of same-sex marriage, powerful forces remained arrayed against it. In a reminder of what a political third rail gay marriage still was in 2008, the *New York Times* noted that all major candidates for the 2008 presidential election—Democratic and Republican alike—opposed it. Only one party, however, stood to exploit California's ruling, as it had done in past court cases. "Republicans could use a surge in same-sex marriages in the country's most populous state to invigorate their conservative voters," the article said.[12]

There was no doubt that the religious right would capitalize on the case. Maggie Gallagher, now president of the National Organization for Marriage, denounced the California decision as "wrong from top to bottom," saying the court had "brushed aside the entire history and meaning of marriage in our tradition."[13] Mathew Staver, founder of Liberty Counsel, the more strident of the two conservative groups that had stepped in to fight the Newsom weddings, condemned the decision, taking aim not just at same-sex marriage but at what, to him, was the ruling's implicit approval of homosexuality. Calling the decision "outrageous" and "nonsense," he said, "No matter how you stretch California's Constitution, you cannot find anywhere in its text, its history or tradition that now, after so many years, it magically protects what most societies condemn." Staver predicted the ruling would "ignite California voters to amend their state Constitution to protect marriage and prevent judges from wrecking" it.[14] Liberty Counsel asked the court to stay its decision until the November election, when voters would be asked to support a state constitutional amendment that would override the court's decision by defining marriage as for straights only.[15]

The court declined Liberty Counsel's request, but the group was not leaving anything to chance. Even before the ruling came down, it had begun raising money and collecting signatures for a ballot initiative to amend the state constitution. By March 2008, conservative activists had raised nearly $9 million to fund four voter initiatives for that November's ballot, including one on same-sex marriage along with abortion restrictions and get-tough-on-crime measures that increased penalties for certain offenses.[16] By the time of the pro-gay-marriage ruling in May, the ballot question had already been filed with the state.[17]

In June, the initiative became known as Proposition 8, as it was the eighth ballot question to be officially certified by the secretary of state to appear on that fall's ballot. To qualify, proponents needed to gather 694,354 signatures, 8 percent of the number of votes cast in the last governor's election. By the time of the June certification, Proposition 8's backers had obtained 1,120,801 signatures, well over the required number.[18] The official ballot question read simply: "LIMIT ON MARRIAGE. CONSTITUTIONAL AMENDMENT. Amends the California Constitution to provide that only marriage between a man and a woman is valid or recognized in California."[19]

The battle lines were now drawn for a dramatic confrontation between backers and opponents of same-sex marriage in the state, with the eyes of the nation upon it. But as late as that summer, the anti-gay efforts were still operating largely under the radar of the general public. Although more and more people had tuned in and gotten involved since 2004, particularly in California, the public, if following gay marriage developments at all, was most likely to have noticed the California high court's ruling and the exultant same-sex marriages that took place the next month. Fewer noticed the fervor and growing efficiency of the anti-gay-marriage organizing efforts quietly bubbling up in the state and elsewhere. Some gay advocates expressed confidence, citing pro-gay support by the public and lawmakers, including the passage of marriage equality by the California legislature, as cause for hope that Proposition 8 would fail.[20] Political observers in California noted glibly that more than 90 percent of initiatives where opponents spend more than $1 million end up losing.[21]

Support for gay marriage seemed only to grow after images of jubilant marrying couples infused the airwaves. On Monday, June 16, at 5:00 p.m. Pacific time, gay Californians were once again allowed to wed—this time not just at the say-so of a few local officials, but by the court-ordered authority of the nation's most populous state. In San Francisco, a crowd formed outside the office of Mayor Newsom, who at 5:01 officiated at the (second) marriage of Del Martin, now eighty-seven, to Phyllis Lyon, four years her junior. "This is love made visible," said Newsom to a gleeful throng, gesturing at the octogenarian couple as a media crowd 200 strong watched rose petals rain down on the festivities. Outside city hall, about a thousand supporters gathered to celebrate. Nearby, a tiny group of protestors stood, including one holding a sign that read HI. GOD IS ANGRY WITH YOU GAY PEOPLE. STOP NOW.[22]

Yet love made visible was contagious. In front of the Alameda County clerk-recorder's office, a crowd of journalists gathered to witness the county's first same-sex wedding performed that evening—begun about thirty minutes late because computer software that had only provided space for "bride" and "groom" was still being updated. Sixty same-sex couples received marriage licenses from that office alone. Around the corner, Ron Dellums, the mayor of Oakland, which lay within Alameda County, married eighteen same-sex couples at city hall. "This is an incredible day," Dellums said before a crowd of hundreds of newlyweds, celebrators, and well-wishers. "The energy in this room is infectious." At last, he said, "the law is on our side." The first couple Dellums married was Karen Boyd and Samee Roberts, two city officials who had also first wed in 2004 before their marriage was voided by the same court that had now relaunched marriage equality in California. The crowd roared its approval.[23]

In Los Angeles, Robin Tyler and Diane Olson readied themselves to be among the first same-sex couples to legally marry in the state, before a rabbi in front of the Beverly Hills courthouse. The county clerk announced plans to issue an early marriage license to the couple "in recognition of their unique role in the court's decision," bringing Tyler's mind all the way back to her efforts to organize a mass wedding demonstration at the 1987 march on Washington when few in the gay community had any sympathy for the idea.[24] In West Hollywood, George Takei, the famous *Star Trek* actor, married his longtime partner, Brad Altman.[25]

By July, the first major poll on where the public stood on Proposition 8 found that most Californians opposed changing the constitution to revoke marriage rights from gay couples. In a Field Poll, 51 percent of respondents opposed the measure (a no vote on the ban), while only 42 percent approved (a yes vote). Just 7 percent of respondents were unsure, meaning that only a small number were likely to move into the yes camp. Back in May, when the court first struck down the gay marriage ban and a month before gay marriages actually began, a *Los Angeles Times* poll had found far more enthusiasm for banning gay marriage, with 54 percent backing a constitutional amendment and only 35 percent opposing it. The more recent numbers gave gay rights advocates hope that the measure would fail to yank away their right to wed. Still, the Field Poll had underestimated anti-gay support for the Knight initiative in 2000, making the future far from certain.[26]

Underestimating resistance was not the only parallel between Proposition 8 and its predecessor, Knight's Proposition 22; another was the organized support of Christian conservatives. As in 2000, church organizations played an enormous role in building support for Proposition 8. Weeks after the May court ruling that legalized gay marriage in California, the archbishop of San Francisco reached out to Mormon leaders in the state and in their home base, Salt Lake City, and invited them to join strategy discussions with Catholic leaders, evangelicals, and other religious conservatives. Mormons responded fervently, releasing statements throughout their churches encouraging members to commit themselves to fighting gay marriage.[27] According to emails and memos written by Catholic and Mormon church officials, both churchgoers and churches themselves provided hefty financial, strategic, and human resources for the Proposition 8 effort. One Mormon church memo said California's campaign to ban gay marriage was "entirely under priesthood direction" and that all but two of the state's 161 Mormon leaders had joined a conference call to discuss urging church members to donate to the Proposition 8 effort, with a goal of $5 million.[28] Ultimately Catholic and Mormon conservatives succeeded in sending more dollars to the effort than any other entity. In total, supporters of the measure spent nearly $39 million in their fight to pass Proposition 8—nearly half of it donated by Mormons, according to officials' estimates—while gay advocates and their supporters spent more than $44 million; the $83 million total made the battle the country's most expensive ballot fight that year.[29] And at certain points during the campaign, an estimated 80 percent of campaigners who knocked on doors to get out the vote for Proposition 8 were Mormons. In the final two weeks of the battle, more than $9 million in donations flowed to the campaign from out of state, overwhelmingly in support of the marriage ban, and much of it from religious conservatives. Even on abortion, a spokesperson for the Mormon church explained, their members normally "don't get involved to the degree we did on this." Something about the marriage battle triggered an intense reaction that made this one of the most divisive culture war issues ever seen in the nation.[30]

Like backers of the Knight initiative eight years earlier, Proposition 8's proponents—at least the savvier ones—were careful to root their position in concern for the institution of marriage instead of bald expressions of anti-gay hostility. "It is not our goal in this campaign to attack the homosexual lifestyle," read a talking points memo distributed by Mormon leaders, using a dog-whistle phrase that reflected precisely the belief that homosexuality was inferior. It was not their objective, continued the document, "to convince gays and lesbians that their behavior is wrong—the less we refer to homosexuality, the better. We are pro-marriage, not anti-gay."[31]

And yet the millions of dollars raised in that campaign went to create some of the most demeaning, dismissive, and disrespectful ads imaginable, arguably made worse by the subtlety of their anti-gay prejudice. Both reflecting and fueling long-standing fears of gay people as molesters, recruiters, and threats to children, a series of ads created by conservative message guru Frank Schubert warned darkly that allowing same-sex marriage would badly harm children by reinforcing distorting and confusing messages to America's young. In the most tautological and quietly homophobic message of the campaign, ads claimed, not entirely untruthfully, that if gay marriage remained legal, children would be taught in schools that homosexuality was acceptable. The message, that is, was that same-sex relationships must not be deemed acceptable because that would result in deeming same-sex relationships acceptable—something tacitly understood to be so insalubrious that it needed no further explanation.

The strategy, of course, went deeper than this. Research conducted by both sides of the marriage debate was revealing that a major point of concern for gay marriage opponents was the sense that change was being forced on them and their families and that they had little control over their future, particularly over how they raised their kids. This sentiment, when stoked by the sense that alien cultural changes were being "forced down our throats," had the power to deepen resistance to equality that was otherwise only moderately salient. Hence anti-gay strategists created ads that fanned the flames of such fears, claiming that LGBTQ advocates were trying to seize power and take over other people's freedoms and lives. Parents would no longer be able to mold their own children, the ads suggested, predicting "serious clashes between the public schools and parents who desire to teach their children their own desires and beliefs." They argued that while marriage equality advocates "couched" their claims in terms of concepts such as happiness and equality, the battle was "really about gaining control, forcing all of us to give up the very foundation of speech and religious freedom on which this country was founded." One ad ended, "It's *our* future; it's our children's future. Vote yes on Proposition 8."[32] Other ads drove the point home with footage of Mayor Newsom seeming to boast that gay marriage was now legal in California "whether you like it or not."[33]

In the most famous of the Schubert ads, an excited little girl races home from school and says to her flabbergasted mother, "Mom, guess what I learned in school today? I learned how a prince married a prince, and I can marry a princess!" An affable but concerned-looking man, apparently an earnest professor, then appears, warning, "Think it can't happen? It's already happened." Another ad showed anguished school leaders lamenting a new curriculum forced upon them by the legalization of gay marriage. It contains lessons, they complain, that would not educate the state's children but "confuse" them and "mess them up." Another showed two dads shifting uncomfortably as they try but fail to explain to their daughter where babies come from and what marriage is for. "Let's not confuse our kids," the ad concluded.[34] The message was clear, and it traced a thread directly back to Anita Bryant's Save Our Children campaign in 1977: gay people and their perverse ways—even when they are simply aiming to settle down and live their lives like anyone else—are a dire threat to the nation's young and hence its future, all the more so for seeming so innocuous.

The campaign worked. A month before the election, polls showed Proposition 8 losing. As October wore on and more of the Schubert ads ran, support began growing.[35] It surged as proponents of the measure ran misleading ads suggesting that churches could be forced to perform gay marriages or risk losing their tax exemptions.[36] Tempers flared. Despite efforts by anti-gay-marriage advocates to appear civil, a shoving match broke out at a rally the day before the election in a town outside San Francisco, underscoring the rage the issue spurred in people's veins. Two supporters of Proposition 8 were arrested after punching and spitting at their opponents.[37] The next day, California voted 52 percent to 48 percent to revoke the right of same-sex couples there to wed.

The failure to block Proposition 8 dealt a crushing blow to gay rights proponents. The vote had been "a stunning, stinging defeat," noted David McCuan, a political science professor at Sonoma State University, observing that "this is a Democratic blue wave and standing out in one of the bluest of the blue states is this huge red result."[38] Kendell called the loss an "awakening to people out of their complacency," and the lesbian journalist Karen Ocamb dubbed the vote "a political awakening" for gays and lesbians and "a mini-Stonewall in the LGBT soul."[39] Disproportionately liberal and supportive of Democratic political candidates, gays and lesbians throughout the country felt the strange, bittersweet sensation of shedding tears of joy at the election of the first African American president and, on the same day, tears of rejection as the "bluest of the blue states" yanked away their right to marry.

Reflecting the racial blind spots of the movement and the disproportionate whiteness of its leadership, the campaign against Proposition 8 failed to adequately break through to African American and Latino voters, who backed the anti-gay measure in higher numbers than the population at large. While 52 percent of state voters overall supported the measure, an estimated 58 percent of African Americans did. There were several likely explanations for this. Polling data consistently showed that while racial minorities skewed liberal and were likely to be sympathetic to civil rights causes, many did not view gay rights as a civil rights issue, even bristling at the comparison. Backers of Proposition 8 exploited this sentiment with robocalls targeting African Americans that touted President

Obama's opposition to gay marriage. Although the president had come out against Proposition 8 as "divisive," he simultaneously continued to oppose same-sex marriage itself, which was music to Frank Schubert's ears. "Here is Barack Obama in his own words on the definition of marriage," said the robocalls, quoting the president's remarks that "marriage is a union between a man and a woman" and that "for me as a Christian, it is also a sacred union."[40]

The largely white leadership of the campaign to reject Proposition 8, including the heads of Equality California (a party to the lawsuit that initially won marriage equality in the state), NCLR, and the Los Angeles LGBT Center, bore the brunt of community criticism for the loss—both for inadequate outreach to racial minorities and for running a campaign some saw as tepid and complacent. In truth, the campaign had conducted some outreach to minority communities, but it acknowledged it should have done more. It had also invested enormous resources in testing messages and running advertisements, ultimately operating a highly sophisticated, if clearly imperfect, campaign. (Among the loudest complaints, however, was the assertion that the campaign was too reliant on professional consultants who failed to feature enough ads with gay people themselves, since such ads had not tested well.)[41]

The challenges the campaign had faced in its outreach were both familiar and distinct. The disproportionate support for Proposition 8 from racial minorities, which turned out to be exaggerated by some outlier polls and an embellished media narrative, was largely a feature of their tendency to be more religious. Nationwide, campaigners for LGBTQ equality faced that same challenge with religious people generally. Conservative black pastors campaigned zealously for Proposition 8, yet many African American political leaders spoke out eloquently for marriage equality. In other words, many aspects of engaging racial minorities were no different from those seen with anyone else. Likewise, within the African American LGBTQ community, like the gay population at large, viewpoints ranged widely. Some black gays and lesbians felt an added sting on election day as they witnessed a dream come true in the presidential race together with a wrenching and stigmatizing loss of their legal rights. Others fiercely resented the attention being given to marriage in the first place, preferring to prioritize other pressing needs in their communities. The African American lesbian commentator Jasmyne Cannick alleged a "white bias" not just in the tactics of the No on 8 campaign but in the very fight it was waging. Writing in the *Los Angeles Times,* Cannick argued that "at a time when blacks are still more likely than whites to be pulled over for no reason, more likely to be unemployed than whites, more likely to live at or below the poverty line . . . the right to marry does nothing to address the problems faced by both black gays and black straights." She viewed marriage as a "luxury" for wealthy whites. "Many black gays just haven't been convinced that this movement for marriage is about anything more than the white gays who fund it."[42]

As with any population, people of color's views on marriage were diverse, and passionately held principles often clashed. And yet white movement leaders seem to have missed some important differences that marked how both gay and straight people of different races and backgrounds might view same-sex marriage. For straight African Americans contemplating whether to support marriage equality, unique or added concerns could come into play: about whether they could keep a gay child of their own safe from violence, for instance, or about how well legal marriage rights served the needs of their own families or social networks. For LGBTQ African Americans, racial blinders could be detected in a wide range of issues and strategies that the largely white movement leadership chose to adopt. Given all the campaign was up against, however, it is possible that the best-run campaign in the world would not have secured enough votes for marriage equality at this particular place and time.

While Proposition 8 was a devastating setback—the first time that state-sanctioned gay marriage rights were reversed—it had an immediate catalyzing effect that drew in and mobilized far more than dejected movement activists. Building on the momentum created by the events of 2004, a fresh wave of gays and lesbians who had never before considered themselves activists, who had barely tuned in to the battles and debates swirling around them for decades, were awakened by the outrage they felt that millions of California voters had decided to summarily eliminate their rights and try to erase their dignity. "When do I get to vote on your marriage?" said a popular placard in the ensuing protest rallies across the country, capturing the sentiment of many who previously viewed gay marriage as an impossibility or a fringe luxury.[43] The protests, in fact, were a continuation of rallies begun before the Proposition 8 vote. In San Diego, more than 7,000 people gathered in the Hillcrest neighborhood the Saturday before the election to urge the measure's defeat. On

Sunday, a hundred people gathered on the side of a canyon in Vallejo County, forming the phrase NO 8 with their bodies.[44] Protests were not confined to California. Pro-gay Mormons held a rally Sunday night that drew 600 people to a rainy candlelight vigil in Salt Lake City, Utah. Referencing "mother bears who defend their cubs," the event was spearheaded by Mormons with gay children. "This is what happens when people in California say mean things about our gay kids," said Millie Watts, the chief organizer. "The mothers come out of the closet."[45] Opponents of same-sex marriage were similarly inspired, as 15,000 religious conservatives met that weekend in an area stadium for a prayer service to support passage of Proposition 8.[46]

All this happened before the election. But the vote itself shocked tens of thousands into action, with a groundswell of street action primarily engaged in by gay rights supporters. In California, daily protests began filling the streets directly following the election. On Wednesday hundreds gathered around San Francisco's city hall and in West Hollywood and other Los Angeles neighborhoods demonstrating and disrupting traffic. On Thursday what began as a press conference organized by the Los Angeles LGBT Center to condemn the heavy involvement of the Mormon church in the Proposition 8 campaign swelled to a popular protest of more than 2,000 people in front of the sprawling Mormon temple complex in Westwood, another section of Los Angeles. Several were arrested for disorderly conduct, but overwhelmingly the protests remained peaceful.[47]

By the following weekend, a new breed of organizers had gotten word out across the country and in several foreign countries that solidarity marches would be held in all fifty states and abroad. As a result, tens of thousands took to the streets. Ten thousand marched in San Francisco. In Los Angeles, Mayor Antonio R. Villaraigosa, a straight supporter of gay rights, arrived by helicopter to rally a similar-sized crowd. Despite the anger shared by so many as a result of Proposition 8's passage, Villaraigosa struck a positive note, reflecting a new wave of excitement the defeat had galvanized among not just gays but straights. "I've come here from the fires because I feel the wind at my back as well," he said, referring to a string of wildfires then threatening parts of the city. "It's the wind of change that has swept the nation. It is the wind of optimism and hope." Four thousand marched in New York City and a thousand in Las Vegas, where the comedian Wanda Sykes was so angered by the vote, saying she

In November 2008 thousands of marriage equality supporters blocked traffic in California and elsewhere in a string of demonstrations against Proposition 8. Often bloggers captured the images and shared the photos on their blogs, helping attract more crowds. This rally in San Diego was photographed by Keith Darcé.

felt "personally attacked," that she made a surprise appearance and came out publicly for the first time. Nearly 1,000 demonstrated in Washington, D.C., despite a tornado watch in effect.[48] Similar protests occurred in hundreds of cities and towns across the country.[49]

The genesis and scope of the protests reflected an important development in the battle for marriage equality, as the impetus behind much of the popular participation was not the urging or organizing of major national gay rights groups. Instead, the near-spontaneous rallies were sparked largely by online networks: emails, Facebook, Twitter, and text chains.[50] Major gay groups did, of course, use online networks to help mobilize troops against Proposition 8, both before and after the vote. At the postelection Los Angeles press conference chastising Mormons for their involvement in the Proposition 8 battle, Lorri Jean, head of the Los Angeles LGBT Center, announced the creation of a new website, www.InvalidateProp8.org, that would allow people to donate to legal or ballot efforts to reverse the ban while sending postcards to the Mormon church expressing anger at its support of the measure.[51]

But many of the key efforts in the weeks after the vote came from gays and lesbians (and some straight supporters) who were not longtime movement participants but who were angered by the elimination of marriage rights. "We're doing an end run around the mainstream organizations that run our causes," said one protest organizer. "While we knew we'd been discriminated against in the past," said Matt Palazzolo, a twenty-three-year-old newly minted activist who founded the grassroots Equal Roots Coalition, "we'd never felt it until now." The passage of Proposition 8, he said, "woke me up." Kate Kendell acknowledged missteps by the mainstream organizations in their effort to fight off Proposition 8, citing a "wish list of things I would have done differently." She said it was "totally legitimate to say that the normal way of doing things did not get us to the finish line," but she also noted that the setback had stirred gay people "out of our stupor" and made way for new energy and leadership. Some of the established groups, she said, "need to move over a couple of lanes to make room."[52]

The day after the vote, Willow Witte, an Ohio activist struggling to turn out supporters for a protest against the measure in Cleveland, called her friend Amy Balliett, a young Seattle Internet entrepreneur who had developed expertise in search-engine marketing. Tapping contacts with Web companies, in a matter of days the pair created a group called Join the Impact, which harnessed the power of social media platforms such as Facebook to spread the word about rallies nationwide. "Why are we going to wait for the organizations to have a protest?" Balliett asked herself. "Why don't we just do it?" By the end of the weekend, the site was getting 50,000 visits per hour. Deployment of the Internet at this astonishing level became a media story in itself, further increasing visibility and making the organizing tool into a self-fulfilling prophecy. Even before the huge rallies held in all fifty states eleven days after the Proposition 8 vote, major news outlets wrote about them in anticipation, often citing the online organizing tools as the focus of the story.[53]

LGBTQ writers and bloggers immediately noted the outsider status of those organizing the protests. "Stonewall 2.0. Is that what Saturday might be?" asked veteran gay journalist Rex Wockner, noting that the "über-establishment" San Diego LGBT Community Center had nothing on its website about the events, but did have an enormous ad for the department store Nordstrom. (The center did organize a rally of several thousand the weekend before the vote.)[54] "Totally grassroots. Totally fascinating," he continued, singing the praises of the new tools of the people's power: "You don't have to listen to the gay 'leaders' who failed you anymore, you don't have to give them any more money, you just have to figure out what you want to do next with the power that now is yours—to get what you want: Full equality."[55] The activist and writer Wayne Besen wrote that "the leaders of what is being billed as Stonewall 2.0 are not coming from large, established organizations, but Internet savvy activists who can use a mouse to mobilize the masses." He spoke of a "paradigm shift in the movement" following the passage of Proposition 8. "We are not the same movement we were prior to Nov. 4," he commented, observing a "wide-eyed sea of fresh new faces" among the street protests, where he found "an injection of raw energy and an infusion of new inspiration that has eluded our movement for more than a decade."[56]

To some extent the new, outside energy of the marriage equality movement was spurred by a widespread sense, as noted by the bloggers, that established gay rights groups had failed to lead and were relying on a tired strategy that wasn't working. Yet in truth, the existing strategies of gay legal advocates were yielding enormous fruit. Movement groups had brought civil unions to Vermont and marriage to Massachusetts with successful lawsuits by GLAD and fieldwork by other activists. Those successes had rippled instantly across the country and helped inspire both the backlash of social conservatives, including President Bush's support for the Federal Marriage Amendment, and Newsom's push for marriage equality in San Francisco. NCLR had joined and helped win the litigation for gay marriage in California that had prompted Proposition 8. And movement lawsuits and legislative campaigns that were in progress were about to secure marriage equality in several more states in October 2008 and the first half of 2009. Meanwhile, public opinion polls showed support for marriage equality ticking dramatically upward starting just after Proposition 8 passed.[57]

Still, the experience of losing rights in California, precisely because it occurred in a context where expectations of equality had grown so high, had an enormous mobilizing effect on grassroots activists, bloggers, ordinary same-sex couples, and increasing numbers of straight allies. "Having our marriage rights stripped away by a slim majority in California was a transformational experience for many gay, lesbian, bisexual and transgender individuals," Besen explained, saying the ensuing protests "marked the end of the Passive Era of gay politics." Echoing the sentiment of Wockner, who extended "a gigantic *thank you* to the Yes on Prop 8 folks," Besen declared the Proposition 8 ballot loss a triumph for the same-sex marriage movement. With it, he claimed, "anti-gay forces unleashed a ferocious storm with powerful winds of change that will only end with the sound of wedding bells."[58]

Other observers shared the sentiment. Fred Karger, a California gay activist and long-shot presidential contender, called the Proposition 8 vote "the greatest thing that could have happened" because it mobilized gay activism. "This narrow loss has awakened Godzilla," he said. "It lit a fire under the gay community and our allies." The vote, he said presciently, would "change history forever and speed up our civil rights movement by probably a generation."[59] A California newspaper article raised the question of whether the fight over Proposition 8 could be "a pivot historians will someday see as a definitive turning point."[60]

As with so many bursts of more radical energy in social change movements, the rhetoric could be grandiose. It would prove difficult to sustain the vigor and excitement of all these new voices, and to parlay them into tangible gains. "Stonewall 2.0" was perhaps a stretch. And yet the new climate was unmistakable: one in which gays and lesbians awoke to a new sense that their dignity was at stake but could be secured if enough showed up, came out, and fought back. Some months after the Proposition 8 vote, Robin McGehee, an activist from Mississippi, organized a march in Fresno, called Meet in the Middle for Equality, that drew several thousand marriage equality supporters. Angry with established movement groups for their inability to defend against Proposition 8, McGehee also felt that the movement and other liberal groups were too urban and homogenous. She billed Meet in the Middle as the start of a new "effort toward full federal equality" that would do more to include rural and minority grassroots activists whose excitement she felt was being wasted. The small but successful march led to a much larger grassroots march in Washington in 2009, and to permanent new organizations including McGehee's direct-action-oriented GetEQUAL.[61]

It was not only new LGBTQ energy that infused the battle following the Proposition 8 ballot loss. Many straight people, for the first time, became fully aware of the genuine, profound, and consequential inequality resulting from the denial of marriage rights to the gays and lesbians they knew, and it angered them. For some, the election result and the heightened focus it brought to gay rights marked the beginning of a new understanding of that unfairness and a commitment to working against it. This development manifested itself in many ways. Signs reading STRAIGHTS AGAINST HATE filled the streets along with the tens of thousands of demonstrators, including the straight Mormon "mother bears who defend their cubs."[62] Press reports of the street marches following the Proposition 8 vote were filled with references to marchers who were "gay and straight, married and single, young and old and in between."[63] A frequent chant was "Gay, straight, black, white, marriage is a civil right."[64] "We're not married and we're not gay," a California demonstrator told a reporter, holding a sign that read DISCRIMINATION IS NOT A FAMILY VALUE. "We just believe all people should have the right to live as they choose."[65]

The presence of Villaraigosa, the straight mayor of Los Angeles who addressed the large crowd even as wildfires were raging throughout parts of his city, was also a testament to the involvement of prominent straight allies in the marriage equality battle—as well as the increasing political value of publicly supporting the issue.[66] The straight mayor of California's second-largest city, San Diego, was also disheartened by the passage of Proposition 8. A year prior, GOP Mayor Jerry Sanders had reversed his opposition to marriage equality in an emotional speech in which he announced that his daughter was a lesbian and he could no longer in good conscience work to block the freedom to marry. "In the end," Sanders said, speaking of his daughter and gay friends and staff members, "I couldn't look any of them in the face and tell them that their relationship—their very lives— were any less meaningful than the marriage I share with my wife Rana," who stood by his side.[67] His announcement came as the mayor faced a decision on whether to sign or veto a bill making San Diego a party to an amicus brief supporting marriage equality in the 2008 California Supreme Court case—and in his speech he now indicated he would sign the bill, after having initially vowed a veto. Sanders's next major public appearance to speak on the issue was at a rally the weekend before the Proposition 8 vote. Standing with his daughter and wife, he told the crowd that "if you love your family then there's no other way to go," and that he was there to help "give everybody permission to vote No on 8."[68]

The tide was now turning so decisively in some quarters that pro-gay-marriage conservative Republicans such as Sanders increasingly no longer stood alone. Among the other straight conservative Republicans who were spurred to support marriage equality in the wake of the Proposition 8 vote was Ted Olson, the former solicitor general under George W. Bush. Olson was most famous as the powerful attorney who helped secure Bush's place in the White House by representing him in the *Bush v. Gore* lawsuit over the disputed 2000 election. A member of the Federalist Society who served under both Reagan and George W. Bush, he was known as a white-glove conservative. He was also a brilliant, admired appellate lawyer, having argued more than fifty cases before the Supreme Court—and winning nearly four-fifths of them. Although Olson says he never opposed same-sex marriage, he allowed that "one's memory is always favorable to oneself," and to date he had never made public comments in support of it.[69] Few would have put him anywhere on a list of the lawyers most likely to take up a case to win marriage equality in court.

Just over a week after the Proposition 8 vote, as Olson was taking note of the reaction around the vote, Chad Griffin was lunching at the Polo Lounge in Beverly Hills with the film director Rob Reiner and his wife, Michele. Griffin was a gay political consultant who had worked in the Clinton White House at the age of nineteen. Reiner was a friend, client, and supporter of Griffin's and had been brought in late in the game to work on the effort to block Proposition 8 from passing. Joined by Griffin's business partner, Kristina Schake, the group discussed the demoralizing election result, the reasons the campaign failed, and the future of gay rights.[70]

Noticing the group, Kate Moulene, an acquaintance of Michele's, stopped by their table to chat. When Moulene learned that they had been discussing Proposition 8, she commiserated, sharing their disappointment. She later called the Reiners to suggest that they talk to her former brother-in-law, Ted Olson. She explained that, despite all his conservative credentials, his disposition was actually libertarian, and they might be surprised by his position on marriage equality.[71]

When Reiner conveyed the idea to Griffin, he was skeptical but intrigued. He grasped immediately that if Olson supported marriage equality—and was willing to put muscle behind it—it could be a major coup for the effort and could help put a bipartisan sheen on the issue. One of the ideas Griffin was contemplating was filing a federal lawsuit challenging Proposition 8 as a violation of the U.S. Constitution. He quickly reached out to Olson, and within a week found himself on a plane to Washington for a dinner with the renowned lawyer.

At their meeting, the two discussed the high suicide rate among gay and lesbian teens, the damage done to families when young people came out and were rejected by disapproving parents, the hopelessness of gay boys and girls for whom the denial of marriage seemed to promise a life lived forever alone. Griffin told Olson about the huge disparities in public benefits and government protections that resulted from being denied the right to marry. "We also discussed the hurt people feel because they're put into a separate category," said Olson, who added that he has always been "very uncomfortable with the idea that we're going to discriminate against people or put them into a separate category based upon their sexual orientation." Echoing the conservative argument for marriage equality first outlined by Randy Lloyd, Andrew Sullivan, and others, Olson said that "when people come together and respect and love one another and want to live in a committed relationship, it seems to me that's good for society, good for families, good for the communities they live in, good for the economy." He concluded, "I cannot think of a reason why we wouldn't want people who feel that way about one another to have that opportunity."[72]

Without hesitating, Olson told Griffin that if he planned to move forward with a federal lawsuit, Olson was in.

9

"Brick by Brick"

PROGRESS IN THE STATES

THE SPONTANEOUS STREET ACTIVISM OF THOUSANDS OF GAYS AND lesbians in 2004 and 2008 had signaled a new form of energy devoted to marriage equality. But it was energy that was tough to sustain and whose concrete objectives remained uncertain. Yes, the people sought marriage. But how was their energy to be applied to the achievement of specific political or legal aims? The 2004 Winter of Love had crashed into an autumn of popular anti-gay resistance as state after state altered their constitutions to block gay marriage. And the political awakening spurred by Proposition 8's passage did not, by itself, constitute or dictate the path to getting rid of it. Instead, it was the grinding, persistent, incremental work of state efforts—in particular, lawsuits begun in the years before Proposition 8—that advanced the fortunes of marriage equality during 2009. All the while, political work and public education continued, as advocates patiently pushed the issue forward.

———

Barack Obama campaigned for president as a "fierce advocate of equality" for gays and lesbians and expressed his support for every major gay rights cause except one: marriage equality. Even here, he wanted to see DOMA repealed, but only so that each state could decide whether to allow gay marriage or not, a position that would earn him harsh criticism for its echoes of the "states' rights" argument historically used to justify racial segregation in the South. Obama had struggled with his position on same-sex marriage since early in his political life. In a questionnaire filled out during his 1996 Illinois state senate campaign, he unequivocally supported marriage equality, responding to a local gay newspaper's question on the issue, "I favor legalizing same-sex marriages, and would fight efforts to prohibit such marriages."[1] Yet by 2004, when he rose to national prominence with a speech to the Democratic National Convention introducing presidential candidate John Kerry, Obama had reversed course. Never very convincing in his opposition to gay marriage, Obama cited his religious faith in response to questions about the subject. He told a Chicago radio audience that as a Christian, his "religious beliefs say that marriage is something sanctified between a man and a woman."[2] In an October 2004 candidate forum he said he did not believe that marriage was "a civil right," and that marriage as a heterosexual institution constituted "a set of traditions" that should be preserved. But he was quick to pivot back to his support for civil unions and for equality for gay people in every other way possible, a position that was quickly coming to seem contradictory.[3]

Throughout his 2008 presidential campaign, although it was clearly not something he liked to discuss, Obama reaffirmed his opposition to gay marriage. At times his reference to the religious basis of his position seemed calculated to allow for a distinction between his personal opposition and the possibility of a more liberal policy position—the equivalent of being pro-choice on abortion while personally opposing it. But by the 2008 election, gay marriage was becoming a major political issue and Obama was ultimately unable to avoid taking a stark position on it. "I'm not in favor of gay marriage," he told MSNBC in April, repeating his comments throughout the campaign.[4]

In June 2008, hoping to demonstrate his commitment to gay rights, Obama wrote a letter to the Alice B. Toklas LGBT Democratic Club of San Francisco expressing his opposition to the Proposition 8 ballot initiative in California.[5] Yet the letter stopped well short of endorsing marriage equality itself. At the time, gay rights advocates seemed content with Obama's position, reflecting where expectations lay in 2008.[6] "I was thrilled to see the senator step up to the plate and say how he feels about discrimination," said Julius Turman, cochair of Toklas, describing Obama as "well on the way to being educated." Others agreed. "It's great to see Sen. Obama's statement, which is consistent with what he has said in the past about allowing each state to make its own decision," said Geoff Kors, head of Equality California, the main group fighting Proposition 8.[7] At the time, backing a "states' rights" position was the most that seemed reasonable to hope for from a major presidential candidate, even though it reeked of the segregationist history that had barred marriages like that of Obama's mother to his father. Kors acknowledged it was not "ideal" that the candidate opposed gay marriage itself, "but it's important when political leaders say gay and lesbian couples should be treated equally." (Obama's support for ending DOMA went further than that of Hillary Clinton, long popular among many gays and lesbians, who only supported ending DOMA's federal recognition ban while maintaining its provision allowing states to ignore gay marriages in other states.)[8]

On January 20, 2009, Barack Obama took office as the first African American president. Feelings among the largely liberal gay and lesbian population were a mixture of excitement and lingering anguish about the Proposition 8 vote eliminating their right to wed in the nation's largest state. Such sentiment likely contributed to the hopes they pinned on the new occupant of the White House to advance gay equality—as well as the watchful eye they kept on him early in his tenure. Things got off to a rocky start when the incoming president chose Rick Warren to deliver the invocation at his inauguration. Warren was a best-selling author and evangelical pastor of a conservative megachurch in California, and he had been a vocal supporter of Proposition 8. His 20,000-member Saddleback Church banned gay people from membership if they were "unwilling to repent of their homosexual lifestyle."[9] Warren had urged his members—and his millions of fans via video—to vote for Proposition 8, and had compared same-sex marriage to incest, pedophilia, and polygamy.[10]

This was not the kind of representative that many supporters of Obama had in mind when he had promised to transcend old divisions and move past a generation of culture wars, and it sparked an early firestorm among LGBTQ advocates and organizations, bringing bad press to the new White House.[11] The Warren choice was not an intentional slap to the gay community, but it revealed a young administration that was not adequately attuned to the anger of one of its key constituencies and did not understand how to deal with it. If the choice of Warren demonstrated the administration's simple inattention to the pastor's public positions on gay rights, it also reflected an underestimation of the importance of the LGBTQ community's feelings, the demands for equal dignity that followed in the wake of Proposition 8, and the gay community's growing power to exert political pressure through both traditional means and new media channels.[12]

In the first few months of Obama's tenure, the headline-grabbing gay rights issue was not the struggle for same-sex marriage rights but efforts by gays and lesbians to be able to serve openly in the military, and it was here that gay and lesbian advocates were able to flex that muscle and demonstrate the need for a new political calculus on gay rights. Just six weeks after the new president took office with a Democratic majority in Congress, the House introduced legislation to repeal "don't ask, don't tell," which Obama had vowed to get done. It seemed a far easier lift than marriage, as public support for openly gay military service hovered around 75 percent, compared to just 40 percent in favor of same-sex marriage rights.[13]

Yet as sympathetic as many Democrats were toward gay rights, the issue remained a source of fear for many politicians, something both Obama and gay activists knew well from recalling the political fallout of Bill Clinton's failed effort to end the military's gay ban. Even a decade later, many Democratic advisors had taken as the lesson from John Kerry's 2004 loss that gay rights were still the third rail in American politics, even though the role of gay rights in causing that loss had been debunked. On top of these concerns, Obama had inherited two wars and the deepest economic recession since the Great Depression—and still sought to pass a national health care law where all previous presidents had failed. His support for LGBTQ equality was real, but he had little appetite for spending political capital on it in his first year in office.[14]

Gay rights advocates, for their part, did not have much time to waste, as it was a rare advantage to have both a supportive president and a Congress controlled by that president's party. Obama had once told progressive advocates, "I want you to hold our government accountable. I want you to hold me accountable." It was a variation of Franklin D. Roosevelt's plea to liberals to force him to do what they all wanted: "I agree with you, I want to do it, now make me do it." Yet Obama seemed unprepared for the pressure that LGBTQ advocates put on him early in his administration. By April, the Servicemembers Legal Defense Network, the main lobbying group pushing to end the gay ban, published an ad in the military newspaper *Stars and Stripes* demanding that Obama move a repeal bill forward by including the measure in his Pentagon spending bill. The group warned him, "If you don't, you will soon be approving the firing of men and women for being gay. That infamous law will become your infamous law, your albatross."[15]

That spring, Army First Lieutenant Dan Choi, an Arabic-speaking West Point grad, appeared on the *Rachel Maddow Show* and announced he was gay, in violation of the policy. His appearance was the start of a string of direct actions that would land Choi and others under arrest amid embarrassing headlines that Obama and the Pentagon were wasting essential military talent.[16] Gay advocates began to turn up the pressure on the White House by pointing out that the president had the power to suspend military firings without depending on congressional action, effectively ending "don't ask, don't tell" until Congress mustered the will to wipe it off the books. The resulting headlines painted Obama as forgoing a simple opportunity to carry out a promise he had made on gay rights.[17]

Those headlines became a thorn in the side of the administration, reflecting the strengthened leverage of an LGBTQ community that had become increasingly vocal after Proposition 8. Over the next several weeks Obama's press secretary was inundated with questions from mainstream journalists wondering why the president was willing to compromise national security by allowing the firing of gay Arabic-speaking service members. The Associated Press reported that Obama "has taken the heat from his political base" for a decision to "hold off debate on contentious social issues" for the first year of his presidency. The piece said gay advocates were "unhappy the administration is moving at a snail's pace" to end the military gay ban.[18] "Gay Groups Grow Impatient with Barack Obama," blared a *Politico* headline. Human Rights Campaign president Joe Solmonese offered modest criticism of the White House, saying that HRC was "frustrated at the pace of progress" but that no one could expect anti-gay laws to be "miraculously changed overnight"—a comment that angered many in the community by seeming to excuse the president. The gay writer and activist John Aravosis, who founded the website AMERICAblog, told *Politico* that gays and lesbians were "far angrier than they're saying publicly" and that many in the movement had the feeling that they had "entered a danger zone where the administration is backing away from us fast." He said most gay activists in Washington felt "a sense of impending betrayal."[19]

Gay advocates and other progressives began to lean on the White House not just over the gay troops issue but regarding gay rights more generally. Opinion leaders—mostly liberals at first—began turning up the volume on Obama's position on marriage. The *Washington Post's* Eugene Robinson wrote that it was "time for President Obama to stand up for gay marriage." Views on gay rights, he wrote, had "changed dramatically—more than enough for a popular, progressive president to speak loudly and clearly about a matter of fundamental human and civil rights." Richard Socarides, a former advisor to President Clinton on gay rights and the son of the notorious anti-gay psychiatrist Charles Socarides, agreed that attitudes were quickly changing and that the current president risked being left behind the curve. Citing recent state-based gay rights victories on which Obama had remained silent, "a youth-driven paradigm shift in public opinion and the election of our first African American president," the younger Socarides argued that it was "a uniquely opportune moment to act." Instead, Obama was "disappointing" LGBTQ advocates with his inaction, after having promised to be a "fierce advocate of equality."[20]

One of the president's sharpest critics among his supporters was Andrew Sullivan, whose influence on the administration was confirmed when Obama publicly cited him as one of his favorite bloggers.[21] In an *Atlantic* piece entitled "The Fierce Urgency of Whenever," Sullivan described "a sickeningly familiar feeling in my stomach" that deepened "with every interaction with the Obama team on these issues." The message from Obama's critics was becoming uniform: events were moving too quickly for this president to remain on the sidelines. "Here we are, in the summer of 2009," wrote Sullivan, "with gay servicemembers still being fired for the fact of their orientation. Here we are, with marriage rights spreading through the country and world and a president who cannot bring himself even to acknowledge these breakthroughs in civil rights, and having no plan in any distant future to do anything about it at a federal level."[22]

In late May Choi, who had increasingly become the face of gay rights to the mainstream media, spoke across the street from an Obama fundraiser at a protest rally organized by the Courage Campaign. The group was circulating a petition with 140,000 signatures on it demanding that

Obama put a stop to the military's discharges of gay service members. The fund-raiser was being held at the Beverly Hills Hilton, and in one of the men's rooms there Jim Messina, the president's deputy White House chief of staff, was accosted by a frustrated attendee who lamented that Obama talked the talk but was allowing Choi to take a walk. By that time former vice president Dick Cheney, a man reviled by much of the left, had expressed support for same-sex marriage (his daughter was openly gay). Howard Dean, former head of the Democratic Party had, too, along with 40 percent of the public as a whole, including 55 percent of Democrats and 75 percent of self-identified liberals. The president, as even high-profile supporters were beginning to express, was coming to seem out of step with his party.[23]

Into this context—frustration and impatience among LGBTQ advocates, and an increasing sense even among non-gay political observers that Obama's reticence on gay issues was unsustainable—the administration dropped a bomb. On June 11 the Justice Department wrote a stern legal brief defending DOMA in a lawsuit filed by Arthur Smelt and Christopher Hammer, a gay couple married in California in 2008. As gay rights advocates quickly pointed out, the content of the brief sounded as though it had come not from an administration that opposed DOMA but from one that fervently supported it. The brief called opposite-sex marriage the "traditional and uniformly-recognized form of marriage" and argued that DOMA was "entirely rational" in seeking to privilege it over same-sex marriage. It called the law a "measured response to society's evolving understandings of marriage" and a "cautious decision simply to maintain the federal status quo while preserving the ability of States to experiment with new definitions of marriage." It argued starkly that there was no constitutional right to same-sex marriage. It drew on precedents upholding prohibitions on incestuous and underage marriages to argue that gay unions could be banned as well, infuriating gay advocates with its apparent comparison of gay marriage to incest and pedophilia. And in a final insult, the brief seemed to borrow an approach taken by social conservatives who had long believed that homosexuality was a choice—that it did not exist as a genuine identity or the natural expression of gay people's love, but was the sinful behavior of broken heterosexuals.[24] "DOMA does not discriminate against homosexuals" at all, said the brief, because it "does not distinguish among persons of different sexual orientations, but rather it limits federal

benefits to those who have entered into the traditional form of marriage."
In other words, since DOMA did not explicitly target gay people but
merely privileged heterosexual marriages, it did not discriminate against
gay people, who could simply choose to marry someone of the opposite
sex.[25] Anyone at all, the Obama administration seemed to be saying, could
simply opt to embrace the "traditional and uniformly-recognized form of
marriage."

These claims threatened to deprive gay marriage proponents of some
of the strongest potential arguments against DOMA, arguments they
would need for the scores of state and federal lawsuits the movement was
counting on to legalize marriage across the nation. Among the earliest and
loudest critics of the brief was John Aravosis on AMERICAblog. Calling
the document "despicable" and "gratuitously homophobic," he wrote,
"I cannot state strongly enough how damaging this brief is to us. Obama
didn't just argue a technicality about the case, he argued that DOMA is
reasonable. That DOMA is constitutional. That DOMA wasn't motivated
by any anti-gay animus."[26] Richard Socarides, who was in the White House
when Bill Clinton signed DOMA, complained that the Obama brief "had
such a buckshot approach to it, a veritable kitchen sink of anti-gay legal
theories, that it seemed expressly designed to inflict maximal damage to
our rights."[27] The gay legal and national advocacy groups immediately released a statement saying they were "surprised and deeply disappointed in
the manner in which the Obama administration" was defending DOMA.
The letter faulted the administration for "using many of the same flawed
legal arguments that the Bush administration used," arguments that had
already been rejected by numerous courts as "legally unsound and obviously discriminatory."[28] Solmonese of HRC, who had largely avoided criticizing the administration to this point, wrote the president a public letter
lamenting the "pain that we feel as human beings and as families when
we read an argument, presented in federal court, implying that our own
marriages have no more constitutional standing than incestuous ones."[29]

These laments were picked up by mainstream media outlets, adding
to a growing public relations headache for the Obama administration.
In "A Bad Call on Gay Rights," the *New York Times*'s editorial page called
the brief "disturbing" and used the occasion to chastise the White House
for having "not done much" on gay rights despite its promises. "The administration," it said, "needs a new direction on gay rights."[30] Other head-

lines such as "Gay Rights Groups Irate After Obama Administration Lauds Defense of Marriage Act," "Obama Admin Hearts DOMA (for Now); Do Gays Still Heart Obama?" and "Obama Justice Department Defends Defense of Marriage Act—That Candidate Obama Opposed" undermined White House efforts to retain the votes and dollars of gay constituents, and to maintain control over the political narrative.[31] It was difficult to talk about health care reform if journalists in the press room were constantly asking why the president was defending the ban on gay marriage.[32]

The Justice Department brief was part of the typical pattern in which an administration defends existing laws, including ones a president opposes. But as advocates immediately pointed out, there was ample precedent for declining to defend laws that the administration deemed unconstitutional. Indeed, bloggers cited decisions by all four presidents immediately preceding Obama to decline to defend laws they opposed. Noting that "the Obama administration's own word will now be used against us" in legal efforts to overturn gay marriage bans, Aravosis slammed this misstep by a Democratic, biracial president who had campaigned as a "fierce advocate" of gay rights and had relied on gay votes and dollars to take the White House: "You don't make your first official legal statement on gay rights an outright attack on the underpinnings of our entire civil rights."[33]

The next week the White House announced an order giving several new benefits to same-sex couples, including sick leave, long-term care insurance, and some health care access for partners of Foreign Service officers abroad.[34] In a sign of how mainstream gay rights had become in both politics and culture, Frank Kameny stood beside the president as he signed the memorandum in the Oval Office. The cumulative impact of these and other executive actions—including the appointment of a record number of LGBTQ and gay-friendly officials, which made similar advances more likely—would turn out to be sizable.[35] Yet at the time these steps were easily denigrated as crumbs or simply overshadowed by continuing waves of anger over the legal brief and the lack of more robust progress. Some donors expressed their frustration by pulling out of a Democratic National Committee fund-raiser planned for later in the month, the second time in two weeks that gay demonstrations had stolen headlines and dollars from a fund-raiser headlined by the president.[36] Although the president's new benefits announcement had been in the works for months, Aravosis cast

President Obama, in the Oval Office, hands a pen to longtime gay activist Frank Kameny during signing of a presidential order granting limited same-sex partner benefits in June 2009. Also pictured (left to right) *are Vice President Joe Biden, Rep. Barney Frank, Sen. Joe Lieberman, and Sen. Tammy Baldwin. Partly obscured is Joe Solmonese, then president of the Human Rights Campaign.*

it as a meager consolation prize for the damage done by the legal brief. "The only reason we're getting anything," he complained, was that "the gay ATM ran dry."[37]

With progress looking unlikely on Capitol Hill, LGBTQ advocates that spring continued to press forward with their incremental strategy to win marriage equality. Mary Bonauto and her colleagues at GLAD had long thought about how best to attack DOMA and use its death as a "stepping-stone" to full marriage equality. Bonauto rarely used that phrase in public, however, not wanting to make individual steps look like a quiet effort to smash the entire anti-gay-marriage edifice. That was the end game, of course, but Bonauto thought that getting there would take time and require a set of narrowly crafted legal steps. Unlike a direct challenge to state gay marriage bans, a lawsuit against DOMA would not require the courts to declare gay marriage legal; rather, it would only stop the federal government from discriminating against married gay couples living in states where such marriages were permitted. Further narrowing the lawsuit, GLAD would mount an "as-applied" challenge: target specific programs such as social security, tax advantages, and veterans' benefits and argue that withholding these from otherwise eligible gay or lesbian spouses was unconstitutional. "It was the most conservative, limited approach," Bonauto explained, "and we thought the most conservative outcome would be a fatal blow to DOMA." As part of the conservative legal strategy, only Section 3 of DOMA, involving the question of federal recognition, would be targeted, not Section 2, the provision that states did not need to recognize other states' same-sex marriages.[38]

GLAD had begun conceiving of a DOMA challenge in 2004, as soon as it had succeeded in making same-sex marriage legal in Massachusetts. Immediately GLAD began hearing of the difficulties that married same-sex couples faced when the state recognized their marriage but the federal government did not. Still, Bonauto felt strongly back in 2004 that the Massachusetts marriages needed time to "settle in" before a federal lawsuit could succeed. Some in the movement thought GLAD would file a federal suit right away. "That would be nuts," Bonauto recalled thinking. She had sought in the aftermath of *Goodridge* to discourage federal lawsuits. In addition to wanting to let the world absorb that these same-sex couples were "really and truly married," she knew that the freedom to marry in Massachusetts was not yet safe from being trumped by a state constitutional amendment. Bonauto worried that judges might scoff at being asked to force the federal government to recognize a marriage that even the state in question might not ultimately recognize.

After that concern was put to rest in 2007 with the failure of the last attempt to amend the Massachusetts state constitution, GLAD commissioned polls to learn more about public attitudes, the judicial climate, and what legal approach might work best in attacking DOMA. The results showed that most of the public had never heard of DOMA, and those who had did not understand how it hurt gay couples. The polls also found that while most Americans did not yet favor same-sex marriage, a majority opposed anti-gay discrimination, and so GLAD developed a message emphasizing that DOMA denied gay couples federal rights and protections that straight couples enjoyed. GLAD staff also looked at every federal statute that involved any aspect of marriage. This deep dive into legislative history uncovered something significant: DOMA marked the first time the federal government had singled out one class of married couples and denied them recognition or benefits. While different states had always made their own rules about who could marry (for instance, specifying age of consent, restrictions on cousins getting married, and so forth), the federal government had always deferred to the states' rules. That meant if a state blessed a marriage, the federal government accepted it as valid—until DOMA, when the federal government chose to designate same-sex marriages as second-class. All of this helped build a record showing that DOMA was nothing more than discrimination, a key point that would be used in successful court cases against the law, and eventually against gay marriage bans themselves. It also helped GLAD and other litigators to see the wisdom of using an equal protection theory to challenge DOMA, something that may seem obvious in retrospect but took time, thought, and experience to develop.

The DOMA challenge was hotly debated at the Litigators' Roundtable. "We had a lot of controversy with our closest friends," remembered Bonauto. One participant described "some big ugly meetings at the Roundtable" over whether and when to file a DOMA suit, with some voices expressing particular concern over a possible backlash playing out in the 2008 election, which everyone hoped a Democrat would win. The ACLU and Lambda had recently lost a federal suit challenging an expansive Nebraska measure that banned not only gay marriages but the provision of any similar rights to same-sex couples. The loss was so bad that they chose not to appeal, with an ACLU attorney saying, "With the current climate in the courts, I think it's a very bad time to attack this problem." The Roundtable lawyers had watched several state and federal lawsuits fail between 2004 and 2008, having actively discouraged some from moving forward because of the prospect of setting bad precedent, and the losses proved their concerns well-founded. Now lawyers from the groups were made nervous by the possibility of a high-profile federal suit with highly uncertain prospects being mounted by one of their own.

Mostly, however, the Roundtable forum served its purpose well: it became almost a moot court where all possible objections from judges could be anticipated and answered. How could they tell the federal government that it could not define marriage for its own purposes? Didn't the government have a right to prioritize one kind of marriage over another? Couldn't the argument that marriage was for procreation and same-sex couples don't procreate hold water with the judges? All these hypothetical objections were cause for worry. But eventually Bonauto felt they could all be overcome. "The reason we were ready to file," she said, "was that we had answered every question, and we had what we thought was a winning answer."

The decision to move forward with a federal DOMA challenge was made easier when in October 2008, to little fanfare, the high court of Connecticut ruled that gay couples had a constitutional right to marry. That case had also been brought by GLAD, working with the single-issue group Love Makes a Family. By early 2009, with the momentum of the Connecticut win, the presidential election out of the way, and outrage over Proposition 8 having ratcheted up national attention and community pressure, the staff at GLAD felt the time was right for a federal lawsuit. On March 3 GLAD filed suit in federal district court in Boston challenging DOMA's denial of federal benefits to couples who had legally married in Massachusetts.

The plaintiffs in GLAD's suit were eight couples and three widowers, and each had applied, and been rejected, for benefits for which they would have been eligible if their partners were the opposite sex. Nancy Gill, the suit's named plaintiff in *Gill v. Office of Personnel Management,* was a postal worker who had tried to put her wife, Marcelle Letourneau, on her family health plan. Because of DOMA, her employer, the federal government, rejected her claim. A second plaintiff was Dean Hara, widower of Gerry Studds, the first openly gay congressman. The pair had been together for sixteen years and legally married for two when Studds, sixty-nine, failed to return one morning in 2006 from walking the couple's dog. He had collapsed from a blood clot, and died ten days later. Studds's pension would have provided his surviving spouse with $62,000 every year, along with health insurance benefits—if Hara were a woman. Instead he got nothing. Other plaintiffs incurred thousands of dollars in added tax bills each year because they couldn't file their federal taxes jointly; lost thousands in social security survivor benefits; paid extra taxes on insurance benefits because they were denied the spousal right to deduct the benefits as income; were unable to update their passports to reflect a new last name after marrying; and were denied the right to extend employer health coverage to their spouses.[39]

GLAD's strategy was multipronged and long-range: to ask the court to make the lightest possible lift that would still result in substantial change; to place media stories about the harms its plaintiffs suffered from marriage discrimination, furthering the public's—and judges'—understanding of DOMA's discriminatory effects; to gather amicus briefs from influential and unexpected voices; and to hone its arguments for their day in court. Carisa Cunningham, GLAD's director of public affairs, said the group believed the case could reach the Supreme Court "in about four years."[40]

A few months later, on July 8, Martha Coakley, the attorney general of Massachusetts, filed a second suit against the federal government. In early 2007, just before Coakley took office, GLAD staff had met with her to discuss their efforts to challenge DOMA, and to plant a seed in her mind: the only state in the nation to allow same-sex marriage had a unique opportunity to show the harm done by federal marriage discrimination. Why should these valid state marriages be the only ones to be treated by the federal government as nonentities? After two years of discussion, Coakley (who was considering a run for the Senate, perhaps to replace Sen. Ted Kennedy, who had been battling brain cancer) agreed to file a suit—the only one of its kind. In passing DOMA, said the lawsuit, Congress had exceeded its constitutional authority, violating the Tenth Amendment, which reserves to the states any powers not explicitly granted to the federal government. Massachusetts should not be forced "to disregard the marriages of same-sex couples when implementing federally funded programs," Coakley said. "We cannot and should not be required to violate the equal-protection rights of our citizens in Massachusetts who choose to be married."[41] Much had changed in the six short years since the *Goodridge* case, when another Massachusetts attorney general had defended the state's gay marriage ban as serving "the Commonwealth's legitimate interest in fostering and protecting the link between marriage and procreation [and] fostering a favorable setting for child-rearing."

The Coakley suit focused, in part, on Darrel Hopkins, a twenty-year army veteran, who had married his partner, Thomas Hopkins, in 2004 in Massachusetts, just months after the state became the first in the nation to allow it. As a decorated veteran—Darrel Hopkins had served in Vietnam, South Korea, and Germany, earning two Bronze Stars, two Meritorious Service Medals, an Army Commendation Medal, and four Good Conduct Medals—he would be eligible for burial in a government-owned cemetery created for veterans and their families. Through a federal grant program, the state received funding from the U.S. Department of Veterans Affairs (VA) for the cemeteries it operated. But that funding was contingent on the state complying with VA rules, and since the VA is a federal agency, it made clear that under DOMA, family burial eligibility did not extend to same-sex spouses. Thomas Hopkins would be denied the right to be buried next to his husband, a man who had ably served his state and nation.[42]

Not only that, but the grant program had such strict funding requirements that the VA was entitled to demand past repayment for any money it ever gave a state if the state was seen as running afoul of federal rules on how to operate the cemetery. Massachusetts had received more than $20 million in grants for building, expanding, and operating two veterans cemeteries. The VA told the state that burying a veteran's same-sex spouse (if he was not eligible based on his own service) was not permitted, and that it might demand the money back from the state if Massachusetts insisted on viewing the couple as married, as its own state law dictated.[43]

The other part of the strategy to win gay marriage, of course, was to ratchet up legal victories in the states. Since the tough 2004 elections, the lawyers of the Roundtable had continued meeting, as they had for two decades. But after the heady Winter of Love and the stinging ballot defeats, their table was getting bigger, with other key players joining in their discussions. As ever, the meetings were contentious, the more so now that the circle had grown beyond the lawyers. Disagreements were palpable, with the more radical participants continuing to view marriage skeptically while established groups such as HRC signaled they would prioritize other work because marriage was too difficult a goal for the short term. But there was general consensus that movement groups must find a way to better coordinate their efforts and to stem the tide of anti-gay laws and ballot initiatives proliferating in states across America. "People were saying, 'We've got to figure out how to turn this around,'" said Matt Foreman of the Task Force.[44]

Increasingly, big funders took an active role in these meetings. While their involvement promised to direct badly needed funds to the overall marriage effort, it was also controversial. Traditionally, funders participating in advocacy work did not drive the process; they decided which efforts to fund but rarely called the shots on how those efforts moved forward. Yet with new levels of direct participation by inside-the-movement donors and program officers, funders began raising their expectations about exactly how their investments would be used and the returns they would produce. While some activists grumbled about losing a degree of independence in their work, the greater involvement of the funders—with their impressive Rolodexes, their technological savvy, and their ability to get nearly anyone on the other end of the phone, from movement leaders to senior White House officials—quickly proved itself a boon to the work at hand.

In May 2005 the Gill Foundation funded a meeting in Jersey City, New Jersey, that brought together the legal groups, the national political groups, and the leaders of the state groups. Freedom to Marry was there, along with the Equality Federation, HRC, the Task Force, and several other organizations. At the meeting they identified the states where marriage litigation had the best chance of succeeding, as the Roundtable had long been doing, but they also discussed how the broader movement could better coordinate its efforts by sharing knowledge among the many state campaigns that big donors were promising to fund. The next month the group created a document, called "Winning Marriage: What We Need to Do," that would serve as a blueprint for their strategy moving forward. The document, written primarily by Matt Coles, noted that both supporters and opponents of marriage equality were geared up for battle, energized and determined as never before. Both sides had one thing in common: they believed that marriage equality was on the cusp of becoming inevitable but wasn't yet locked up. And that meant that while supporters saw positive trends and major opportunities, opponents were taking a last stand, recognizing that the window to stop equality was closing. "Thus, as we try to take advantage of the best opportunity for progress we have ever had," said the document, "we are met by the most determined opposition we have ever faced." A section called "Long-Term Strategy" suggested that the state-by-state approach the groups were pushing could bring about national marriage equality in as little as fifteen years or as much as twenty-five years. "But we cannot stop our opponents," it concluded, "if we simply continue doing what we are doing now."[45]

The "Winning Marriage" document was also known as "10 / 10 / 10 / 20," which referred to a prospective timeline for winning national marriage equality: in fifteen to twenty years, the group hoped, the movement would count ten states with marriage equality (at the time, there was one), ten more with full civil union laws, ten with limited partnership or nondiscrimination laws, and the remaining twenty showing positive trends in the states' laws or social views. "Winning Marriage" even sorted all fifty states into four categories to show which states might land where. The plan reflected the incrementalist strategy that the gay legal groups had been advancing since Hawaii, not only because of its long time frame but also because of its reliance on a mix of incremental steps that could gradually familiarize the public—and the Supreme Court—with the reality and worth of same-sex relationships. Obtaining pro-gay legislation short of marriage, said the document, was a critical way to help change attitudes and open people up to the prospect of supporting marriage.

Of course, some activists, including contributors to the document, continued to believe that marriage was being too highly prioritized at the expense of either other priorities or alternative forms of family recognition. The document nodded to this perspective in a section called "Why Marriage?" While some members of the working group, the document acknowledged, would have preferred to address the needs of same-sex couples "with different tactics and / or with different conceptual models," or not at all, "crucial legal, political, and social issues are being debated and decided in the framework of marriage." It would likely be impossible to "move the central focus away from marriage." Reflecting a new, pragmatic consensus among leading LGBTQ advocates, the document argued that "right now, marriage is the legal and social system that provides the most comprehensive protection for the relationship of two people who make a life together." It concluded: "There is no way that gay people can be full participants in American life as long as society and the law treat our relationships as if they were inferior or as if they did not exist."[46]

Finally, the document offered an encapsulation of why the leading thinkers of the marriage movement foresaw a state-based strategy advancing before a federal one: "At first, marriage will have to be won in the states, through state courts and state legislatures. Only after we have won in many states are we likely to be able to get the Supreme Court or Congress to insist that 'hold out' states get in line. Despite widespread beliefs to the contrary, historically, Congress and the Supreme Court have been much more willing to insist that 'hold out' states abide by widely accepted social norms than they have been willing to set norms for the nation generally."

The document noted that a federal constitutional amendment remained a threat, especially if the Supreme Court ruled in favor of marriage equality before the public was adequately onboard. And it said that a DOMA challenge would likely precede a full-on right-to-marry lawsuit in federal court, for just the reasons Bonauto would explain in filing the *Gill* case four years later. Challenging DOMA, said the document, "can be a crucial part of winning the public." But "until fairly late in the process, the focus for establishing marriage will be on creating the national context for change—a climate of receptivity—and making change through state legislatures and state courts"—not yet in federal court.

The strategy, then, would be to build toward the state benchmarks that the document laid out by professionalizing the coordination of the numerous state gay rights campaigns, conducting and sharing public opinion research, and updating and streamlining the messaging contained in public education campaigns, all while continuing the litigation and legislation campaigns in states ripe for change. In return for this cooperation, groups would be rewarded with a level of funding many were not used to enjoying—and the movement would be rewarded with marriage equality. "Nothing quite like this has been done in the LGBT movement so far," the document concluded. "But the LGBT community has never faced a challenge so ripe with the prospect for success and carrying such risks if we fail."

One of the goals the Roundtable thought crucial was to avoid the impression that marriage equality was something that could only be accepted by the nation's coastal elite. Lambda, which now had a Chicago office, reported a continuing onslaught of requests by would-be plaintiffs to represent them in marriage cases. And so the staff there began discussing whether a midwestern state might be ready for a marriage suit. Camilla Taylor, a straight lawyer who had joined Lambda in 2002, began focusing on Iowa immediately. The Roundtable agreed that a win in Iowa would send a powerful message that marriage equality could be embraced in the heartland. Still, "there were a lot of advocates who thought we were crazy," Taylor said, recalling the early discussions about Iowa. She listed all the typical assumptions that coastal people held about the state: too conservative, too religious, too rural, not cosmopolitan enough to accept gay marriage. "Some thought we were pushing too hard too fast."[47]

For a while Taylor herself would have been among them. For years, every time her office was approached by same-sex couples considering a marriage suit, Lambda did what nearly all the gay legal advocates at one time had to do: asked them to hold off until, as Taylor put it, "the time was right." But by 2005, the staff began to feel they could no longer justify asking people to wait. In addition to all the irrepressible passion unleashed among gay couples by the Newsom weddings and the 2004 elections, the Lambda staff started to think it had an opportunity to open the door to marriage equality in the Midwest. There were several good reasons for this. Iowa had a strong tradition of civil rights leadership. It had desegregated its schools nearly a century before the U.S. Supreme Court outlawed segregation in 1954. It was the first state to admit women to the bar. A historic court case in the nineteenth century had boldly challenged the Fugitive Slave Law, which required anyone who found an escaped slave to return him or her to the slave owner. In general, Iowa's courts had a record of progressive independence, frequently interpreting the state's constitution as having broader guarantees of both liberty and equality than the federal Constitution.[48]

The groundwork that Taylor and her staff had engaged in—collaboration with state groups such as One Iowa, and the listening and learning that Taylor did as she crisscrossed the state—was critical to Lambda's decision to file. While Iowa did not have the pro-gay reputation of a place such as Massachusetts, its people were known for being respectful and tolerant. This perception was confirmed by her own research and engagement. Couples she spoke to about becoming plaintiffs in the case told her they were treated with respect. Even in areas where homosexuality was frowned upon, neighborliness often trumped intolerance.

Taylor was aware she could lose in Iowa—or win a victory that would be snuffed out by a ballot initiative. But she knew she had to be willing to stick her neck out. "We're in the business of trying to advance laws as far as we can," she said. "Inherent in that is taking some risks." In December 2005 her Lambda office took the plunge and filed suit on behalf of six Iowa couples (the children of some of the couples were later added to the suit).[49]

The challenge was based on the equal protection and due process clauses of the Iowa Constitution. In August 2007 the district court ruled for Lambda but stayed its decision pending appeal. It would take two more years for the case to wind its way up to the state's high court. Although the media followed in some detail the twists and turns of the California cases as they proceeded through the courts during this same period, the Iowa case garnered less attention. Which was why on April 3, 2009, many Americans were surprised to learn there was even a case pending in Iowa, not to mention the outcome: a unanimous decision that "the exclusion of gay and lesbian people from the institution of civil marriage does not substantially further any important governmental objective," as Justice Mark S. Cady wrote in the court's ruling, which Camilla Taylor read, in front of rolling cameras, to the plaintiffs and an elated crowd gathered in a conference room at the Hotel Fort Des Moines.

Opponents vowed to amend the state constitution. But the Iowa legislature was by then controlled by Democrats sympathetic to the gay donors who had helped put them in power. Same-sex marriage had come to the heartland and didn't appear to be going anywhere.

The same could not be said for all the judges who handed down the controversial ruling. The following year, three of the seven judges on the Iowa Supreme Court, including the chief justice, were removed from office in a retention election spurred by their marriage ruling. Christian conservative groups spearheaded the campaign, which outspent supporters three to one in an unprecedented election that cost nearly $1 million.[50] As the first noncoastal state to legalize same-sex marriage, Iowa marked a huge victory in the battle. But the ouster of the three judges sent a loud message to other elected judges that a vote for marriage equality might be their last. The only thing to do, marriage equality advocates recognized, was to continue to win the public over to their side.

A crucial marker of having done that work—and a strategy that would likely avoid the threat of reversal—was to persuade a legislature to legalize same-sex marriage instead of relying on the courts. California had done so twice, in 2005 and again in 2007, but saw the bill vetoed by Gov. Schwarzenegger. Meanwhile, Beth Robinson's group, the Vermont Freedom to Marry Task Force (VFTMTF), was developing a five-year strategy to win marriage in that state's legislature. In 2004 the Democrats had retaken the Vermont statehouse. A lawyer in Burlington's small legal community, Robinson knew Shap Smith, who recently had become Speaker of the House, and he held several conversations with members of VFTMTF. So did William Lippert, who, as the only openly gay member of the legislature in 2000, bore the brunt of much anger from Vermonters during the battle over civil unions. As a measure of just how much had changed between 2000 and 2009, Lippert pointed out that this time around, there were five openly gay lawmakers. In 2000 no one in the business community had backed same-sex marriage; by 2009 businesses saw full equality as a plus because it helped attract the best talent. In 2000 Burlington's largest paper had opposed civil unions; nearly a decade later it favored marriage. These changes reflected the impact of the belief that the most important thing gays and lesbians could do was to come out. "It's simply not possible for people to pretend they don't know gay and lesbian people in Vermont anymore," said Lippert. "The negative myths and stereotypes simply can't be sustained in the same way once people know you as their neighbor up the road or the person who sells you food at the farmer's market or teaches your child at the school."[51]

And in 2000 the future governor of Vermont, Peter Shumlin, then president of the state senate, had believed that if Democrats in the legislature pushed for full marriage for gays and lesbians, "we were going to push Vermonters farther than it was going to be wise to push them." He had promised the gay and lesbian community that when the time was right, the legislature would pass marriage. "We understood that we were making a political compromise that was unfair to gay and lesbian Vermonters but was a matter of political survival," Shumlin said. "I felt bound to deliver on that promise."[52]

In 2007, at Robinson's urging and with Shumlin's backing, Vermont created a Commission on Family Recognition and Protection that traveled the state and took testimony on how civil unions differed from marriage in the lives of gay Vermonters. In 2008, the commission reported that gay couples did not experience civil unions as equivalent to marriage, and it recommended that the state "take seriously the difference between civil marriage and civil union."[53]

Late that year, Speaker of the House Gaye Symington asked Shumlin if he thought it was time to try to pass gay marriage. California's vote on Proposition 8 struck Shumlin as deeply unfair. "When I saw the results of California," he said, "I felt stronger than ever that politicians were not going to stand in the way of justice." Inspired but contrite, he felt "that we had wimped out in not taking action sooner." Growing up, he never would have imagined that his children would go to school with children of same-sex couples. But for years now he had been dropping off his kids at a school they shared with kids who had two moms or two dads. "Those parents are as dedicated to their families as I am to my own," he realized. Like Newsom, Shumlin lamented that gays and lesbians were the only group that politicians could publicly demean and "see their numbers go up." And the more he thought about it, the more he realized that his long-standing belief in gay equality demanded action. If Canada, Spain, and South Africa could legalize gay marriage, if Massachusetts and Connecticut could do it, why not Vermont?[54]

Smith was elected Speaker in December, replacing Symington, and between that time and March 2009, Shumlin, Smith, Lippert, and others spoke with the folks at VFTMTF to determine if it was time to move forward. For all of them, the reality of marriage equality elsewhere in New England and in Canada played a major role in their thinking, as did the sense that so much groundwork had now been done. In the small state of Vermont, each representative has only a few thousand constituents, which can make gauging constituent opinion fairly straightforward. "When you start hearing from neighbors in the community saying, 'Please take this up,' that gives a strong impression" that voters are ready, said Lippert. "Thousands and thousands of conversations about this are what laid the groundwork for this grassroots movement."[55]

In March 2009 at a town meeting, the annual gatherings where lawmakers and Vermonters congregate to discuss the business of their towns and the state, Smith and Shumlin decided to move on the marriage bill. The Vermont Senate was safely Democratic, and they felt the votes for marriage equality were secure. But support in the House was up for grabs. As deliberations drew to a close, Vermont's Republican governor, Jim Douglas, announced he would veto a marriage equality bill, angering many legislators who were surprised the governor would weigh in before they had finished their own debates. In an initial vote, the bill passed, but not with enough votes to override a veto.

In advance of the veto-override vote, lawmakers and advocacy groups focused on a handful of Democratic legislators who they thought might switch their vote to affirm the will of the people. One was Jeff Young, a retired federal immigration employee who later became a master gardener. Young supported civil unions. "I was trying to be reasonable," he recalled. "I thought we should be respectful of traditional marriage." But, he said, he only felt "51/49" about it. New to politics in 2008, Young penned an op-ed in the *St. Albans Messenger* saying he planned to vote against marriage equality. As soon as it appeared, the phone rang; it was his statehouse colleague Kathleen Keenan, telling him he had made a big mistake. "Never tell them how you're going to vote," she said. It became an enduring lesson. "If I hadn't nailed myself to the floor with that stupid op-ed piece," said Young of the marriage bill, "I probably would have voted for it the first time."

Young got an earful from friends, constituents, and colleagues about his opposition to the marriage bill. A gay couple he knew from church told him how upset they were. Shap Smith sat him down and explained the Democrats needed his vote. Young said he'd think about it. But part of what finally tipped him were the forces that aligned themselves with him after that first vote. "This wing-nut group started saying wonderful things about me because I'd taken a position against gay marriage," he said, "but I wouldn't have agreed with them on anything else." He also realized the political costs of breaking with his leadership. There were many other items on his agenda. As a master gardener, he was hoping to be able to work on environmental laws, and he began to recognize that voting against the leadership on this could sink his leverage. Weighing both the moral and political considerations, Young ultimately provided the crucial vote to override Governor Douglas's veto and establish same-sex marriage legislatively for the first time in America.[56]

The Vermont vote came one week after the Iowa court ruling, and the two were not unconnected. In perfect incremental fashion, one state built on the next. "There's no question the fact that Massachusetts had marriage, and that Connecticut had court-ordered marriage, and then Iowa—definitely this leadership from the courts was tremendously important," Shumlin said shortly after leading the state's legislature to pass gay marriage.[57]

The vote in Vermont, in turn, started more dominoes falling. Immediately after the Vermont win, Shumlin got on the phone to his counterpart in New Hampshire, Sylvia Larson, president of the senate there. As she pushed marriage equality forward, so did advocates in Maine, where Equality Maine had been working with GLAD and others for several years to get marriage on the agenda. The next month, Maine's Democratic governor, John Baldacci, signed a marriage bill, having overcome his prior opposition. "It's not the way I was raised and it's not the way that I am," Baldacci explained. "But at the same time I have a responsibility to uphold the constitution. That's my job, and you can't allow discrimination to stand when it's raised to your level."[58]

Maine became the first state whose legislature and executive joined together to pass marriage equality, without need for a veto override or a court intervention. But, with the state's marriage law not yet in effect, the fate of actual gay marriages there faced uncertainty throughout the year, as opponents threatened a ballot initiative that fall that would reverse the law and block gay couples from tying the knot. That allowed an opening for New Hampshire to spring past Maine. In June, just two months after Iowa and Vermont legalized same-sex marriage, the New Hampshire legislature, now held by Democrats, followed suit, with Governor John Lynch putting his signature on the bill to make it law.

The steady, strategic work of the legal advocates was paying off. In the span of eight months starting in the fall of 2008, notwithstanding the harrowing passage of Proposition 8, marriage advocates won gay marriage in Connecticut, Iowa, Vermont, and New Hampshire. The victories included a state in America's heartland, and wins not just in courtrooms but through elected legislatures. Although LGBTQ advocates in Maine were deflated when voters there overturned the legislature's approval of same-sex marriage late that year (as were advocates in New York when that state's legislature failed to pass marriage equality legislation), the District of Columbia the next month became the sixth U.S. jurisdiction to legalize marriage equality, and the third to create it by legislative vote.

Nevertheless, for some, especially members of a younger generation of activists with fewer battle scars to show, the pace of change still seemed slow. For this younger generation of activists, and for all those gays and lesbians who spontaneously became active in the wake of Proposition 8, patience was in short supply, and contemplating a long, state-by-state slog felt incommensurate with the sting of stigma they felt from losing marriage in California and reading the Obama administration's demeaning court brief. For some in this group, there was great appeal in a silver bullet that could knock out every last state marriage ban at once and confer a psychic equality like no other force in the United States: the Supreme Court.

10

"Make More Snowflakes and There Will Be an Avalanche"

BATTLES OVER STRATEGY

COME TO A HEAD

Since the Proposition 8 vote in late 2008, Chad Griffin had continued his talks with Ted Olson about how the famous conservative's foray into the marriage equality movement might shake things up in California and beyond. Young, ambitious, and well-connected, Griffin was frustrated that the leading LGBTQ movement groups—both legal and political—had chosen not to challenge Proposition 8 in federal court, opting instead to build up more public support over time and return to the ballot box a year or even several years down the road.[1] Finding that option too timid, he resolved to do what he could to push things along more quickly. "To say we shouldn't move forward until public opinion is there is not a convincing argument," Griffin thought. With gays' and lesbians' anger and impatience mounting, he saw Ted Olson's participation as providing the crack in the door that could make a federal challenge to California's gay marriage ban possible. "There was a moment when I realized that I was perhaps sitting across from someone who could become a real game changer," he said.[2]

Griffin and Olson made their plans in utter secrecy. Like others contemplating impact litigation, they were aware that their challenge could be controversial and difficult to control—anyone could file a lawsuit at any time—so they would need to work quickly and under the radar to ensure that they would be the ones to file just the right lawsuit. They also recognized that the blessing of established LGBTQ movement leaders—those

217

who had been pushing marriage equality forward for decades—would be critical to their plan, or at least that movement opposition could be a major thorn in their side. And they knew that winning such an imprimatur might not be easy. For starters, few gay advocates would view the archconservative Ted Olson as a promising partner in the task of forwarding equal rights. Perhaps more important, the strategy these movement outsiders were proposing was an indictment of the established, incremental playbook, pushing instead a fast-track approach that grew out of dissatisfaction with the pace and results of existing efforts.

In March 2009, Griffin and Olson decided to float a trial balloon at the upcoming OutGiving conference. Griffin had recently been introduced by a Hollywood friend to Dustin Lance Black, the thirtysomething gay screenwriter of the film *Milk,* which had won him an Academy Award that February. Griffin and Black were part of a new breed of gay activists that mixed Hollywood glamour and a growing populist impatience with established movement forces. Born after Stonewall, they lacked the war wounds of an earlier generation of gay activists and the firsthand experience with the grueling, time-consuming, against-the-odds work often required to effect lasting change. But they frequently spoke of their loneliness and pain as gay southerners, and both of them welcomed the chance to parlay their growing public profiles into a platform to tell an even younger generation of gays and lesbians that they mattered. In his Oscar acceptance speech, Black channeled Harvey Milk: "I think he'd want me to say to all the gay and lesbian kids out there tonight who have been told that they are 'less than' by their churches or by the government or by their families, that you are beautiful, wonderful creatures of value and that no matter what anyone tells you, God does love you and that very soon, I promise you, you will have equal rights, federally, across this great nation of ours."[3]

Black's speech at the Oscars was meant not just as an inspiration to gay youth but as an expression of frustration with the current generation of gay leaders. Yet as a fresh face in the world of LGBTQ activism, the newly prominent Black earned an invitation to speak at OutGiving, which would be attended by some of those very same leaders. Black had yet to accept that invitation when Griffin reached out to him seeking his help in getting the gay community's blessing for a federal lawsuit. Griffin urged Black to accept the speaking invitation and test how a message of impatience would be received right in the belly of the beast. Besides, Ted Olson's legal representation was not coming cheap, so the support of these high-rollers could be a big help. Black agreed.

In his remarks to the donors at the Ritz-Carlton Lake Las Vegas, Black ramped up his criticism of the gay rights establishment. "We are at a critical moment in the gay and lesbian movement," he said. Drawing again on the subject of his film, Harvey Milk, as inspiration for a bolder, faster, more demanding path to equality, he contrasted his hero's efforts to those of the veteran gay activists before him. "Unlike the gay and lesbian movement today," said Black, "Harvey Milk fought for the rights of his people and he won on election day. I believe that his history holds the keys to winning our freedom again today." It had been thirty years, he said, "since Harvey Milk gave his life in our struggle for equality, and we will not wait 30 years longer. It is time for us to stop asking for crumbs and to demand the real thing."[4]

Black cast existing gay rights leaders as timid, complacent, ineffective, and apparently untutored in civil rights history. Many found his remarks disrespectful and callow. He sometimes spoke in platitudes ("If you don't know your history, you are doomed to repeat it"), and quoting Harvey Milk and Martin Luther King Jr. about the "tranquilizing drug of gradualism" to a room full of veteran gay activists seemed to many patronizing and naive. These battle-scarred gay leaders—strategists, funders, legislators, litigators, lobbyists, protesters, and others, many of whom cut their teeth as young activists in the black civil rights and student movements—were irked by the suggestion of this thirty-four-year-old screenwriter that they had stumbled haplessly into their gay rights work and were carrying it out without a basic understanding of how civil rights progress occurs.

Black took particular aim at the movement's incremental approach to building support in the states. He, Griffin, and other movement outsiders regarded the state-by-state approach as part of the problem, as did many other younger and grassroots LGBTQ activists, along with some veteran activists such as Cleve Jones, the former Milk aide, who had also recently met with Griffin and Black. "The example set by the Civil Rights Act of 1964," said Black, had shown that "full and equal civil rights can only come from the federal government." In his view, "the strategy of the past decade has failed. We have lost state and local fights time and again in over 30 states and if we look at our history books, this should come as no surprise. No group has ever won their civil rights going state by state or county by county." Now on a roll, Black urged the donors to give money not to the staid organizations of the past but to those from a "new generation of politics," people who understood the role of grassroots activism, public education, broad collaboration, and genuine outreach.[5]

Black's speech was given a respectful hearing and polite applause. Tim Sweeney, now president of the Gill Foundation, which sponsored the conference, appeared onstage to thank Black and praise his "righteous, real energy" as part of what Sweeney agreed was urgently needed in the movement. But others found Black's remarks arrogant, uninformed, and ungrounded in the history that many of his listeners had created. "When that gay kid out there tonight in San Antonio, Texas, hears for the first time," Black had said, that "we are finally fighting for his full equality, he will know there is a bright future ahead, and he will no longer think of taking his own life." What, some thought, did Black believe these and other activists had been doing for the past fifty years that made his call to action the "first time" anyone was fighting for full equality?[6]

Despite the applause, Black and Griffin themselves viewed the response to the speech as hostile. Griffin had hoped Black's speech would help persuade the LGBTQ movement to embrace, and perhaps help underwrite, the Olson lawsuit.[7] Judging from Tim Gill's response, the plan was not going well. "I have a little bit of a rebuttal to make" to Black's speech, Gill said the next morning, taking the stage. He said that using "gradualism as a pejorative denigrates the hard work of tens of thousands of people over more than three decades to achieve equal rights for gay and lesbian people," and that it "oversimplifies reality and completely misrepresents history." Citing black emancipation, women's right to vote, and Prohibition, Gill argued that "history is created by people doing small things in small ways over a long period of time." Of those three examples, Gill noted, only Prohibition had jumped the gun, failing to build consensus before pushing through a federal measure that was reversed just years later. Gill offered a countertheory to the "instantaneous discontinuity" approach that was becoming fashionable among younger gay activists. "Change is the falling of snowflakes on a slope and eventually you have a landslide," he said. "I want you to go home, remember that you're a snowflake, make more snowflakes and eventually there will be an avalanche."[8]

Black's critique was not nuanced, and it risked alienating the audience rather than winning them over. But it did reflect the views of many, both gay rights activists and movement observers, who had come to see certain sectors of the movement as crusty and ineffective. Indeed, for years, voices in the gay community had complained that the movement's largest players, particularly the Human Rights Campaign, had become behemoths, corporate organizations that sucked up enormous resources and produced little to show for it. Andrew Sullivan, for instance, a longtime critic of both the left and of the gay movement in particular, reserved special disdain for HRC, and often expressed his contempt in his blog and elsewhere. In one pointed post, he wrote that the movement had had "no strategy" since the early 1990s and that its leaders had spent the period "pushing the gay movement nowhere slowly." HRC, he wrote, was the worst offender. He complained that the group was too close to power and was "scared of tackling the military ban and absolutely terrified by any notion of civil marriage rights." Despite spending tens of millions of dollars each year, it failed to deliver change. The group's top priority since 1989 had been passing the Employment Non-Discrimination Act, but twenty years later "HRC's top priority is still passage of the Employment Non-Discrimination Act," not yet achieved despite an increase in public support for the law over that time. "Any organization that places its top priority on a law that has 90 percent approval but cannot get it passed in 20 years is doing something wrong."[9]

Sullivan expressed a common view within the gay community—although one often missed by mainstream press and straight observers who were not in the trenches—that the movement had been captured by leaders who cared more about hobnobbing with celebrities and expanding their paychecks than about having an impact. He ridiculed the very thought that the leaders of the biggest gay rights group in the country had any genuine passion for civil rights. The idea that any of them "had ever had a dream," he wrote, referencing King's famous speech "—apart from meeting Cyndi Lauper—was ludicrous." After all, "you don't build a civil rights movement by selling rainbow fucking candles and teddies-for-equality in gay neighborhoods where nobody needs persuading in the first place." Real change "requires professionals with more interest in getting shit done than basking in celebrities' reflected glory or sending out press releases."[10]

This particular critique closely paralleled Black's sentiment at Out-Giving, where he cautioned the big gay donors against substituting commercial gain for the civil rights dream. "Before you pull out your check-books," he had told them, "make sure the organization you are writing your check to is not driven" by personality, ambition, or ego, and don't waste money on a group that is "stitching the name of Harvey Milk on its hoodies and selling them at champagne dinners," as they only ask "for crumbs from our elected officials." As Harvey Milk had taught him, "big dreams are how change really happens."[11]

Black's critique struck a nerve. Yet in many ways he was preaching to the wrong crowd. Although some gay bloggers and activists referred derisively and amorphously to "Gay, Inc." to describe all the established, well-funded gay rights groups that they felt were ineffective and wasteful, there were, in reality, enormous differences among those groups. Black's reference to selling images of Milk on a sweatshirt applied to HRC, which the next year Black would accuse of co-opting Milk's name by turning the site of the martyr's San Francisco photo shop into a store to sell the group's merchandise.[12] But the OutGiving donors were largely distinct from HRC's staff or members. OutGiving was an invitation-only, large-donor conference that usually welcomed only those who gave more than $10,000 to gay causes, along with a select group of movement leaders and organizational staff who were beneficiaries of that largess. In taking aim at this group, Griffin and Black conflated the failings of HRC with the work of the scrappy gay legal groups—largely underfunded until recently, given the workload they took on—that were largely responsible for the successes that had even made it possible to feel impatient for full equality. That distinction was why Sullivan had praised, as a contrast with the monied HRC, the work of the monied Tim Gill, whose support for state-focused campaigns was yielding fruit in creating gay-friendly legislatures and laws. Sullivan suggested that because of this sort of effort (along with his own writing), "our message has reached millions in the best way possible—through a cultural revolution, an intellectual argument, and a non-lefty mainstreaming strategy."[13]

The divide between the established, professional gay advocates and the outsiders represented by Griffin and Black reflected strategic and gen-erational differences that were hardly new to the LGBTQ movement—and which marked the history of nearly all social movements. Indeed, the out-sider critique aired at the OutGiving conference seemed to miss a parallel split that had taken place over just the last five years: the newly coordinated efforts of funders, state groups, and Freedom to Marry, which in an important sense constituted a fresh, critical reaction of their own against the previous two decades of advocacy that these leaders found wanting. Yet the Griffin-Olson cadre was swept up in the belief that it was they, as Olson liked to put it, who would "change the course of history." They viewed their involvement in the marriage battle not so much as the continuation of a long civil rights struggle but as its start. Olson wrote some years later that the group's goal was to transform public opinion on same-sex marriage, and that doing so would "require a sustained, prolonged effort in every forum available." Their efforts, he commented, were "just the start," a feeling echoed by a young gay lawyer on their legal team who, as he began his involvement in the case, thought, "This is the first step toward marriage equality. It happened today. Right now."[14]

In April Griffin, a public relations whiz kid who had long hobnobbed with celebrities, began wooing donors from Hollywood and the business world to help pay for a lawsuit, though it hadn't yet been decided if it would go forward. Griffin brought on a film team to document their efforts and allowed *New York Times* reporter Jo Becker to be embedded with an eye toward writing a book. Everyone involved seemed to feel the excitement of starting a brand-new movement. Black had suggested at OutGiving that gay people must demand full equality "for the first time," as though the incomplete achievements of the movement so far were the product of simply not making adequate demands. At one fund-raising event, Norman Lear, the legendary entertainment writer and producer who had founded the liberal group People for the American Way, became misty-eyed over the prospect of helping end marriage discrimination and announced that one day "we're going to look back and remember this as the beginning."[15]

Griffin and Black were passionate, impatient activists. And in that role, they could display the kind of blinkered, righteous urgency that can characterize popular awakenings, including a blind faith in their own creation myth. The previous month the Oscar-winning Black had panned gay leaders for prizing celebrity and ego, and had disparaged the futility of champagne dinners while speaking at a champagne dinner. Now his group was raking in money from Hollywood celebrities at a high-dollar fund-raiser, and teaming up with a superstar lawyer with an outsize personality. Although hardly populists themselves, Griffin, Black, and Olson were aligned with the populist energies and frustration of a younger generation now so used to tasting equality that many thought it could be secured by simply demanding it loudly enough. It was an increasingly popular belief, and one that, by this point in the struggle, was not entirely inaccurate. But as a criticism of the marriage movement, it demonstrated a lack of familiarity with the long game that had created this moment. Far from starting something brand-new, this Hollywood crew was seeking to advance a struggle that had been decades in the making, aiming at something for which movement strategists and an earlier generation of persistent gay marriage champions had paved the way.

By the end of April, armed with passion, ambition, money, connections, and talent, Griffin and Olson had decided to file suit. They created a new group called the American Foundation for Equal Rights (AFER), purposely named with neutral terminology that avoided branding itself as a gay rights group, the better to cast marriage equality as a broad, nonpartisan issue. With a single phone call from Olson, AFER secured David Boies as cocounsel in the case. The two lawyers had been on opposite sides of the notorious 2000 *Bush v. Gore* case that had landed George W. Bush in the White House, but their families had become friends in subsequent years. The optics of having two prominent lawyers who had symbolized opposite sides of the partisan divide were meant to make a strong statement that marriage equality was something that Americans on both sides of the political aisle could support—and were also meant to help generate media and public interest in the case and the issue, a critical ingredient of their plan.

The lawsuit, of course, needed plaintiffs. The people they chose had to be folks who had not already married during the 2008 window, or else they would lack legal standing to sue. Griffin reached out to his large network of gay friends, colleagues, and acquaintances. One couple that appeared on his radar was Paul Katami and Jeff Zarrillo of Burbank, who had been together nine years. The men had made a video mocking alarmist ads backing Proposition 8. They wanted to be married but, as they watched the Proposition 8 effort gain steam, had opted not to wed in California given the uncertainties of the legal status there. Another couple, Kris Perry and Sandy Stier, a lesbian pair from Berkeley, had also been together for nine years and had four children. Perry and Stier, who were friends of Griffin's, had married in 2004, and so their marriage had been invalidated by the court that August. Since they hadn't yet married again,

Chad Griffin (far right), who later became president of the Human Rights Campaign, conceived of the federal lawsuit against California's Proposition 8 in 2008. He secured attorney Ted Olson (next to Griffin), to lead the team, and David Boies (far left), who had argued before the Supreme Court opposite Olson regarding the disputed presidential election of 2000. The team recruited two same-sex couples as plaintiffs: (left to right) Sandy Stier and Kris Perry, and Jeff Zarrillo and Paul Katami.

they could have standing in the AFER suit. The couples talked over what involvement in the suit would mean. Perry and Stier assumed they would "sit quietly on the sidelines" as the court case proceeded, but they also knew that becoming plaintiffs in a case like this was a major commitment that could affect their work lives, their family's privacy, and their relationship. Both couples decided that joining the effort was one of the most worthwhile things they could do. They were in.[16]

Everything seemed to be falling into place. There remained, however, one important step. AFER hoped to get the blessing of the LGBTQ legal groups before moving forward. So Griffin reached out to Lambda

Legal and the ACLU of Southern California and invited their top staff to a confidential lunch meeting at Rob Reiner's Los Angeles home on May 14, 2009. Jennifer Pizer and Jon Davidson represented Lambda, and Ramona Ripston and Mark Rosenbaum represented the ACLU of Southern California, while AFER sent, in addition to the Reiners, Griffin, his business partner, Kristina Schake, the producer Bruce Cohen, and Ted Boutrous from Olson's firm. Griffin made the case that the time was right, the risks were minimal, and Olson's involvement would be instrumental in moving both public opinion and that of the justices. Boutrous argued that the filing of a federal marriage suit was virtually inevitable, and having Olson and this team at the helm was the best possible scenario.[17]

Lambda and the ACLU were unshaken in their opposition, explaining that the incremental strategy they had put in place was yielding results— indeed, was what got the movement to this point. They cited the victories in Massachusetts, Connecticut, Iowa, and Vermont, and noted that just a week before the present meeting, the governor of Maine had signed a law that would bring marriage equality to a fifth state, barring a voter reversal. This was impressive momentum, they argued, and the state-by-state approach must be allowed to take its course, since it was highly unlikely the Supreme Court would step in and recognize a national freedom to marry when only a handful of states allowed it. Public approval, another part of the big picture, was also marching forward. Although support for marriage equality had fallen in recent years, it was still more than 10 percentage points higher in Gallup polls than it had been in 2004, when voters in thirteen states chose to ban same-sex marriage. The risks of upending this successful approach, they argued, were substantial, as anyone who remembered the *Bowers* decision should realize. Pizer did not feel the Los Angeles group fully grasped the situation. Davidson perceived "a lot of disrespect" for the expertise and longevity of movement insiders. "Who are you?" he wondered to himself.[18]

Michele Reiner remembered the meeting as a "disaster."[19] Boutrous recalled being angered that his team was being asked to "just wait" but that he listened seriously to the views of the veteran gay lawyers. Consulting with Griffin and Olson, he considered every dimension of the case before quickly concluding that the federal lawsuit was the right path.[20] In a memo entitled "The Time is Now," the AFER legal team made its formal recommendation to Griffin. Inspired by King's 1963 "Letter from Birmingham Jail," they pointed out that in the 1967 *Loving* case, which ended bans on inter-racial marriage, the Supreme Court "did not wait for the South to change; it changed the South." With just 20 percent of the public supporting that decision, they argued, the Court had led rather than followed.[21]

The more relevant data point, in the view of the gay legal groups, was that at the time of the *Loving* decision, interracial marriage had been illegal in only sixteen states, just as when the 2003 *Lawrence* ruling struck down sodomy bans, only thirteen states had such bans, down from twenty-five when *Bowers* had upheld those laws seventeen years earlier.[22] This, the legal groups argued, was why more states needed to win marriage equality—at that time forty-six still banned it—before the Court was likely to act.[23]

The AFER leaders thought the gay legal groups were exaggerating the risks of a loss. Even in the worst-case scenario, the memo explained, the Court would throw the question back to the states, which was where gay advocates were urging that the battle be fought anyway. There was every-thing to gain, they thought, and little to lose.[24]

On May 22, AFER filed suit in the U.S. District Court for the Northern District of California. The case was called *Perry v. Schwarzenegger.* In an unusual step, Enrique Monagas, a gay associate lawyer at Olson's firm, Gibson, Dunn, and Crutcher, filed the complaint in person as part of AFER's commitment to keeping the suit secret until a press conference scheduled for the following week. Until then, when it could better control the media story that was sure to erupt, the group wanted to avoid making public any version of the ugly strategic disputes that had surfaced at the Reiners' home. California's Proposition 8, said the complaint, denied to same-sex couples "the basic liberties and equal protection under the law that are guaranteed by the Fourteenth Amendment to the United States Constitu-tion." As a result of the measure, the "state is stigmatizing gays and lesbians, as well as their children and families, and denying them the same dignity, respect, and stature afforded officially recognized opposite-sex family relationships."[25]

On May 27, the group held a press conference in downtown Los An-geles to announce the formation of AFER and the group's federal law-suit. Flanked by nearly two dozen American and California flags—and, by design, no rainbows—Griffin, the lawyers, and the plaintiffs took their positions before a room full of national media. "Ted and I, as everybody knows, have been on different sides in court on a couple of issues," Boies said dryly. "But this is not something that is a partisan issue. This is some-thing that is a civil rights issue."[26] The rhetorical formulation made little sense—civil rights issues had long also been partisan issues. But AFER was making a concerted effort to bring reachable conservatives over to the side of marriage equality. Responding to critics from the gay rights movement, some of whom went so far as to wonder if this card-carrying conservative was taking the case merely in order to throw it, Olson insisted that the plan was sound. "We feel that this is the right time," he told reporters. "When an individual comes to you and his or her constitutional rights are being violated, what do you tell them? Do you tell them yes I'm a lawyer, but I won't take your case? Do I tell them to go wait a year until the time is right? I don't think so."[27] The line was somewhat disingenuous, as this was not a situation where plaintiffs had organically sought out the legal help of Ted Olson's firm. As is often the case with impact litigation, advocates had recruited plaintiffs to move their issue forward. Olson had wanted child-less plaintiffs to avoid having to deal with the gay parenting debate. Ideally he would have wanted a teacher, a cop, and a shop owner—ordinary folks people could relate to. And Griffin and Schake had hoped to find some racial minorities to lend the face of diversity to their efforts and to help at-tract minority support. Those were not the plaintiffs they ended up with. Still, Olson repeatedly deployed the sentimental argument of not being able to say no to a plaintiff as a way of deflecting criticism over bringing the suit prematurely.[28]

That criticism was severe. Nan Hunter, the founding director of the ACLU's Lesbian and Gay Rights Project, called it a "reckless" step with a "significant chance of failure if the case reaches the U.S. Supreme Court." Hunter said that "one of the best examples of any aspect of the LGBT movement is the Roundtable" with its "very careful and deliberate, collab-orative" approach to impact litigation, and "to have someone come from out of the blue and upend that strategy was extremely frustrating."[29] Others piled on. "Federal court? Wow. Never thought of that," said Matt Coles, his words dripping with sarcasm.[30] Changing the world, he explained, "involves building blocks. You build constitutional principles alongside efforts at the societal and legislative levels. They're jumping over the process and going straight to the end. From where we sit, this is a very high-risk proposi-tion."[31] Pizer called it "risky and premature."[32] Kate Kendell of the National Center for Lesbian Rights called it a "very high-stakes move." She allowed that it could be "a total game changer," but if it went wrong, it could "have devastating consequences."[33] Court observers from outside the movement generally agreed, pointing out that the Bush years had made not only the Supreme Court but the bulk of circuit courts more conservative.[34] One called it a "dangerous ballgame,"[35] and another characterized it as a risky "poker move," given the difficulty of counting five friendly votes at the Supreme Court.[36]

The same day that AFER held its press conference announcing a federal lawsuit, nine major gay rights groups released a letter denouncing the idea of a federal lawsuit. The letter's signers said it was a response not to AFER's announcement but to a court ruling the previous day upholding Proposition 8. That suit, a challenge on procedural grounds to the ban's legality, had been brought by several of the parties who had been behind the original lawsuit that won marriage in California. The LGBTQ groups had been aware that if the state supreme court upheld Proposition 8, non-movement parties might have considered filing a federal lawsuit to have the ban struck down. And given their years of strategizing around an incremental approach, the movement groups feared the consequences of such a step.

The letter that was released in May 2009 was actually an update of a similar letter that had been released in June 2008, weeks after the initial California court win. In that document, entitled "Make Change, Not Lawsuits," nine groups, including the four main gay legal groups along with Freedom to Marry, the Human Rights Campaign, the Task Force, Equality Federation, and Gay and Lesbian Alliance Against Defamation, warned sharply against rushing to court in the wake of the California win. They were especially concerned about a federal challenge to state marriage bans, including any reactive measure that might arise in California. "Now that we've won marriage in California," the document read, "should we be bringing cases in other states or suing the federal government?" The answer, in a word, was no. "We all need to be smart about how we go about making progress on this issue," wrote the lawyers. Certainly activists should use the court's "brilliant reasoning and stirring language" to move public opinion, push state legislators forward, and perhaps bring suits in select states where courts might be ready to hand down a positive ruling. But only after winning "in a critical mass of states" should advocates "turn to Congress and the federal courts."[37]

Pointing out that marriage suits had been lost in five states (Arizona, Indiana, Washington, New York, and Maryland), the 2008 document had made clear why its authors thought that suing willy-nilly—especially at the federal level—was a dangerous idea: "One thing couples shouldn't do is just sue the federal government or, if they are from other states, go sue their home state or their employer to recognize their marriage or open up the health plan. Pushing the federal government before we have a critical mass of states recognizing same-sex relationships or suing in states where the courts aren't ready is likely to get us bad rulings. Bad rulings will make it much more difficult for us to win marriage, and will certainly make it take much longer."[38]

The May 2009 update of the previous year's letter was designed to issue the same caution in anticipation of the court upholding Proposition 8. But, despite claims by the letter's signers that it was not a response to the AFER suit, many assumed that it must be, since it came out the same day as AFER's announcement and opposed precisely the kind of lawsuit AFER had filed. In any case, the letter functioned as a retort to AFER and to Olson's eyebrow-raising rationale for moving forward with a lawsuit: that it was unfair to "look into the eyes" of plaintiffs and tell them they must wait.

Yet once the AFER suit was filed, the gay legal groups knew there was no sense in fighting it. Instead, they decided to cooperate and tried to salvage what alliances they could. If they failed to seize momentum generated by those outside the movement, the gay legal groups stood to lose control of their strategy—a reprise of what had happened after the Newsom weddings in 2004. So they dove in. They joined conference calls to share their knowledge, prepared legal briefs, even agreed to participate in a moot court session with the Olson legal team.[39] Kate Kendell told Olson during a phone meeting that she was anointing him "an honorary lesbian." Although Kendell had raised concerns about the Olson suit and signed the letter opposing federal litigation, she also saw the potential value in this enormous step. "Shannon and I thought it was pretty effing brilliant," she said. "Even in our wildest imaginings, we had not considered that the most celebrated conservative attorney would be on our side. We thought, if anyone can win, it would be this team." Kendell conceded that part of the resistance to the Olson suit was a feeling among movement lawyers that if anyone was going to win marriage nationwide, it should be the legal groups that "have been toiling for decades on this work." But she ultimately welcomed the entry of straight supporters. "In every civil rights movement," she said, "you have to have unlikely allies show up to provide a whole new level of fuel and attention. I felt like that was exactly the moment we were in."[40]

At the end of June, however, came a development that threw the fragile alliance back into disarray. The federal judge assigned to the case, Vaughn Walker, surprised almost everyone by ordering a full-blown trial instead of the more minimalist legal proceeding that could have decided the case through court motions. Neither Olson nor his opposing counsel, Charles Cooper, had wanted a trial, preferring to proceed as quickly as possible to the Supreme Court. But there was no changing the judge's mind. When the gay legal groups heard the news, the stakes grew even higher. Now, it seemed, the AFER case would prompt a national airing, in a federal court of law, of nearly all the questions around marriage and sexual orientation that they had been working for years to bring to the American public's attention in an accessible way. The case was quickly coming to look historic. And the LGBTQ lawyers who had put the pieces in motion were intent on having a place at the table.[41]

Immediately Lambda, along with NCLR, the ACLU, and the City of San Francisco—which had had the experience of litigating on this issue when it defended the Newsom marriages—sought to join the case as interveners. "We think it will be very helpful to Judge Walker and the ultimate resolution of the questions in the case for the litigation to have the benefit of the presence of the community in all its diversity," Jennifer Pizer of Lambda told the press.[42] The Olson team slammed the idea, wanting to keep control of the case for their plaintiffs, and resenting the efforts to intervene from groups that had lambasted the case in the first place. In a fuming letter of opposition addressed to the gay groups and released to the press, Griffin expressed his dismay over the intervention effort. "You have unrelentingly and unequivocally acted to undermine this case even before it was filed," he wrote. "In light of this, it is inconceivable that you would zealously and effectively litigate this case if you were successful in intervening." What enraged him further was that Griffin felt AFER had reached out to the groups for input notwithstanding their hostility to the case moving forward. They had bashed the case, and here they were trying to join it.[43]

While AFER opposed the intervention, they were less vociferous in objecting to the City of San Francisco's effort to join the suit. They recognized that they might look unreasonable if they sought to block all parties from participating, and the city was the least objectionable.[44] Judge Walker ultimately denied the request by Lambda, NCLR, and the ACLU, explaining that these groups were not in a sufficiently different position to warrant their added involvement, which could cause "interference and delay." But he allowed San Francisco to join the case, reasoning that the city brought a governmental perspective that the other parties lacked. The trial—the first test in federal court of whether states could ban gay marriage—would begin in January.

— 11 —

"Without Any Rational Justification"

PROPOSITION 8 ON TRIAL

THE *PERRY* TRIAL OPENED ON MONDAY, JANUARY 11. THAT WEEK, AS part of the public relations campaign to accompany the litigation, Olson published an article in *Newsweek* laying out his argument. While the essay contained elements of the case gay marriage advocates had been honing for years—about the dignity of equality, the parallels to the black civil rights quest, and the inadequacy of civil unions—Olson's article was also designed to explain his position to conservatives and win them over. His "The Conservative Case for Gay Marriage" was essentially an echo of the gay marriage arguments articulated first by Randy Lloyd and then by Andrew Sullivan. "Same-sex unions promote the values conservatives prize," Olson wrote. "Marriage is one of the basic building blocks of our neighborhoods and our nation," involving a "stable bond between two individuals who work to create a loving household and a social and economic partnership." Marriage is to be encouraged, he argued, because the commitments spouses make "provide benefits not only to themselves but also to their families and communities," and in compelling people to think beyond just themselves, marriage "establishes a formal investment in the well-being of society." Marriage by same-sex couples fits the bill, and "conservatives should celebrate this, rather than lament it."[1]

With the groundwork laid, Olson was ready to take his case to trial. The court, in San Francisco's federal building, was just blocks from city hall, where Mayor Newsom had helped launch the Winter of Love five years earlier by authorizing the marriage of Del Martin and Phyllis Lyon. (Martin had died in August 2008 at the age of eighty-seven, just two months after the pair became the first same-sex couple to legally wed in California, amid a crowd of well-wishers a thousand strong. Lyon said that her deep loss was lessened somewhat by "knowing we were able to enjoy the ultimate rite of love and commitment before she passed.")[2]

The plaintiffs Olson was representing were the two couples recruited by AFER—Perry and Stier, Katami and Zarrillo—and the city of San Francisco. The defendants were California's governor, Arnold Schwarzenegger, and attorney general, Jerry Brown, both of whom had chosen not to defend the law but were still named in the suit, and ProtectMarriage.com, the official proponent of Proposition 8, who had intervened to defend the measure when the state authorities opted out. Their lawyer was Charles Cooper, who had defended Hawaii's same-sex marriage ban back in 1997 as part of the state's appeal of earlier decisions.[3]

The job of Olson's team was to persuade Judge Vaughn Walker that Proposition 8 was based on nothing more than animus toward gays and lesbians. The lawyers would use a two-pronged approach. First, they would argue that the heightened scrutiny standard should apply to their challenge, since gays and lesbians had a history of suffering discrimination for an "immutable" trait. Second, they would argue that the law served no legitimate purpose that could justify such an infringement, regardless of which standard of review the justices applied. That meant going through all the possible explanations for the gay marriage ban and showing they were irrational.

The defendants would need to show that Proposition 8 had a sound purpose, demonstrate what that purpose was, and explain why barring gay marriage was necessary to achieving it. The arguments they used to make this case were threefold. First, they would argue that the purpose of marriage was to regulate procreation, making it reasonable to exclude same-sex couples, who couldn't create biological offspring of their own. Second, they would claim that expanding how the public viewed marriage by altering its parameters could hamper the state's ability to regulate procreation by destabilizing the institution altogether. This was the argument that if gay people could marry, straight people might not, since they might come to view marriage as no longer an essential prerequisite for a procreative union. As a result, children would be more likely to grow up in unstable environments. Finally, they would insist that something as important as marriage ought to be defined by the people through the democratic process, not the courts.

Underneath these three main points swirled many smaller issues that would be deployed as supporting arguments. Disputing the idea that being gay or lesbian was a genuine, unchangeable identity, Proposition 8 supporters would argue that the gay marriage ban did not, in fact, deprive anyone of rights, since anyone was free to get married so long as he or she abided by the rule applied equally to everyone: marry someone of the opposite sex. Even if letting gays wed was a good idea, they would further argue, such a right was not in the Constitution, and in fact the nature of marriage as a male-female union was a long-standing tradition that should not be changed without great caution and good reason. In addition to claims that gay marriage could destabilize straight unions and threaten optimal child-rearing environments, gay marriage opponents would argue that children raised by same-sex couples faced added risks of harm, something anti-gay advocates had been trying to establish for years, with little success and no evidence. Finally, throughout the trial Proposition 8 lawyers would try to show that gays and lesbians did not suffer from a history of discrimination or political powerlessness—an effort to ensure that the judge did not apply heightened scrutiny to the plaintiffs' claims.

That Monday morning, hundreds gathered in the San Francisco fog outside the courtroom holding signs and chanting in support of, or opposition to, same-sex marriage. Inside, the gallery was packed with press and spectators. As they would on each day of the trial, Olson and Cooper, friends from their days serving together in the Reagan Justice Department, embraced before the proceedings began.[4]

In his opening arguments, Olson said the case was about "marriage and equality." The plaintiffs, he said, "are being denied both the right to marry and the right to equality under the law." From the start, he quoted the powerful language of the Supreme Court in past cases on the importance of marriage itself, an effort to tie views about the dignity of both marriage and same-sex love to constitutional guarantees of equality. "The right to marriage," he described the Court as saying, is "one of the most vital personal rights essential to the orderly pursuit of happiness," a "basic civil right," an "expression of emotional support and public commitment, the exercise of spiritual unity, and the fulfillment of one's self." In short, in

the "words of the highest court in the land, marriage is the most important relation in life, and of fundamental importance for all individuals."[5]

Judge Walker interrupted early and often with questions on all aspects
of Olson's points. Never losing his footing, Olson parried the questions and
continued to make eloquent arguments about the harm that marriage discrimination visited on gays and lesbians. "What Prop 8 does is label gay and
lesbian persons as different, inferior, unequal and disfavored," he said. Banning
gay marriage "stigmatizes gays and lesbians. It classifies them as outcasts. It
causes needless and unrelenting pain and isolation and humiliation." Tying his
argument to citations of earlier Supreme Court rulings, he said that Proposition 8 "ended the dream of marriage, the most important relation in life, for
the plaintiffs and hundreds of thousands of Californians."[6]

For the defense, Charles Cooper had a tall order competing with the
inspirational language of love and equality that gay marriage proponents
had in their arsenal. Cooper was consequently reliant on a more quotidian
set of arguments despite being able to draw on the principles of popular
democracy and longstanding tradition. All Proposition 8 had done, he argued, was "restore and preserve the traditional definition of marriage as
the union of a man and a woman," something that 52 percent of California
voters had decided to back. This restricted view of marriage, he argued,
was "a definition that has prevailed in virtually every society in recorded
history, since long before the advent of modern religions." Indeed, only
five states in the Union allowed gay people to marry, and California had
done so only because four judges voted against three others to override the
will of the people.[7]

If democracy and tradition were Cooper's main defenses against court-
imposed change, he also offered a proactive argument for the state's interest
in opposite-sex marriage. "The purpose of the institution of marriage," he
said, "is to promote procreation and to channel narrowly procreative sexual
activity between men and women into stable, enduring unions." Marriage,
he insisted, was a "pro-child" institution that stood to be "deinstitutional-
ized" if it was opened up to same-sex unions. Pressed on how allowing gay
marriage could undermine the "pro-child" purpose of straight-only marriage, Cooper said the risk was the "gradual transformation of marriage
from a pro-child societal institution into a private relationship designed
simply to provide adult couples with what the plaintiffs say is personal
fulfillment."[8] It was a sinister echo of the old canard that homosexuality

was primarily about indulging individual selfishness, while somehow heterosexual pairing was about contributing to the greater good.

But showing that same-sex marriage actually harmed society and was therefore a reasonable thing to prohibit was going to be tough. At a hearing the previous fall held to determine if the case would go to trial, Judge Walker had asked the lawyer how allowing gay couples to marry "would harm opposite-sex marriages." Given the centrality of that question to the case and to the whole decades-long debate about gay marriage, it was a question Cooper should have been prepared to answer. Yet he had shocked many observers when he appeared not to have a response. He had first tried to avoid the question by saying it was not "legally relevant." He then turned to an argument that social conservatives had been honing for the past dozen or so years. Previously, marriage equality opponents had claimed that procreation lay at the heart of marriage, and hence same-sex unions didn't fit. But this crude reasoning was fatally flawed, since procreation was never a requirement for marriage, and surely no state policy was necessary to encourage people to have procreative sex, which happened all the time. So a refinement of this position emerged, which added the qualifier "responsible" to "procreation." Society, went the new argument, has an interest in encouraging heterosexual sex to occur only inside the bounds of a marriage since children can result from such sex, and children do best when raised by two parents who are committed to each other for the long haul. The state, in other words, has an interest in promoting marital sex as a social norm, and discouraging extramarital sex as taboo, but only for heterosexuals. Since same-sex sex can't result in procreation, society's interest in "responsible procreation" is not served by calling a same-sex union a "marriage." The trouble was that this argument still failed to answer a central question that the judge continued to ask Cooper: Though "responsible procreation" may demonstrate why marriage was important for straights, it hardly explained why it was necessary to exclude gays. "What is the harm to the procreative purpose or function of marriage," the judge wanted to know, "of permitting same-sex marriages?" And how was barring same-sex marriage necessary to fulfilling the "responsible procreation" purpose of opposite-sex marriage?[9]

Repeatedly pressed during the hearing, Cooper had finally responded, "Your Honor, my answer is: I don't know. I don't know." Seconds later, he had tried to elaborate, perhaps recognizing the enormous consequences of what he had just admitted—that he couldn't say why the state had a compelling interest in preserving its gay marriage ban. It wasn't so much that he didn't know the answer, he ventured, as that the consequences of something as novel as gay marriage were still unknown, and therefore too risky. "When dealing with radical proposals for change," he said, Californians were entitled to proceed "incrementally, to move with caution and to adopt a wait-and-see attitude." Same-sex marriage was so new, he suggested, that its wider implications and its "impact on marriage over time can't possibly be known now."[10]

At trial, showing the harms wrought by gay marriage was still proving tough, but showing the harms wrought by barring gay couples from marriage was easy. And no one made the case more powerfully at trial than the plaintiffs themselves. Kris Perry described marriage as "the most important decision I was going to make as an adult" and said, "There's something so humiliating about everybody knowing that you want to make that decision and you don't get to." She recounted showing up with Stier for a football game at their children's high school. When other parents greeted them on the bleachers, all she could think was, "They are all married and I'm not." She told the court that when their 2004 license was revoked, her first thought was, "I'm not good enough to marry."[11]

Stier said that she, too, had felt "outraged and hurt" when she saw the letter from the state invalidating their marriage. But the impact, she said, was not limited to her and Perry. "I felt like everybody who had come to our wedding and gone out of their way and brought us lovely gifts and celebrated with us must feel a level of humiliation themselves, too." The comment helped demonstrate how the harms of stigma and discrimination affected not just the immediate victims but the broader community, and suggested how marriage—whether for same-sex or opposite-sex couples—was a positive good for society, as it wove into its web of support many more people than just the married couple. Stier described the constant need to explain to people her relationship to Perry and to her own children. Picking them up at school, she would have to say she was their stepmother or the domestic partner of their mother. The term, she explained, was not commonly understood. And even if it had been, it hardly described their true bond. "We have a loving, committed relationship," she said. "We are not business partners. We are not social partners. We are not glorified roommates. We are—we are married. We want to be married."[12]

Plaintiff Jeff Zarrillo added yet another layer of humanity to the trial. Asked to talk about his relationship with Paul Katami, he called him the "love of my life" and said, "I love him probably more than I love myself." He quoted the traditional wedding vows, committing to sticking things out in sickness and health, for richer or poorer, until death. His voice cracked with emotion. "I would do anything for him," he said. "And I want nothing more than to marry him."[13]

For the next two weeks, an extraordinary array of the nation's top scholars on marriage, family, and anti-gay discrimination endured hours of questioning from both sides as expert witnesses. The testimony began with Nancy Cott, a Harvard historian and author of numerous books about marriage, women, and family. Cott had supported the marriage equality effort since Mary Bonauto first reached out to her in 2000 as part of the effort to secure marriage rights in Vermont. Bonauto had come to believe it was imperative to show that marriage had always been continuously changing, and thus same-sex marriage was continuous with that history rather than a radical departure from it. Cott's scholarly work, which Bonauto had admired since her college days, made this crystal clear. So Bonauto had called her up and found her eager to help. Cott had testified in Vermont and also had helped recruit the twenty-five other experts who signed the scholars' brief for the *Goodridge* case. Now an expert in *Perry,* she explained how marriage as practiced in America was a modern and even innovative institution, since much of the globe in the years before the American Revolution embraced polygamy rather than monogamy. Simple history, she showed, proved Cooper's assertions inaccurate when he claimed that marriage had been limited to a man and a woman universally "across history, across customs, across society." Echoing what the scholar E. J. Graff had laid out in her 1999 book *What Is Marriage For?* Cott concluded that the roles and purposes of marriage— maintaining social order, forming stable households, distributing economic benefits, and regulating procreation, to name a few—had never been constant but had always been evolving. Rebutting Cooper's suggestion that allowing gay couples to marry would make the institution "adult-centered," Cott said that marriage "has always been at least as much about supporting adults as it has been about supporting minors." Marriage is broad, she concluded, but also unique. "There is nothing like marriage except marriage."[14]

Yale historian George Chauncey, who along with Cott had signed the historians' brief for the *Lawrence* case, chronicled a century of anti-gay discrimination in America, showing how the degrading campaign to pass Proposition 8 fit squarely within that history. His purpose was to demonstrate both the animus at the root of the marriage ban and the long record of discrimination that ought to trigger heightened scrutiny.[15] Lee Badgett, an economist at UCLA's Williams Institute and the University of Massachusetts, Amherst, echoed testimony by the city of San Francisco that marriage discrimination created financial burdens for the city and affected the state's economy, and that allowing same-sex marriage had no negative impact on heterosexual marriage. Gregory Herek, a psychology professor, testified about the harmful impact of social stigma, such as that created by Proposition 8, on gay men and lesbians and their families.[16]

Since a crucial sticking point in debate over gay marriage was the impact it could have on children, the Olson team had hired one of the world's top experts on child development to unpack the social science evidence. Michael Lamb, a psychologist who was head of Cambridge University's Department of Social and Developmental Psychology and had published more than 500 articles, described the overwhelming scholarly consensus that growing up with same-sex parents did not put children in harm's way. Under cross-examination, defense attorney David Thompson cited a study purporting to show that having same-sex parents raised risks for kids, but Lamb pointed out that none of the children studied had actually been raised from birth by an intact same-sex couple. In a trick that social conservatives had been playing for years, research conducted on children of single and divorced parents was used interchangeably with research on households headed by two adults of the same sex. In both cases, families lacked either a mother or a father, creating a convenient talking point that, superficially, sounded like common sense: children need a mother *and* a father. In reality, scores of studies showed that, so long as additional factors were held constant—the most important of them being family stability—kids with same-sex parents fared no worse than those with opposite-sex parents.[17]

While the defense failed to show that children in same-sex households fared worse than their peers, they did show something else: the shocking inhumanity of raising that point in the first place. After all, no other group had to demonstrate their intent or ability to procreate before gaining the right to marry, or prove that they would turn out perfectly adjusted kids before they enjoyed the right to parent. As Judge Walker had mused to Cooper during the pre-trial hearing, the last marriage he had performed involved a ninety-five-year-old groom and an eighty-three-year-old bride. "I did not demand that they prove that they intended to engage in procreative activity," Walker had told the attorney. "Now, was I missing something?"[18] Giggles had rippled across the courtroom. But the relentless demand that gay families pass a litmus test that no other group was required to take could be seen as evidence itself of the pattern of discrimination the plaintiffs claimed gays and lesbians have historically suffered. Hour after hour after hour, Thompson drilled Lamb on whether children with lesbian mothers had inferior cognitive skills, lower grade point averages, lower IQ scores, less resistance to drug use, and other adverse outcomes. The "cognitive competence" of children with two heterosexual parents, Thompson demanded to know, is "higher than the children of the lesbian mother families, correct?" When Lamb challenged the statistical significance of the research being cited, Thompson snapped back, "Well, it's certainly a worse outcome, isn't it?" After four hours of cross-examination, Judge Walker signaled that enough was enough: when Thompson referenced research claiming that lesbian parents had trouble "setting limits" for their children, Walker said, "This is not the only area in which setting limits would be helpful."[19]

It was, ironically, a witness for the defense who laid bare the double standard being applied to gay families. David Blankenhorn was one of two experts who ended up testifying for ProtectMarriage.com. At least four other scholars whom the defense had initially listed as expert witnesses withdrew at the eleventh hour under mysterious circumstances. The defense claimed that the main reason for the withdrawals was witnesses' fear of harassment at the hands of their pro-gay antagonists, a fear that increased after Walker announced that he was considering videotaping the trial. Yet it was later found that the pre-trial depositions had thoroughly rattled these witnesses, casting doubt on their expertise, eviscerating their arguments, and in some cases revealing that their positions were more favorable to the plaintiffs than the defense. Blankenhorn, one of the only defense experts left standing, would turn out to present the same problem. Blankenhorn was not an academic. As founding president of the Institute for American Values, he had written books on family and the role of fatherhood in contributing to child well-being. But he had authored only one scholarly publication: his master's thesis on nineteenth-century British cabinetmakers' unions. Judge Walker narrowly accepted him as an expert witness, commenting, "Were this a jury trial, I think the question might be a close one."[20]

Blankenhorn's testimony came just days after defense lawyers had spent hours trying to wrench from Michael Lamb a concession that children of same-sex parents had worse outcomes than their peers. Yet when David Boies put to the defense's star witness the question "Are you aware of any studies showing that children raised from birth by a gay or lesbian couple have worse outcomes than children raised from birth by two biological parents?" Blankenhorn said no. Boies then asked him to confirm that, "in fact, the studies show that all other things being equal, two adoptive parents raising a child from birth will do as well as two biological parents raising a child from birth, correct?" Up until this point Blankenhorn had spent hours locked in a tense battle of wits with Boies, angering both the lawyer and Judge Walker by repeatedly refusing to give yes-or-no answers without elaboration (which is not an uncommon phenomenon with expert witnesses). To this question Blankenhorn once again refused to answer Boies with a simple yes or no—but this time there was a twist. It was not true, Blankenhorn said, that children of adoptive parents did as well as their peers, and that was because they actually did better. Outcomes were often superior because of the rigorous screening process prospective adoptive parents were required to undergo. Likewise, outcomes were sometimes better among children of same-sex parents who used assisted reproduction, presumably because they had to jump through extra hoops to become parents, making unwanted or unplanned children less likely. Blankenhorn's testimony was turning out to be a boon for the plaintiffs. Toward the end, Boies quoted back to Blankenhorn a passage he had previously written and asked him if he still agreed with it. He did. The passage was: "We would be *more* American on the day we permitted same-sex marriage than we were on the day before."[21]

The defense's other witness, Kenneth Miller, was a professor of government at Claremont McKenna College whose testimony sought to show that gay people were not politically powerless. Boies spent nine hours cross-examining Miller, who eventually conceded that he had not read very much on the topic he was testifying about. The thin showing of the defense's witnesses prompted one journalist covering the trial to write, "Memo to Proposition 8 defense team: perhaps have the defense experts read a few more books and scholarly articles before they take the stand."[22]

In June, finally, Judge Walker held closing arguments. The judge had delayed the last step of the trial to give him time to review the evidence presented to him, but the break had dragged on as the parties resisted submitting various documents as part of the process. Now, for closing arguments, the press had returned in full force. Mayor Newsom sat in the front row. Olson spoke first. "We conclude this trial, Your Honor, where we began," he said. The state of California had rewritten its constitution to take away from gay people the fundamental right to marry. It had placed same-sex couples into a "special disfavored category where their most intimate personal relationships are not valid, not recognized, and second rate." A true understanding of what Proposition 8 was really about, asserted Olson, came not from the carefully crafted legal arguments put forward in court but from the political campaign that its advocates launched to persuade the voters of California. What "animated Proposition 8," he said with disdain, was the notion that it was necessary to "protect our children" from learning that gay marriage is okay. The underlying idea was that being gay was different, inferior, and not normal. (The Olson team called as a "hostile" witness Bill Tam, an original Proposition 8 proponent who, like several expert witnesses, had dropped out of the suit on the eve of the trial. A leader of California's Chinese evangelical community, Tam had linked homosexuality to pedophilia, incest, prostitution and moral decay, at one point citing "the Internet" as his source, giving David Boies a delicious opportunity in court to link Proposition 8 to the bigotry that most of its defenders were straining to downplay.) Clearly, Olson concluded in his closing remarks, the law was based on "discriminatory animus," which was not acceptable under the Constitution. "Mr. Blankenhorn is absolutely right. The day that we end that, we will be more American."[23]

Against this onslaught of arguments both logical and emotional, the defense's case withered. Try as they might, defense attorneys had little to offer Judge Walker. "The historical record leaves no doubt," Cooper said in his closing arguments, "that the central purpose of marriage in virtually all societies and at all times has been to channel potentially procreative sexual relationships into enduring stable unions to increase the likelihood that any offspring will be raised by the man and woman who brought them into the world." He went on to say that marriage is "uniquely imbued with the public interest."

But the judge cut him off, asking whether people really decided to get married because they wanted to serve the public interest. "When one enters into a marriage, you don't say, Oh, boy, I'm going to be able to benefit society by getting married." Instead, what you think is, "I'm going to get a life partner." Walker's retort helped upend the narrative of social conservatives that marriage (like the military and the church) is something that straight individuals embrace for purely selfless reasons, rather than for how it serves them—a vein of thought Cooper had tapped into when he argued that same-sex marriage would turn marriage into an adult-centered institution.

While the nation awaited Judge Walker's decision, two other important rulings were handed down. On July 8, 2010, Judge Joseph Tauro ruled in both *Gill v. Office of Personnel Management,* the Defense of Marriage Act challenge brought by Gay and Lesbian Advocates and Defenders, and *Commonwealth of Massachusetts v. U.S. Department of Health and Human Services,* the related challenge brought by Martha Coakley's office. In the Coakley suit, Judge Tauro found that "DOMA imposes an unconstitutional condition on the receipt of federal funding," and that the federal government, "by enacting and enforcing DOMA, plainly encroaches upon the firmly entrenched province of the state, and, in doing so, offends the Tenth Amendment. For that reason," he concluded in granting the plaintiffs summary judgment, "the statute is invalid."[24]

While the judge's ruling in Coakley's case was heavy on process, his *Gill* ruling handily dispatched each substantive argument that gay marriage opponents had offered. First Tauro refuted Congress's claim that DOMA was necessary for "defending and nurturing heterosexual marriage." Not only was reserving marriage for one group at the expense of another an avowedly supremacist—and therefore unconstitutional—goal, but, as Tauro noted, DOMA didn't even achieve it, and couldn't logically be expected to. In dry language that seemed to exude tacit amusement at the absurdity of DOMA's rationale—that preventing gays from being able to marry would make straights more likely to—the court deemed such a causal link to be essentially a non sequitur: "DOMA cannot possibly encourage Plaintiffs to marry members of the opposite sex because Plaintiffs are *already* married to members of the same sex." The court found it impossible to understand the logic, asserted by DOMA's defenders, that denying benefits to same-sex spouses could somehow encourage gay people to marry members of the opposite sex—essentially to turn them straight. Recall that the 1996 House of Representatives report on DOMA had cited "encouraging heterosexuality" as one of the important governmental interests the law would advance. By 2010, few people continued to believe that any such thing was possible, much less desirable. And encouraging responsible procreation was not a sound basis for banning same-sex marriage because, Tauro wrote, procreation had never been a required ingredient of marriage. Tauro noted that even Justice Scalia had made this point, in his *Lawrence* dissent. Scalia, of course, had done so to issue a warning: eliminating moral disapproval as a basis for passing laws, such as the sodomy bans in question in *Lawrence,* left many such laws with no remaining justification. It was with some irony that Tauro cited Scalia's dissent in his own ruling in favor of federal recognition of gay marriages.[25]

Tauro then panned the claim that DOMA was designed to create "uniformity" in how the federal government defines marriage. The idea, he wrote, "strains credulity." For one thing, even if the law appeared to create uniformity on the face of things, in practice it actually created chaos, with couples married in one state not knowing if their marriage, or even their parental rights, would be recognized when they crossed a state line. For another, the legislation marked "a stark and anomalous departure" from the federal government's customary deference to state marital determinations, just as the Bonauto team's research had uncovered. The only conclusion a rational observer could draw from all this was that with DOMA, Congress had passed a law singling out same-sex relationships "for the one purpose that lies entirely outside of legislative bounds, to disadvantage a group of which it disapproves."[26]

Reflecting one of the most important social developments on the path to marriage equality, the ruling dwelled for a key moment on the effort by anti-gay opponents to cast gay people as fundamentally different, something the Supreme Court's *Romer* ruling had declared impermissible as a basis for making legal distinctions and which the gay rights movement had long recognized as an impediment to equal treatment. Creating or exaggerating differentness was a time-tested way to dehumanize unpopular minorities, further eroding support for their rights by corroding the natural links of empathy that otherwise tie humans together. This Judge Tauro would not allow. Creating separate classes of married couples based upon whether they were of the same or different sexes "is to create a distinction without meaning," he wrote. And when a court can find "no reason to believe that the disadvantaged class is different" in any relevant way from others in the same position, the court "may conclude that it is only irrational prejudice that motivates the challenged classification."[27]

Both of Tauro's rulings were stayed pending appeal, but the twin decisions were a decisive blow against marriage discrimination—the first time a federal court had struck down the Defense of Marriage Act.

The next month, as a national CNN poll found for the first time that a majority of Americans favored same-sex marriage, Judge Walker handed down his decision in the Proposition 8 suit. The ruling was a stinging rebuke to decades of emotionally driven opposition to gay equality and denigration of same-sex love. It drew even greater power from resting on a thorough federal trial litigated and ruled on by respected Reagan-Bush conservatives. (Judge Walker had been appointed to the bench by George H. W. Bush. His original nomination by Ronald Reagan had been held up, ironically, over concerns by Democrats that he was biased against gays. It was later confirmed that Judge Walker was himself gay, something defenders of Proposition 8 unsuccessfully tried to use to vacate his ruling.) "Proposition 8 cannot withstand any level of scrutiny under the Equal Protection Clause," Walker wrote in a 136-page decision. "Excluding same-sex couples from marriage is simply not rationally related to a legitimate state interest." Specifically, Walker concluded that Proposition 8 "does not make it more likely that opposite-sex couples will marry and raise offspring biologically related to both parents," dealing another blow—after Judge Tauro's—to the "responsible procreation" argument. The plaintiffs, he found, had "demonstrated by overwhelming evidence" that Proposition 8 violated their due process and equal protection rights. He was persuaded that the campaign to pass Proposition 8 was based on nothing more than moral disapproval, fear, and bias against gay people, and was "without any rational justification." The measure "was premised on the belief that same-sex couples simply are not as good as opposite-sex couples" and that "opposite-sex couples are morally superior to same-sex couples," neither of which, the judge said, citing *Romer* and *Lawrence,* was a "proper basis on which to legislate."[28]

The judge stayed his decision pending appeal; the battle for marriage equality would now advance to the next rung on the legal ladder. But Walker's ruling had put the dignity of gay love, and its disparagement by anti-gay opponents, at the center of the case for marriage equality.

═ 12 ═

"A Risk Well Worth Taking"

EDIE WINDSOR AND

WINNING MARRIAGE IN NEW YORK

THE LGBTQ LEGAL GROUPS HAD OPPOSED THE SUIT BY THE AMERICAN Foundation for Equal Rights, seeking to join it only after it was filed and they determined there was little else they could do but add their weight to the effort. The groups had fervently debated the more incremental step of challenging the Defense of Marriage Act. And yet when Gay and Lesbian Advocates and Defenders went forward with filing such a suit, that hardly assured that other parties wouldn't press ahead with their own lawsuits. Ordinary couples faced extraordinary pain on a daily basis when their marriages were rebuffed by the federal government, and they became increasingly likely to sue as more states legalized same-sex marriage and more Americans became aware of the fight for equality, especially after the high-profile setback of Proposition 8's passage.

One month before GLAD submitted its petition in the *Gill* case, Edie Windsor, nearing her eightieth birthday, suffered a wrenching loss when, after a forty-year engagement and two years of marriage, Thea Spyer died at age seventy-seven. Spyer had been diagnosed with multiple sclerosis in 1975, but it hadn't changed their relationship one ounce. If anything, the disease gave the pair a heightened zest for their love and their lives, which continued to include glamorous travel and socializing. And the two women who had begun their relationship dancing so long into the night that Windsor had worn a hole in her stocking continued to dance every chance they could, eventually dancing with the aid of a wheelchair—

Windsor would sit in Spyer's lap as they zipped around the dance floor.[1] "We never danced together that we weren't at some point yelling, 'I love you. God, I love you!'" Windsor recalled some years after Spyer's death.[2]

Windsor's path from community outsider to engaged activist was illustrative of the journey to awakening taken by many gays and lesbians of her era. Although Windsor had reacted coolly to Stonewall when she first brushed past it that June weekend in 1969, the years of gay consciousness and activism that followed the uprising—so much of it swirling right around her Fifth Avenue apartment—soon inspired her to further involvement with the gay community. Having initially dismissed the event as the work of misfits and queens with little relevance to her life, she eventually absorbed the significance of their resistance. "When Stonewall happened, that was the beginning of my looking and seeing who they really were," she said of the gay and transgender rioters. She watched as gays and lesbians and gender-nonconforming people around her came out and began to live less furtively. She recognized that a community of which she was inevitably a part was saying no to intimidation and violence and shame. "They were finally not going to take this kind of abuse," she said. Some years later, she loaned her convertible to the gay pride parade, a way of stepping gently into the fray.[3]

In the 1980s the pair got involved with several lesbian social and advocacy groups. One was based in East Hampton, near where they shared a vacation house. The East End Gay Organization was primarily a social group for lesbians, with an annual seasonal kickoff party each Memorial Day weekend, sometimes held at Windsor and Spyer's house. But the group also engaged in political and charitable work. At one point members took a vote on whether they preferred civil unions or civil marriage as a movement priority. Civil unions won. Windsor was part of the cohort that thought marriage itself should be a paramount goal, so she helped start a committee to educate people about the differences between civil unions and marriage. "The feeling for many people at the time," she recalled, was that civil unions were "all that was possible. They would never get marriage."[4]

Men and women of the gay community often dwelled in separate worlds in the early years of gay activism, butting heads over politics and priorities or simply keeping to their own as the natural result of the search for partners. "Gay men had all of the big events," remembered Windsor;

"lesbians didn't have any money," and "rarely did the groups meet." Then came the AIDS epidemic, which shattered the community. The disease disproportionately infected gay men. But as Windsor recalled, "The lesbians came pouring in to pick up the garbage, to clean the floors, to do serious caretaking," something that soon resonated with the straight world, as the display of new levels of care and commitment undercut views of gays as carefree, irresponsible hedonists. It brought gay men and lesbians together in unprecedented ways as well. "My sense of community grew in the midst of this tragedy," Windsor recounted. She understood anew "not just [that] we belong to each other but [that] we have to take care of each other."[5]

Windsor spent decades as Spyer's primary caretaker, lifting her in and out of the pool to get her exercise, devoting hours to getting her ready for bed or dressed to leave the house in the morning; it must have made the AIDS years that much more personal to the couple. By 2007, after marriage equality lawsuits had failed in New York and New Jersey, Spyer's condition was growing worse. When doctors told her she might have one year left, the two decided they had some unfinished business that was very important to both of them: getting legally married. Despite the enormous burden of travel—Spyer was by now paralyzed from the neck down—they decided to marry in Toronto, where same-sex marriage had been legal since 2003.[6] Given their age and Spyer's health, the trip was not easy. A small entourage of friends and aides attended to help move medical equipment, the wheelchair, and the women safely to Canada and back. Enduring the voyage was a testament to their commitment and the power, to each, of legal marriage.

Spyer beat the odds by a year. The weeks after her death on February 2, 2009, were agonizing for Windsor. In the space of a few short weeks that nevertheless felt endless, she lost her greatest love and constant companion, suffered two heart attacks (diagnosed as stress cardiomyopathy, or "broken-heart syndrome") and, on top of all this, faced a federal estate tax bill of $363,053 that she wouldn't have been charged if her wife had been her husband. Spyer had left her a sizable inheritance, a certain amount of which was assessed a hefty tax—unless it went to a recognized spouse. Writing the enormous check just compounded Windsor's pain. "I have a documented marriage," she thought. "This woman I lived with and loved and was loved by for all those years was being treated like a stranger by the government." She felt stuck in sixth grade civics class. "I believe in the Constitution, I believe in justice, I believe in fairness, and I was so indignant," she remembered.[7]

Windsor and Spyer had been supporters of Lambda for many years, and late in 2009 she reached out to the organization to gauge support for a lawsuit. To hear Windsor tell it, she was initially ignored by Lambda, then rebuffed. "It's the wrong time for the movement," she remembered hearing on the other end of the phone. She was beginning to wonder what was wrong with that movement. A year or so earlier, Windsor had been at a community event where a Human Rights Campaign spokesman rattled off the group's agenda. Marriage equality wasn't on it. She remembered someone from the audience yelling out, "What about marriage?" to which the HRC representative answered, "That's years down the road." Windsor then shouted out her own response: "I'm seventy-seven years old and I can't wait that long!"[8]

While the perception of movement lethargy around marriage was increasingly widespread during this period, the reality was more complex. For starters, one doesn't secure representation from a legal aid group simply by calling the front desk; failing to get a commitment on the phone is not the same as being spurned. In addition, Windsor felt frustrated at both Lambda and HRC, perhaps viewing the movement as a monolith, which was easy to do. But unlike HRC, the legal groups were already deeply engaged with marriage litigation; for them the question was just which cases to push forward. Indeed, while Windsor remembered being told it was "too soon" for a marriage case, that was no longer the perception across wider and wider swaths of the movement, and particularly within the legal groups. To many, now *was* the time for a federal lawsuit, which was why GLAD had already filed its DOMA challenge earlier that year with its *Gill* suit (and the state of Massachusetts filed a second DOMA suit that summer). GLAD was also preparing another federal suit in Connecticut, and Lambda was preparing a DOMA challenge in California, both of which would be filed in 2010.[9] It was the success of the state-by-state marriage equality campaign, which chalked up five new wins between fall 2008 and the end of 2009 (along with a 2008 New York court decision directing the state to recognize out-of-state same-sex marriages), that made the challenges to DOMA viable in the first place, as a federal constitutional challenge without the existence of state-sanctioned marriage would have been a long shot.

With no interest from gay legal groups in representing her, Windsor found a private attorney she later described as "some jerk lawyer" who drained $70,000 from her pocket before she dismissed him and was put in touch with the lesbian attorney Robbie Kaplan.[10] Kaplan was a corporate litigator who normally represented banks and other large firms. But she was not a total outsider to the gay rights movement. In 2006 she had teamed up with the American Civil Liberties Union to bring a marriage equality suit in New York, and lost. She had served as clerk to the chief justice of New York's Court of Appeals, the state's highest court, and as the ACLU considered bringing a lawsuit, Matt Coles, then serving as ACLU's LGBT Rights Project director, suggested Kaplan as a potential cocounsel, thinking her connections with judges and insight into the court could be useful in the case. She was happy to take on the work, and proud of their efforts despite the loss, which she nevertheless viewed as helpful in moving the needle on public and judicial opinion—what Evan Wolfson called "losing forward." Kaplan's wife, Rachel Levine, had been active in gay rights and Democratic politics, and the two were friendly with many of the lesbian legal thinkers working full-time on gay rights litigation. Kaplan and Levine married in 2005 in Toronto, as had Windsor and Spyer. "Getting married had a huge impact on me," she said, helping solidify her commitment to marriage equality as an issue.[11]

Fortuitously, Kaplan had seen Spyer, a therapist beloved in the New York lesbian community, in counseling long ago as an anxious and depressed twentysomething struggling with her sexuality and coming out. When she got the call from Windsor, the past connection dawned on her and she was eager to hear more. Kaplan walked over to Windsor's Manhattan apartment—four blocks from her own—for a visit and showed her a video of her oral argument in the New York case she had lost. "Do you still want me, knowing I lost the case?" Kaplan asked her, offering on the spot to take the case pro bono. Windsor thought Kaplan's performance was brilliant. "Absolutely," came the reply.[12]

Windsor praised Kaplan as the only one who would help her because Kaplan "knew there was no wrong time for justice." Yet Kaplan herself called that idea "a little bit bullshit" because, though she shared with the movement lawyers a concern for strategic timing, this "*was* the right time." Yet Kaplan maintained that she did not view the case as a vehicle to slay DOMA. "I wasn't thinking this is going to be the case to go to the Supreme Court,"

Attorney Roberta Kaplan argued the case before the Supreme Court that brought down the Defense of Marriage Act.

she recalled. That prospect seemed too "pie in the sky." She knew that GLAD had filed *Gill* more than a year before and was much further along in the process. But she was struck by Windsor immediately, and found her and Spyer's love story irresistible. "Talk about marriage in sickness and in health," she said. "It's hard to imagine a couple—gay or straight—who lived those vows more than Edie and Thea did, which is what I liked so much about it." She badly wanted to help get Windsor's money back from the government, and thought she could prevail. And Windsor's indignation at the injustice of her situation struck her personally.[13] In passing DOMA, the U.S. government had deemed marriages like Kaplan's and Windsor's unworthy. The House of Representatives said the nation's "collective moral judgment" was that "heterosexuality better comports with traditional (especially Judeo-Christian) morality." It was the right time, Kaplan felt, to challenge that groundless judgment, and for Windsor to get her due.[14]

She was aware, however, that opposition could come not only from the government—the defendant—and the right wing but also from the LGBTQ movement, which had vehemently opposed another outsider lawsuit not long ago in California. Kaplan showed Windsor the spring 2009 letter signed by the nine movement groups opposing federal litigation. Kaplan had agreed with the groups in opposing the AFER lawsuit as too risky. But she later said she found the resistance excessive, especially after it became clear there was no stopping the suit. She figured that a DOMA challenge would not be as controversial as AFER's more sweeping right-to-marry suit, and GLAD had already filed the *Gill* case, indicating that there was at least some movement support for a careful federal challenge. But that only gave Kaplan more reason to worry that she could be seen as operating on other people's turf. Also, from what Windsor had told her about getting a poor response from Lambda when she first sought help, Kaplan had the perception that the legal groups would not be supportive. Ultimately she dismissed her worries. But she warned Windsor that her suit could provoke criticism from within the movement and that she would need to be ready. "It could get ugly," Kaplan told her.[15]

Windsor never wavered. But once the two were sure they would file suit, Kaplan, seeking movement buy-in, reached out to James Esseks of the ACLU to invite the group to join her as cocounsel. Esseks had succeeded Coles as head of ACLU's LGBT and AIDS Project, and had litigated cases on parenting, employment discrimination, and marriage, including working on the California *In re Marriage* cases. Kaplan felt a certain warmth toward the ACLU since she had been invited to work on the 2006 New York lawsuit, and she recognized, too, that she could use not only the imprimatur of the movement but its help and expertise.

Esseks was among those who routinely worried about pressing lawsuits forward too quickly or with insufficient skill or groundwork. There were also questions about whether Windsor's case would be helpful to the cause. Back in 2004, Bonauto had said she couldn't imagine a "less sympathetic" plaintiff than a wealthy person facing a large tax burden. Evan Wolfson raised the same concern. Esseks did, too: in the abstract, an estate tax problem for wealthy people was not the story he would have chosen to tell America, nor did he think it was the quickest way to a judge's heart. Moreover, the legal groups had long believed that single-plaintiff cases were not ideal vehicles for impact litigation. When possible, they preferred to showcase a range of couples who suffered different kinds of harms that would be more likely to resonate with all kinds of people.

But by the time Esseks received Kaplan's call in September 2010, he fully understood how quickly the gay marriage landscape was changing.

At that point he and his colleagues were ready for the ACLU to take part in a DOMA challenge. He was also touched by Windsor's tale, which fit nicely into the framework of what recent movement opinion research had found to be publicly resonant: focus on love and commitment when talking to the nation about same-sex marriage. Windsor was going to come across not as a wealthy woman living on Fifth Avenue but as a charming old lady who had stuck by her partner for forty-four years, through a period of considerable sickness, and was now being treated unfairly. These women had gotten engaged two years *before* Stonewall! Theirs was a "killer story," Esseks thought. "The facts were so good, it seemed a risk well worth taking." Windsor and Spyer's love story bespoke a dignity and commitment that anyone—gay or straight—could admire and envy.

But Esseks worried about one more thing: in addition to its already filed *Gill* case, GLAD was preparing to file a second DOMA lawsuit in Connecticut. Both Connecticut and New York lay in the Second Circuit, which meant the two suits could end up essentially competing with each other for a hearing in the appeals process. Esseks was concerned that Mary Bonauto would resent the prospect of another case being mounted simultaneously. He encouraged Kaplan to speak with Bonauto about timing and strategy, but Kaplan refused, assuming that Bonauto would try to talk her out of filing. "No good could come out of that," she decided, as much as she deeply respected Bonauto. She figured the two would need to work together if their cases went up together, and she did not want to start that process with an argument. But it was also clear that neither needed the other's blessing to proceed. After some hesitation, Esseks committed to joining Kaplan's suit, Bonauto accepted that Windsor's case would move forward, and all parties agreed it would be best to coordinate and assist each other's efforts. They decided to file the Windsor suit and GLAD's Connecticut suit on the same day, which they did on November 9, 2010.

———

In February 2011, Obama's attorney general, Eric Holder, released a letter addressed to John Boehner, the Republican Speaker of the House, that would help dramatically speed the death of DOMA. The letter explained a new position the administration was taking on the law. The Justice

Department served as the federal government's lead attorney in all challenges to federal law. That was why it had written the controversial 2009 brief defending DOMA against the *Smelt* suit. Since then, the Obama administration had faced the full wrath of the vocal LGBTQ community for its robust defense of the law, along with sustained lobbying by gay rights groups pressing the White House to view DOMA challenges under heightened scrutiny. From the start of the Obama administration in 2009, both White House and Justice Department lawyers, as well as political advisors, had been wrestling with the question of DOMA's constitutionality, aware that the swelling list of federal lawsuits would require them to weigh in on the matter as they decided whether to support appeals to lower court rulings. White House lawyers quickly concluded that the law could not withstand constitutional challenge, but Justice Department lawyers were slower to join in that opinion.[16]

Following the summer 2010 rulings by Judge Tauro in Massachusetts that DOMA was unconstitutional, gay advocates—legal groups along with HRC—met repeatedly with a cadre of Justice Department lawyers and made the case that defending DOMA as constitutional was legally and politically unsustainable. Doing so would not only require the president to continue vigorously defending a law he opposed but also mean presenting other legal and historical claims the president would be hard-pressed to make with a straight face: that laws constraining gay rights did not warrant special scrutiny because gay people did not historically suffer from discrimination, or that their orientation was changeable—two of the factors that helped determine whether a group was subject to heightened scrutiny.[17]

The president had already told the *Advocate*'s Kerry Eleveld in a wide-ranging interview that gay people were, in fact, victims of discrimination and stereotyping—hardly a revelation to anyone, but an indication of the president's thinking on the question of scrutiny, which turned, in part, on those determinations. After the disastrous administration brief defending DOMA in 2009 and the shock it prompted among not just gay activists but the mainstream press, it would strain credulity for his administration to now argue the opposite. And that was exactly what the administration would have to do, gay advocates argued, if it continued to defend DOMA as constitutional.[18]

For the White House, the decision whether or not to defend DOMA was thorny both politically and legally. The president had signed a law in

December 2010 repealing "don't ask, don't tell," the ban on openly gay military service, and had seen that none of the dire military or political consequences that opponents had warned of for years had come to pass. To the contrary, repealing the military ban quickly established itself as a political and military success story, gaining the support of many top military officials and several Republican supporters in Congress, earning kudos from military scholars for its smooth implementation, and giving Democrats and progressives a solid political and cultural win at a time when the president's party had just lost control of the House of Representatives. Above all, the success of ending "don't ask, don't tell" seemed to finally shake off the decades-old perception among Democratic politicians that gay rights was a losing issue for them. The first major federal bill to support gay rights had passed into law, and there was no political fallout.[19]

That autumn, the president had also arranged meetings with a number of progressive and gay rights bloggers and advocates. Obama had continued to take incoming fire from LGBTQ leaders for his failure to support marriage equality and the confusing positions he was forced to take in public: supporting gay rights but not gay marriage, opposing Proposition 8 as discriminatory but tolerating discrimination when it came to marriage. After the trial court ruling against Proposition 8, while gays and lesbians celebrated, the president's top advisor, David Axelrod, went so far as to reiterate Obama's opposition to marriage equality, even though the president had spoken out against California's gay marriage ban and insisted he supported full equality. The awkward reaction spurred a fresh wave of criticism from the gay community, including a post by Andrew Sullivan entitled "Obama's Marriage FAIL," which complained that "if the president does not support my right to marry, then he does *not* support my equality."[20]

Disappointment from Obama's base, dubbed the "enthusiasm gap," was the impetus for the meetings set up by the White House in the fall of 2010, an effort to shore up support for Democrats heading into the midterm elections. In one meeting, the blogger Joe Sudbay, who worked with John Aravosis at *AMERICAblog*, asked the president about his views on same-sex marriage, citing dramatic changes in public opinion. "Attitudes evolve, including mine," the president said titillatingly. While he was not prepared to "make big news" at that moment, he said gay marriage was something he wrestled with often, spurred on by having friends and staff members who were openly gay and in committed relationships.[21] The interview set politicos speculating about whether the president planned to reverse his public opposition to marriage equality in the near future, and whether such comments might reflect anything about the administration's position on DOMA.

As a legal matter, the administration had repeatedly claimed that it was compelled to defend DOMA against constitutional challenges, despite precedents of presidents declining to defend laws for various reasons. Now gay legal groups had given the White House a way out of this tenuous position of strenuously defending a law the president opposed. Both the *Windsor* case and GLAD's case, *Pedersen et al. v. Office of Personnel Management,* were filed in the Second Circuit Court of Appeals, which, unlike the First Circuit, where *Gill* had been filed, had no precedent on whether gays and lesbians were subject to heightened scrutiny in constitutional claims. That meant the Obama administration would have a fresh opportunity— indeed, an obligation—to offer its legal opinion about what level of scrutiny should be applied. GLAD had chosen this circuit in part to force the hand of the administration on this very question. But if doing so created a pressure point, it was also a political gift to the White House: the fact that the Second Circuit had no precedent on level of review gave the president a convenient rationale for switching his position on whether to defend—at just the moment when political pressure to stop defending DOMA was becoming impossible to ignore. When the Justice Department went to examine the cases, the administration would be able to explain that, in assessing the scrutiny question in a venue where there was no precedent on it, it had determined that heightened scrutiny should apply, and that under that level of review, it must conclude that DOMA was unconstitutional, and opt not to defend it.[22]

This is exactly what Attorney General Holder did in his February 2011 letter to Boehner. "The President and I have concluded that classifications based on sexual orientation warrant heightened scrutiny," Holder wrote, "and that, as applied to same-sex couples legally married under state law, Section 3 of DOMA is unconstitutional." The attorney general explained that the Justice Department's customary position was to defend all statutes as constitutional so long as "reasonable arguments can be made in their defense." Yet, he wrote, the Justice Department "does not consider every plausible argument to be a 'reasonable' one," particularly if it has concluded that heightened scrutiny applies. As a result, the present situation was "the rare case where the proper course is to forgo the defense of this statute."[23] Holder based his decision on standards laid out by the Supreme Court about when heightened scrutiny ought to apply: if the group has suffered a history of discrimination, if "immutable" characteristics make the class into a "discrete group," if the group has limited political power, and if its defining characteristics are unrelated to either an important government purpose or to group members' ability to contribute to society.[24]

To meet the heightened scrutiny standard, the law must be "substantially related to an important government objective." But, raising the bar even higher, courts must look at the "actual state purposes, not rationalizations for actions" dreamed up by a judge that *could have* explained the actions of a legislature or voter initiative. As Holder explained, this meant that the government could not defend DOMA "by advancing hypothetical rationales, independent of the legislative record," as it could do in cases where only the "rational basis" test applied. This made it a slam dunk to find DOMA unconstitutional once sexual orientation was looked at as a suspect class, because the only way to defend it was "by invoking Congress' actual justifications for the law." Those justifications were an object lesson in anti-gay animus, as Holder pointed out in his letter. "The legislative record underlying DOMA's passage," he wrote, "contains discussion and debate that undermines any defense under heightened scrutiny. The record contains numerous expressions reflecting moral disapproval of gays and lesbians and their intimate and family relationships—precisely the kind of stereotype-based thinking and animus the Equal Protection Clause is designed to guard against."[25]

The result of this monumental decision was that the Justice Department would not defend DOMA in the *Pedersen* or *Windsor* cases (and possibly other DOMA challenges brought while Obama was in office). Robbie Kaplan wept as Assistant Attorney General Tony West told her by phone of the decision, propelling her case forward and giving her constitutional argument the imprimatur of the president of the United States. Three straight African American men—West, Holder, and Obama, all too aware of the history of discrimination—had convened to determine if they could write a brief claiming that gay people did not face a history of discrimination. She felt they had put politics aside to answer in the right way.[26] The Obama administration itself had begun to evolve, and would now put the dignity and self-evident love of this remarkable couple ahead of any other calculus. Windsor, too, was ecstatic. "The very fact that the president and the Department of Justice are making such a statement is mind-blowing," she said. "It removes a great deal of the stigma. It's just great."[27]

While the Justice Department would not defend the law, the executive branch would continue to enforce it, "consistent with the Executive's obligation to take care that the laws be faithfully executed." Enforcing the law was also necessary in order for the cases to move forward; without that step, Windsor would lack standing to continue the suit.[28] When the Justice Department declined to defend the law, the Bipartisan Legal Advisory Group (BLAG), a legal arm of Congress with authority to direct legal action on behalf of the House of Representatives, stepped in to defend it instead. Calling it "regrettable" that the Obama administration had "opened this divisive issue" when most Americans were focused on economic hardship, Speaker Boehner said in a statement that he would convene BLAG to defend the law. "The constitutionality of this law," said the statement, "should be determined by the courts—not by the president unilaterally—and this action by the House will ensure the matter is addressed in a manner consistent with our Constitution." BLAG consisted of three Republicans and two Democrats—the leadership of each party in the House. While the committee's two Democrats opposed using BLAG to take up DOMA's defense, the three GOP leaders held the majority, and their wishes prevailed. There was, in fact, nothing bipartisan about BLAG but the name.[29] The group hired Paul Clement as its lawyer. Clement had succeeded Ted Olson as U.S. solicitor general under George Bush when he was just thirty-eight years old. After a public uproar over Clement's decision to defend what the public had increasingly come to view as simple discrimination—2011 was the first year when polls consistently showed a majority of the American public in favor of marriage equality—his law firm, King and Spalding, withdrew from the case and Clement resigned from the firm to continue as DOMA's legal champion.

While Republicans in the nation's capital busied themselves defending the federal marriage recognition ban, momentum for marriage equality was gathering in the nation's cultural capital, New York. Two years earlier, in

2009, the movement had suffered a trying setback when the State Senate failed to pass a marriage equality bill, dashing the hopes of activists who had poured time, money, and strategic prowess into the effort. Tim Gill and the group of wealthy donors who had been pushing marriage forward for a decade pumped dollars into the state's political races and helped flip the Senate into Democratic hands in 2008 after a four-decade GOP reign. The Democratic-controlled Assembly had voted for marriage in 2007, but at the time the Senate allowed the bill to die. In 2009, several lawmakers who had enjoyed the largess of the gay donors promised to bring marriage to a vote and back the bill. Governor David Patterson was an outspoken marriage equality supporter who promised to sign a bill into law if only the Senate would get the job done. Key players from both the marriage movement and the world of New York politics were confident that this time New York would pass marriage.

But it was not to be. On December 2 the famous dysfunction of Albany joined with the political and emotional fears that continued to fill the ether around gay equality, and the marriage bill failed by a vote of 38 to 24—not even close. Several Democrats who had clearly promised gay political players that they would back the bill pulled their support at the last minute.[30] The loss devastated gay advocates at a time when frustration with the pace of change was coming to a head. After the vote, hundreds of protesters gathered in Times Square to vent their anger. Although early 2009 had seen monumental advances with marriage wins in Iowa and New England, by the end of the year some thought momentum was stalling, and there was little certainty about where things would go next.

Movement leaders, however, stayed focused on the long game. Bill Smith, the deputy executive director of the Gill Action Fund, was crestfallen the moment the New York vote failed. But when he glanced at his phone, he saw a characteristic email from Tim Gill: "That was sad. What's next?" What was next was a new chapter in Tim Gill's plan to "punish the wicked." Even when substantial gay dollars flowed to Democrats, who professed support for gay marriage and promised to vote accordingly, nothing ensured that these lawmakers delivered. There had to be consequences to crossing the gay community, or else the leverage of the donors and the protests and marches of the activists would amount to nothing.[31]

In 2010, teaming up with a small group of New York political operatives, Smith created a new political action committee with Gill seed money, called Fight Back New York. The aim of the group was to relentlessly target state senators who had failed to back marriage equality and were vulnerable to losing their seat. Fight Back New York was unique in the history of political issue campaigns: rather than speak directly about the issue it sought to advance, the campaign ruthlessly exploited any weakness it could identify in lawmakers to unseat its opponents. That meant declining to engage in a debate on the merits of gay equality and opting instead for a political fight on totally unrelated grounds. And it meant targeting Democrats as well as Republicans. This was an approach that reflected a new willingness by progressive gay advocates to prioritize their own equality even at the expense of party loyalty. And it was also consistent with the increasingly bipartisan effort to win marriage equality.

Bill Smith was the perfect operative to carry out this campaign. A Karl Rove protégé from Alabama, he understood brass-knuckle tactics and had little trouble picking off Democratic lawmakers in the service of advancing gay equality. With Smith in charge of the day-to-day, Fight Back New York identified three vulnerable senators who had voted against marriage equality, two Democrats and a Republican. The group solicited money from other gay donors both to fund its campaign efforts and to support replacement candidates. It sent a barrage of direct mailings to carefully targeted voters using pioneering "microtargeting" techniques that had been used by Republican operatives to help George W. Bush win reelection in 2004. It ran radio and television ads, created a social media presence, and made robocalls, all to highlight not the politicians' opposition to marriage equality but their other sins: domestic abuse, financial improprieties, excessive spending, opposition to women's health, and more. Fight Back New York spent nearly $800,000 to replace three of their enemies with pro-gay-marriage candidates. The enormous effort by the PAC relative to the normally modest expenses that went into state political campaigns—together with very small margins in some of the losses—suggests that the effort paid off, swaying races that might otherwise have had different outcomes. In any event, all of Albany was now on notice that the savvy, bipartisan, well-funded marriage equality movement meant business: no more coddling old friends or party allies. They would use all tools at their disposal to punish those who stood against gay equality.[32]

Despite the successes of Fight Back New York, 2010 saw the State Senate fall back into Republican hands, part of a national wave that ejected incumbents across the country amid anger over the floundering economy, ongoing wars, and a sense of government excess and ineptitude. The new margin in the New York State Senate, 32 to 30 with control held by the GOP, now meant that if marriage equality was to become law, it would be dependent on the willingness of Republican leaders to bring the issue to a vote.

Key to winning marriage in a GOP-controlled Senate was tapping the support of influential Republicans with the social capital to cast marriage equality as a bipartisan issue. Shortly after Ted Olson got involved in the marriage battle, his friend Ken Mehlman invited him to lunch to discuss the case Olson had helped launch. Mehlman had been George W. Bush's campaign chair in 2004 and subsequently chairman of the Republican National Committee. What few people knew was that Mehlman was gay. At lunch the two conservative stalwarts discussed the conservative case for same-sex marriage. It wasn't until a year later that Mehlman told Olson he was gay and wanted to play an active role in marriage advocacy. It was an ironic coda to a political career that involved the rank exploitation of anti-gay sentiment by the campaign and party he led. But Mehlman, who later apologized to the gays and lesbians who had been hurt by his party's efforts, felt he was now in a position to do good after years of complicity with his party's ugly and divisive actions.[33]

Mehlman came out publicly in 2010 to heavy media coverage and dove headfirst into rallying conservative support for marriage equality in New York and elsewhere. Joining the board of AFER, he contributed and helped raise substantial funds for the lawsuit and related marriage efforts, and lobbied other pro-gay conservatives to voice support for marriage equality. One such figure was Paul Singer, a billionaire investor and major Republican donor, on whom Mehlman prevailed to cochair an AFER fund-raiser in 2010. Singer and Mehlman then worked together with New York gay advocates over the next year to bring more conservative donors onboard and—crucially—to use their influence to win the support of Republican senators. Singer, who had a gay son and had donated smaller amounts to the marriage effort for some years, now rallied to the cause, writing a $425,000 check to Freedom to Marry, and helped bring in another half million dollars from friends.[34] Taking up Andrew Sullivan's conservative argument for gay marriage, Singer recounted thumbing through the photo album of his gay son's wedding album and feeling that "no moment better encapsulated for me the contribution to societal stability than that moment of normalcy in leafing through that album."[35] Sullivan had titled his 1995 book *Virtually Normal,* and to some gay advocates, achieving gay equality at the cost of "mainstreaming" gayness was too high a price. But for many conservatives and even mainstream liberals, groups that were coming to embrace their gay and lesbian friends, family, and coworkers, viewing gay people as "normal" was the path to endorsing gay marriage (and vice versa).

Among the most important factors in bringing marriage equality to the Empire State was Governor Andrew Cuomo, son of the famed liberal governor Mario Cuomo. Although Cuomo was a Democrat, he had demonstrated an ability to work across the aisle and was expected to be able to deliver some crucial Republican votes. When Cuomo first sought the governorship, he was attorney general of New York, and many gay advocates were initially not sure what to make of the hard-talking Italian American who liked to ride motorcycles. But as state attorney general, Cuomo was developing a reputation as a serious, effective liberal political leader, and as his sights settled on the governorship in the lead-up to the 2010 election, gay leaders had no choice but to take notice. People began to like what they were learning. The attorney general had filed a brief on behalf of same-sex couples in earlier New York marriage litigation. He had openly gay friends, colleagues, and financial supporters and had told one that the state's marriage ban was an "abject injustice" that he thought greatly about. "Let me make a promise to you," he had said in a 2007 conversation. "We're going to change this."[36]

During Cuomo's 2010 campaign he met with Bill Smith and his boss, Patrick Guerriero, who headed the Gill Action Fund. Cuomo told the men that he felt New York was behind where it ought to be on this issue, and he planned to make it a top priority. "I don't want to be the governor who just proposes marriage equality," he said later that year, addressing the Empire State Pride Agenda, New York's biggest gay rights group. "I want to be the governor who signs the law that makes equality a reality in the state of New York."[37] He won his election that November by almost a two-to-one margin over a Republican opponent who had called attending a gay pride parade "disgusting."

In March 2011, one year after he had met with Gill Action, Governor Cuomo called marriage equality advocates together for a strategy meeting. There he demonstrated his commitment to delivering marriage, showing that he would be personally involved and that he expected the various advocacy groups, which had often failed to work together effectively, to be far more disciplined this time around. He put his top staff on the issue, told the LGBTQ leaders that he expected them to fully coordinate with his office, and called on them to do the heavy lifting of lining up the various state constituencies whose support would be needed for a win in the Republican-controlled senate. Gay advocates responded enthusiastically. At Freedom to Marry, Marc Solomon now worked directly under Evan Wolfson as national campaign director, and under his leadership a coalition was created called New Yorkers United for Marriage. The group included Freedom to Marry, Empire State Pride Agenda, HRC, Marriage Equality New York (which had spawned the national grassroots group, Marriage Equality USA), Log Cabin Republicans, and Gill Action, and had the support of the major gay funders. With several new state senators installed who were supportive of marriage—their presence in part due to the efforts of coalition members—along with a popular and strong new governor and growing public approval of same-sex marriage in the state (and nationally), the participants were optimistic that this could be the year for New York.[38]

The most pressing task for the coalition would be to lobby about a dozen lawmakers seen as reachable but not yet committed to marriage. But such a campaign was always about more than just reaching out to politicians. It required winning the support of their constituents, creating a drumbeat of media stories to repeatedly win the news cycle, keeping campaign coffers full, securing support from public personalities and organizations willing to speak out in support of the issue, and more. To help coordinate the work and to ensure a uniform public message, the campaign hired a political consultant who enjoyed Cuomo's imprimatur, and it committed funds and held weekly phone calls and regular meetings.

Freedom to Marry and Marriage Equality New York helped provide stories of same-sex couples to the media. Drawing on its strengths in lobbying and organizing, HRC identified specific districts throughout the state where targeted advocacy was most likely to yield results and set up field operations there, including devoting thirty full-time organizers to the effort. The group's high profile and history of cultivating celebrity supporters and spokespeople allowed it to attract sports and entertainment stars as public "validators" of marriage equality, a topic they often spoke about in speeches, videos, and ads. HRC secured video statements of support from Barbara Bush, daughter of President George W. Bush; New York Rangers star Sean Avery; Mike Bloomberg, the billionaire mayor of New York and onetime Republican; hip-hop producer Russell Simmons; and many others, focusing especially on broadening voices of support to include the unexpected such as minorities and conservatives. Some of the recruits threw additional levels of support to the effort. Mayor Bloomberg, for instance, a major donor to GOP politicians, gave $100,000, hosted a high-dollar fund-raiser, and personally lobbied senators in Albany.[39]

By spring of 2011, 58 percent of New Yorkers favored marriage equality, field organizers had mobilized an impressive voter response, and word had reached state senators that there was substantial support among their constituents for marriage equality. A crucial breakthrough came on a Monday in June when three Democratic senators who had opposed marriage equality in 2009 announced they were changing their votes after hearing greater support from constituents. That afternoon, Governor Cuomo, who had personally lobbied senators, called the marriage coalition into his office, where he expressed confidence that there would be enough votes to pass the bill. He then ushered a guest into the conference room. Sen. Jim Alesi, Cuomo said, wanted to be the first Republican senator to publicly commit to backing marriage equality. To eager applause, Alesi greeted the members and singled out Tom Duane, a toweringly tall, openly gay senator from upstate who had long pushed gay rights in emotional speeches and lobbying of his colleagues. "I feel terrible about the 2009 vote," Alesi told Duane, referring to his vote against marriage equality. "It was a political vote. And I apologize to you, Tom, for that vote." That month, Alesi signaled, he would right the wrong.[40]

On June 24 the GOP-controlled New York State Senate followed the lower Assembly in passing a marriage equality bill. The senate vote was 33 to 29, with four Republicans voting in favor. When Governor Cuomo signed the bill just before midnight, as a joyous celebration unfolded around the Stonewall Inn, New York became the fifth and largest state to permit same-sex marriage (not counting California, which had allowed and then revoked it in 2008). Overnight, the share of the American population living in a marriage equality state had doubled. Press coverage was extensive, surprising even Cuomo and his top staffer, Steve Cohen, who had led the effort from inside the governor's office. Just three years earlier, media coverage of

California's pro-gay-marriage court ruling had stressed the potential of that development to boost Republican political fortunes by driving angry social conservatives to the polls. Now media reports praised Cuomo's strong leadership—both for its political efficacy and its moral stance—and cast the successful marriage equality campaign as a feather in his cap as he looked toward higher office.[41]

Not everyone was celebrating. Catholic, Mormon, evangelical Protestant, and Orthodox Jewish leaders vowed to keep fighting the spread of gay marriage. And voices of the gay left continued to ring out, articulating why the focus on marriage had costs in the quest to achieve a broader, now-fading vision of liberation. The night before the vote in Albany, Katherine Franke, a Columbia Law School professor with long ties to alternative-family champions such as Paula Ettelbrick and Nancy Polikoff, wrote an op-ed in the *New York Times* dedicated to keeping that vision alive. "While many in our community have worked hard to secure the right of same-sex couples to marry," she wrote, "others of us have been working equally hard to develop alternatives to marriage." For those advocates, she explained, domestic partnerships and civil unions were not a substitute for marriage, but "an opportunity to order our lives in ways that have given us greater freedom" than what marriage had long offered to respectable society. And for some pocket of the LGBTQ community, the alternatives were still more noble and alluring than marriage. "As strangers to marriage for so long," Franke wrote, "we've created loving and committed forms of family, care and attachment that far exceed, and often improve on, the narrow legal definition of marriage."[42]

Franke's op-ed reflected the passionate liberationism of an older generation of lesbian and gay activists who insisted on full citizenship and equal respect without the need to conform. But it was swimming against the tide of thought occurring in homes across the country, including the White House. Even among the Litigators' Roundtable, there were few members still critiquing marriage equality as a goal. The crush of media praise for Governor Cuomo's triumph in passing landmark gay rights legislation—a telling commentary on how far the nation had come from the days when gay rights were a third rail in politics—and the jubilant celebrations of marriage equality at Stonewall two days later were the true markers of the shape of the gay rights movement a decade into the twenty-first century.

13

"The Nation Is Ready for It"

A PRESIDENT AND A COUNTRY EVOLVE

IT HAD BEEN TWO YEARS SINCE THE LAST STATE WIN FOR MARRIAGE equality and the stinging disappointment of Proposition 8, and New York's passage of marriage equality in June 2011 energized the gay and progressive communities, advancing momentum and buoying hopes. But the development was a swelling headache for the Obama White House, which faced growing public criticism as it was contrasted to Governor Cuomo's glowing leadership role in New York. After the vote there, the columnist Maureen Dowd complained that the president, who continued to publicly oppose gay marriage, was "not leading the public" but following, just as he had on "don't ask, don't tell." He was even "lagging behind a couple of old, white conservatives," she griped, referring to Dick Cheney and Ted Olson, who both favored same-sex marriage.[1] The popular pollster Nate Silver praised Cuomo's boldness as "a brand of leadership that many Democrats I speak with feel is lacking in President Obama."[2] Increasingly, the president could not avoid sharp questioning by the mainstream press on the issue of gay marriage, with several wondering aloud why Obama refused to say what they assumed he really believed about it: that there was no better reason to ban gay marriage than there had been to ban interracial marriages like that of his own parents.

There was another problem for the White House. A reelection campaign was heating up, something for which Obama would continue to rely on LGBTQ votes and dollars. The night before the New York vote, the president was heckled at a speech to a group of gay donors, and sorely disappointed listeners when he failed to weigh in on the next day's crucial legislative vote on gay marriage. It was becoming increasingly awkward for Obama, the nation's first biracial president, a stalwart liberal, an intellectual, and someone who had favored same-sex marriage on a questionnaire in the 1990s, to tell his gay and lesbian supporters and the pesky mainstream press that he did not support the freedom to marry.

As 2011 wore on, the president and his advisors intensified their internal debate about whether and when Obama should shift his public position on gay marriage. On one side were some senior staff members who worried that endorsing it would turn off his African American supporters, many of whom belonged to conservative churches that preached against homosexuality, and depress voter turnout among that group and other culturally conservative cohorts. On the other side were those who argued that most voters who strenuously opposed gay marriage were not likely to vote for Obama anyway, that his contorted positions on marriage were increasingly transparent and untenable, and that the president's reputation as an authentic leader was being irreparably harmed by his insistence that he opposed same-sex marriage.

Meeting with top staffers including senior White House advisor Valerie Jarrett, Evan Wolfson brought to the administration the LGBTQ community's message that supporting marriage equality was a logical next step for Obama after choosing not to defend the Defense of Marriage Act. It was a way to get the president out of the awkward situation of seeming both for marriage equality and against it. And Wolfson proposed a way to do it. In 2010, the president had publicly declared that his feelings on the issue were "evolving." For many gay advocates, the word resonated, evoking the awakening to the equal worth of same-sex relationships that millions of Americans—including gay ones—had experienced in recent years. The president, Wolfson advised, drawing on research that suggested Americans identified with the concept of a journey toward acceptance of gay rights, should tap into that experience. Obama had stressed the impact of getting to know his gay friends and staff, and how conversations with his own family had propelled him forward on this issue. Here, perhaps, was a lever with which to push the president's administration to evolve along with the president.

As the White House debated what to do, it also had the benefit of polls now showing consistently not only that the majority of Americans favored same-sex marriage, but also that the voters that Obama most needed to attract were highly motivated by the issue—and that those who opposed same-sex marriage were less and less motivated to vote based on this issue. This was a change from an earlier era when conservatives were thought to flock to the polls when offered anti-gay ballot proposals to vote on. Now young people in particular, a key part of Obama's voting coalition and always a challenge to get to the polls, were motivated by the opportunity to support gay marriage.[3]

Finally, in the fall of 2011, Obama told his senior staff that he was tired of ducking the issue and wanted to find a way to come out for same-sex marriage. For help in deciding when and how to make the announcement— including, crucially, whether to do so before or after the 2012 election—the administration turned to Ken Mehlman, someone Obama had known in his law school days and respected despite their very different politics. Mehlman, now willing to do all he could for gay rights as a way to atone for his damaging role in reelecting George W. Bush at their expense, was happy to advise the White House. He was consulting closely with the American Foundation for Equal Rights and Freedom to Marry, and all the groups dedicated to ending same-sex marriage bans were conducting polls and strategizing about public education and legal approaches to furthering marriage equality. Everyone involved in the movement was aware of just how important the president's opinion would be to further advancements. Both state and federal judges referenced the president's public opposition to same-sex marriage as apparent evidence that it was perfectly reasonable to support gay rights but oppose gay marriage. And the president was the most authoritative single voice in the nation. His blessing would be enormously influential both to voters and legislators in state battles and to gay and lesbian Americans, whose quest for recognition of their love could only be immeasurably enhanced by the imprimatur of the president of the United States.[4]

In a lunch with the president and a follow-up memo to his advisors, Mehlman offered the White House counsel from his own political research and experience and from the LGBTQ groups and leaders he consulted with. Consider, he suggested, a sit-down with a friendly interviewer, perhaps a woman, and explain to the nation that the president and his family had been on a journey alongside so many other Americans, who had gotten to know their gay and lesbian loved ones, and now embraced their love as equal to everyone else's.[5]

Yet by 2012 the president still had not moved on the issue. To add pressure, Marc Solomon came up with an idea: why not try to add support for marriage equality as a plank in the Democratic Party platform? If support caught on among party leaders and elected officials, the president would be pressed to lend his support as well to avoid being at odds with his own party's position—and to avoid the inevitable slew of questions from journalists demanding yet another explanation of his slithery position on marriage equality.[6] The plan worked perfectly, as leading Democrats embraced the plank idea and the press pounded the president's advisors on whether he would close ranks or continue making a far-fetched case for opposing equality and his own party. "Why can't he say what he believes on this issue?" a frustrated George Stephanopoulos, of ABC News, asked senior advisor David Plouffe on Sunday morning television. Some White House insiders, including Valerie Jarrett and the First Lady, were encouraging the president to do just that, arguing that it would free him to be himself.[7]

The president was ready to back marriage equality, but his team still had not come up with the right time and way to make the announcement. What finally pushed the issue to the fore was, by all accounts, the kind of rare, unscripted political development for which Vice President Joe Biden had become lovably famous. In May 2012, after weeks of media pressure on the administration in response to anger and impatience by gay advocates, David Gregory of NBC News asked the vice president on *Meet the Press* what he thought about same-sex marriage.[8] Biden said it was the president who set the policies of his administration, but that he himself was "absolutely comfortable" with same-sex marriage. All married couples, he said, should enjoy the same rights, a position in sync with the administration's opposition to DOMA, which denied federal benefits even to gay couples legally married in their state. Still, the vice president's comments were major news. In his emotional remarks to David Gregory, he had gone into some detail about his feelings about gay families and marriage equality. He described a fund-raiser the previous month in which Chad Griffin, who had just been named the next leader of Human Rights Campaign and who had helped organize the event at the Los Angeles home of a gay couple and their two young children, asked him pointedly what his views were about gay equality. Biden characterized Griffin's question as "one of the most poignant questions I had ever been asked in my life." It was as if he had been asked, "So tell us, Mr. Vice President, what do you think of us?" Biden described his visit warmly, recounting how the couple's kids had greeted him excitedly with flowers. He could only think: "I wish every American could see the look of love that those kids had in their eyes" for their two dads. Then no one would "have any doubt about what this is about." It had been abundantly clear, said Biden, that those children were loved and well cared for. And more and more, he said—ever since the rise of shows such as *Will and Grace,* which "probably did more to educate the American public than almost anything anybody's ever done so far"—the world was coming to see that love as, simply, love. "Things are changing so rapidly, it's going to become a political liability in the near term for an individual to say, 'I oppose gay marriage.' Mark my words."[9]

Amid breathless news reports about Biden's comments—had the vice president just gotten ahead of the president on gay marriage?—the White House and Biden's office sprang into damage control mode, insisting that Biden had expressed the president's established position: that gay couples deserved the exact same rights as straight ones (in other words, that they deserved civil unions with all the rights of marriage except use of the word itself). White House advisors worried that Biden had just caused them a major headache, and Jarrett, who wanted the president to back same-sex marriage, was furious at the vice president for speaking out of turn.[10]

Yet the White House quickly recognized the development as the right moment for the president to finally resolve the issue—far enough ahead of that fall's election not to appear as a campaign stunt, but still a bold step given that the political consequences were far from certain. What his advisors knew was this: national polls had consistently showed majority American support for same-sex marriage since 2011; advancing gay marriage was a motivating issue for young voters—and would-be young voters—in Obama's coalition; and even those who sat outside the progressive coalition, such as conservatives, Republicans, and certain corporate leaders, were registering support for same-sex marriage. Nearly fifty large companies had signed an amicus brief in Edie Windsor's lawsuit supporting her effort to strike down DOMA, and with the help of HRC and other gay advocacy groups, corporate titans including Goldman Sachs chairman Lloyd Blankfein had become public spokespeople for the cause.

Within days the White House had set up a sit-down interview with ABC's Robin Roberts, an African American woman friendly with the Obamas and known by media insiders to be a lesbian.[11] In the interview, for which ABC broke into its regular programing, Obama used the framing and themes that Wolfson and Mehlman had proposed, emphasizing common values and a progression in his thinking that millions of other Americans had also experienced. He spoke of conversations with his own family and with staff, friends, and neighbors who were gay or supported marriage equality. Ultimately, he said, he simply could not find any reason to deprive loving same-sex couples of the protections and recognition that other committed couples enjoyed. "At a certain point," he said, "I've just concluded that, for me personally, it is important for me to go ahead and affirm that I think same-sex couples should be able to get married."[12]

The president's announcement had an enormous impact on both gay and straight Americans. In one reflection of this, a number of affluent gay advocates announced they would max out contributions to Obama's reelection campaign—after some had withheld money in anger at his foot-dragging. Even though his announcement had no direct effect on policy, some gays and lesbians seemed to be surprised at how moved they were by finally having the president personally on their side—a signal of how much public recognition really mattered. Obama's support also influenced feelings about marriage across the country. The same month, national support for same-sex marriage hit a new high at 53 percent, while opposition hit a new low of 39 percent. The NAACP, meanwhile, released a statement endorsing same-sex marriage. Indeed, African American support for marriage equality showed the most dramatic turnaround in polls, with 59 percent now favoring same-sex marriage in contrast to only 41 percent registering support immediately prior to Obama's public shift. Another poll conducted in North Carolina, whose voters had backed a constitutional amendment banning gay marriage one day before Obama made his turnabout, found that resistance to same-sex marriage among blacks dropped 11 percent almost overnight.[13]

The poll numbers mattered, not only for Obama's reelection campaign but also because four states—Maine, Washington, Maryland, and Minnesota—were preparing for ballot fights over marriage equality that November. Gay rights leaders were hoping to break a thirty-one-state losing streak with the first voter-approved state marriage wins in some or all of the states. (The first three were measures to legalize same-sex marriage, while Minnesota's measure was the more typical variety: a ban proposed by gay-marriage opponents.) In the 2008 campaign for Proposition 8, Obama's views seem to have carried important weight with voters. As the 2012 ballot fights approached, the president's support could only help advance marriage equality.

Although Obama's remarks reflected the language that the conservative Mehlman had recommended, the idea of framing social change in terms that resonated with common, even traditional values had, by 2012, become a crucial strategy shift that helped spur major gains by the LGBTQ movement. This approach of capturing the center had proven effective in the successful battle to end discrimination against gay and lesbian service members, as advocates had touted the principles of patriotism, unit cohesion, and selfless service to help win over military and political conservatives to their side. Indeed, the very choice to fight for military service, marriage, and parenting rights (along with mainstream religious inclusion) reflected an awakening to the crucial fact that full equality meant having the choice to fully belong to the mainstream, and that the more gay people who occupied that space, the harder it would be to cast them as a threat to the nation's most cherished customs and ideals.[14]

By 2012, this message had found its way to the president in one of the most momentous political shifts of his presidency (although, given his 1996 statement in support of gay marriage, it was most accurately described as a shift *back;* in fact, David Axelrod later acknowledged that Obama's public opposition to same-sex marriage was dishonest, and that part of the reason the president wanted to come clean was that, as he put it, "I'm just not very good at bullshitting"[15]). His "evolution," Obama told Roberts, had come about after years of getting to know members of his staff "who are incredibly committed, in monogamous relationships, same-sex relationships, who are raising kids together," and from thinking about the "soldiers or airmen or marines or sailors who are out there fighting on my behalf, and yet feel constrained, even now that Don't Ask, Don't Tell is gone, because they're not able to commit themselves in a marriage."[16] Monogamy, family, military service—these had become almost the default currency for speaking about gay equality. Their echo of conservative values owed a debt to Randy Lloyd and Frank Kameny, as well as Andrew Sullivan and Mehlman. But their development also reflected an understanding by both gay leaders and the president that the most effective way to change opinions and beliefs was to frame them in the terms that were most palatable to those being asked to evolve.

Now this principle was showing up in research by LGBTQ movement organizations, whose focus groups and psychological studies were confirming the wisdom of pursuing change incrementally, an approach that some in the movement had been advocating for years. Ever since the stinging ballot losses in 2004, gay groups had been strategizing about how to turn the tide with voters. Not only was this crucial to actual state marriage wins, but it was key to creating national momentum by crushing the conservative talking point that all the ballot losses proved that Americans opposed gay marriage. To advance public support for gay marriage, Equality California, with support from the Task Force, had started a small project in 2005 called Let California Ring (LCR), a public education campaign that researched and tested what marriage equality messages best resonated with the diverse California public. By 2007, the group had hit upon a novel approach to talking about same-sex marriage: the way folks talked about marriage itself. Rather than emphasize the political rights and legal benefits that marriage offered, LCR began testing messages that stressed the commonality of shared values across sexual orientations and that tapped the capacity of ordinary Americans to empathize with those who might seem different by having people share their own views of why marriage mattered. The goal was to switch the focus from the political to the personal, to discuss not the Constitution or tax benefits but the feelings people have about what marriage means, and to activate in people's hearts what it must feel like to be excluded from something so fundamental. In an ad called "Garden Wedding," a bride prepares for the big moment and makes her way to the altar, but gets tripped up by a series of obstacles, her face revealing growing consternation. As her fiancé—a groom—comes into view, the message appears: "What if you couldn't marry the person you love? Every day, lesbian and gay couples are prevented from marrying. Support the freedom to marry."[17]

Although the group's budget was too small to scale the ad in time for the Proposition 8 campaign, it did conduct a rare field test with a control group. First the group polled residents in Santa Barbara County and in Monterey County. Then it ran the ad repeatedly in Santa Barbara County, but not in Monterey. Finally it conducted the polls again after weeks of the ad run in Santa Barbara. Astoundingly, support for gay marriage shot up eleven points in Santa Barbara County, while it stayed level in Monterey County. Sure enough, the results were confirmed in the real world: Proposition 8 passed easily in Southern California that November, but in one county—Santa Barbara—it lost by ten points.

Equality California's LCR was one of several organizations that began to ramp up its messaging research after the 2004 losses. Others included Third Way, a gay-friendly centrist think tank; the Movement Advancement Project, a think tank for the LGBTQ movement begun by top gay funders; Gay and Lesbian Alliance Against Defamation, which had long focused on media portrayals of gays and lesbians; and some state-based gay advocacy groups, such as Basic Rights Oregon, which had taken a lead role in conducting polls and research to try to determine the most effective ways to fight anti-gay ballot initiatives.[18]

The research during these years—the second half of the Bush presidency, when little seemed winnable at the federal level—was beginning to yield intriguing new insights into what messages and tactics were most likely to change the hearts and minds of the "movable middle": those not yet firmly supportive of marriage equality but considered reachable with the right message. What the movement was learning was that the non-gay public was failing to relate to the aspirations, wishes, and needs of gay couples, even though most of those couples wanted the very same things as straight couples, for the very same reasons. This was partly the result of the early history of the gay rights movement. Ever since gay liberation emerged in the 1970s, gay rights activists had fought their battles using the language of demands for equal rights. In the quest for same-sex marriage, at least since the 1990s, they had generally focused on the financial and government benefits that marriage offered, highlighting the deprivation that came with being denied a government license to wed. The result was that many straight Americans who tuned in came to view the gay rights cause as demanding and confrontational, and they failed to register the wishes and feelings of gay couples as equivalent to their own.

Now, as the movement took stock of roadblocks hindering its effort to introduce gay life even further into the mainstream—with marriage rights taking center stage—the emphasis, said the research, had to shift from confrontation to commonality, from demands for rights to appeals to shared dignity. As a result, "we went to work developing core messages about core values," recalled Tim Sweeney. "We quit talking about legal benefits—talking from the head—and started talking about those shared sets of values like love and commitment that we all share."[19]

These early research efforts were promising but not well coordinated. Each time a gay group in a given state faced a battle—nearly always in a defensive crouch against an upcoming ballot initiative—advocates, often working in isolation and with limited money and knowledge, had to reinvent the wheel. But after the 2009 ballot loss in Maine, which compounded the despair of the previous year's loss in California, gay leaders gathered, as they had following the 2004 ballot losses, to channel their anger and energy into assessing their strategy and increasing their coordination. Matt Coles oversaw an update of the "Winning Marriage" document created in 2005. Chief among the next set of priorities would be to break the thirty-state losing streak of gay marriage ballot measures (at the time, North Carolina had yet to become the thirty-first state loss). "As long as marriage has lost every popular vote, it will be almost impossible to build a sense that the nation is ready for it," said the document. The major marriage donors also made the tough decision to consolidate their funding to focus on only the most promising states, reasoning that making larger investments in the most viable states was crucial to creating state-by-state momentum toward victory nationwide. After 2010, the Civil Marriage Collaborative cut the number of states where it invested in half, from ten to five, so as to funnel more dollars to each critical state. In an effort to ensure efficient investments in laying the groundwork for legislative, ballot, or court wins, the donors laid out specific criteria that state-based groups would have to meet in order to demonstrate the likelihood of achieving majority public support in their state.[20]

Even before the Maine loss, in the summer of 2009, Evan Wolfson had proposed a plan to transform FTM from a kind of marriage movement consulting shop to the nerve center of the campaign itself. In an outline of the plan, he wrote that new opportunities and needs "continue to require attention *state by state,* but are also in need of new *central, federal,* and *national* strategy and capacity." The "cobbled together" approach of the marriage movement thus far was "not sufficient for today's opportunities and challenges." In the Obama era, and with a Democratic-controlled Congress, federal work could now move forward. "The next 5 years have the potential to create the foundation for the culminating sweeping change that will rid the country of marriage discrimination," his paper said.[21]

With a new dose of funding, the group ramped up its staff from five people to forty, and its spending from $3 million annually to more than

$12 million. Wolfson hired Marc Solomon as national campaign director and Thalia Zepatos to oversee messaging research. Zepatos was an experienced campaign consultant and had worked in organizing at the Task Force, where she collaborated with LCR in the effort to build marriage support in California. Arriving at FTM, she began an ambitious project to review as much of the movement's polling and messaging research as she could find, twisting arms to persuade groups to share data they had often paid for and guarded as their own.[22] FTM wanted to aggregate lessons learned, but not for its own sake—it now had the funding and the mandate to share this information with groups across the country who had sometimes taken a ragtag approach to building public and political support for marriage. Wolfson had long preached the importance of conducting a sustained campaign to win hearts and minds, not just in the immediate run-up to elections but between ballot fights, so as to avoid the problem of scrambling to launch an effective defense at the last minute. It was also a waste of scarce resources for groups in dozens of states to undertake their own research. And organizations with minimal professional staff often lacked the resources or know-how to collect solid data, much less deploy it in a winning campaign based on the latest understanding of public opinion research. Finally, the movement was sufficiently motivated, coordinated, and funded to create a proactive, unified campaign to help advance public support for the freedom to marry.[23]

Zepatos's findings, which were collected in a confidential portal called the Marriage Research Consortium, synthesized and built upon what earlier researchers had begun to uncover: rights-based, sometimes confrontational language—the kind with which liberals and the left were historically comfortable—was failing to appeal to the movable middle on marriage. As a result, many straight people thought gay people wanted to marry for wholly different reasons than their own. Shaped by age-old stereotypes about gay people being selfish and hedonistic—attitudes stoked in a masterly way by the religious right—many thought that gay couples wanted to marry just for the basket of goodies marriage offered. When researchers asked straight people in focus groups why they got married, they said it was to express love and commitment to another person. But when asked why a gay couple might get married, respondents thought it was just for personal gain—they wanted the health care coverage or the tax benefits, or perhaps they were just trying to make a political statement. These distinct views of marriage for straight and gay couples were precisely the reason Wolfson had long insisted on using the phrase "freedom to marry" instead of "gay marriage"—because, he explained tirelessly, there is no separate legal structure that ought to apply to gay unions; instead, there is only one "marriage," the common institution that same-sex couples deserved the freedom to join.

The belief that gay people sought something distinct and more radical than what straight people enjoyed was inadvertently (when not purposely) perpetuated by the language historically used for gay rights demands. An oft-repeated statistic was that marriage came with more than a thousand rights and benefits that were denied to gay couples—a figure contained in a Government Accountability Office report issued after DOMA was passed.[24] This focus on rights and benefits had an alluring logic for a variety of LGBTQ constituencies, particularly in the first decade following the Hawaii lawsuit. For the gay lawyers well versed in the language of constitutional rights and long partial to marriage alternatives, which carried the promise of legal protections but not the cultural baggage of the "*m*-word," equal rights formed a natural vocabulary for their quest. Ditto for liberals of all stripes, who prized equality but tended to play down the collective power of marriage as a shared cultural institution. Many gays and lesbians shared this political heritage, and when it was added to a personal history colored by fury over years of stigma and discrimination, the result could easily be a combative tone. Angered by the injustice and deprivation they personally had endured over decades of anti-gay policy and sentiment, inspired by the social and legal framework of the black civil rights movement, and increasingly frustrated by the persistence of homophobia among political leaders and ordinary Americans alike, it felt wholly natural to many gays and lesbians to assert their demand for marriage equality in the language of rights and benefits, and to do so in a tone of righteous and sometimes accusatory rage. Finally, much of America responded to the push for gay marriage with ridicule, scorn, or incredulity. In the face of such reactions, speaking of equal treatment and protection against discrimination could seem far more reasonable than mounting a moral case for marriage equality rooted in empathy and common emotions. For some in the movable middle, the statistics about benefits surely helped awaken them to the rank unfairness of depriving same-sex couples of the right to wed.[25]

Yet because of gay rights advocates' comfort with the language of rights, what the new research said worked best with the voters they now needed to attract felt highly counterintuitive to many of them. Rather than confronting people and calling them "bigots" or seeking to shame them into taking a pro-gay position, gay advocates needed to activate emotions—their own and those of the people they were trying to reach. What must it feel like to be excluded from so central an institution? The task was to emphasize not entitlement but points of commonality: We want to get married for the same reasons you do, to express our love, commitment, and care for a life partner. We are, for the most part, just like you. We are, as Andrew Sullivan put it, "virtually normal."

The new messaging approach, which reflected a commitment of several years and millions of dollars' worth of research, represented a sea change in how gay marriage advocates made their case. Now, instead of demanding equality in the confrontational language of the movement's early days—methods that served a purpose in their era, and which surely helped win some segments of the population, including gays and lesbians themselves, over to the cause of marriage—gay advocates invited straight people to empathize with their experience of exclusion, while assuring them that they wanted not to upend their way of life but to join it. The approach evoked Frank Kameny's insistence on conforming to the dictates of respectable society in order to earn a place within it. It reflected messages that Andrew Sullivan had been promoting since 1989 and that other gay conservatives such as Bruce Bawer and Jonathan Rauch expressed in books in 1993 and 2004.[26] All these strands were now converging in the research of gay groups and the instincts of a new breed of gay and pro-gay conservatives such as Ken Mehlman.

But if the newest way of talking about same-sex marriage hit upon broadly conservative themes, it also reflected Evan Wolfson's original vision of a liberal state whose people are constantly seeking to expand their capacity to empathize with the rights of others. His 1983 law school paper, while naturally emphasizing legal rights, linked those rights to the moral dimension of same-sex love as a positive good for gay people, and to the capacity and duty of Americans to recognize and respect it. Rejecting as too narrow both the left's privacy-based conception of freedom and the right's Puritan understanding of morality, he instead sought to link legal rights to an expanded view of moral autonomy. "The Constitution morally respects the freedom of individuals to create, live, and love in the happiness they can make for themselves in the world, consonant with the rights of others," he had written. "For gay women and men, who also love, samesex marriage is a human aspiration, and a human right. The Constitution and real morality demand its recognition." It was an early blueprint for a constitutional view of human autonomy that included within it the right of people not only to live but to love freely. And it was a vision that was now becoming a reality.

In response to the latest research findings, FTM helped create a new public education campaign, Why Marriage Matters, to emphasize a message of "love, commitment, family" rather than the rights and benefits of marriage. "Why do gay and lesbian couples want to get married?" asked its website. "For similar reasons as anyone who wants to marry. To stand in front of friends and family to make a lifetime commitment to the person they love. To share the joys and the sorrows that life brings. To be a family, and to be able to protect that family." More than thirty state and national organizations became partners in the campaign, allowing for a heightened level of cooperation and efficiency unusual in social movements. Proposed messages, polls, or ads could be fed into a central clearinghouse and quickly enjoy the benefit of a national pollster analyzing their effectiveness. Results were shared widely and tailored to each specific campaign or battle, all using the speed and resources of the professional experts associated with the coalition.[27]

As the 2012 ballot contests heated up, the Why Marriage Matters coalition sprang into action. While it ran ads pushing the message out far and wide, it also went much further than that. Its work with Ken Mehlman was connecting its leaders to an odd bedfellow: a firm called TargetPoint Consulting, founded in 2003, which Mehlman had used to help George W. Bush win his reelection campaign in 2004. TargetPoint was a pioneer of "microtargeting," a method that used the latest technology for gathering personal data to identify and mobilize reachable voters and turn them out for a particular issue or candidate. The idea was to model voting behavior and then tailor a campaign's outreach to target the most likely supporters and to reach them with messages most likely to resonate. This was the key to the new science of microtargeting. Granular consumer data help predict voting behavior. Republicans, for instance, were more likely to support same-sex marriage if they were also NASCAR fans. That meant that knowing who was a NASCAR fan could help determine where to focus campaign outreach, a far more efficient way to mobilize likely supporters than sending direct mailings or making phone calls to every house in the state. Even more important, such data could also determine which specific messages worked best. Mehlman called microtargeting "the political equivalent of smart bombs," allowing campaigns to reach their targets in an ultra-efficient way.[28]

And the coalition didn't stop there. Working with Analyst Institute, a progressive group of academics who studied voter contact results, it field-tested which messages worked best with which cohorts. The key was in following up with potential voters after one group received one message and another received a different message or none at all. Applying micro-targeting and field-testing to a live issue campaign was a revolutionary approach that gay marriage activists embraced with a zeal that pleasantly surprised the researchers. "I love working with the marriage people," said Jennifer Green of Analyst Institute, "because their thinking is long-term and strategic."[29] What impressed her was that advocates were not—or at least not any longer—waiting for specific battles to arise that put them on the defensive, but were coordinating with one another and plotting a professional, incremental, data-driven approach to building support for their issue.

Throughout 2012, versions of this new approach were applied in all four of the states facing ballot votes in November. Maine saw a tightly run campaign led by Matt McTighe, who had worked for HRC and Mass-Equality. There advocates spoke directly to 250,000 people, nearly a fifth of the state's population. And because of microtargeting, those likely voters were probably the ones most open to—but not yet committed to—supporting same-sex marriage. In Washington and Maryland, the state legislatures passed marriage equality early that year, with Democratic governors signing each bill into law. But in each case, opponents placed the measure on the ballot before it could go into effect. In Minnesota, conservatives launched a ballot initiative to ban same-sex marriage via a constitutional amendment.

On election day, gay marriage proponents won big. Voters in all four states backed marriage equality, resulting in the addition of three states that let gays and lesbians wed. In Maine, this meant reversing a voter-approved gay marriage ban just three years after it was created. Anti-marriage-equality champions were not helped by their strident campaign rhetoric:

claiming that homosexuality "center[ed] around anonymous sexual encounters" and was "largely predatory" had come to seem sorely outdated and fundamentally hateful.[30] Minnesota still banned same-sex marriage legislatively, but the defeat of a constitutional ban was a major turning point. (Until then, only Arizona voters had rejected a constitutional ban, in 2006, but they passed one two years later.) Now, all at once, four states had chosen not to block gays and lesbians from getting married—a reversal of the thirty-one-state sweep between 1998 and 2012. Wisconsin elected the country's first openly gay senator, Tammy Baldwin, as openly gay candidates in elections large and small across the nation won in record numbers.

The battle in Maryland, in particular, showcased how marriage had become a top priority for LGBTQ political groups such as HRC. With shaky confidence in how effectively the local Marylanders for Marriage Equality group was shaping up to defend the state's pro-marriage law at the ballot, Wolfson's FTM organization was helping to fund the efforts in Maine, Washington, and Minnesota but not in Maryland. HRC stepped in with more than $1.5 million, and other Washington-based political groups such as the progressive Center for American Progress also supported the marriage effort (in Maryland and beyond). HRC's president Joe Solmonese had announced in 2009 that the LGBTQ movement's "central organizing principle" should be working to repeal DOMA and end marriage discrimination. But he acknowledged that equality would take time, telling the *Washington Post* that "the real measure for me is not so much what happens today as what happens tomorrow." Increasingly viewing marriage as a winnable issue, and one that its member surveys showed was now a top priority, HRC became a significant presence in the state battles for marriage, helping build support for wins in Washington, D.C., in 2009, New York in 2011, and the ballot votes of 2012. Solmonese had hired Mass-Equality's Marty Rouse to direct field operations in 2006, and that meant a long-term commitment to fighting against anti-gay-marriage amendments, expanding national public education efforts, and mobilizing political muscle at the state level. The group's funding, communications, lobbying, and field work for marriage were now showing results, and as Chad Griffin took the helm, its commitment to nationwide marriage equality was not about to waver. HRC would always face community criticism from activists who felt the behemoth organization was either doing too little to support their particular battle or too much on marriage at the expense of other important issues. But its concrete assistance to smaller, state-based marriage outfits in the years leading up to 2012 was a far cry from the days when these groups had complained about minuscule $5,000 "equality grants."[31]

The unprecedented ballot victories were a huge boon to the marriage movement. Not only did they add three marriage states to the running tally and break the undefeated streak of anti-gay-marriage activists at the ballot, but they gave a popular endorsement to the quest for marriage equality, depriving opponents of the talking point that the American people—as shown in vote after vote—wanted to reserve marriage for straights. The momentum was palpable, coming a year after public approval for gay marriage had crossed the 50 percent threshold in national opinion polls, and months after winning the support of the president of the United States. On top of this, after endorsing the freedom to marry, that president won his reelection handily, beating Mitt Romney by a four-point margin, larger than either of George W. Bush's victories. Exit polls showed that gay and lesbian voters backed the president by a three-to-one margin, and some political analysts concluded the gay vote may have been critical to Obama's win.[32]

Even more important, Obama's broader coalition of young people, Catholics, Latinos, and African Americans held fast, breaking for the president. Young people had been motivated to get to the polls, exit surveys showed, by a wish to support marriage equality—and Obama for his support of it. Incredibly, 52 percent of African American and Latino voters told pollsters they supported same-sex marriage, a massive increase from just two years earlier, when a mere 30 percent of African Americans and 41 percent of Latinos backed marriage equality.[33] Maryland's marriage equality ballot win was itself a significant barometer of growing African American support, as nearly a third of the state was African American. Despite the uncertain political ramifications, Obama had decided earlier that year to endorse same-sex marriage before his reelection campaign. Not only had he survived but, demonstrating true leadership, he appeared to have helped advance public support for the issue among key constituencies. In doing so, he helped show that gay equality need not be a toxic issue for politicians. He was hardly the first national politician to do so, and his big step forward—taken a year after polls showed majority support for marriage equality—said as much about the patient, persistent work of

gay strategists and the popular participation of gay activists and their supporters since 2008 as it did about political courage. Still, Obama had had
a choice to make, one that carried risks on both sides, and he'd chosen to
place himself and his administration on the side of equality, sealing his
legacy as a leader before it was too late.

The ballot victories also reflected years of incremental change efforts
by grassroots activists and political groundwork, including the cultivation
of out politicians, which were undertaken to breed familiarity and create
a positive climate for marriage. For years preceding the 2012 vote in Washington, Ed Murray, an openly gay State House member who went on to
become a state senator and then mayor of Portland, had helped lead a successful drive for a nondiscrimination law and then a domestic partnership
bill in the state. As the legislature and electorate became more familiar
with gay people and same-sex relationships, Murray and other gay lawmakers brought their partners and children to dinner with the governor, to
holiday gatherings, and to the statehouse itself. "Getting to know you and
your family, I saw it differently," one conservative lawmaker told an openly
gay representative, in explaining her changed position on same-sex unions.
Another undecided lawmaker told a lesbian colleague that the more he
saw and learned about her family, the more she was "getting" him over to
her side. In 2012 a heartfelt speech lit up YouTube as Republican Rep. Maureen Walsh described what she missed as a straight widow: not the sex but
"that incredible bond that I had with another human being," something
marriage captures in a unique way. She broke ranks with her party to vote
in favor of marriage equality because, she explained, she had concluded it
would be cruel to deny others the great joy she had known. The legislature
passed marriage equality and the voters of the state ratified the decision
that fall.[34] Clearly, the fight to legalize marriage both reflected and further
advanced familiarity with gay people and same-sex love.

Meanwhile, a series of federal lawsuits was working its way through
the legal system. During the summer of 2011, the Bipartisan Legal Advisory Group and Kaplan's team had traded legal motions on the *Windsor*

case, each hoping to win without need for a trial. Attorney Paul Clement's strategy in defending DOMA had two main prongs. Casting the right of gays to wed as "redefining" marriage itself, he first argued that such a major social change should be left to the "democratic process"—voters and their elected officeholders. Second, he insisted that heightened scrutiny did not apply to this suit, a key point that stood to make or break the whole case. If DOMA merely needed a rational basis to be ruled constitutional, any number of hypothetical rationales that might strain credulity could be used to justify the law. "DOMA easily passes the rational basis test," Clement's motion stated, and therefore did not violate the Constitution.[35]

Yet the arguments Clement had to make in order to prevent the court from applying heightened scrutiny were hard to take seriously: that gay people had not faced a history of discrimination; that sexual orientation was a choice and therefore not an immutable trait; and that gay people did not suffer from political powerlessness (the last of these was perhaps an easier one to make, given recent advances for gays and lesbians, but was still a stretch given the very barriers to marriage equality that Clement was defending).[36] A parallel argument that was equally difficult to swallow was that DOMA was necessary because it saved the federal government money and ensured a uniform application of federal benefits across states. For one thing, any law that withheld benefits to some citizens would save money, but that hardly spoke to whether doing so was fair, wise, or constitutional. And regarding the uniform benefits argument, it had the clear whiff of a rationalization for discrimination: offering federal benefits "equally" to all the states clearly meant offering them only to straight couples, even while some states had chosen to honor same-sex marriage. Congress, in other words, wanted the right to pick and choose which marriages it approved and which it dubbed inferior.

Such arguments only seemed to bolster the plaintiffs' claim that DOMA was rooted in nothing more than animus and served no legitimate government interest. The plaintiffs also asserted that the case should indeed be subject to heightened scrutiny, and that the law was a clear violation of the Fifth Amendment's guarantee of personal liberty. All were arguments that were familiar from the *Perry* trial the previous year, but the plaintiffs now had the benefit of citing the U.S. Justice Department's view that the law warranted heightened scrutiny and was unconstitutional.[37]

Clement did all he could to avoid answering specific questions asked of him in discovery, the period early in a lawsuit when both parties can be required to submit requested information to the other. In a dryly amusing exchange, Kaplan complained to the court that BLAG was refusing to answer twenty-three of the questions her team had posed in discovery, including basic questions about its position on fundamental matters in the case: whether the defendant believed that gays and lesbians had faced a history of discrimination, whether sexual orientation was related to job performance, whether gay people could be decent parents—even stating the very purpose of the law they were defending, something Kaplan noted it would have to do in order to win the case. All these were questions the plaintiffs had a right to have addressed before the suit proceeded, argued Kaplan. BLAG claimed it did not need to answer the questions because they were, among other reasons, "undefined and vague." Kaplan shot back: "There is clearly nothing even remotely vague about terms like 'discrimination' 'unequal treatment,' 'stereotypes,' 'denied jobs,' or 'terminated from jobs.'" How could the U.S. government, she asked rhetorically, not understand the term "discrimination," given that it was the force behind both years of formal exclusion and numerous laws protecting some Americans—though not gays and lesbians—from such exclusion? Such phrases, she wrote, are "common English words, and mean precisely what their plain language indicates."[38] The court called some of BLAG's reasoning "disingenuous" and ordered it to answer certain questions, while allowing that a number of others were too "sweeping" and not sufficiently relevant to compel an answer.[39]

Across 2012, federal court rulings pounded DOMA, and several related legal developments made the climate increasingly friendly to marriage equality—just as LGBTQ legal advocates had planned. In February, the liberal Ninth Circuit upheld Judge Walker's meticulous decision invalidating California's Proposition 8 in the *Perry* case. (The decision was stayed.) Weeks later, a district judge ruled against DOMA in the case of *Golinksi v. Office of Personnel Management,* the 2010 case that Lambda had filed in California seeking to allow a court employee to add her wife to her health insurance plan. In April Lambda filed a federal right-to-marry challenge in Nevada, a similar case to *Perry,* and the first to be filed by a movement group. And in May, for the first time, a circuit court struck down DOMA, in GLAD's 2009 case, *Gill v. Office of Personnel Management,* now consolidated with the

Massachusetts suit filed by state attorney general Martha Coakley, *Massachusetts v. Department of Health and Human Services*. With that ruling by the First Circuit Court of Appeals, it became nearly certain that the Supreme Court would hear a DOMA case, as historically the court usually grants review after an appeals court finds a federal law unconstitutional.[40]

In June, Judge Barbara Jones of the U.S. District Court for the Southern District of New York ruled against DOMA in Edie Windsor's case, becoming the fifth judge to strike down the law. Jones's ruling rested mainly on the grounds that Congress had improperly intruded on the province of the states, violating the Constitution's principles of federalism.[41] The law, declared the judge, assumes that the federal government has authority to reconsider decisions by states about whether to legalize same-sex marriage, when in fact the federal government should not be in the business of picking and choosing which state laws to approve and which to reject. "Such a sweeping federal review in this arena does not square with our federalist system of government," she wrote, "which places matters at the 'core' of the domestic relations law exclusively within the province of the states." Jones's decision cited the First Circuit ruling in the Massachusetts cases, a reminder of the importance of patiently building a record when it comes to legal advances. A month later, a federal district judge in Connecticut, Judge Vanessa L. Bryant, struck down DOMA in GLAD's *Pedersen* case.[42]

During Windsor's appeal, her lawyers made the unusual request that the circuit court hear the case on an expedited basis, citing the plaintiff's age, her ailing health, and her wish to have her case resolved while she was still around to see justice served. In a similar move, they asked the Supreme Court to make the unusual decision to hear the case without waiting for the appeals court to render judgment. But things moved so quickly that this turned out not to be necessary. Oral arguments at the circuit court were held in September. In October, the Second Circuit upheld Windsor's district court victory, calling DOMA "an unprecedented breach of long-standing deference to federalism" that did nothing to advance the government's goals of "responsible childrearing"—thus rejecting one of the chief arguments Clement's team had proffered in court. The decision marked the first time a circuit court applied heightened scrutiny to gays and lesbians, a crucial turning point in the battle for legal equality. If one of the nation's twelve appellate courts now used this standard, lower courts, state courts, and other appellate courts could soon follow, making it exceedingly difficult for gay marriage bans to pass constitutional muster.[43]

On December 7, the Supreme Court announced it would hear both Windsor's case and AFER's challenge to Proposition 8. Ten consecutive lower court rulings had recognized the freedom to marry. GLAD's challenge in the *Gill* case was passed over by the Court, likely because of a quirk of history: Justice Elena Kagan had discussed the case when she was Obama's solicitor general before joining the Court. That could have forced her to recuse herself from the case, potentially leaving the Court deadlocked at 4–4, something the justices would rather avoid. Instead it chose to hear two cases brought by movement outsiders that had rattled the marriage equality playing field and rocked the nation in the process.[44]

"You'd have to be an inanimate object not to be disappointed," Bonauto said after learning her case would not make it to the Supreme Court. But the modest lawyer was known among colleagues for having so little ego as to be self-effacing. So far from wallowing about what could have been, she focused on being of use to the cases now headed to the Court. Upon hearing that Windsor's case had been granted review, Robbie Kaplan lost no time calling Bonauto. The two had ultimately collaborated well when their cases were heard at the lower levels, and the initial suspicions they had felt toward each other had largely dissipated. Kaplan asked Bonauto to coordinate the amicus briefs for Windsor's Supreme Court battle, a task she eagerly accepted.[45]

The job was enormous, and enormously important, as the briefs would not only help make the broadest possible case to the justices but would signal—and help expand, in the process—the support of a wide range of American voices for marriage equality. These included, crucially, a brief signed by 278 businesses and employers, including Fortune 500 companies, who complained that DOMA required them to treat their employees differently depending on their sexual orientation and the state they lived in, an administrative nightmare and a detriment to company morale. This brief, like many others signed by religious leaders, scholars, political officials, professional organizations, and more, grew out of the efforts GLAD had begun for the *Gill* case. The business brief created for that suit was the first of its kind, and helped lay the foundation for a key element in winning same-sex marriage: the vocal support of business and corporate leaders who endorsed equality both because they saw public opinion evolving and because they increasingly viewed marriage bans as discriminatory, and that was becoming anathema to a business culture that prized (or at least sought to project that it prized) meritocracy. GLAD and the other legal groups also helped collect briefs for the Olson team, which lacked the deep experience and connections of the movement (though it could fill some of the gaps with conservatives and corporate leaders—for example, Ken Mehlman recruited more than a hundred Republican leaders to sign a brief supporting same-sex marriage). By early 2013, lawyers from the gay legal groups, the Kaplan team, and the Olson team were, despite serious divisions in the past, cooperating closely, holding joint conference calls, meetings, and moot courts, and sharing strategies and contacts as this extraordinary alliance built the strongest cases possible to end federal marriage discrimination. The effort was made even trickier by the need to ensure that neither party said something in briefs or oral arguments that might help their case while harming the other's.

Although President Obama had come out for marriage equality in May 2012, he had disappointed some advocates when he qualified his endorsement by saying that a "healthy process" was playing out in the states, and that he hesitated to see the process "nationalize[d]." The first African American president, it seemed, favored a "states' rights" approach to equality, something that during the black civil rights movement had been used to block equality in several states. This did not sit well with many gay advocates. Worse, their opponents were using Obama's words against their efforts. In an opening brief to the Supreme Court, attorney Charles Cooper quoted Obama's interview for his own argument. If as strong a supporter of gay rights as the president, went Cooper's reasoning, still thought that each state should be able to decide for itself how to define marriage, then the courts should let the democratic process play out state by state, just as the president proposed. And if, as Obama had said, many opponents of gay marriage "are not coming at it from a mean-spirited perspective" but because they cared about families or had strong religious beliefs, then surely DOMA could not have been motivated simply by anti-gay animus, a constitutionally impermissible basis for such a law.[46]

So Olson's team pressed the Justice Department to file a brief supporting their claim that the California ban violated the U.S. Constitution.[47] Now, weighing his options, Solicitor General Donald B. Verrilli Jr. reread the words of the Rev. Dr. Martin Luther King Jr.'s "Letter from Birmingham Jail," and also noted the suicide statistics of gay youth, something Chad Griffin had discussed with Ted Olson in their first meeting. He recommended to Attorney General Holder that the department file the brief. Holder, the first African American to hold the office, agreed. He, too, saw the comparisons to the black civil rights movement, and at this point he viewed anything short of marriage as a "separate but equal" status. Remaining on the sidelines, he decided, "was just not consistent with where we wanted to be tactically, legally or morally."[48]

Meeting with the president and his top legal advisors, Holder and Verrilli made their case to a receptive Obama to weigh in with a brief. But the team was leery of coming on too strong. Along with other legal observers, they were focused on Justice Kennedy, who, while he had authored two major pro-gay Supreme Court rulings, was politically (and by disposition) conservative. He might balk, some worried, at the prospect of striking down either DOMA or Proposition 8 if the only way to do so was to find a constitutional right to same-sex marriage in all fifty states— something the DOMA suit did not seek and the Proposition 8 suit did not require.[49]

The president and his team decided to file the brief, which they did in February 2013, but to write it on narrow grounds, arguing that only those states that already granted domestic partnerships or civil unions were constitutionally obligated to grant same-sex marriage. (The reason was that if the only thing being withheld from gay couples was the word "marriage," this actually demonstrated that the gay marriage ban's "sole purpose was to deny same-sex partners access to marriage"—that is, that nothing but animus could explain excluding gay couples from what straight couples enjoyed.) Echoing the president's personal endorsement of same-sex marriage the previous May, which had highlighted the importance of ongoing dialogue among well-meaning Americans and respect for the state-by-state process of inching toward marriage equality, the Justice

Department's 2013 brief against Proposition 8 was characteristic of the Obama administration, with its support for an incremental approach to picking off state marriage bans without resorting to an immediate national resolution.[50]

It was also consistent with the incremental strategy that LGBTQ legal advocates had formulated and refined over two decades: carefully assess the legal landscape; understand those you need to persuade, including judges; build familiarity with committed same-sex couples through discussion and exposure to gay families; and accumulate state wins as building blocks to national marriage equality at the right time. For many gay advocates, the White House's approach, like that of many gay advocacy groups, had been too slow, as evidenced by the enormous anger and impatience they had expressed since 2009. The White House had not always shared the same game plan as the gay rights movement (itself so often divided), and when Obama's actions were considered inadequate, the public outcry from LGBTQ activists and the media clearly had an impact on the White House all the way up to the top.[51] By 2013, the Obama administration was working virtually in lockstep with the gay rights movement. It was a testament to Obama's management abilities, his values, and his power to further awaken both gay and straight Americans to the dignity of same-sex love. It was also a demonstration of the stunning effectiveness of a movement that had once been confined to tiny and often faceless protests at the distant margins of polite society.

14

"Love Survives Death"

THE WINDSOR RULING

AND ITS AFTERMATH

By the time oral arguments in the Windsor and Proposition 8 cases rolled around in March 2013, the movement had created a climate that few legal observers thought could fail to at least bring down the Defense of Marriage Act. That month, Bill Clinton wrote an op-ed saying that the law he had signed just seventeen years earlier was unconstitutional (and his then press secretary, Mike McCurry, admitted that the president's position back then had been "driven by the political realities of an election year").[1] Tougher to predict than the outcome of the DOMA challenge was whether the American Foundation for Equal Rights would prevail in establishing a right to marry for gay couples nationwide. The first of two mornings of oral arguments that month at the Supreme Court was devoted to the Proposition 8 challenge, now called *Hollingsworth v. Perry*. Olson began his argument by summarizing the harms caused by Proposition 8, much as he had in the trial before Judge Walker. The measure, he began, "walls-off gays and lesbians from marriage," which this Court had called "the most important relation in life." It stigmatized a whole class of people based on their status, "labeling their most cherished relationships as second-rate, different, unequal, and not okay."[2]

At this point Olson was interrupted. "When did it become unconstitutional to exclude homosexual couples from marriage?" Scalia wanted to know, throwing out a number of possible dates. For Scalia, an icon of constitutional originalism, the only possible answer was "never."

Olson refused to put a date on it, but eventually found his footing. "We've learned to understand more about sexual orientation and what it means to individuals," he said, adding a quote from Justice Ruth Bader Ginsberg that he said resonated with him: "A prime part of the history of our Constitution is the story of the extension of constitutional rights to people once ignored or excluded."

Chief Justice John Roberts suggested that the plaintiffs were obsessed with the label of marriage, as if the term meant any less to those urgently trying to keep gay couples from using it. "All you're interested in is the label," Justice Roberts asserted, and he accused the plaintiffs of insisting on changing the definition of that term. Why, he asked Olson, was that word so important to gay and lesbian couples? Olson responded in kind. If one were to say, "You can vote, you can travel, but you may not be a citizen," would that not matter to those excluded from the label "citizen"? In the *Loving* case on interracial marriage, Olson went on, you could have told such couples, "You can't get married, but you can have an interracial union." Everyone would have known this was a separate label and its purpose was to confer on one group an inferior status.

As he had in Walker's trial, Charles Cooper struggled to make headway with his argument. Hoping to show that governments could have a rational basis for banning same-sex marriage, he argued it would be reasonable to believe that "redefining marriage to a genderless institution" could cause harm over time. Asked to explain what that harm could look like, and how it would result from same-sex marriage, he said that including gay unions in the definition of "marriage" could sever the institution's "abiding connection to its historic traditional procreative purposes." There again was the importance of the label itself. But such abstract and imprecise phrases seemed to continually fall on deaf ears, especially when viewed next to the tangible harms experienced by the plaintiffs and the concrete constitutional claims that those real-life stories now made graspable.

The next day, oral arguments were held for Edie Windsor's case. As a strategic matter, it was by now clear to DOMA's defenders that any hint of anti-gay sentiment underlying the law could spell its death knell in court. Approval of gays and lesbians had simply grown too widespread to try to defend the law the way the House Republicans had in their report during the 1996 DOMA debate: as a way of encouraging heterosexuality while expressing "moral disapproval" of homosexuality. Whatever one thought of gay people at this point, in 2013 it was only a minority of Americans who believed that encouraging heterosexuality was a good use of time. And since the 1996 *Romer* ruling and the 2003 *Lawrence* ruling, moral disapproval had become constitutionally suspect as a basis for discriminatory law. Instead, moral disapproval was increasingly falling on opponents of same-sex marriage, who, far from guarding a universally accepted moral order, were coming to be seen as bigots.

As a result, defense attorney Paul Clement focused more and more of his claims on a banal pretext that was failing to gain him traction in the lead-up to the oral arguments: "uniformity," the idea that the federal government was intervening in the marriage industry merely because it wanted to "treat same-sex couples in New York the same as in Oklahoma." Clement used the example of a military couple who could lose benefits if they were transferred from a marriage state to a non-marriage state, creating a disincentive for the couple to accept the transfer. The idea drew skepticism from Solicitor General Verrilli, who was arguing against DOMA for the Obama administration, and who noted that the law was "not called Federal Uniform Benefits Act; It's called the Defense of Marriage Act." It drew equal skepticism from Justice Kennedy, who pointed out, as had the appellate court, that the law singled out only one aspect of marriage to regulate—gender. "It's not really [about] uniformity," he snapped, because if it were, federal law would regulate "all of marriage," and not just step in when gay couples wanted to join. That it drew a line around gay marriages suggested that uniformity was a pretext, as the federal government apparently had no interest in making uniform any of the numerous other aspects of marriage that historically varied by state—age requirements, definitions of parental status, divorce proceedings, et cetera. This was an argument Bonauto and Gay and Lesbian Advocates and Defenders had been making since GLAD mounted its DOMA challenge with *Gill*. It was convincing to the *Windsor* appellate court, which viewed the double standard as "a reason to look upon Section 3 of DOMA with a cold eye." And it now appeared convincing to Kennedy.[3]

That was certainly what the more liberal justices were doing. Justice Ruth Bader Ginsburg spurred laughter and created a brand-new meme when she suggested that DOMA created "two kinds of marriage: the full marriage, and then this sort of skim-milk marriage." Justice Elena Kagan dug further. "Maybe," she suggested to Clement, "Congress had something

different in mind than uniformity." When Congress singles out an unpopular group, it waves a "red flag" that its judgment may have been "infected
by dislike, by fear, by animus." Indeed, she said, quoting from the House
report, DOMA's backers had written their animus right into the historical
record: "Congress decided to reflect and honor a collective moral judgment and to express moral disapproval of homosexuality." Wasn't that,
Kagan wanted to know, really what had happened when Congress passed
DOMA in 1996?

In the courtroom could be heard soft murmurs of disbelief. Clement
said that if the admission in the report was enough to strike the law down,
then so be it. But "just because a couple of legislators may have had an improper motive" to support the bill should not doom it in court. The conservative justices stepped in with backup for Clement. Justice Roberts noted
that eighty-four of one hundred senators had voted for DOMA in 1996, and
that the standard-bearer of the Democratic Party, Bill Clinton, had signed it.
Could it really be, he wanted to know, that all those American leaders had
been motivated by animus and moral disapproval of gay people? And at a
time when no country or state in the world permitted gay marriage?[4]

In responding to such challenges, Kaplan and Verrilli were engaged
in a delicate dance. It was no secret that the conservative justices asking
these questions were aligned with supporters of the law. And while it was
one thing to disagree respectfully about whether a law was wise or unwise,
it was quite another to suggest that someone was a bigot—especially a Supreme Court justice whose vote a lawyer was trying to win. Of course they
were not insinuating that all those folks had been motivated by anti-gay
animus, Kaplan and Verrilli both replied. "I certainly would not suggest
that it was universally motivated by something other than goodwill," tried
Verrilli. But, he maintained, even a "more subtle, more unthinking" kind
of discrimination was not a constitutionally permissible basis for the law.

Kaplan agreed. "I'm not saying it was animus or bigotry," she explained,
but rather an "incorrect understanding that gay couples were fundamentally different than straight couples." It was an echo of Shannon Minter's
claim to the California Supreme Court in 2008 that the nation had "awakened to the full humanity of gay people and to a fuller notion of what liberty and equality requires." Kaplan then quoted Kennedy's 2003 opinion in
Lawrence: "Times can blind," she said, and "we can all understand that people
have moved on this" and now recognize that such distinctions are false.

Indeed, said Kaplan, articulating her broader argument to the Court, there was no legitimate difference between straight and gay married couples "that can possibly explain the sweeping, undifferentiated and categorical discrimination of DOMA."

Outside the courtroom after the hearings, Edie Windsor, predicting victory, reveled in her star power. Mobbed by well-wishers who seemed to literally hold the eighty-three-year-old woman up, Windsor effortlessly charmed the crowd of reporters and supporters. "Hi. I'm Edie Windsor," she said. "Somebody wrote me a large speech which I'm not going to make." Instead, she spoke from her heart. "I am today an out lesbian, who just sued the United States of America, which is kind of overwhelming for me." She marveled at how far the nation had come in just a decade. "I'm speaking to you guys freely," she told the press, saying that just ten years earlier, "I'd have been hiding in the closet." For all the talk of rights and benefits in the courtroom, Windsor helped the nation focus on the personal and emotional—on the intangible aspect of dignity that marriage equality signaled. "It's a magic word," she said of marriage. "For anybody who doesn't understand why we want it and why we need it, it is magic."[5]

In May, likely buttressed by the attention garnered by Windsor's case, the state-by-state strategy yielded more fruit, racking up three additional wins, as Democratic governors signed freedom-to-marry bills in Rhode Island, Delaware, and Minnesota, whose voters had cleared the way for marriage equality when they rejected a constitutional ban the previous November. When Minnesota passed its bill, Rep. Michele Bachmann predicted that God would destroy Minneapolis as he had Sodom and Gomorrah. "I don't want my family to be the last ones out," she told a local television reporter.[6]

With the addition of three marriage equality states that spring, twelve states, including all of New England, as well as the District of Columbia allowed same-sex marriage on the eve of the Supreme Court's decision in the *Windsor* and *Hollingsworth* cases, covering 18 percent of the American population. (Also that spring, France, Uruguay, and New Zealand became the twelfth, thirteenth, and fourteenth nations to allow same-sex marriage.) National polls in the United States found that nearly 60 percent of Americans favored marriage equality.[7] That figure was significantly higher than the number of Americans who supported interracial marriage when the Supreme Court struck down bans against it in 1967. But the twelve

Edie Windsor, pictured here at age eighty-three, greets an adoring crowd on the Supreme Court steps after oral arguments in her case in 2013. She holds a crumpled-up speech that she declined to read, instead charming well-wishers by speaking from the heart. For those wondering what marriage meant to gays and lesbians, she said, "It is magic!"

states allowing same-sex marriage constituted a much smaller number than the thirty-four states that had permitted interracial marriage by 1967. That meant that while the climate for a DOMA win was auspicious, the prospect of declaring a federal right to same-sex marriage in the Proposition 8 case—the broadest possible ruling that the Olson team was hoping for—still seemed dim.[8]

On June 26, 2013, ten years to the day after the *Lawrence* ruling that struck down sodomy bans, the Supreme Court handed down its decisions in both

Windsor and *Hollingsworth*. In the *Hollingsworth* challenge, as some members of the Olson team had quietly feared, the Court declined to decide whether Proposition 8 was unconstitutional, ruling that the decision by California's governor and attorney general not to appeal the trial ruling should have been the end of the road. The proponents of Proposition 8 who had stepped in to take on that appeal, said the Court, never had the right to do so, and so Judge Walker's ruling striking down the ban was the final word. The Court's ruling restored marriage equality to the state of California, making the nation's most populous state the thirteenth to allow marriage equality, and placing 30 percent of the American population in a jurisdiction that allowed gay couples to marry. Olson's team was pleased, of course, that its legal challenge had returned marriage equality to California. But it was disappointed that it failed to achieve its larger goal of establishing a nationwide right to marry at the Supreme Court, an objective that nearly all the movement lawyers had said was too ambitious.[9]

Unlike the Proposition 8 ruling, which failed to reach a decision on the merits (the case did set a precedent on the procedural matter of standing, but not on the substantive question of whether same-sex marriage bans were constitutional, having sidestepped that question when it dismissed the appeal as wrongly heard), the *Windsor* ruling would turn out to have an enormous impact on the path toward national marriage equality. In his opinion, Justice Kennedy first established the constitutional and moral legitimacy of the decision by New York to recognize and perform within its own borders marriages like that of Windsor and Spyer's. Here his language reflected what was likely a personal—but also quite widespread—journey of awakening to the moral justness of same-sex marriage. "It seems fair to conclude," he wrote, "that, until recent years, many citizens had not even considered the possibility that two persons of the same sex might aspire to occupy the same status and dignity as that of a man and woman." For most Americans, he wrote, the heterosexual nature of marriage was inherent in its definition. When the concept of a same-sex marriage began to take root, reactions were often split. For some, the fundamental heterosexuality of marriage "became even more urgent, more cherished when challenged." But for others "came the beginnings of a new perspective, a new insight." Those states where the former view prevailed banned gay marriage, while in other states, these exclusions came to seem unjust. New York's decision to permit gay marriage reflected the community's "evolving understanding of the meaning of equality," he wrote, in an echo of his declaration in *Lawrence* that "as the Constitution endures, persons in every generation can invoke its principles in their own search for greater freedom." In 2011, he recounted, New York had "acted to enlarge the definition of marriage to correct what its citizens and elected representatives perceived to be an injustice that they had not earlier known or understood."[10]

Woven through Kennedy's opinion were repeated references to the "pride," "dignity," "integrity," "worthiness," and "respect" that marriage conferred on individuals. Although he noted the more than 1,000 benefits and protections that marriage afforded, his focus was squarely on the intangibles—the emotional and psychological returns of marriage that the LGBTQ movement had begun to highlight since its more recent messaging research showed that those approaches resonated better with Americans than did touting the rights and benefits marriage afforded. Marriage "is more than a routine classification for purposes of certain statutory benefits," Kennedy wrote. It is "a far-reaching legal acknowledgement of the intimate relationship between two people." In this morally tinged language about the power of marriage to ennoble a union and the role of the law to constitute a marriage could be heard distinct echoes of Evan Wolfson's paper from exactly thirty years earlier. "Samesex marriage," he had insisted, was a human right and "the Constitution and real morality demand its recognition."

Indeed, the Court's ultimate determination that DOMA was unconstitutional relied extensively on the emotional injuries the law imposed on gay couples by refusing to recognize their marriages, and in particular by depriving them of the "label" marriage, as Olson had argued in the sister case. The purpose and impact of DOMA, as Kagan had suggested, was succinctly expressed in the legislative record of its enactment, its text, and its very name, which laid bare a belief that marriage must be "defended" against the harm that including gay people would cause to it. Although opponents of gay marriage had tried hard in recent years to avoid sounding anti-gay, there was no escaping what was written into the record as DOMA was being debated and passed: that reserving marriage for straights was an expression of "moral disapproval of homosexuality." Hence DOMA's "avowed" purpose, Kennedy concluded, is "to impose a disadvantage, a separate status, and so a stigma upon all who enter into same-sex marriages."[11] Kennedy also noted the argument that Bonauto and Kaplan had prominently featured in the briefs: In creating a federal definition of marriage, DOMA made an unusual foray—Kennedy called it a "deviation"—into what was normally the province of the states, throwing the law into the territory of what *Romer* had called "discriminations of an unusual character." That deviation, Kennedy concluded, was "strong evidence" that the law was about stigmatizing gay people rather than about serving a legitimate government purpose.

The remainder of Kennedy's opinion reads like a legal rampage against the rationalizations invoked to defend the law. "DOMA writes inequality into the entire United States Code," said the Court. It declares every same-sex marriage to be "second-tier" and "less worthy." It "humiliates tens of thousands of children now being raised by same-sex couples" by telling them and the world that their parents' union is illegitimate. It only serves "to disparage and to injure" couples whose dignity the state of New York chose to protect with its own valid law. The opinion concluded by stating that "the principal purpose and the necessary effect of this law are to demean those persons who are in a lawful same-sex marriage. This requires the Court to hold, as it now does, that DOMA is unconstitutional as a deprivation of the liberty of the person protected by the Fifth Amendment of the Constitution."

Kennedy's opinion had begun with the observation that many Americans had never even considered that a gay couple might want to become a married pair. Viewing marriage as inherently heterosexual was not, in this reading, a matter of bigotry, but reflected age-old habits of thought that had simply not yet evolved to conceive of marriage from "a new perspective." This line of thinking could have served as an escape hatch for declining to strike down DOMA. If the law had not been rooted in animus against gay people, it would have been easier to regard it as having a constitutional foundation because it could have been seen to have a legitimate government purpose—any of the more positive-sounding rationales proffered by its more high-minded backers, such as preserving the functions of a traditional institution or creating uniformity in how the government treats marriages. But Kennedy's opinion ended with a forceful repudiation of the impermissible hostility that clearly lay at the root of the law. That the Court was able to note the more innocent side of Americans' resistance to gay marriage while ultimately finding animus at DOMA's core suggests that the law itself, passed in 1996, appeared too late in the nation's collective awakening to gay dignity to plausibly reflect such innocuous intentions.

Upon hearing the news that she had won her suit, Edie Windsor, sitting with Robbie Kaplan in her lower Manhattan apartment, declared, "I want to go to Stonewall!" First managing to receive—and accidentally hang up on—a congratulatory call from President Obama, Windsor toured Greenwich Village in a hired SUV and alighted to a hero's welcome at the Stonewall Inn, so near and yet so far past, where she had begun her journey as a lesbian more than half a century ago. As she climbed a stage set up for the rally, hundreds gathered to celebrate the news, crying joyously and thanking this self-described "goofy old lady" whose lawsuit brought down one of the last bastions of discriminatory federal law in the country.[12]

Of course, not everyone was celebrating. Rep. Vicky Hartzler of Missouri called the ruling "a dangerous precedent which strips power away from Congress with respect to defining national marriage policy." Tapping long-standing stereotypes about gay hedonism and irresponsibility, Rep. Timothy Huelskamp of Kansas, a fellow Republican, complained that the decision "allowed the desires of adults to trump the needs of children."[13] In a characteristically fiery dissent that castigated his colleagues' opinion as "legalistic argle-bargle" whose vague legal principles amounted to "nonspecific hand-waving," Justice Antonin Scalia warned of a cavalcade of lawsuits against state marriage bans that, in light of the Court's majority opinion, could not survive a challenge. "No one should be fooled," he wrote. "It is just a matter of listening and waiting for the other shoe." By deeming anyone opposed to same-sex marriage "an enemy of human decency, the majority arms well every challenger to a state law restricting marriage to its traditional definition." Scalia then made a bitter promise: "The only thing that will 'confine' the court's holding is its sense of what it can get away with." Like so many social conservatives watching as the nation embraced the dignity of gay people, Scalia seethed at the idea that supporting a position that had long been viewed as common sense could now render someone a bigot. "In the majority's telling, this story is black-and-white: Hate your neighbor or come along with us. The truth," Scalia declared, "is more complicated." Yet if DOMA was motivated simply by constitutionally impermissible animus, as the majority declared, "how easy it is, indeed how inevitable, to reach the same conclusion with regard to state laws denying same-sex couples marital status." Justice Clarence Thomas and Justice Roberts joined, in part, Scalia's dissent. Roberts also wrote his own dissent, as did Justice Samuel Alito.[14]

Scalia, it would turn out, was exactly right. In the first month after the *Windsor* ruling, gay and lesbian couples filed at least half a dozen new lawsuits in both federal and state courts challenging marriage discrimination in Pennsylvania, Arkansas, Louisiana, Virginia, Ohio, and Kentucky. The first of these, in Pennsylvania, was brought by the American Civil Liberties Union, but many others were brought by private law firms representing plaintiffs, sometimes pro bono, who had generally reached out to them for relief from real-life harms. The logic of *Windsor*—and the momentum of the gay rights movement's successes—had made the challenges irresistible, not only to LGBTQ legal groups but to gay and lesbian plaintiffs and to lawyers across the country eager to join the cause. Now there seemed to be a particularly strong case that same-sex marriages validly performed in one state must be recognized by other states, even if granting the freedom to marry in those states might not be required. After all, if the Supreme Court declared that the federal government must recognize same-sex marriages, why shouldn't the states have to do the same?

The *Windsor* ruling ultimately unleashed dozens of new lawsuits, and breathed life into existing suits that had been filed months or years earlier.[15] By the end of 2013, the smattering of new suits had become a torrent, with at least forty pending in twenty states.[16] And the "Windsor effect" began to make itself clear. The first state to win marriage equality after the *Windsor* decision was New Jersey. The state had passed a civil union law in 2006, after the state supreme court handed down a decision in a Lambda lawsuit first filed in 2002. The ruling paralleled that of Vermont in 1999: gay couples are entitled to all the same rights as straight couples, and the legislature must determine how to provide those rights. Like Vermont, New Jersey chose civil unions instead of outright marriage. But the legislature simultaneously established a commission that would study the reality of civil unions and report on whether the arrangement adequately fulfilled the court order. In 2008 the commission found that the state's Civil Union Act was, as the president of the New Jersey State Bar Association put it in testimony, "a failed experiment." The commission noted that "the separate categorization established by the Civil Union Act invites and encourages unequal treatment of same-sex couples and their children," and recommended that the law be changed to allow marriage itself.[17] The legislature took no action until 2012, when it passed a marriage equality bill. But Gov. Chris Christie vetoed it, saying that a social change "of this magnitude and importance" should be decided by the voters.[18]

In 2011 Lambda filed another state lawsuit on behalf of New Jersey's main gay rights group, Garden State Equality, and several same-sex couples. In that suit, Lambda argued that, as the state commission's report had found, civil unions failed to provide same-sex couples with benefits and protections on a truly equal footing with other couples. A decision was still pending in that case when the *Windsor* ruling transformed the legal landscape overnight. The 2006 New Jersey court ruling had mandated that same-sex couples enjoy the same rights as straight couples, and the legislature had responded with civil unions. But now that *Windsor* had extended all the federal benefits of marriage to gay couples who were married by state law, having a civil union in New Jersey was an even clearer deprivation: not only did gay couples suffer the indignity of having to call their union by a lesser name and the uncertainty of having both public and private entities potentially not recognize their partnership, but now they were passed over for hundreds of material benefits doled out to married couples by the federal government. Elsewhere gay married couples—so long as their state allowed them to wed—now enjoyed these rights.

So on July 3, 2013, Lambda lawyers filed a new brief arguing that, under the changed circumstances following the *Windsor* ruling, the couples' inferior status as civil union couples was depriving them of rights that their own state constitution guaranteed them—as interpreted by the New Jersey Supreme Court back in 2006. Superior court judge Mary C. Jacobson agreed with the plaintiffs. "Whereas before *Windsor,* same-sex couples in New Jersey would have been denied federal benefits regardless of what their relationship was called," she wrote in her decision, "these couples are now denied benefits solely as a result of the label placed upon them by the State."[19]

Governor Christie, who was now considering a run for president, at first signaled his intent to fight the ruling. His administration filed a brief arguing that it was the federal government and not the state of New Jersey that was withholding benefits from gay couples because of the way they are classified—never mind that it was New Jersey that was forcing the classification on gay couples. In October the state supreme court determined that the *Windsor* ruling had "changed the contour of the pending lawsuit," and it rejected Christie's defense of the state's ban as unpersuasive. "The state has advanced a number of arguments," wrote the court, "but none of them overcome this reality: Same-sex couples who cannot marry are not treated equally under the law today. The harm to them is real, not abstract or speculative." The court also rejected efforts to delay letting same-sex marriages go forward pending an appeal. As a result, New Jersey began allowing same-sex marriages on October 21, 2013, making it the fourteenth state to legalize gay marriage—and the first of many that followed directly from Edie Windsor's successful lawsuit.[20] Christie, sensing the legal futility and political unpopularity of an appeal, announced that week that his administration would not continue to fight the ruling, ending the battle for marriage equality in New Jersey.

In November, within the span of one week, legislatures in Hawaii and Illinois voted to legalize same-sex marriage. Hawaii's bill was signed into law by Governor Neil Abercrombie twenty years after the state's high court had first put gay marriage on the map with its surprise ruling in *Baehr v. Lewin.* Adopting the identical reasoning of the New Jersey court, the Hawaii bill began by acknowledging its debt to the *Windsor* ruling, which had spurred Governor Abercrombie to call the legislature to a special session to consider the legislation. The "recent decision of the United States Supreme Court," said the bill's preamble, meant that gay married couples—but not those in a civil union—would now enjoy full federal rights and benefits. Hawaii had granted gay couples civil union status in 2011, so, as in New Jersey, the *Windsor* ruling had relegated such couples to a distinctly inferior status with a clear deprivation of tangible rights and protections for their union. Therefore, the legislature announced, it would now "ensure that same-sex couples are able to take full advantage of federal rights, benefits, protections, and responsibilities" granted to other couples "by allowing same-sex couples to marry under the laws of this state." This the legislature had the power to do, because although voters had approved a constitutional amendment in 1998, it did not ban gay marriage outright but put the decision in the hands of the legislature.[21]

Hawaii's path to marriage equality followed a classic incremental course that—fittingly, given its formative role—epitomizes the change model that LGBTQ legal advocates plotted out for the broader national marriage equality effort—*after,* as was so often the case, the suit was first launched by activists outside the professional movement against the advice of its leaders. The model was this: a lawsuit launched a public dialogue, which occasioned countless conversations among gay and non-gay residents, which showcased the stories of ordinary gay people who simply wanted to live their lives on equal terms with their straight counterparts; voters reacted in the early years by pushing back against change, resulting in laws and sentiment that blocked marriage equality; the state passed first a reciprocal-beneficiaries law that granted limited rights and protections to same-sex couples, and fourteen years later a more comprehensive civil unions law; and finally the state, through its legislature, was ready to legalize same-sex marriage.

Like Hawaii, Illinois had passed a broad civil unions law in 2011. Advocates had hoped to make the state the first in the Midwest to legalize marriage by a legislative vote, but fierce opposition, especially by Catholic and African American religious and political leaders, slowed the process, and Minnesota took the honor in the spring of 2013. Illinois's diverse LGBTQ activist community was fractured and angry that summer as disappointment about the stalled bill sunk in, and blame was directed in particular at statehouse Democrats for failing to deliver. But the failure of the legislature to pass marriage equality became a unifying force in the activist community, where an "insider-outsider" game of donors, lobbyists, and out gay politicians ultimately joined forces with street protestors and gay publications—Tracy Baim, publisher of the *Windy City Times,* was particularly active in trying to bring pro-gay forces together—to salvage the Illinois marriage effort. The coalition garnered endorsements by labor groups, progressive religious leaders, and even a statement of support by President Obama, the first time he spoke out directly in favor of a specific state's marriage battle. A lawsuit brought by Lambda and ACLU added further pressure on the legislature to get the job done.[22]

By November, with the winds of *Windsor* at its back, the bill finally had the support needed to pass, including three votes from GOP members of the house. At a festive signing ceremony with live music, Gov. Pat Quinn sat before a backdrop of state and rainbow flags and signed the bill with one hundred different pens. The documents sat on the desk of Abraham Lincoln, who was referenced repeatedly as a champion of the principles of liberty and equality that were being celebrated that day for gay couples. With Illinois becoming the sixteenth state and seventeenth jurisdiction, including Washington, D.C., to allow gay marriage, more than half the U.S. population lived somewhere that let same-sex couples wed. (The law was set to take effect June 1, 2014, but the movement lawsuit yielded a ruling by a federal judge in February that, in certain places and situations, gay couples had the right to wed immediately. The first couple to legally marry in the state included Vernita Gray, an African American lesbian and longtime activist who fought for the right to wed as hard as she fought her cancer, adding poignancy to her court-ordered marriage just four months before she died.)[23]

Hawaii and Illinois had passed bills long held up in their legislatures, which were dislodged with the momentum of *Windsor.* But in December 2013 the dominoes truly began to fall. On December 19 the New Mexico Supreme Court struck down the state's same-sex marriage ban in a suit begun by ACLU, the National Center for Lesbian Rights, and private lawyers earlier that year. The court held that "the State of New Mexico is constitutionally required to allow same-gender couples to marry and must extend to them the rights, protections, and responsibilities that derive from civil marriage under New Mexico law." The ruling came a few months after a summer of frenzied activity in which state courts, noting that no law actually specified that same-sex couples could not get married, ordered certain counties to issue licenses, and several clerks in other counties followed suit.[24]

The next day, on December 20, not yet six months after the *Windsor* ruling came down, a federal court first cited that decision in finding a constitutional right to marry for gay couples in—of all places—Utah. The suit bubbled up from a grassroots effort begun by Mark Lawrence, who after the passage of Proposition 8 started a Facebook group called Restore Our Humanity to raise money to challenge Utah's gay marriage ban. Lawrence, who had cut his teeth protesting Anita Bryant's anti-gay campaigns and now found himself battling lung cancer, met with little interest from national gay groups, although he eventually got support from two Utah gay rights groups, Equality Utah and the Pride Center. The coalition raised money from individuals and businesses and was able to hire a small law firm, Magleby and Greenwood, to represent three couples seeking to marry or have their marriage recognized in Utah. The team filed suit in the spring of 2013.[25]

The lead attorney at Magleby was Peggy Tomsic. Kate Kendell, who was from Utah, had known Tomsic for years. When she heard about the lawsuit, she wondered why Tomsic didn't plan to wait to file until the *Windsor* decision came down, since such a major case could contain analysis that would be helpful to shaping the arguments in a new filing. She phoned Tomsic to air her concerns. In recent years Kendell herself had thought about bringing suit in Utah, but she was "laughed out of the room" just for mentioning it to other gay and lesbian lawyers. Many Roundtable lawyers hoped Tomsic would not bring the case. Kendell, although not opposed to the suit, remained nervous about prospects for success in the Tenth Circuit, and wanted to make sure any lawsuit there was well-conceived and properly timed. Tomsic listened to Kendell's concerns—and filed anyway. Kendell and her NCLR colleagues quietly helped behind the scenes, recognizing that at this point, the idea of carefully plotting the path to marriage equality—of bringing lawsuits with the best odds of success only in the best circuits before the best judges—had "gone to hell in a handbasket."[26]

As it turned out, Tomsic's timing was perfect. In his December ruling, U.S. district judge Robert J. Shelby made Utah—the conservative headquarters of the Mormon church, which had done so much to thwart marriage equality—the second state after California to have its marriage ban struck down in federal court. The *Windsor* ruling had emphasized the sovereignty of states in making decisions about marriage, raising questions about whether its impact would be limited primarily to state authority issues or would extend to constitutional principles about gay marriage itself. If the Utah decision was any indication of the future, the answer was the latter. "The State's current laws deny its gay and lesbian citizens their fundamental right to marry," Shelby wrote, "and, in so doing, demean the dignity of these same-sex couples for no rational reason. Accordingly, the court finds that these laws are unconstitutional."[27] Gay marriage bans were on the run, along with their sometimes stupefied and increasingly embittered advocates.

Seeming to relish the irony, Judge Shelby, an Obama appointee, credited Justice Scalia for providing the reasoning Shelby used in his pro-gay-marriage decision. Scalia, wrote Shelby, had helpfully "recommended how this court should interpret the Windsor decision when presented with the question that is now before it." Whether it was a federal or state law denying marital status to same-sex couples, Scalia had noted, the Constitution's equal protection guarantee applies to gays and lesbians. "The court agrees with Justice Scalia's interpretation of *Windsor,*" Shelby concluded, "and finds that the important federalism concerns at issue here are nevertheless insufficient to save a state-law prohibition that denies the Plaintiffs their rights to due process and equal protection under the law."[28]

Shelby then bid a decisive farewell to the pesky *Baker* precedent that so many judges had cited to rebuff marriage discrimination lawsuits. Since the Supreme Court had dismissed that 1972 challenge "for want of a substantial federal question," Shelby wrote, significant "doctrinal development" (including three pro-gay high court decisions written by Justice Kennedy) meant that the legal landscape had officially changed: "There is no longer any doubt that the issue currently before the court in this lawsuit presents a substantial question of federal law. As a result, *Baker v. Nelson* is no longer controlling precedent."[29]

Starting the night of Shelby's ruling, first dozens and then hundreds of couples lined up outside state marriage bureaus. The chaotic but jubilant scene at the Salt Lake County clerk's office forced the chief deputy clerk to return from vacation to handle the crowds. Utah's Republican governor, Gary Herbert, denounced the ruling by an "activist judge" as counter to the people's will, and vowed to "defend traditional marriage" by seeking a stay and appealing the decision. But both Judge Shelby and the Tenth Circuit Court of Appeals declined to issue stays. It wasn't until January 6, 2014, more than two weeks later, that the Supreme Court stayed the decision and halted further marriages. By then, more than 1,200 same-sex couples had married in one of the most conservative states in the nation.[30]

—

As Christmas 2013 approached, James Obergefell awaited news of a ruling in a case he had brought with the help of the Cincinnati law firm Gerhardstein and Branch. Obergefell was the widower of John Arthur. The two had met in 1992 as young men and created a life together that had lasted over twenty years. In 2011 Arthur was diagnosed with amyotrophic lateral sclerosis (ALS), known also as Lou Gehrig's disease, and, as in the relationship between Edie Windsor and Thea Spyer, the illness brought out the true measure of the couple's devotion. The debilitating disease quickly took its toll, confining Arthur to his bed, with Obergefell tending to his daily needs.

The men were increasingly aware of Arthur's deteriorating health and of the excitement in the air over a number of states legalizing same-sex marriage. But if they decided to wed, they wanted to do it in their home state, and that was something Ohio would not allow. News of the *Windsor* ruling in July 2013 moved the couple deeply. Obergefell reacted immediately upon seeing the verdict on television. He embraced Arthur in his bed and proposed.

A Facebook post went out in hopes of securing assistance in getting the two men to Maryland, where they could legally marry. As luck would have it, someone with ties to a medical jet responded, and friends and family rallied to raise $13,000 to charter the plane needed to get them to marriage-friendly terrain. On July 11, following in the footsteps of Edie Windsor and Thea Spyer six years earlier, they set out accompanied by a small cadre of medical assistants, pilots, and Arthur's enthusiastically supportive aunt, Paulette Roberts, who obtained an online ordination so she could officiate at their nuptials. Landing in Baltimore, the couple held a brief ceremony right on the plane, promising each other their love, support, and commitment. And then the group set off for home.

A week later, as they absorbed the news that Obergefell still would not be listed as the surviving spouse on Arthur's death certificate since Ohio refused to recognize same-sex marriages from Maryland, the couple was referred to civil rights attorney Al Gerhardstein. A forty-year veteran of private civil rights litigation, Gerhardstein's first foray into gay rights advocacy was an effort to help his brother, a popular Catholic-school teacher who in the 1980s had married a man in a church ceremony, only to be swiftly dismissed from his job as a result. There was no legal recourse, but Gerhardstein saw the pain that blatant discrimination created, and took several cases over the years defending gay and transgender clients, including cooperating with Lambda and the ACLU. Never, though, had he thought of leading an effort to win same-sex marriage. "I thought Evan Wolfson was nuts," he said. Because he lived in socially conservative Cincinnati, which he called "Reactionaryland," marriage seemed an impossible option, and he thought it a far better tactic to fight for job protections, the right to public accommodations, and other issues around discrimination. "I was wrong and he was totally right," he later concluded about Wolfson's pushing of marriage, "and I'm o glad he did the work he did to pioneer that concept."[31]

When the *Windsor* ruling came down, Gerhardstein found it tremendously exciting and thought immediately about how it could apply to Ohio. Like the LGBTQ legal groups, Gerhardstein thought incrementally. In such a conservative part of the country, he didn't think it wise to sue for the full right to marry. "I thought I should just copy *Windsor*," he explained, which was a marriage recognition approach. And he realized that both the federal government (with DOMA) and states such as Ohio (that refused to recognize other states' gay marriages) were applying a double standard to gay unions: they deferred to state determinations of which marriages were valid—unless they were same-sex marriages. Ohio, for instance, did not allow fourteen-year-olds or first cousins to marry, but if they wed in a state that did allow such marriages, Ohio would recognize the unions as valid. "This was an equal protection issue," Gerhardstein quickly realized, just as GLAD had recognized when first developing its attack on DOMA. "If Ohio is going to recognize other out-of-state marriages that can't be performed here, they should also recognize gay marriages from the states that allow them." The idea was to ask the court for the lightest lift, to climb only to the next rung on the ladder. "I wanted to take the smallest step I could possibly take," said Gerhardstein.

Fortuitously, a friend introduced him to Obergefell and Arthur, fresh off the plane from their tarmac wedding in Baltimore. After an emotional meeting, the couple decided to fight for the right to a proper death certificate. They filed suit against the state in federal court on July 19.

Like Kaplan, Gerhardstein was not a total outsider to the LGBTQ movement. Both had worked with the gay legal groups on important cases, and followed developments as well as they could. So the Ohio lawyer was not surprised to get a call from James Esseks of the ACLU expressing his concerns about the case. Cincinnati was not a very progressive place, and, more to the point, the Sixth Circuit, where it was located, seemed like a hostile place to bring a gay marriage claim. Gerhardstein knew that filing a federal suit in Ohio wasn't part of the movement lawyers' plan. Yet he felt that his suit fit squarely within that plan. He was adjusting to the conservative turf he was on by filing only a recognition case, not a right-to-marry case, thus seeking less from the court and minimizing the risk of setbacks in case of a loss. And unlike Peggy Tomsic's Utah suit, Gerhardstein had waited until after the *Windsor* ruling came down before filing in Ohio. "I'm just over here copying *Windsor*," he thought. He understood the movement lawyers' caution, but felt he had thought it through. "That's why my case is so narrow," he explained to Esseks. "I get that you guys have a plan. You're making good progress and I'm excited for it. But I don't think I'll hurt you too much." There was nothing to worry about, he reassured the ACLU.

Gerhardstein was right. With record speed, the suit was scheduled, heard, and decided. On July 22, mere days after the filing, U.S. district judge Timothy S. Black, applying the principles of *Windsor,* ruled in favor of Obergefell and Arthur, issuing a preliminary injunction against the state. In his ruling, Black noted that Ohio generally recognized all validly performed marriages from other states—except when it came to those of gay couples. "How then can Ohio, especially given the historical status of Ohio law, single out same-sex marriages as ones it will not recognize?" Black asked. "The short answer is that Ohio cannot." Black called the uncertainty around the question of how Arthur's death certificate would read "the cause of extreme emotional hardship" for the two men: "Dying with an incorrect death certificate that prohibits Mr. Arthur from being buried with dignity constitutes irreparable harm." Obergefell was deeply touched. What a new and profound emotion, he thought, "to have a federal judge say, 'You know what, John and Jim, your relationship exists and it's just as valid as any other married couple.'" It was, he told the press, "an incredible feeling—that we do matter."[32] When Arthur died that October, Jim Obergefell appeared on the death certificate as his surviving spouse, just as any different-sex spouse would have. This was a case, Gerhardstein said, "about love surviving death."

Five months later, on December 23, Judge Black made his temporary injunction permanent in another ruling that encompassed Obergefell and Arthur's claim along with another, in a consolidated case. Judge Black cited the *Windsor* ruling as a new foundation for the reasoning that states can no more constitutionally withhold recognition of lawfully performed marriages than the federal government can—no matter the sex of the spouses. The December 23 ruling, wrote Black, "flows from the *Windsor* decision," and its implications "speak for themselves." Although *Windsor* had not put before the court the second section of DOMA—the question of whether states must respect other states' same-sex marriages—Judge Black could see no logic left after *Windsor* for allowing states to bar recognition of gay marriages. "The question is presented whether a state can do what the federal government cannot—e.g., discriminate against same-sex couples" just because a majority of voters "don't like homosexuality." Judge Black's answer: "Under the Constitution of the United States, the answer is no." It was just beginning to become clear, and would be made more so over the next year, but the *Windsor* ruling—its constitutional power, its emotional resonance, and its historical reach—had made imminent the end of legal marriage discrimination in the United States.[33]

= 15 =

"The Responsibility to Right Fundamental Wrongs"

A CIRCUIT SPLIT SETS UP A SHOWDOWN

By the start of 2014, seventeen states plus the District of Columbia allowed same-sex marriage. State courts in five of those states—Massachusetts, Connecticut, Iowa, New Jersey, and New Mexico—had legalized same-sex marriage. Legislatures in eight—Vermont, New Hampshire, New York, Rhode Island, Delaware, Minnesota, Hawaii, and Illinois, as well as Washington, D.C.—had enacted marriage equality. Ballot propositions in Maine, Washington, and Maryland had created marriage equality in three states. And a federal court had legalized it in California (five years after the state's highest court had done so with a decision that was overturned by the voters). Because of the Supreme Court's *Windsor* ruling, married same-sex couples in all those states enjoyed all the same federal rights and protections as any other married couples. Half of Americans lived in a jurisdiction that allowed same-sex couples to marry.[1] Meanwhile, several other federal court rulings had struck down marriage bans but the decisions had been stayed pending appeals.

The *Windsor* ruling set in motion a cascade of legal challenges—more than thirty federal suits would be filed in 2014—whose outcomes would collectively decimate the constitutional defense of gay marriage bans. This was precisely the thinking behind the decision Mary Bonauto and other movement lawyers made to file a challenge to the Defense of Marriage Act before filing right-to-marry challenges in federal court: brick-by-brick legal change. Although the legal intricacies of the *Windsor* case were distinct from those implicated in state marriage bans, the logic and language of the *Windsor* ruling were so powerful and far-reaching that, just as Justice Scalia had predicted, state bans began tumbling at the hands of federal judges, nearly all of them invoking the *Windsor* decision. And the positive rulings in some of the more limited cases inspired new and broader challenges. After his initial victories in Obergefell's case, Gerhardstein, joined by Lambda, filed another suit seeking to have dual-parent birth certificates recognized for children of same-sex couples married outside of Ohio. "At both ends of our lifespans," Gerhardstein explained, poignantly tying together the two Ohio suits, "a marriage is a marriage. A family is a family." The presence of visibly pregnant plaintiffs helped drive home the point that marriage bans caused immediate and irreparable harm, as the lawyers reminded the judges that these babies—who were poised to start their lives without the legal protections of married parents—would not "wait to be born."[2]

Early in 2014, key rulings began coming down. On January 14 a federal judge in Oklahoma struck down that state's 1996 gay marriage ban in a lawsuit first filed by two lesbian couples back in 2004. The *Windsor* court, wrote Judge Terence Kern of the U.S. District Court for the Northern District of Oklahoma, based its decision on "the law's blatant improper purpose and animus." Likewise, Oklahoma's ban was "an arbitrary, irrational exclusion of just one class of Oklahoma citizens from a governmental benefit" that does nothing to advance a legitimate government interest. Echoing the response of Utah's governor to Judge Shelby's ruling, Republican governor Mary Fallin condemned the ruling as judicial overreach, saying she was "disappointed in the judge's ruling and troubled that the will of the people has once again been ignored by the federal government."[3] Unlike Shelby, Kern stayed his decision pending appeal.

The next month, on February 12, U.S. district judge John G. Heyburn of Kentucky ruled for the plaintiffs in *Bourke v. Beshear,* a lawsuit seeking to compel the state to recognize same-sex marriages performed elsewhere. The suit was filed in July 2013, a month after the *Windsor* ruling, by a small Louisville firm run by two attorneys, Shannon Fauver and Dawn Elliott. The firm represented Greg Bourke and Michael DeLeon, a couple for more than thirty years, who had legally married in Canada. They had two children whom they had had to adopt separately because joint adoption was not available to unmarried couples in Kentucky, and since the state did not recognize same-sex marriage, Bourke and DeLeon were considered unmarried.[4]

Judge Heyburn's ruling, the first in the South to strike down a gay marriage ban, found that the state had failed to produce evidence showing "that recognizing same-sex marriages will harm opposite-sex marriages" or cause any other damage to the state or its people. "What this opinion does, however, is make real the promise of equal protection under the law," and elevate same-sex marriages "to an equal status in the eyes of state law."[5] It is almost unimaginable that a judge—let alone one in the South, and one nominated by George H. W. Bush on the recommendation of the state's staunchly conservative senator, Mitch McConnell—could have viewed gay unions as entitled to equal dignity just ten years earlier, a signal of sweeping, rapid change not in constitutional theories but in perceptions of same-sex love across America.

Over the months the lawsuit was proceeding, the pressure and complexity of the case mounted. Fauver and Elliott, whose firm was a small family-law practice, also received additional requests from same-sex couples for representation, some wishing to marry in their hometowns without having to leave the state to obtain a license. The lawyers sought the help of experienced civil rights litigators, inviting the Kentucky firm of Clay, Daniel, Walton and Adams to join their effort. When the expanded team read Judge Heyburn's opinion in the first case that February, they could hardly believe what they saw: Heyburn loudly hinted how he might rule in a right-to-marry challenge, given the logic of his marriage recognition decision. "The Court was not presented with the particular question whether Kentucky's ban on same-sex marriage is constitutional," he wrote, even though no one had asked. "However, there is no doubt that *Windsor* and this Court's analysis suggest a possible result to that question." It was an echo of what had happened in 2004 when the California Supreme Court seemed to invite a full challenge to the state's marriage ban after gay lawyers had begun litigation with a narrower, defensive case. Two days later, on Valentine's Day, the Fauver team brought a right-to-marry challenge before the same judge—something they had to carefully craft to ensure it would stay in front of Heyburn himself. The case was named, suitably, after the lead plaintiff, *Love v. Beshear*.[6]

In March, the attorney general of Kentucky, Jack Conway, saying the state's marriage ban was indefensible, announced he would not appeal Judge Heyburn's February decision in the *Bourke* case. Conway was a Catholic Democrat considering a run for governor, and he cited remarks by Pope Francis about welcoming gays and lesbians ("Who am I to judge," the new pope had said, a striking change in tone from that of earlier pontiffs) in explaining his decision to "draw the line at discrimination."[7] Without explicitly supporting his state's marriage ban himself, Governor Steve Beshear, also a Democrat, said he would hire outside counsel to defend the ban in court.

Conway was the eighth attorney general (serving in seven different states) to decline to defend a marriage ban. Preceding him were Jerry Brown and later Kamala Harris of California, Lisa Madigan of Illinois, Kathleen Kane of Pennsylvania, Mark Herring of Virginia, Catherine Cortez Masto of Nevada, and Ellen Rosenblum of Oregon.[8] All were Democrats, and many had won office with the help of strategic gay donors. The commitment of these states' top legal officials, as well as similar decisions by the U.S. Justice Department, to decline to defend marriage discrimination, reflected just how mainstream a position marriage equality had become. Still uncertain, for the moment, were the clashes that would arise as equality opponents realized they were becoming defenders of a minority-held opinion.

In July, Heyburn issued a second ruling, this one for the right-to-marry plaintiffs in *Love v. Beshear,* striking down the state's same-sex marriage ban altogether. Not only did the U.S. Constitution require Kentucky to respect gay marriages conducted out of state, but, as Heyburn had foreshadowed in his previous ruling, it required that the state perform such marriages at home. Although both rulings were ultimately stayed, the successful role of incremental litigation was clear.[9] Justice Scalia had warned that the logic in *Lawrence* dictated one day allowing same-sex marriage. He had wrung his hands in his *Windsor* dissent, complaining there was no way to protect the rights of states to bar same-sex marriages now that the feds had been forced to treat them unequally. Judge Black of Ohio had agreed, positing there was no reason that "a state can do what the federal government cannot—e.g., discriminate against same-sex couples," and had built that logic into his decision that Ohio must recognize the marriage of Jim Obergefell and John Arthur. And now Judge Heyburn had drawn on the reasoning of marital recognition lawsuits to advance a constitutional argument that the state must also grant its own licenses to same-sex couples.[10]

And the dominoes continued to fall. The day after Heyburn's first February ruling in Kentucky, a federal judge in Virginia struck down that state's same-sex marriage ban. The suit originated in a July 2013 filing by plaintiffs Tony London and his partner, Tim Bostic. London was a real estate agent who had gotten to know Bob Ruloff, a straight lawyer at the Virginia Beach firm Shuttleworth, Ruloff, Swain, Haddad and Morecock, when Ruloff handled a business matter for him. Ruloff, an idealistic coal miner's son with dreams of representing underdogs like his dad, had ended up as a real estate attorney instead, but he had never lost his interest in fighting for social justice. Chatting with London just as news of the *Windsor* ruling broke, Ruloff grasped the couple's predicament—they were considering leaving the state to get married, but in that case Virginia would not honor their marriage anyway—and he jumped at the chance to represent the couple in a challenge to the state's gay marriage ban.[11] The team filed suit on July 18, and later allowed Ted Olson and the American Foundation for Equal Rights team to join as cocounsel. That same summer, Lambda and the American Civil Liberties Union, joined by Paul Smith, who had argued the *Lawrence* case, filed a separate class-action suit on behalf of all Virginia same-sex couples who either had been married out of state or wanted to marry in the state.[12]

The February 2014 ruling in Virginia was for the *Bostic* case, and was handed down by federal district judge Arenda Wright Allen. Citing the *Windsor* ruling and mindful of the historic role of her own state in originating the successful challenge to interracial marriage bans, Allen described the common humanity of gay people to which so many had recently awakened. "Gay and lesbian individuals share the same capacity as heterosexual individuals to form, preserve and celebrate loving, intimate and lasting relationships," she wrote. In granting them the right to wed, "we have arrived upon another moment in history when 'We the People' becomes more inclusive, and our freedom more perfect." The judge wrote that "tradition alone cannot justify denying same-sex couples the right to marry any more than it could justify Virginia's ban on interracial marriage." The Supreme Court eventually stayed her decision just one day before gay marriages were set to begin.[13] The other suit, brought by movement groups, was later merged with the *Bostic* case for consideration by the Fourth Circuit Court of Appeals.

Then on February 26 a federal judge in Texas declared that state's gay marriage ban unconstitutional. In denying same-sex couples the right to marry, wrote Judge Orlando Luis Garcia of the United States District Court for the Western District of Texas, the state's laws "demean their dignity for no legitimate reason. Accordingly, the Court finds these laws are unconstitutional." Garcia stayed his decision pending appeal. In what had become a seemingly obligatory response by conservative Republicans, Texas governor and sometime presidential candidate Rick Perry responded to the decision by denouncing activist judges for blocking the will of the people. Yet his and others' confidence in the people's will was about to be tested.[14]

Meanwhile, the rulings kept coming. On March 14 a federal judge in Tennessee ruled that the state must honor the marriages of three same-sex couples who were legally married elsewhere. The couples were represented by the National Center for Lesbian Rights and the private firm of Abby Rubenfeld, who had helped form the Litigators' Roundtable three decades earlier.[15] As with the Utah suit, Kate Kendell and her NCLR colleagues had considered bringing a suit in Tennessee earlier in 2013, but met with little enthusiasm from their colleagues. "There was pretty open ridicule" among other Roundtable lawyers, Kendell remembered. "For us it demonstrated how, in some quarters, the LGBT legal advocacy organizations were slow to recognize how much the landscape had changed." By the time *Windsor* came down, Kendell said, "we had totally lost control of whatever litigation was going to be filed." Minter, her colleague, agreed. "After *Windsor*," he said, "It took a little while for the litigation groups to recognize that it wasn't going to be business as usual." For the remainder of 2013, many "were still in the old mold, running around saying, 'Don't bring cases.'" But to others it was quickly becoming clear that the old idea of carefully selecting the jurisdiction and chalking up strategic victories was no longer an option. Now, said Minter, "there was going to be an explosion of litigation all over the county, including in unlikely places."[16]

Tennessee was among those places. And for some, regional concerns were personal. "Many of the groups were against doing a case in the South," said Rubenfeld, born in Florida and now a Tennessean. "Those working from the big cities don't always appreciate what's going on in the fly-over states." That may have been true. But for the movement lawyers, it wasn't a question of ignoring middle America but an effort to build momentum by securing victories in the most winnable states—a strategy crucial to making the incremental approach a success. That's why the Civil Marriage Collaborative had decided to reduce the number of states where it threw its financial support, in favor of larger, more focused grants to groups in those states it did think winnable.

After the *Windsor* ruling, a reporter called Rubenfeld, who had become a go-to source for commentary on gay issues in Tennessee, which still had few other openly gay leaders known to the local press. Would there now be a marriage challenge in Tennessee? the reporter wanted to know. Rubenfeld didn't have one lined up. "Hell yes!" she replied anyway. The invitation from the *Windsor* decision seemed irresistible. Upon seeing the headline from the story—"Nashville Attorney to Move Quickly on Gay Rights"—she realized she needed a case. Luckily, Regina Lambert, another lesbian Tennessee lawyer, reached out to her to discuss helping with a challenge. Lambert taught at a law school and was well connected in both the lesbian and the legal worlds of Tennessee. She was able to bring in plaintiffs, including the pregnant couple Valerie Tanco and Sophie Jesty, and the prominent corporate lawyer Bill Harbison, soon to become president of the Tennessee Bar Association. "He was such an unlikely person to work on this case," said Rubenfeld. Having him and his prestigious firm onboard "instantly added credibility to the whole effort," one of the first marriage challenges in the South. One of Rubenfeld's other early calls after *Windsor* had been to Shannon Minter at NCLR to ask if the group was interested in coordinating on a case. Without hesitation Minter and Kendell said they were in. The team constructed a narrow case that, consistent with the incremental strategy, wouldn't ask too much of the court—it applied only to those specific plaintiffs, and it was a marriage recognition case instead of a full-on challenge to the marriage ban. "We were still thinking incrementally," said Kendell, explaining why the team crafted a limited challenge. Lambert called it a "baby step." As "one of the first southern states to file," she said, "we thought 'recognition only' might be a better start."[17]

The strategy worked. Five months after it was filed, with Tanco about to burst with the couple's daughter, Emilia, Judge Aleta Trauger, of the United States District Court for the Middle District of Tennessee, ruled in favor of the three plaintiff couples. Two weeks later, with legal forms not updated, Emilia became the first baby born in the state to have a woman listed as "father" on her birth certificate. An "as-applied" case, the ruling, *Tanco v. Haslam,* only affected the three couples who were party to the suit, and was appealed by the state, throwing Emilia's legal relationship to her mother Sophie into question.

A week later, a federal judge in Michigan struck down that state's gay marriage ban after a high-profile trial that marked only the third time gay marriage bans had been put on trial (after the 1996 Hawaii trial and the 2010 Proposition 8 trial). The suit, *DeBoer v. Snyder,* began in 2012 as an adoption case. It centered on April DeBoer and Jayne Rowse, both emergency care nurses, who were in an eight-year relationship. The couple were raising three children with special needs, including one born prematurely to a drug-addicted prostitute. Abandoned at birth, he had weighed 1 pound 9 ounces and had shown signs of having been exposed to marijuana, cocaine, and methadone. He was not expected to live, but DeBoer and Rowse took him in as a foster child anyway, and stunned the boy's doctor by nursing him back to health. ("There's only two things in this world that could have saved your son," the doctor had told the couple. "God and a mother's love, and apparently he had both on his side.") Yet while Michigan considered the couple good enough to foster children no one else wanted, even saving their lives, the state only allowed couples to adopt jointly if they were married, and it banned same-sex couples from marrying. Such laws, championed by conservatives who claimed to care about children and "intact" families, ironically made it impossible for children to have two legal parents, leaving families vulnerable and unprotected by the law.[18]

Like many same-sex couples, DeBoer and Rowse sought legal workarounds. In 2011 they learned of a lesbian lawyer named Dana Nessel, who practiced family and criminal law, and asked if she could draw up paperwork to help protect their parenting rights in the absence of joint adoption. When Nessel learned of their story—of their heroic work as nurses who took in unwanted children—she called her suitemate, Carole Stanyar, another lesbian lawyer who had experience in federal appeals courts. "We have to help these people," Nessel said, and Stanyar agreed to work on the case. DeBoer and Rowse thought about what it would mean to become plaintiffs in a federal lawsuit, and decided to go for it. Their lawyers thought it would be a fairly straightforward suit. After all, it was not a direct challenge to Michigan's marriage ban. "I thought adoption was an easier fight," Nessel

*April DeBoer and Jayne Rowse, pictured here with their children, were among the
many plaintiffs who filed suit to challenge marriage discrimination throughout
the country. The DeBoer-Rowse suit was brought in Michigan originally as an
adoption case, and was filed by lawyers outside the LGBTQ movement.*

recalled, noting that at the start of 2011 only five states allowed gays to
marry. The couple was already raising kids and could easily elicit public
sympathy, and Nessel could see "no rational basis for the court to find a
legitimate reason for the state to have this law in place."[19]

Others weren't so sure. Michigan lay in the Sixth Circuit, known to
be conservative, so even a victory at the district level might easily be overturned. When the legal team reached out to the local ACLU for support,
they instead faced discouragement and the expectation that they would
lose. Nessel was aware of the resistance by national gay legal groups to
the Olson suit and figured her case could face something similar. Yet as
an adoption case, her suit was narrower than Olson's, and a lot had happened in just two years. Like Rubenfeld, Nessel was also sensitive about
being told by representatives of gay rights groups—with headquarters in
progressive coastal cities where gays and lesbians often enjoyed more legal

protections than they did in Michigan—that southern or red states should wait to file suit because "it's not your time yet." Nessel wondered what the rationale was: "Are we lesser people because we're residents of this state? Are the needs of our families any different?"[20] It was a sensitivity that was widespread but which read strategic disagreements as personal or geographic bias. Still, the ultimate success of controversial lawsuits such as those brought in Michigan, Ohio, Kentucky, and Tennessee showed that some movement lawyers were still playing catch-up in a dramatically changed landscape.

While Nessel's case, filed in January 2012, began as a simple adoption challenge, it didn't remain that for long. In August Judge Bernard Friedman of the United States District Court for the Eastern District of Michigan, a Reagan appointee, urged the plaintiffs to broaden their claim to include a challenge to the state's marriage ban, which he called the "underlying issue." Nessel and Stanyar were bowled over. " 'Surprised' doesn't adequately describe it," said Nessel. "We were absolutely shocked and dumbfounded." They had expected a relatively quick win or loss, not a nudge from the judge to try to bring down Michigan's gay marriage ban. It was yet another example of a judge encouraging a wider challenge in a suit that had initially taken an incremental approach, suggesting that, as prudent and successful as this approach turned out to be, in some cases the caution of both private and movement lawyers turned out to be excessive.

Four months later, uneasy about what had become a federal challenge to Michigan's marriage law, a coalition of national and local gay rights groups filed an amicus brief that appeared to give Judge Friedman an escape hatch from ruling on gay marriage: It outlined an option for the judge to strike down the state's adoption ban "without addressing the question of whether Michigan may deny same-sex couples the ability to marry." By then the movement groups had begun to collaborate with Nessel's team, and Lambda's Camilla Taylor said the brief was written at the request of the Michigan lawyers. But Nessel said her team never asked for a brief offering the judge an out on a marriage ruling, and she interpreted the movement groups' brief as an effort to undercut their challenge.[21]

Judge Friedman, however, had no interest in sidestepping the marriage question, particularly after the *Windsor* ruling came down the next year. Instead, he shocked nearly every lawyer involved with or observing the case by ordering a full-blown trial. "The parties must be afforded the opportunity to develop their own record in this matter," wrote the judge, "with the benefit of calling witnesses and subjecting them to cross-examination." He envisioned the trial, he said in court, as a "battle of the experts." Nessel couldn't believe the case was going to trial. It would be historic—only the second federal trial ever to air the arguments on same-sex marriage—but time-consuming and expensive. At this point, she needed help. "We literally had no money," she remembered. "I didn't know if we were going to have to withdraw our case." Her team had obtained written testimony from some expert witnesses, but hiring the nation's best social scientists to testify live in a trial was of a different magnitude, requiring time and money for which they were wholly unprepared. Nessel called Mary Bonauto immediately, and after a quick conversation with GLAD's Gary Buseck, Bonauto agreed to help. With a couple of phone calls, Bonauto could persuade renowned experts such as George Chauncey as well as Gary Gates of the Williams Institute to testify, something Nessel didn't have the power to do on her own. And now that the case was going to trial, national groups came onboard quickly. Leslie Cooper of the ACLU agreed to play a role in cross-examinations, and limited funds and the star power of experts were provided to help the case.[22]

For the trial, which began in February 2014, the state of Michigan hired star witnesses from the religious conservative brain trust, who contended that social science cast serious doubt on the wisdom of letting gay couples marry and raise children. The most famous of these was Mark Regnerus, a sociologist at University of Texas at Austin, who had made waves with a 2012 academic article claiming to have found that children of same-sex parents face added disadvantages that undercut the wisdom of blessing same-sex relationships. The study made him a darling of social conservative circles working against gay equality and helped allow the more restrained voices of the bunch to seem reasonable in opposing same-sex marriage: this was not about animus, they could now claim with the weight of scholarship behind them, but a simple concern for child welfare.

Regnerus's study was full of holes, the most notable being that while he touted a large, representative sample, that sample contained virtually no households headed by two adults of the same sex in which children had actually been raised from birth. The sample thus contained a level of family instability that was sure to skew the outcome. As a result, his research was denounced in an audit conducted by the journal that had published the piece, as well as by the chair of his own department and in a letter signed by two hundred fellow social scientists—a highly unusual public rebuke for a journal article. Further investigation found that the study's genesis was a series of meetings among social and religious conservatives and foundations beginning in 2010 at the Heritage Foundation—ties that, as Leslie Cooper showed in cross-examining Regnerus, the scholar had sought to conceal. It quickly became clear that use of a tiny sample of stable households headed by a same-sex couple was not an oversight but a continuation of the deceptive tactics social conservatives had been using for over a decade: conflating gay families with those that experienced disruption, creating a predictably distorted result.[23]

Indeed, many of these conservative thinkers who gathered at the Heritage Foundation to plan for battle were veterans of the effort to pass the Federal Marriage Amendment a decade earlier, including Princeton's Robert George, the professor who, with Maggie Gallagher, had founded the major gay marriage opposition group, the National Organization for Marriage. This time around, the strategy was to showcase a young, fresh-faced academic who seemed eminently reasonable to the public but who would offer research conclusions that could help justify the dire warnings of gay marriage opponents about a threat to children and families. And participation in the lawsuit was part of the strategy. After the conservative scholars testified—in addition to Regnerus, they included Loren Marks, a professor in human ecology at Louisiana State University; Joseph Price, of Brigham Young University; and Douglas Allen, a Canadian economist—lawyers and officials for the state closed ranks by echoing the message that the research was too preliminary to warrant tinkering with the institution of marriage. "Social science is just too uncertain," said the state's attorney, Kristin Heyse, in her closing argument, adding vaguely that "the evidence shows that there are benefits to a child being raised by a mom and a dad."[24] After the trial ended, a spokeswoman for state attorney general Bill Schuette amplified the talking point, saying that "the science on this remains unsettled" and that anyway it should be voters, not social science, that decided the issue.[25]

Judge Friedman was unconvinced. In a stinging repudiation of the state's full slate of experts, the judge wrote, "The Court finds Regnerus's testimony entirely unbelievable and not worthy of serious consideration," that it was "unable to accord the testimony of Marks, Price, and Allen any significant weight," and that the research that the group relied on had been "hastily concocted at the behest of a third-party funder" that sought a predetermined outcome. He ruled that the state's law banning same-sex marriage and adoption "impermissibly discriminates against same-sex couples in violation of the Equal Protection Clause because the provision does not advance any conceivable legitimate state interest."[26] The Michigan ruling was the fourteenth consecutive court loss for anti-gay advocates in nine months. More than 300 same-sex couples were married in Michigan the following day in a frenzy of joy, excitement, and uncertainty about the ruling's status. The marriages were halted hours later by a stay, dashing the hopes of thousands. But, as in Utah, the simple reality of same-sex weddings made it harder for opponents to argue that God's wrathful destruction would rain down on those places that allowed them.

Then, across two days in May 2014, a major step: federal judges in Oregon and Pennsylvania struck down their states' marriage bans with such force, and amid such jurisprudential momentum and public approval, that neither state officials nor the courts fought or stayed the rulings, making them the first states after the tortuous California case to permanently legalize same-sex marriage at the hands of federal courts. Oregon's marriage laws, wrote Judge Michael McShane of the U.S. District Court for the District of Oregon, "burden, demean, and harm gay and lesbian couples and their families." While McShane seemed taken by the stories of the plaintiffs in his case, he noted coolly that gay couples should not have to prove their good character to qualify for marriage. "Oregon law recognizes a marriage of love with the same equal eye that it recognizes a marriage of convenience," he wrote. It grants the same rights to literature's most storied romantic lovers as it grants "to a Hollywood celebrity waking up in Las Vegas with a blurry memory and a ringed finger." Yet it denies those rights to a sliver of couples based solely on their sexual orientation. "No legitimate state purpose justifies the preclusion of gay and lesbian couples from civil marriage," he concluded.[27]

Judge McShane, an Obama appointee, seemed both aware of the controversy his ruling might spur and eager to use his platform to wax lyrical about the basis and import of his decision. "On this issue of marriage," he wrote in his conclusion, "I am struck more by our similarities than our differences. I believe that if we can look for a moment past gender and sexuality, we can see in these plaintiffs nothing more or less than our own families, families who we would expect our Constitution to protect, if not exalt, in equal measure." To those who remained skeptical about the wisdom of his decision and fearful of the potential consequences of such social change, he spoke directly: "With discernment we see not shadows lurking in closets or the stereotypes of what was once believed; rather, we see families committed to the common purpose of love, devotion, and service to the greater community." Let us not, he concluded, indulge abstract fears of the unfamiliar. "Let us look less to the sky to see what might fall; rather, let us look to each other . . . and rise."[28]

Oregon lay in the Ninth Circuit, which in January had issued a major decision affecting the standard of review it would apply in gay rights cases. The case, *Smithkline Beecham Corp. v. Abbott Laboratories,* concerned whether prospective jurors could be excluded from an antitrust case based on their sexual orientation. Citing *Windsor* and applying heightened scrutiny, the San Francisco appeals court decided they could not. The *Windsor* court, of course, had not applied heightened scrutiny explicitly, instead relying on what has become a characteristic of Justice Kennedy's gay rights rulings: casting the rights in question as fundamental while stopping short of using the technical legal category "fundamental right," and likewise applying added scrutiny to the case without explicitly declaring that "heightened scrutiny" must always apply in such cases. Judge Stephen Reinhardt, writing for a unanimous three-judge panel, explained that his court had analyzed the *Windsor* ruling and applied its precedent "by considering what the court actually did, rather than by dissecting isolated pieces of text." That is, he read from the Supreme Court a decision it had made not in word but by its actions.[29]

The result of the ruling was that all nine states that lay in the Ninth Circuit were now bound by the application of heightened scrutiny in future gay rights claims. That development may have eased the way for Oregon's Democratic attorney general, Ellen Rosenblum, to announce that the state would not defend its marriage ban. Yet Rosenblum emphasized that a heightened standard was not even necessary to deem the ban unconstitutional. Writing in a federal court filing in February, she argued that the law "cannot withstand a federal constitutional challenge under any standard of review." Along with several other state attorneys general, she had also submitted amicus briefs arguing for marriage equality in both the *Windsor* and *Hollingsworth* suits.[30] With no state official defending the ban, the

National Organization for Marriage sought to intervene. Judge McShane, the Ninth Circuit, and the Supreme Court repeatedly denied the group's requests, and same-sex couples began marrying in Oregon directly following McShane's ruling.

In Pennsylvania, while the Democratic attorney general, Kathleen Kane, also chose not to defend her state's marriage ban, Republican governor Tom Corbett promised that he would. Yet when Judge John Jones III of U.S. District Court for the Middle District of Pennsylvania, a George W. Bush appointee, struck down the state's gay marriage ban the day after Judge McShane's Oregon ruling, it become clear even to Corbett that the battle was lost. "We hold that Pennsylvania's Marriage Laws violate both the Due Process and Equal Protection Clauses of the Fourteenth Amendment to the United States Constitution," wrote Judge Jones. "That same-sex marriage causes discomfort in some does not make its prohibition constitutional. Nor can past tradition trump the bedrock constitutional guarantees of due process and equal protection."[31]

Citing the "high legal threshold" established by the decision, the governor ultimately chose not to fight the ruling, saying an appeal was "extremely unlikely to succeed."[32] But the real calculation was likely political. Corbett had taken flack for comparing same-sex marriage to marriage among siblings, and he was now facing a tough re-election against a pro-gay Democrat.[33] Pennsylvania was the only state in the Northeast not to offer either marriage equality or civil unions. Corbett risked becoming the face of this increasingly unpopular status quo. And hovering over the politics was the soaring language of Judge Jones's ruling. "We are a better people than what these laws represent," he wrote, "and it is time to discard them into the ash heap of history."[34] The efforts of a sole county clerk to carry on the ban's defense failed repeatedly, with Justice Samuel Alito denying her motion at the Supreme Court. With Jones's decision, the twelfth consecutive federal court ruling to strike down a gay marriage ban, same-sex couples began marrying in Pennsylvania immediately.

That summer the winning streak continued in both state and federal courts. In May an Arkansas state judge struck down the state's marriage ban, but the Arkansas Supreme Court stayed the ruling after 400 same-sex couples married. In June, a federal judge in Indiana ruled for the plaintiffs, allowing some same-sex couples to wed before the decision was stayed. A federal judge in Wisconsin invalidated the marriage ban there but stayed her ruling. A judge in Florida issued a preliminary injunction against enforcing the state's marriage ban in August. In September a federal judge in Louisiana upheld the state's gay marriage ban, breaking a twenty-one-state winning streak for gay advocates in federal court (the streak had been at nearly forty when state court decisions were included).[35]

Across the second half of 2014, appeals courts increasingly began upholding district court rulings in favor of same-sex marriage, adding weight to the judicial consensus post-*Windsor* that marriage discrimination of any kind was unconstitutional. At the same time, a second showdown at the Supreme Court now seemed inescapable. The chances would be even greater if there was a "circuit split"—if one of the twelve U.S. circuits bucked the trend and handed down a decision allowing same-sex marriage bans. For now, all circuit court rulings were in favor of gay marriage. The Ninth Circuit had been the first when in February 2012 it upheld Judge Walker's decision on Proposition 8 (although the Supreme Court later threw out the appeal because Proposition 8's defenders lacked standing, which left Judge Walker's pro-gay-marriage ruling in place). In June 2014 the Tenth Circuit followed suit, upholding the decision in Utah that invalidated the state's marriage ban. NCLR, which had quietly helped the lawyers at Magleby and Greenwood prepare the case at the district level, officially joined the suit as cocounsel for the appeal. The team then asked Mary Bonauto to join as well, and charged her with the massive task of coordinating amicus briefs for the appeal, as she had done for so many cases before. Once again, the years of deep experience that the legal groups had in developing expertise on constitutional theories, precedent, messaging, and outreach infused the Utah case through the participation of NCLR and GLAD, even though the case had first been launched by a modest grassroots outfit. Bonauto was pleased to be able to help. "I'm in," she had said of the ongoing marriage equality effort after the *Windsor* victory. "I want to be a part of helping take it over the finish line."[36]

Applying strict scrutiny in its decision, the Tenth Circuit ruled that, "under the Due Process and Equal Protection Clauses of the United States Constitution, those who wish to marry a person of the same sex are entitled to exercise the same fundamental right as is recognized for persons who wish to marry a person of the opposite sex." Crucially, in just a few sentences, the court summarily repudiated the procreation argument that gay marriage opponents had relied on for their case. Running through all the defendants' arguments, said the court, is the contention that same-sex marriage "would break the critical conceptual link between marriage and procreation." Yet the state's gay marriage ban does "not differentiate between procreative and non-procreative couples. Instead, Utah citizens may choose a spouse of the opposite sex regardless of the pairing's procreative capacity." The next month the same court issued a similar ruling in upholding Judge Kern's decision striking down Oklahoma's marriage ban. Both rulings were stayed.[37]

That summer, the Fourth Circuit upheld Judge Allen's ruling tossing out Virginia's same-sex marriage ban in the consolidated case that Ted Olson, and later the ACLU and Lambda, had joined. During oral arguments, sparks flew between Judge Roger Gregory, appointed by President Bill Clinton, and defending attorney David Nimocks, who had been hired by the conservative Christian Alliance Defending Freedom. Debating the benefits of marriage to children, the judge pointedly raised the question of what impact gay marriage bans had on children of same-sex parents: "Why do you want to deny them all those warm and wholesome things about marriage?" Gregory asked. "Do you think the child loves the parents any less because they're same-sex parents?" Nimocks said of course not, but had little to add in his defense. Then Judge Paul Niemeyer, a George H. W. Bush appointee, stunned the courtroom when he declared, "Every person in this room is the product of a marriage. You need a man and a woman to have a family."[38]

Few besides Judge Niemeyer needed to be reminded that millions of Americans were not, in fact, born to married parents—gay or straight. But much had been made clear by that spring day in 2014 about how the gay rights movement had pushed its strategy forward in a changing world. On one side stood those, like Judge Gregory, who echoed Justice Kennedy in reflecting a rising awareness that family could fully include gay parents with children. If the "warm and wholesome things about marriage" signaled the deployment of an idealized version of family, indebted more to the family values of conservatism than to anything resembling the early aspirations of the alternative-families movement, at least it was an idealism that looked toward the future and embraced the role of gays and lesbians within it. And on the other side stood judges like Niemeyer, who so thoroughly dwelled in an idealized past that he seemed literally unable to consider that married couples were not the wellspring of every child born in America. Failing to notice how the world had changed, Americans like Niemeyer would be hard pressed to incorporate a role for gay equality in their vision of society or how the law should govern it. But judging from the majority opinions coming down from court after court, America was no longer dependent on people like Paul Niemeyer for such determinations. However, the Supreme Court blocked that decision from going into effect the next month, less than twenty-four hours before same-sex couples would have begun getting married.[39]

In September the Seventh Circuit struck down marriage bans in Indiana and Wisconsin by upholding lower court decisions. Ruling on equal protection grounds, the appellate judges slammed the states' limp defense of their marriage bans. "The challenged laws," wrote the prolific judge Richard Posner, who had eviscerated the states' arguments in court appearances, "discriminate against a minority defined by an immutable characteristic, and the only rationale that the states put forth with any conviction—that same-sex couples and their children don't *need* marriage because same-sex couples can't *produce* children, intended or unintended— is so full of holes that it cannot be taken seriously." The court stayed the ruling pending appeal, so couples in those two states remained unable to wed.[40]

On October 6, 2014, the Supreme Court made an unexpected move with major consequences for the spread of marriage equality. It denied requests for review in all seven cases seeking it—brought in five different states located in three different circuits. Since bans had been struck down in district or appellate courts in all those cases, the result was to let those rulings stand, and thus to make gay marriage legal immediately in those five states, where stays had blocked gay marriage pending review: Indiana, Wisconsin, Oklahoma, Virginia, and Utah. The development also meant that same-sex marriage was now imminent in six more states with gay marriage bans that lay in those three circuits (because lower court judges in those states would essentially be required to rule for the plaintiffs): Colorado, Kansas, West Virginia, North Carolina, Wyoming, and South Carolina. Sure enough, either by direction of state officials or by court order, over the next six weeks same-sex marriage came to all six of those states. While a smattering of clerks and county officials resisted, particularly in Kansas, the marvel was that same-sex couples were marrying more or less without issue in deeply conservative and southern states just ten years after liberal

Massachusetts became the first state in the nation to legalize same-sex marriage. With the Supreme Court's decision not to act, the number of marriage equality states jumped from nineteen to thirty in under two months. A majority of states in the Union now allowed gay and lesbian couples to legally wed.[41]

In opting not to intervene, the Supreme Court, which in theory had the power to leapfrog over a state-by-state path to marriage equality, seemed to be embracing precisely the incremental change strategy that gay legal advocates had advanced. Even the more liberal justices—perhaps they especially, since they likely supported marriage equality in principle—preferred to let gay marriage spread from state to state, rather than to impose it judicially upon the nation. Justice Ginsburg, in particular, feared that the Court's 1973 decision in *Roe v. Wade* had spurred a public backlash to abortion rights by moving "too far, too fast"—"things might have turned out differently if the court had been more restrained," she said in a 2012 lecture, referring to the ongoing controversy over the *Roe* decision—and she seemed to imply that a high court ruling on gay marriage could similarly damage the cause if handed down too soon.[42] Likewise, some legal observers believed that both the court and the public could be more likely to accept gay marriage if it came gradually rather than all at once. "The more liberal justices have been reluctant to press this issue to an up-or-down vote until more of the country experiences gay marriage," said Walter E. Dellinger III, a top lawyer in the Clinton administration. "Once a substantial part of the country has experienced gay marriage, then the court will be more willing to finish the job."[43] Since granting review required only four votes, at least six justices had declined to support it, meaning there were conservative justices who effectively agreed with the path the court was taking.[44] By all accounts, the Court was loudly signaling how it would eventually rule on a same-sex marriage case: it would be shocking for the court to allow same-sex marriage to spread, only to invalidate countless marriages months or years later. Clearly the Court had tipped its hand.

And then came the circuit split. On November 6, the Sixth Circuit, which covers Michigan, Ohio, Tennessee, and Kentucky, reversed six rulings in those four states and became the first circuit court to uphold same-sex marriage bans. The decision stood to reverse the Ohio rulings, wiping Jim Obergefell's name off John Arthur's death certificate, and to void the dual-parent birth certificates issued by the state when Judge Black ruled in favor of the four couples who had brought suit earlier that year. The Sixth Circuit reversal also meant that appeals would go forward in the suit by the Michigan nurses April DeBoer and Jayne Rowse, in Abby Rubenfeld and NCLR's Tennessee case, and in the Kentucky case of Greg Bourke and Michael DeLeon and the additional plaintiffs who brought *Love v. Beshear*.

The Circuit Court opinion, written by Judge Jeffrey S. Sutton, a George W. Bush appointee, invoked the 1972 *Baker* ruling that had dismissed same-sex marriage claims "for want of a substantial federal question." Judge Sutton claimed that the Sixth Circuit was still bound by that precedent and that, in any event, such an important matter as who gets to marry should be determined not in a court like his but by the "reliable work of the state democratic processes." He dismissed the "plaintiffs' theories" as failing to make the case "for constitutionalizing the definition of marriage and for removing the issue from the place it has been since the founding: in the hands of state voters." It was a claim that could be made only by ignoring what DOMA had done in federalizing marriage between 1996 and 2013. A sharp dissent by Judge Martha Craig Daughtrey, a Bill Clinton appointee, slammed the majority opinion as "a largely irrelevant discourse on democracy and federalism." Noting that she had taken an oath to administer justice "faithfully and impartially," she wrote, "If we in the judiciary do not have the authority, and indeed the responsibility, to right fundamental wrongs left excused by a majority of the electorate, our whole intricate, constitutional system of checks and balances, as well as the oaths to which we swore, prove to be nothing but shams."[45] At the time of the ruling, nearly fifty pro-gay-marriage decisions had been handed down.[46]

As expected in the case of a circuit split, the Supreme Court announced on January 16 that it would hear the Sixth Circuit case. If it ruled for the plaintiffs, the legality of same-sex marriage would finally be settled nationwide.

= 16 =

"It Is So Ordered"

MARRIAGE EQUALITY
COMES TO ALL FIFTY STATES

COUNTLESS PEOPLE—IT IS IMPOSSIBLE TO PUT A NUMBER ON IT— were responsible for getting the gay rights movement and the nation to the moment in 2015 when same-sex love was poised to land on equal legal footing with heterosexual love. Scores of lawsuits had been filed for marriage equality. Now six of them, from four states, were consolidated into one case for argument before the Supreme Court in *Obergefell v. Hodges.* That left a major question for LGBTQ legal advocates, now consisting not just of longtime movement activists but also numerous lawyers from private firms who had built on their years of work and leaned on their carefully crafted legal arguments to bring suits of their own: who would have the honor—and responsibility—of arguing what might be the final case on the freedom to marry, before the highest court in the land?

It was not an easy decision to make. In granting Supreme Court review, the justices indicated they would devote an unusually long period of two and a half hours to oral arguments, which would be divided into two questions. Question #1 was "Does the Fourteenth Amendment require a state to license a marriage between two people of the same sex?" Question #2 was "Does the Fourteenth Amendment require a state to recognize a marriage between two people of the same sex when their marriage was lawfully licensed and performed out-of-state?" If the Court answered yes in Question #1, then Question #2 was moot, while if it answered yes only in Question #2, then gay couples could function as married everywhere but might have to travel to another state to actually get married, something that was not always easy, as the stories of Windsor and Obergefell had shown. The challenges in those cases were health-related, but for poor, rural, or working people, financial and geographic constraints could also make out-of-state marriage a genuine hardship.

The two questions—on the right to marry and on out-of-state recognition—would be argued separately, and Solicitor General Donald Verrilli would be one of the oralists. That meant that dozens of lawyers involved in the four cases would need to figure out how to choose two to stand before the Court, one to argue each question. For many lawyers of the Roundtable, the stakes couldn't be higher. Egos had been bruised over the course of decades of strategic disagreements over how and whether to advance marriage equality. And this decision could have an enormous impact on millions of lives and on equal protection law for generations to come. For many, their life's work seemed to hang in the balance.

More recently, a new breed of lawyers, largely from outside the movement, had entered the fray, and in three of the four cases now being considered—all but the Tennessee case—what had landed before the Supreme Court were lawsuits that originated with private attorneys, just as Ted Olson and Robbie Kaplan's cases were the ones to land there in 2013. (Even the Tennessee suit brought by the National Center for Lesbian Rights, the one case originated by a movement group, was originally conceived by Abby Rubenfeld's private firm.) On the strength of their high profiles from those suits, both Olson and Kaplan had sought to join additional cases in hopes of helping carry the issue back to a finale at the Supreme Court. Olson had succeeded at this when the American Foundation for Equal Rights joined the *Bostic* case in Virginia, welcomed by the private firm that originated the case. Kaplan had joined a case in Mississippi. But even though Kaplan had invited the American Civil Liberties Union to serve as cocounsel in *Windsor,* the ACLU had opposed her involvement in the *Obergefell* suit—which it had only recently joined as cocounsel—explaining that it wished to avoid "the disruption and prejudice that would flow from new claims and parties at this late stage."[1]

Kaplan and Olson had both been denied the right to join the Utah suit; Olson had also hoped to join the Oklahoma suit first filed by private attorneys in 2004. Some felt their efforts to muscle their way into cases were unseemly or ego-driven. (Olson took criticism for charging roughly $6 million for his firm's role in *Hollingsworth v. Perry*, a steeply discounted rate but a hefty sum when considering that firms with far fewer resources took on gay marriage cases entirely pro bono, charging their clients nothing at all.) Kendell said that a "little footnote" to her otherwise significant esteem for the Olson and Boies team was the attempt to intervene in cases that were "already very well-lawyered," including NCLR's Utah suit. "I felt it demonstrated a lack of respect for the lawyers already on that team."[2]

Of course, many lawyers from small firms felt similarly when movement groups sought to join cases others had begun. But both Olson and Kendell said they simply wanted to make sure suits were litigated as exquisitely as possible. Olson felt the reason he was hired for the California suit in the first place was the worry that less experienced lawyers would not have the knowledge and experience to effectively "take a case all the way to the Supreme Court." He said it was impossible to overstate "how meticulously handled it must be in order to ensure the best outcome." On that front, Kendell agreed, explaining, "We had private attorneys filing suit who had never done a marriage case, who had never even done a gay case before. That is not a recipe for a victory; that's a recipe for disaster."[3]

Tapping the resources and know-how of national experts was one reason all three of the cases that were not originated by movement groups eventually sought or welcomed support from the national groups. Bonauto, from Gay and Lesbian Advocates and Defenders, had joined the Michigan team as its case went to trial and then again on its petition to the Supreme Court. The ACLU had sent Leslie Cooper to grill Regnerus in the Michigan trial and had begun helping Gerhardstein's firm in 2013 after its initial win in Obergefell's case. Despite having earlier eyed the case with some concern, it joined as cocounsel in January 2014 when the state appealed. Lambda also provided support in Ohio and joined as cocounsel in February 2014, adhering to a common pattern where legal groups offered crucial behind-the-scenes assistance, without or before formally joining a case.[4] In Kentucky, the ACLU joined the case at the end of the year, in time to help as the suit went to the Supreme Court.[5]

Some outsider lawyers, like Nessel, had grumbled about efforts by the legal groups to join cases they had first spurned, echoing complaints by grassroots and other activists that the establishment movement was slow and risk-averse. There was some truth to this complaint, although those who resisted cases from inside the movement were never a mono-lith; hence sometimes the critique only properly applied to a handful of lawyers. Other times, the pressure to hold off was forceful. This happened in 1991 with *Baehr,* a suit that, while it spurred enormous backlash, was re-sponsible for launching a movement that triumphed in less than a genera-tion. It happened with the *Goodridge* and *Gill* suits brought by GLAD but which some Roundtable lawyers initially opposed. It happened with *Perry,* which was uniformly rebuked by the major LGBTQ movement groups, and which failed to achieve its coveted Supreme Court victory but had won marriage equality in California and propelled public approval of same-sex marriage forward. It happened with *Windsor,* which brought down DOMA. And it happened after *Windsor* with several of the federal challenges to mar-riage bans, largely in "flyover" states, that some movement lawyers eyed warily, only to be surprised by victories. Meanwhile, gay and gay-friendly politicians, including Barney Frank and Dianne Feinstein, along with some movement lawyers, had cringed when Gavin Newsom began issuing mar-riage licenses, worrying he was pressing too far too soon. Time and again, looking at these critical junctures, it can seem that each time movement leaders declined to support a lawsuit or sought to dissuade people from taking action, this is when marriage equality lurched forward. And the astounding speed of ultimate victory is a testament to the virtue of taking such risks.

Yet while the triumph of marriage equality did not unfold exactly as movement lawyers planned, and was ultimately impossible to control, the fact is that it was the strategy delineated by tenacious and persistent marriage movement champions such as Evan Wolfson and Mary Bonauto that ultimately prevailed—and with what can only be viewed as lightning speed. Movement lawyers did take risks at several points, and some law-suits that they opposed indeed turned into setbacks, validating their cau-tion. Many outsider lawyers expressed understanding of the movement groups' need to make tough strategic choices. "The fact that they didn't see Kentucky as a place to focus their resources before didn't bother me in any way," Laura Landenwich, a Louisville lawyer involved in the Ken-tucky case, said about the movement groups.[6] Her colleague Dan Canon agreed. "I understood that they can't put their resources everywhere at all times," he said. "Kentucky was not part of the strategy, in part because they didn't think it could be won. And guess what? They were right: we didn't win in the Sixth Circuit." But Canon was happy to have the help of the ACLU, which provided support both before and after becoming co-counsel. "They were there when we needed them."[7]

Moreover, even the successful lawsuits brought by outsider lawyers embraced, in some fashion, the incremental strategy of crafting cases that carefully built upon one another. Rubenfeld's Tennessee team developed a narrow challenge that applied only to the plaintiffs who brought the suit, and, like the Ohio and Kentucky cases, began by only seeking recognition of out-of-state marriages rather than the right to marry. Likewise, the Michigan suit began as an adoption challenge, which Nessel regarded as a lighter lift than suing for marriage. By the time the four Sixth Circuit cases were granted Supreme Court review in January, "it set the stage beautifully and poetically," Kendell explained, "to have all four legal organizations in 2015 at the Supreme Court. You couldn't have scripted it better if you were [screenwriter] Dustin Lance Black."

This brick-by-brick approach grew out of the interplay between movement outsiders, who came to personally embrace the righteousness of marriage equality, and LGBTQ movement professionals, who on their own or through being prodded by other activists and developments on the ground took up the call to arms and tried to bring order to a boisterous and increasingly impatient populace. As more and more Americans, gay and non-gay alike, came to embrace marriage equality, more and more actors came to play a role in something that had once been plotted and debated and molded by a small group of gay and lesbian social justice dreamers— something that had long been dismissed as crazy, perhaps undesirable, but certainly unachievable.

This was the dramatic backdrop to the negotiations over who would argue for marriage equality before the nation's high court. The decision of who would argue Question #2, on marriage recognition, was made rather easily. The lawyers involved in the Ohio and Tennessee cases winnowed down their candidates to two—Al Gerhardstein, who had brought the Ohio cases, and Douglas Hallward-Driemeier, a highly respected appellate lawyer who had been involved in pro bono LGBTQ rights cases, had worked in the solicitor general's office, and had argued before the Supreme Court fourteen times. Hallward-Driemeier had joined the Tennessee challenge for the appeal, lending the weight of his white-shoe law firm, Ropes & Gray, to the effort. Meeting in Louisville for a "moot-off," the group of lawyers videotaped a mock court session, peppering the candidates with some of the sharpest questions they could anticipate the justices asking. Then the group viewed the videos and cast their votes. Hallward-Driemeier had blown everyone away with his performance— including Gerhardstein, who announced that he supported the Ropes & Gray partner for the job.[8]

The choice of oralist for the right-to-marry question was more complicated, as no consensus candidate readily emerged. While lawyers from the LGBTQ legal groups were in the mix, choosing one of them could be seen as unfair to all the other groups. Besides, three out of four of the cases had initially been brought by private counsel, with the gay legal groups joining later. As February gave way to March, the lawyers from the Kentucky and Michigan teams butted heads. Dan Canon, whom Fauver had brought into the case early on, would have relished the honor. "Everyone wanted to be the one to argue," he recalled. "When you have forty lawyer egos competing over who will argue, it's almost like the Court was setting us up to fight each other." But Canon also believed it was essential for people to put their egos aside for the greater good. And like Gerhardstein, he quickly came to the conclusion that others might be better suited for the job than he was.

One of those was Jeffrey Fisher, a legal wunderkind who had argued roughly two dozen cases at the Supreme Court by age forty-five and now, as codirector of the influential Stanford Law School Supreme Court Litigation Clinic, had joined the Kentucky team. Canon ceded Kentucky's nomination to Fisher. On the Michigan side, Dana Nessel felt strongly that her colleague Carole Stanyar ought to argue the case. Theirs had been the first of the four to be filed—even before the *Windsor* ruling unleashed a torrent of lawsuits, including all three of the others now coming before the justices. Nessel felt that the Michigan lawyers' early filing, hard work, and considerable financial sacrifices had earned them the honor of arguing the case. And Stanyar was also an experienced appellate lawyer. "I thought Carole would be terrific," Nessel said.

The trend in Supreme Court cases, however, was increasingly to bring in one of a few dozen elite lawyers with deep experience arguing before the justices to make the final case—someone exactly like Fisher. A slew of meetings, phone calls, and email chains yielded little progress toward making the harrowing choice of who would argue Question #1. On March 17, with a date set for oral arguments late the next month, the lawyers sent a letter to the clerk of the Supreme Court pleading for a break: could they divide their time among four different attorneys (plus the solicitor general), essentially one from each of the four states in the case? Without ever formally replying, the Court expressed its strong preference for just one attorney per question, and the lawyers found themselves back at square one. They scheduled a Sunday late that month to meet in person in Ann Arbor, Michigan, and hold a moot court.

The lawyers gathered in a room at the University of Michigan, where five "judges" had been chosen from among the nation's top attorneys and legal scholars. Their job would be to cast a vote after watching the moot-off between the two finalists, Stanyar and Fisher. After it ended, Fisher seemed to many of the gathered attorneys to be the clear standout: among the five judges, the vote was four to one in favor of Fisher. But the larger group had not made explicit what the rules were: Did the majority vote win? Was a consensus needed? "Well, it looks like we're at an impasse," said one lawyer from the Michigan team, angering others who felt the majority vote should have carried the day.

Deliberations continued deep into the night. Finally the Michigan and Kentucky teams each left the room to confer among themselves. Some thought egos were getting in the way of consensus. "Everybody puts their whole heart and soul into these cases," said Paul Smith, who had argued *Lawrence*. "You want to be the one who gets the brass ring at the end." Others pointed to a different concern. With Hallward-Driemeier likely to be chosen as the oralist for the recognition question and Verrilli planning to argue for the United States government, choosing Fisher to argue Question #1 would mean that three straight men would stand before the highest court in the land to finish off a battle begun decades earlier by the toil and courage and strategies of LGBTQ people. Straight people had long played a key role in advancing marriage equality, but for some this prospect was too much. "I thought the optics would be awful," said Nessel. "What would that say about us if we had only straight people arguing the case? That we weren't good enough or smart enough to argue our own issues before this court?" Others noted that a gay or lesbian person might have an easier time responding to certain sensitive or complex questions from the justices. In any event, Nessel believed the justices had already made up their minds, especially given that the Court had chosen to let stand several lower court rulings that consequently legalized same-sex marriage in numerous states, so while she had great confidence in Stanyar's ability to argue the case, she also felt that it was important to consider fairness as well as the optics of the choice. By contrast, many in the Kentucky camp seemed set on backing the person they thought was likely to perform the best.

As the night wore on with no resolution in sight, the Michigan team made a proposal: send a letter to the clerk explaining that the lawyers could not decide who should argue and let the Court make the choice. The other lawyers excoriated the idea, saying it was imperative to come to oral arguments as a united front. They were still stalemated, but people had planes to catch at the end of the night, and some said they would have to leave even if no resolution had been found. Someone suggested flipping a coin, another idea panned by everyone else in the room. Finally, a handful of lawyers began discussing an idea: although it was too late to redo the moot court, what about considering a new candidate, someone with a proven track record and decades of experience pushing marriage equality? The person? Mary Bonauto.

Bonauto had not put her hat in the ring. She had not originated the cases going before the Court, and one of her great assets was a level of humility that could be rare among litigators. In any event, the Michigan team, including the plaintiffs April DeBoer and Jayne Rowse, wanted one of their own lawyers to argue the case, and so had nominated Stanyer. But other lawyers, including Abby Rubenfeld and Dan Canon, had mentioned Bonauto's name from the get-go as a natural candidate given her early, effective, and consistent advocacy of marriage equality. Suddenly she was emerging as the one candidate everyone could feel good about. Bonauto was a member of the LGBTQ community. She worked at a gay group, but one with a regional rather than a national focus. She had brought and won the case that made Massachusetts the first state to allow same-sex marriage. While she had never argued before the Supreme Court, she was an accomplished attorney who had lived and breathed marriage equality for more than two decades. The previous year she had won a MacArthur Foundation "genius" award for her work. She was part of the Michigan legal team, which could potentially soothe feelings among its lawyers.

After many appeals to the importance of building consensus and taking the high ground, everyone present agreed on Bonauto. "I have only one month to prepare," she fretted to her colleagues. To which one replied, "You've been preparing for this your whole life."

As oral arguments, set for April 28, drew closer and Bonauto held moot court sessions with a long list of colleagues and strategic allies, polls showed that as much as 60 percent of the public now favored legalizing same-sex marriage, a record high. Showcasing the breadth of interest in marriage equality that now blanketed the country, amicus briefs flooded in, a testament to the years of outreach that LGBTQ advocates had conducted, and specifically to Bonauto's coordination of the briefs in earlier cases. Nearly 150 briefs were submitted from around the nation and world, breaking records last set just two years earlier in the *Windsor* and *Hollingsworth* cases. Slightly more argued for marriage equality than against it, but the signatories of the pro-gay-marriage briefs were impressive—there were backers from think tanks, business (one brief was signed by 379 companies, corporations, and employer groups arguing that diversity and tolerance were essential to how they conducted business), advocacy groups, universities, local and state governments (another brief was signed by 226 U.S. mayors), legal groups, unions, and more, including the U.S. Department of Justice (no surprise at this point in the process, but the fruit of years of advocacy and public education). Signing briefs opposing marriage equality were conservative scholars and advocacy groups, largely southern and Republican government officials and political bodies, conservative religious groups and think tanks, and an outfit called Same-Sex Attracted Men and Their Wives—six men who said they were attracted to other men but still married to women, hence demonstrating, they alleged, that gay men already enjoyed the right to marry.[9]

By the time the Supreme Court was ready to hear the case in April 2015, the number of marriage equality states had rocketed from one in 2004 to thirty-seven. In October 2014, the day after the Supreme Court had set in motion the addition of eleven new marriage equality states by declining to review any of the seven petitions before it, the Ninth Circuit had handed down a ruling that resulted in five more—Nevada, Idaho, Arizona, Alaska, and Montana. Then a ruling in January 2015 made Florida the thirty-sixth state. The next month, in a shock to many who remembered its brutal segregationist history, Alabama became the thirty-seventh state to allow same-sex marriage when a federal judge there struck down the state's marriage ban. That ruling spurred pockets of resistance and a protracted legal battle after Alabama Supreme Court chief judge Roy Moore ordered county clerks not to issue licenses, throwing the status of same-sex marriage across the state into uncertainty.

Yet as the briefs, polls, state advances, and other indicators of popular and political culture made increasingly clear, momentum nationwide was on the side of marriage equality. And it was a momentum that seemed somehow disproportionate to its mere poll numbers, surpassing the saliency of other issues. Large majorities of Americans favored strong gun safety laws, the right to die, and inclusion of gays and lesbians in nondiscrimination law. Yet none of those issues spawned the kind of popular outcry or policy advances that some aspects of the marriage equality battle now could. In March, the state of Indiana drew closer to passing a bill allowing people to opt out of laws protecting gays and lesbians from discrimination if they cited religious objections. The so-called religious freedom bills were the latest strategy of Christian conservatives to fight the spread of gay and transgender rights, and a slew of media stories had emerged about florists and bakers and even pizza shops that were refusing to provide service to same-sex couples. Lawsuits and legislative battles were heating up, with religious conservatives casting their position as a simple affirmation of religious freedom rather than an instance of anti-gay discrimination. Many of the bills went beyond existing laws that simply reaffirmed the First Amendment right of conscience, instead carving out broad behavioral exemptions that applied not only to religious organizations but to private businesses whose owners claimed a religious basis for declining to serve gay people.

The Indiana bill was one of the broadest yet. It allowed anyone in the state to opt out of following virtually any law simply by stating that it conflicted with his or her religious beliefs. The uproar against it was not confined to LGBTQ advocates. After the state legislature passed the bill, Gov. Mike Pence signed it into law on March 26 amid a firestorm of criticism. A joint statement from leaders of the corporate technology sector denounced the law and called for a strong bill that would proactively protect gays and lesbians from discrimination. It was signed by the heads of major companies: Yelp, Twitter, Salesforce, Airbnb, Cisco, eBay, PayPal, and others. Over the course of days, the list grew: Subaru (which built cars in Indiana), Eli Lilly, The Gap, NASCAR, Marriott, the National Basketball Association, and Gen Con, which held a massive gaming convention in the state but was threatening to pull it as a consequence of the law. "#Boycott-Indiana" was trending near the top of Twitter. The White House decried the law. Tim Cook, the new and openly gay CEO of Apple, declared his company "open for everyone."

Governor Pence had a disaster on his hands. Rather than leading his state into the future, the governor risked becoming an irredentist reactionary defending a minority opinion. After a dismal week spent trying in vain to defend the law on national television, he and the Republican lawmakers behind the bill were forced to back down in the face of public embarrassment and threats of economic devastation to the state. The law was modified, but still fell short of protecting gay and lesbian Hoosiers from discrimination. While the step took some of the heat off Indiana, the successful outcry sent a signal across the nation that anti-gay sentiment was decisively out of favor in the political mainstream. If social conservatives planned to respond to the spread of gay marriage with religious exemptions laws, there would be costs.

That spring the Catholic nation of Ireland became the first country to approve same-sex marriage by a popular vote with a decisive 62 to 38 percent victory. Roughly twenty countries now allowed same-sex couples to marry, largely in Western and Northern Europe but also including Canada, South Africa, and some countries in South America.

———

On the clear spring morning of April 28, 2015, as raucous protests raged outside, Mary Bonauto stood to address the Supreme Court. She began by tying same-sex unions together with opposite-sex ones, calling both "the foundation of family life in our society." Denying gay couples the legal protections and responsibilities of civil marriage not only imposed on them material harms but stamped them with a "stain of unworthiness" that violates the Constitution's "commitment to equal dignity." It was fortunate that she squeezed in so many key points in her opening statement, because she was immediately peppered with interruptions by the justices seeking answers to their—or others'—reservations about recognizing a constitutional right to marriage for gay people. Justice Ginsberg wanted to know how to reconcile the *Windsor* decision, which stressed the importance of deference to states, with the declaration of a federal right to marry. Justice Alito wanted to know if Bonauto could defend the suggestion that state marriage bans were really efforts to demean gay people. If so, he wondered, how could one explain ancient Greece, a civilization that was relatively tolerant of homosexuality yet still did not extend marriage to same-sex couples?[10]

But the justices seemed fixated on the historical stakes of recognizing a constitutional right to marry for same-sex couples. "The word that keeps coming back to me," said Justice Kennedy in describing his thinking on the case, "is millennia." In using the term, he was resurrecting it from its odious deployment by Chief Justice Warren E. Burger in his *Bowers* concurrence. Burger had fretted that "millennia of moral teaching" would be unceremoniously discarded if the Court protected the right of gay people to intimate conduct, as if tradition alone were a viable justification for law. Now Kennedy noted that it had been just over ten years since the *Lawrence* decision overturned *Bowers,* giving the country little time to contemplate the issue of same-sex marriage. He seemed wary of imposing a constitutional mandate when the issue had not, in some minds, had sufficient time to percolate. "I don't even know how to count the decimals," he said to drive home how short ten years was relative to thousands. The definition of marriage as a male-female union "has been with us for millennia. And it it's very difficult for the Court to say, 'oh, well, we know better.'"

It was not surprising that conservative justices Roberts and Scalia echoed Kennedy's concerns. "Every definition that I looked up prior to about a dozen years ago," worried Chief Justice Roberts, "defined marriage as unity between a man and a woman," while Scalia complained that the plaintiffs were asking the Court to establish same-sex marriage "when no other society until 2001 ever had it." Justice Alito said that, as far as he was aware, "there never was a nation or a culture that recognized marriage between two people of the same sex" before the twenty-first century. (In fact, such declarations revealed a certain blindness to the work of historians

Attorney Mary Bonauto, who successfully argued the legal case making Massa-chusetts the first state to legalize same-sex marriage, gives a thumbs-up before entering the Supreme Court in April 2015 to do the same for marriage nationwide.

who have suggested that many cultures throughout the ages have recognized at least some version of same-sex marriage.)[11]

But it was more alarming when Justice Stephen Breyer, a liberal, seeming exasperated at Bonauto's refusal to respond to the other justices' queries, joined the interrogation. Male-female marriage, he said, "has been the law everywhere for thousands of years," even in cultures sympathetic to homosexuality, "and suddenly you want nine people outside the ballot box to require states that don't want to do it to change what marriage is to include gay people." Why couldn't those states just wait and see how things played out in the other states—what Justice Louis Brandeis once called "laboratories of democracy"?

Eventually Breyer answered his own question, suggesting that the reason he had asked it was either to help Bonauto's case or simply to get the answer on record. If "people have always done it" were a satisfactory reason to exclude people, he contended, the Court never would have outlawed racial segregation. Marriage, he continued, "is about as basic a right as there is." It is "open to vast numbers of people who both have children, adopt children, don't have children, all over the place. But there is one group of people whom they won't open marriage to. So they have no possibility to participate in that fundamental liberty. That is people of the same sex who wish to marry." Were tradition and religion, he asked, adequate reasons to single out a group and deny its members important rights? He implied not. Yet those were the only two reasons he had heard. And, he concluded dryly, "when I look for reasons three, four and five, I don't find them."

In the *Loving* case, which ended interracial marriage bans, said Justice Kagan, the tradition had been that whites did not marry blacks. But the *Loving* court, she explained, concluded it was "irrelevant" that interracial marriage was not part of the tradition "because there's no good reason for it not to be part of the next tradition."

There was another point to be made, which was to challenge the justices' premise that the definition of marriage had been the same for "millennia" of history. As Harvard's Nancy Cott had explained at Judge Walker's trial, and the scholar E. J. Graff had written in her book a decade before that, the very idea that marriage had always been defined in just one way was historically false, particularly the notion that it was primarily about procreation. Monogamous marriage, Cott had told the trial court, was a modern oddity in America's colonial period, with much of the world at the time still practicing polygamy. Bonauto knew these arguments, and although it was initially tough to interject them, she eventually found her chance. Prompted by Justice Ginsburg, who noted that marriage a millennium ago defined women as wholly subordinate to their husbands, Bonauto expanded on the point. "Because of equality and changing social circumstances" over the last century, she said, marriage has already been transformed. Gay people would not be redefining it but joining "a system in which committed, same-sex couples fit quite well."

Justice Alito was not convinced. Given how widespread heterosexual-only marriage was across the globe, mustn't there be "some rational, practical purpose for defining marriage" this way? Or did the plaintiffs want the justices to believe that the world's cultures across millennia "were all operating independently based solely on irrational stereotypes and prejudice?" It was a grander version of the question Justice Roberts had asked Robbie Kaplan when she argued Edie Windsor's case two years earlier: could the eighty-four out of one hundred senators who had voted for DOMA in 1996 really have been motivated by animus and moral disapproval of gay people? Kaplan had a reply at the ready. Some people might have supported DOMA for reasons that were not rooted in anti-gay animus. But in general, the belief that marriage must be "defended" from gay incursions reflected "an incorrect understanding that gay couples were fundamentally different than straight couples, an understanding that I don't think exists today."

The argument, then, that the plaintiffs in both *Windsor* and *Obergefell* deployed was that they were not asking the Court to legislate from the bench or to step beyond where Americans were on this issue. Like the nation's understanding of gay people, marriage itself had been changing, and had already changed in profound ways that made same-sex unions fit the bill. Indeed, what was most unchanging about marriage in America was how long it had been considered a fundamental right. After decades of court decisions protecting that fundamental right for interracial couples, fathers with unpaid child support, prison inmates, and others, there seemed no other way to view excluding gay couples but as arbitrary and discriminatory. The justices' decision, in an important sense, now hung on the extent to which they had awakened to these changes, and felt the nation had as well.

Kennedy's *Lawrence* decision hinted at the answer and offered a retort to all the musings about breaking with millennia of tradition. "Times can blind us to certain truths and later generations can see that laws once thought necessary and proper in fact serve only to oppress," he had written. "As the Constitution endures, persons in every generation can invoke its principles in their own search for greater freedom." Wisely, Bonauto quoted Kennedy's opinion (as had Kaplan in arguing *Windsor* two years earlier), seeking to soften any insinuation that the plaintiffs were charging all gay-marriage opponents with bigotry, and instead to emphasize the nation's awakening to the reality and dignity of same-sex love. "Times can blind," she told the Court, "and it takes time to see stereotypes and to see the common humanity"—a phrase the Vermont high court had invoked in its 1999 ruling—"of people who had once been ignored or excluded."[12]

In defending the gay marriage bans in Michigan, Ohio, Tennessee, and Kentucky, lawyers had an unenviable job: to bury the dynamism of such historical change, portraying the institution of marriage as static, brittle, and under siege—all while not implying that gay people were a threat, which could cast their arguments as rooted in animus. To do this, they settled on a fairly narrow argument: biology. It was the latest version of the "responsible procreation" argument that social conservative think tanks had been pushing as often as possible. Arguing for the defendants, John Bursch, a former solicitor general for the state of Michigan, rejected Justice Breyer's contention that the only rationales for banning gay marriage were tradition, religion, or anti-gay animus. "The marriage institution," he told the Court, "did not develop to deny dignity or to give second class status to anyone. It developed to serve purposes that, by their nature, arise from biology."

Imagine, said Bursch, a world with no marriage at all. In such a world, men and women would still come together and create children, but there would be no social institution tying them to each other and their children. Marriage, he argued, was the solution to that problem. It was not about excluding gay couples, but it also was not about emotional commitments; it was about tying couples to their biological children for life.

Since Anita Bryant's 1977 Save the Children campaign in Florida, opponents of gay equality had phrased their arguments in terms of defending American families from the alleged threats of gay aggression and hedonism. While defenders of gay marriage bans in 2015 did all they could to avoid appearing anti-gay, the notion that letting gays marry would transform the institution from being "child-centric" to "adult-centric" fit squarely in the tradition of demonizing gay people as selfish and indulgent, and gay rights as the triumph of a narcissistic culture over a responsible and temperate one committed to the common good. If Bursch's argument echoed that tradition too loudly, the justices could be more likely to view gay marriage bans as reflecting nothing more than animus. It probably didn't make Bursch's job any easier that the august proceedings that morning were interrupted by a religious zealot suddenly shouting, "If you support gay marriage, you will burn in hell!" He had to be forcibly removed from the courtroom, and his ranting could be heard for several minutes even after he was ejected.

Justices Kagan and Ginsburg asked Bursch how letting gays wed would harm the institution of marriage as a regulator of procreation. "It has to do with the societal understanding of what marriage means," replied Bursch, invoking the social norms argument that conservative Catholic intellectuals had been honing for over a decade. "If you delink marriage from creating children, you would expect to have more children created outside the bonds of marriage." But how, persisted Justice Kagan, does letting gays marry cause that delinking to happen? Did Bursch think that allowing same-sex marriage would mean "announcing to the world that marriage and children have nothing to do with each other?" Justice Kennedy chimed in. "It's just a wrong premise," he said, to assume that "only opposite-sex couples can have a bonding with a child." Many gay couples have children, several of the justices pointed out, and sometimes straight couples have none. Currently all kinds of people can marry who don't, won't, can't, or can no longer have kids. Why draw the line at same-sex couples?

Bursch answered the justices' questions calmly and without pause, but he had to stretch the boundaries of reason in order to field the toughest challenges. At one point his logic drew a sharp rebuke from Justice Sotomayor. Bursch had summed up his argument this way: by defining marriage to include gay unions, people could come to believe that "marriage is more about love and commitment than about staying bound to your child forever," and such a change in the public understanding of marriage could reduce the rates at which heterosexual couples marry or stay married and hence stay committed to their children. In essence, Bursch was trying to argue that allowing gay marriage would change people's feelings about marriage so much that they would not bother to wed. But Justice Sotomayor dismissed that idea as far too illogical to be taken seriously by the Supreme Court. "Do we accept a feeling?" she asked. "Why would that feeling, which doesn't make any logical sense, control our decision-making?"

Making matters worse, the conservative position now rested on the argument that love and commitment played little role in shaping how Americans understood what marriage was all about. Yet LGBTQ advocates had learned through rigorous research that love and commitment were precisely what most Americans viewed as the purpose of marriage. One important American, in particular, viscerally understood this key component of contemporary marriage, and the dignity that expressing such feelings through marriage bestowed on those who participated. Gay people seek the same "noble purpose" in marriage as anybody else, Justice Kennedy said in an exchange with Bursch. Same-sex couples, too, "understand the nobility and the sacredness of marriage." Their claim, explained Kennedy, was that even though they could not procreate, "we want the other attributes of [marriage] in order to show that we, too, have a dignity that can be fulfilled." It was, it would turn out, a stirring preview of the opinion the Court would hand down two months later.

Solicitor General Donald Verrilli, supporting same-sex marriage for the Obama administration, offered a rousing call for the constitutional and humanistic recognition of the equal dignity of gay people. "In a world in which gay and lesbian couples live openly as our neighbors, they raise their children side by side with the rest of us, they contribute fully as members of the community," he said, "it is simply untenable—untenable—to suggest that they can be denied the right of equal participation in an institution of marriage, or that they can be required to wait until the majority decides that it is ready to treat gay and lesbian people as equals. Gay and lesbian people are equal. They deserve equal protection of the laws, and they deserve it now."

In his remarks on Question #2 in the case—whether states must simply recognize out-of-state same-sex marriages—private attorney Douglas Hallward-Driemeier wove together the stories of the plaintiffs he represented, ending with that of the named plaintiff. If the defense were to prevail, he explained, "Jim Obergefell's husband's death certificate will not reflect the fact that he was married or the name of his husband. The state has no legitimate interest for denying them the dignity of that last fact regarding his life. . . . I urge the Court not to enshrine in our Constitution a second-class status of these petitioners' marriages." Jim Obergefell shifted in his seat and quietly broke into tears.

On June 26, 2015, two years to the day after it handed down the *Windsor* ruling and exactly twelve years after *Lawrence* decriminalized same-sex relationships nationwide, the Supreme Court handed down a 5-to-4 ruling in *Obergefell* written by Justice Kennedy. It was his fourth and most important pro-gay ruling in a constitutional edifice he had built over nearly twenty years that quickly sealed his legacy as one of the high court's gay rights champions. "From their beginning to their most recent page, the annals of human history reveal the transcendent importance of marriage," Kennedy's ruling stated. Immediately two prongs of the long-term strategy for winning marriage equality were vindicated: viewing marriage as a single institution that is not divisible into something called "gay marriage" and "traditional marriage," and the importance of empha-sizing the historical evolution of American traditions. "Far from seeking to devalue marriage," his opinion continued, the plaintiffs in this case "seek it for themselves because of their respect—and need—for its privileges and responsibilities."[13]

Kennedy then proffered a historical account of the importance of marriage, whose "ancient origins" made it central to human history and an integral, ever-evolving part of law and society. Changes in its institu-tional meaning—even when confined to heterosexuals—were "character-istic of a nation where new dimensions of freedom become apparent to new generations, often through perspectives that begin in pleas or protests and then are considered in the political sphere and the judicial process." Reaching back to World War II, he cited the emergence of a "greater awareness of the humanity and integrity of homosexual persons" that had developed across those decades. As he had done in citing the historians' brief in his *Lawrence* decision, Kennedy's reference to an awakening to "new dimensions of freedom" paid tribute not only to the evolving nature of freedom but also to the specific efforts and particular history of gay and lesbian advocacy. An enlarged understanding of freedom for the nation, he suggested, had been made visible over generations through eyes first opened by expressions of protest, and later parlayed into the legal and so-cial mainstream through the political process.

To those who believed a longer process of national discourse should be allowed to play out before a court mandate brought marriage equality to the nation, Kennedy retorted that the country had spent decades debating and considering and slowly coming to understand the nature of same-sex love. There were "referenda, legislative debates, and grassroots campaigns, as well as countless studies, papers, books, and other popular and scholarly writings." Scores of submitted briefs demonstrated the "substantial atten-tion" and "enhanced understanding" the topic had garnered in the public mind. "Numerous cases about same-sex marriage have reached the United

States Courts of Appeals in recent years," and many different courts had by now "written a substantial body of law considering all sides of these issues. That case law helps to explain and formulate the underlying principles this Court now must consider."

That carefully erected legal and historical record—the marriage movement's brick-by-brick masterpiece, the capstone of which Bonauto had laid two months earlier in addressing the high court—seemed critical to Kennedy's ability to surmount his own concern about moving too quickly and short-circuiting the democratic process. The decades-long construction of a same-sex marriage edifice was nothing if not democratic. The turn of the most recent century, Kennedy noted, had occasioned "a quite extensive discussion of the issue in both governmental and private sectors," spurring "a shift in public attitudes toward greater tolerance. As a result, questions about the rights of gays and lesbians soon reached the courts, where the issue could be discussed in the formal discourse of the law." States, he recounted, began opting for marriage equality, taking under advisement their own assessments of the arguments for and against doing so.

The constitutional arguments of equal protection and due process were the same now as they had been in 1970, when Jack Baker recognized their applicability but the Supreme Court dismissed his claim "for want of a substantial federal question," or in 1983, when Evan Wolfson became the first to lay them all out on paper. But so much had had to happen before the courts and the nation could recognize what just a few people had seen decades before. "The nature of injustice is that we may not always see it in our own times," Kennedy wrote in his opinion, echoing his earlier gay rights rulings in what was coming to embody a philosophy of judicial progressivism.[14] Those who ratified the Bill of Rights and subsequent amendments could not have known how freedom, in all its dimensions, would look over time, so they had given later generations the responsibility of "protecting the right of all persons to enjoy liberty as we learn its meaning." What that required was an awakening from slumber and an opening of the eyes to the humanity of gay people and the injustice of excluding them from equal citizenship. "The limitation of marriage to oppo site-sex couples," Kennedy went on, "may long have seemed natural and just, but its inconsistency with the central meaning of the fundamental right to marry is now manifest." Kennedy concluded his decision—and a two-generations-long quest for legal and social recognition of the equal dignity of same-sex love—with a paean not just to marriage as an institution but to belonging: like so many others, many gays and lesbians wished to marry. "It would misunderstand these men and women to say they disrespect the idea of marriage. Their plea is that they do respect it, respect it so deeply that they seek to find its fulfillment for themselves. Their hope is not to be condemned to live in loneliness, excluded from one of civilization's oldest institutions. They ask for equal dignity in the eyes of the law. The Constitution grants them that right. The judgment of the Court of Appeals for the Sixth Circuit is reversed. *It is so ordered.*"

EPILOGUE

In emotional remarks made hours after the Supreme Court ruling, President Barack Obama said that progress toward equality "often comes in small increments" but that on days like this one, "slow, steady effort is rewarded with justice that arrives like a thunderbolt." He attributed victory—in a battle he had publicly embraced only three years earlier—to "the countless small acts of courage of millions of people across decades who stood up" and "came out," who "stayed strong, and came to believe in themselves and who they were. And slowly made an entire country realize that love is love."

That country included, first and foremost, gay and lesbian people themselves, since little advancement was possible before they came to see themselves as members of a legitimate minority rather than isolated degenerates, as fully worthy of equality despite their difference. For decades millions of them had felt too scared and too ashamed to come out, let alone to fight for their dignity and equal treatment. The idea that they might someday legally marry a same-sex partner had been nowhere on most people's radar. This is what Bonauto had meant when she said that many gay people never dared to even think about marriage, shutting down the very contemplation of something they thought they could never have.[1]

Bonauto came to consider this avoidance—at least for some—as a "defense mechanism," and saw its implications play out again and again once marriage began to be legalized. So many had greeted her push for marriage with intense skepticism. Yet many of these very same people—including ardent feminists—who had insisted they didn't want to marry changed their tune and showed up at the altar when marriage became a legal option for them. "I never thought this could matter to me so much," Bonauto recalled many of her lesbian friends and colleagues saying. But after gaining the freedom to marry and then actually tying the knot, "they felt alive in a whole new way," she explained. For some, "it was completely transformative."[2] Bonauto married her long-time partner, Jennifer Wriggins, in Massachusetts in 2008.

This link between public recognition of their love and the unhesitating feeling of equal worth is why Kris Perry told Judge Walker's courtroom that having her marriage license yanked away in 2004 made her feel like she wasn't "good enough." (And this is why she said on the day she won her case that her goal was "to send a message to the children of this country that you are just as good as everybody else no matter who you love.")[3] It's why America's first lesbian senator, Tammy Baldwin, told LGBTQ activists at the 2000 Millennium March (as a congresswoman) that they held crucial reins of power in their willingness to give public voice and visibility to their needs and demands. "There are two things that keep us oppressed," she told the crowd, "them and us. We are half of the equation." Baldwin said that there would be no "magic day when we wake up and it's now okay to express ourselves publicly. We must make that day ourselves."[4] In a similar vein, Robbie Kaplan connected her own self-esteem as a lesbian to her ability to help awaken others. "I had to recognize my own dignity as a lesbian before I could be truly effective as an advocate," she wrote in 2015, just as the queers and misfits of the Stonewall rebellion had to awaken to their equal dignity before they would rise up, fight back, and begin to declare their humanity to the world.[5] It would take Edie Windsor many years to absorb what the Stonewall generation was offering her—a message of pride and the ensuing power to change her life and her country. The significance she ultimately attributed to Stonewall was that it unleashed waves of collective gay and lesbian self-esteem that became self-intensifying. That process would reverberate decades later as federal courts began eloquently declaring the equal dignity of gay people in striking down gay marriage bans. "Suddenly the self-esteem is flowing," Windsor said of the impact of these cases. "I mean even these judges are saying we're respectable."[6]

Of course, not all gays and lesbians were seeking respectability. And even many who felt they deserved respect did not equate that status with being married, an idea that E. B. Saunders and generations of liberationist thinkers had dismissed as antiquated or worse.[7] While some on the left continued to view marriage with deep suspicion and to complain about what was lost in gaining respectability, many viewed both marriage and freedom in a new light as a result of the battle for public recognition of same-sex love. "Since when is marriage a path to liberation?" Paula Ettelbrick had written in her 1989 debate with Tom Stoddard. Now, it seemed, the question could be answered. In his *Obergefell* dissent, Justice Antonin

Scalia, who died early in 2016, eight months after the ruling, aligned himself with feminist and liberationist critics of marriage in at least one regard: they all viewed marriage as not a freedom but a constraint. "If intimacy is a freedom," Scalia wrote in panning Kennedy's suggestion that intimacy was an important form of liberty inherent in marriage, it is one that's "abridged rather than expanded by marriage." If that's not clear, he suggested, just "ask the nearest hippie." For critics of marriage, including LGBTQ people who sought an alternative to it, embracing freedom was precisely why they spurned marriage (while for Scalia and other social conservatives, marriage was valuable precisely because it put constraints on freedom, including the freedom of gay people to join it).[8]

Yet by the time she died from peritoneal cancer in 2011, even Ettelbrick had softened in that view. "I no longer argue against same-sex marriage," she said shortly before then. "I'd look like a dinosaur if I did. That argument's gone, that train's out." She continued to have concerns that some people were being "left behind" in the rush to marriage. But she also had occasion to cry at gay weddings. What she'd come to understand was that the freedom to choose marriage had empowered gay people enormously. The public response to the battle and the national conversations around it had all moved the world "much further along the spectrum of people seeing our relationships as valid than I would ever have anticipated, and at a much quicker pace than I ever would have thought possible."[9]

The ACLU's Matt Coles, never as staunch a marriage critic as Ettelbrick, expressed similar satisfaction with the journey the LGBTQ movement had taken. "I'm very happy about where we are," said Coles. The fight over marriage, he said, "is the fight we've always had to have. Every form of discrimination," he explained, "rests on a belief that the group being discriminated against is less worthy or less good." And the battle over marriage "tees up perfectly" the question of whether gay people are truly equal to everyone else. "Would I have done some things differently, tactically? Sure. Am I always right? God knows, no."[10]

Like Ettelbrick and Coles, Kendell's views on marriage had evolved from the day she first argued to Wolfson at the Roundtable meeting that marriage was an impediment to gay liberation. What she eventually came to believe was that it was not marriage but its denial that "poisoned every possibility for liberation." True freedom, she explained, meant "not only throwing off stigma and shame, but being able to fully participate in civil society, and never having that diminished based on who we are or who we love." Kendell married Sandy Holmes in California during the 2008 window when it was first made legal. "That was an incredible day," she said. "I guess I had undervalued the power of ceremony."[11] But if Kendell was glad to have joined the ranks of the married, she hadn't lost her interest in reforming the institution from the inside, and in using it to continue transforming society. Having secured access to marriage, she expressed confidence that the next generation of young people will rewrite the rules again. "I think we couldn't have gotten to that point without winning marriage first," she said. "We have to go through marriage to remake it."

But what, ultimately, did the embrace of marriage by the LGBTQ movement accomplish? Did it really allow for the remaking of the institution, or indeed the dramatic transformation of society, as some advocates hoped? Consistent with the theory of unintended consequences, many of the veteran gay and lesbian activists who dedicated decades of their lives to fighting for gay equality did not set out to make marriage a top priority. Yet many ended up doing more than they had ever intended not only to attain equal access to marriage, but, in so doing, to achieve equal dignity for LGBTQ Americans and to spur other profound gains for America as a whole.

For starters, the successful battle for marriage, just as early proponents hoped, seems clearly to have improved Americans' attitudes about the dignity and worth of gay people and to have bolstered support for pro-gay treatment, policies, and laws. Moral approval of homosexuality mushroomed in tandem with support for same-sex marriage. Between 1985 and 2015, the percentage of Americans who believed same-sex relations were "morally acceptable," after remaining unchanged for more than a decade, tripled, jumping from 21 percent to 63 percent. Over roughly the same period, national support for same-sex marriage closely tracked those numbers. From a low of between 11 and 23 percent around 1990, approval grew to over 60 percent in 2016, one year after *Obergefell*, according to Gallup. That's an astounding increase of more than 400 percent in about a quarter century, making the embrace of gay marriage one of the fastest-changing issues of any topic polled.[12]

These figures do not indicate whether moral approval increased support for marriage or vice versa, but several other data points indeed suggest that Kameny, Wolfson, Sullivan, and Bonauto were wise to view the marriage issue as a means of advancing the acceptability of same-sex love. For one thing, it is tough to spur thought and conversation about moral abstractions, but easier to ask the public to contemplate the acceptability of something as concrete as marriage. Research from the Williams Institute and elsewhere confirms the self-intensifying effect of advancing rights, in which states that legalize same-sex marriage saw the highest rates of growth in public support for it. Related research has found that states with marriage equality saw the biggest drop in anti-gay sentiment. The findings suggest that the experience of seeing that the sky does not fall after a policy shift helps people embrace both policy and attitudinal change.[13]

Opinion research also shows that the growth in support for same-sex marriage stemmed not simply from generational change but from genuine opinion shifts. Using polling models that project how attitudes would most likely look under various circumstances, pollsters including Nate Silver found that roughly half of the change in marriage equality support is accounted for by older cohorts dying and being replaced by younger people with more gay-friendly attitudes. The other half reflects individuals who actually changed their minds, abandoning earlier opposition to same-sex marriage. These data suggest that the years of opinion research, groundwork, political advocacy, and litigation on behalf of same-sex marriage truly created changes in attitudes and beliefs, hearts and minds, becoming a model for progressive advocacy across the country.[14]

Among those who did change their view on marriage, the most common reason cited was coming to know a gay person. This connection is corroborated by data showing an increase in the number of gay and lesbian Americans coming out in the decades after Stonewall and that those who know gay people are more likely to support equal rights. There is no doubt, of course, that the millions of gays and lesbians who mustered the courage to make themselves visible between the mid-twentieth century and the *Obergefell* decision were absolutely critical both to the triumph of marriage and to the broader progress in attitudes and policies toward LGBTQ Americans that accompanied it. This was indeed one of the key reasons why advocates chose to push marriage, an institution defined by the public recognition of the dignity of a private bond, by the call to bear witness to a couple's love.[15]

As important as public visibility was to both the emergence of marriage equality and advances in LGBTQ approval, such developments leave open a critical question for historians: Why then? Why, exactly, did so many gay and lesbian Americans feel ready to identify themselves—both internally and to others—starting around the last third of the twentieth century?

To answer this, we must return both to the immediate historical context of the Stonewall generation and to the specific nature of marriage as an institution. Both consciousness and visibility of a marginalized group are essential to advancing its rights. In the 1960s, the advent of television, along with the effective organizing of the black civil rights and antiwar movements, meant that searing, inescapable images of pain, abuse, and humiliation, and of dignity, resistance, and resolve were beamed into the living rooms of millions of Americans, helping spur policy and cultural changes across the country and the world. A youth movement and a women's movement emerged from this context, creating a new politics of public visibility, personal identity, and social and political interrogation of existing norms. And in this context, a nascent gay rights movement that was first born at mid-century blossomed, taking flight with the Stonewall uprising. A generation later, a population devastated by a deadly illness but buoyed by innovative activism and a growing consciousness of their own dignity turned the politics of public visibility and personal identity into the first mass civil rights movement of the Internet age. As gay identity came to seem mainstream, marriage—a most traditional institution that weaves together the right to pursue private happiness with a public expression of belonging—came to seem as much a birthright for gays and lesbians as for anyone else. Even some who had scoffed at calls for respectability came to see the freedom to marry as more crucial to both liberty and equality than they had once grasped. It was possible, they determined, to yearn for the respect of others—this is indeed an inherent part of what equality means—without succumbing to the trappings of "respectability."

That public dimension of marriage both reflected and further accelerated the coming out of millions more Americans. Explaining the tremendous increase in acceptance of same-sex marriage early in 2015, Justice Ruth Bader Ginsburg said, "As more and more people came out and said, 'This is who I am,' the rest of us recognized that 'they' are one of us." It was a classic expression of the liberal ideal of ever-widening circles of identification and empathy, something well embodied by the marriage equality effort. On the steps of the Supreme Court building the day her case was heard, Edie Windsor made the same point in her inimitable way: "As we increasingly came out," she told a scrum of reporters and onlookers, "people saw that we didn't have horns. . . . It just grew to where we were human beings like everybody else."[16] (In 2016, Windsor, at age eighty-seven, remarried at New York's City Hall.)

As the Gay and Lesbian Victory Fund had concluded in the early 1990s, out lawmakers would be instrumental to passing pro-gay legislation. This was proven again and again in the quest for marriage, particularly at the state level. Although Barney Frank's impassioned personal remarks on the House floor were not enough to sway the Congress to vote DOMA down, many openly gay and lesbian state lawmakers later inspired wavering colleagues to support their freedom to marry. That was true in California, when the visibility of openly gay assemblyman Mark Leno helped the legislature there become the first to pass a marriage equality law in 2005. It was true in Massachusetts in 2007 when several uncommitted Republican state representatives, after lengthy talks with gay constituents and their openly gay colleague Rep. Carl Sciortino, risked their seats to vote against overturning the *Goodridge* decision. The vote finally ended the fierce battle over whether to allow or reverse gay marriage in the first state in America to make it legal.[17] It was also true in Washington State, where advocates and openly gay lawmakers had pursued an incremental strategy to attain same-sex marriage in the decade leading up to the successful 2012 ballot vote. And it was the reason why President Obama cited getting to know openly gay staff members and their families in explaining his own evolution on same-sex marriage: because his journey mirrored that of millions of other Americans, and numerous other politicians and cultural leaders, who found that their own families and friends included gay people. (In an amusing footnote to history, by the time Charles Cooper argued before the Supreme Court against gay marriage in the Proposition 8 case, he had learned that his daughter was a lesbian; he was soon involved in planning her wedding, telling reporters that his views were "evolving.")[18]

If coming out, speaking up, and becoming visible were crucial to making sweeping gains in public approval of gay lives and same-sex love, the public dimension of gay marriage and of LGBTQ life also had a far-reaching effect on American culture itself. If what Frank Kameny meant by "gay is good" was that being a sexual minority should be experienced by gay people as a moral virtue rather than a source of shame, the push to popularize gay relationships and legalize same-sex marriage was also good for America. This could be seen in reports of young heterosexual couples citing the soaring language of gay marriage court rulings as part of their own wedding vows, a reminder that the scores of court cases themselves occasioned much-needed discussion across the country about what purpose— beyond the simple fealty to tradition or religion—marriage serves.[19] It could be seen in marriage and divorce rates too. While the data are preliminary, the overall marriage rate in Massachusetts spiked after the state legalized same-sex marriage, and remained higher than previous rates even after accounting for the initial jump that resulted from pent-up demand. Looking at the first five states to legalize same-sex marriage, divorce rates dropped there in the years following the policy change, while national rates ticked up slightly, a spot of empirical evidence disproving assertions that letting gays wed would destroy marriage.[20] Quite the contrary, the national debate over marriage appears to have rejuvenated an institution whose social function too few people previously had reason to contemplate.

Whatever one's feelings about the importance that gays and lesbians placed on outside approval, the growing acceptability of gay identity affected more than just gay people. Demographers estimate that 2 million children have a parent who is gay or lesbian, and more than 100,000 are being parented by a same-sex couple. As Justice Kennedy noted, when those children's parents cannot marry, the children "suffer the stigma" of knowing their families have been deemed "lesser," as well as the material costs of being denied the legal protections marriage ensures. Starting out from that point, the ripples are boundless, encompassing millions and millions of Americans whose family, friends, or coworkers are LGBTQ, and who share personally in the stigma and costs of discrimination. There are also very likely fewer sham marriages than there were when more closeted gay people were pressured to form heterosexual families despite the different shape of their hearts—which used to result in shattered families or quiet desperation. There are surely fewer estrangements between parents and their gay children now that parents can better understand and reflexively identify with the relationships their gay children form.

It is an axiom of civil rights movements, if often an underappreciated one, that efforts to conquer prejudice have perhaps as much impact on those who perpetrate discrimination as on those who suffer as its targets. This is what Vice President Biden meant in 2012 when he thanked gay advocates for "freeing the soul of the American people" and when he said that in the wake of advances in gay equality, "so many straight folks have been freed from this straightjacket of what they thought they were expected to support."[21] It's what First Lady Michelle Obama meant when, in a speech at the Democratic National Convention, she cast marriage equality as an essential ingredient of the American promise. "If proud Americans can be who they are and boldly stand at the altar with who they love," she said, "then surely, surely we can give everyone in this country a fair chance at that great American Dream."[22] And it's what President Obama meant when he made virtually the same point upon hearing of the *Obergefell* ruling. "When all Americans are treated as equal," he said, "we are all more free." This principle, that recognizing the equal dignity of minorities also ennobles the majority, was one that Martin Luther King Jr. put at the center of his worldview. "The stirring lesson of this age," King declared after the passage of the Voting Rights Act of 1965, "is that mass nonviolent direct action is not a peculiar device for Negro agitation" but a "historically validated method for defending freedom and democracy, and for enlarging these values for the benefit of the whole society."

In this regard, what can be said about the kinds of changes sought by liberationists distrustful of the idea that marriage could ever be reformed or that incorporating this bourgeois institution into LGBTQ life could be good for LGBTQ people? Did the successful quest for marriage equality advance their vision of America? Did it enlarge the values of freedom and democracy, as King had said, for the benefit of the whole? Certainly, the attainment of marriage equality and its rise to the top of the agenda of the established LGBTQ movement failed to eliminate what E. B. Saunders had called the "stuffy" and "hide-bound" norms of the institution. Winning the battle for marriage stopped short of ushering in a new era of inclusion and legal protections for a much broader array of relationships. Patriarchy, and the sometimes stifling expectations of civilized society, remained intact.

Yet in ways often unforeseen by an earlier generation of gay and lesbian advocates, marriage equality transformed LGBTQ life and the nation alike. As Kendell and others concluded over time, marriage equality furthered a critique of existing social norms, including of gender inequality and even of gender distinctions.[23] After *Obergefell*, transgender rights and new challenges to traditional gender binaries quickly became the subject of popular discourse, which, even as a powerful conservative backlash loomed, helped set new parameters for how to speak about gender and nonconformity. As the nation debated gay marriage, a national dialogue about bullying and youth suicide spilled over to other venues, awakening parents and educators to the risks that not only LGBTQ youth but any youth can face when they feel different or alone. While popular understandings of family and legal recognition of diverse relationships did not broaden to the levels hoped for by alternative-family advocates, familiarity with same-sex relationships did likely have a positive impact on family law: state laws and judges across the country were now far more likely to recognize concepts such as "de facto" parenthood, which could mean protecting ties between children and the adults who actually parented them regardless of legal or blood ties.[24]

The liberationist principle that pleasure is a positive good in itself, rather than a fraught by-product of the sex act, and the related feminist axiom that sexual activity need not be justified by its reproductive ends both gained credence as courts affirmed again and again that marriage and sexual intimacy were not mere instruments of social order but expressions of individual dignity and freedom. Indeed, despairing social conservatives and feminist marriage equality proponents such as E. J. Graff seemed to agree on at least one thing: that, as Graff put it, same-sex marriage had the potential to make marriage itself into an emblem of "sexual choice," a sign of modern life finally "cutting the link between sex and diapers."[25] If marriage equality meant continuing the contested project of making gay life normal, something not all LGBTQ activists sought, it seemed to show even those with continued sympathy for liberationist critiques that everyone deserved to be able to make that choice themselves, that there is no true freedom without the freedom to marry—or not.

Of course, for many longtime marriage equality proponents, victory brought about essentially just what they hoped it would. Both Evan Wolfson and Andrew Sullivan felt, upon getting married themselves, a sort of homecoming. Wolfson had dreamed as a boy of finding love, but the vocabulary of marriage—seemingly so well suited to capturing the kind of love he sought—did not seem to apply to him. In 2002 he met Chang He and the two men fell in love. In 2011, when his own state of New York finally made marriage for them a legal option, it was, fittingly, an appellate judge who officiated at their wedding. Finally, she proclaimed, comes "the ceremony you wanted, in the city you call home."[26] For Sullivan, who got married in Provincetown, Massachusetts, in 2007, the triumph of marriage became synonymous with the promise America held for him as a new home, where he could truly belong. Growing up believing he could never marry made him feel a "deep psychic wound" akin to being "psychologically homeless." Finding love in America helped lift his depression and bring him happiness. "And America for me will always represent it." The day of his wedding, what moved him most was not only having found romantic love but feeling the embrace of his family and friends. "I did not hear civilization crumble" when those wedding bells rang. "I felt a wound being healed."[27]

In any event, the overriding reason why advocates such as Sullivan and Wolfson, and certainly Mary Bonauto, embraced marriage equality as a crucial priority was not because they sought to compel LGBTQ assimilation. It was because they believed that marriage would bring with it, yes, respect for gay people, but also dignity, and not just as a reward for getting married, but simply by virtue of placing same-sex love on equal footing with any other love, thus giving LGBTQ people the sense, finally, that they belonged.

By 2016, that sense of belonging is certainly what Anthony Sullivan felt, despite having been widowed by the death of Richard Adams. The pair was one of six couples granted a marriage license by the Boulder clerk Clela Rorex in 1975. But the U.S. government had rejected the Australian Sullivan's quest for a green card with a notorious letter stating that no marital relationship could exist "between two faggots." Adams died in 2012, and in 2014 Sullivan wrote a letter to President Obama asking that his green card petition be reconsidered. In the wake of the *Windsor* ruling, León Rodríguez, director of the U.S. Citizenship and Immigration Services, wrote Sullivan a formal letter of apology. A U.S. government agency, wrote Rodríguez, "should never treat any individual with the disrespect shown toward you and Mr. Adams. You have my sincerest apology for the years of hurt caused by the deeply offensive and hateful language used in the November 24, 1975, decision and my deepest condolences on your loss." In 2016, nearly a year after the *Obergefell* ruling, Sullivan received his green card, a tacit validation of their 1975 marriage. By the time Adams died, the men had been together for more than forty years.[28]

———

Obama's speech honoring the *Obergefell* ruling came on a bittersweet day. Following his remarks, he flew to Charleston, South Carolina, to deliver a eulogy for Clementa Pinckney, a pastor, state senator, and one of nine African Americans murdered in a racist rampage in one of the nation's oldest black churches. The juxtaposition of the president's palpable emotions in both speeches—exultation at the Court's ruling and anguish over the racist mass shooting, both sentiments perceptible on his face—augured an era of emotional whiplash for the country as pockets of resistance to the dramatic social and economic changes of modern life flared up to cement deep divisions in the nation and the world.

By 2016, a full-fledged populist awakening had emerged, with variations on each end of the political spectrum, crystallized with the rise of both Donald Trump (who, in a nod to anti-gay social conservatives, chose Mike Pence as his running mate) and Bernie Sanders as anti-establishment presidential challengers to Hillary Clinton, the first woman to win a major party's nomination. Trump's stunning upset victory in the November 8 election (in which Clinton nevertheless won the popular vote) reflected a worldwide reaction against the perception that global economic, technological, and demographic and social changes were making life difficult to control for too many people. LGBTQ issues did not appear to play a major role in the U.S. presidential election, and there is little reason to suspect that an anti-LGBTQ backlash played a major role in Trump's rise. Still, it's clear that a significant segment of Americans who had long nursed cultural and racial grievances alongside economic insecurity greeted the waning years of the Obama era with both anxiety and contempt. The first African American president had served for eight years and left office not only having presided over the legalization of same-sex marriage but with impressive overall favorability ratings. It seemed, to many, a time when traditional familiarities were under attack by outsiders enjoying outsize sympathy from coastal elites and establishment forces.

Such resistance to the growing inclusion and equal treatment of minorities served as a constant reminder of the limits of change, of the impossibility of leapfrogging over incremental steps to progress. In the year after the Supreme Court's decision, a dozen counties in Alabama continued to resist granting marriage licenses to same-sex couples (by refusing to grant marriage licenses to anyone at all, or by citing "technical difficulties"). In Kentucky, Kim Davis, a thrice-married Apostolic Christian who served as a county clerk, chose to go to jail rather than hand out marriage licenses to same-sex couples. North Carolina and Mississippi passed so-called religious freedom measures allowing officials to refuse to perform marriage duties for religious reasons. North Carolina became the subject of costly boycotts when it passed another law aimed at gay and transgender Americans that barred discrimination protections and required that bathroom use be dictated by what was written on a person's birth certificate. Celebrities, businesses, and tourists refused to visit or do business in the state, and both the National Basketball Association and the National Collegiate Athletic Association announced they would move high-profile championship games out of the state as a result of the law.[29]

The boycotts reflected how far mainstream opinion had moved toward embracing LGBTQ equality. And in November the reelection loss of Gov. Pat McCrory, who had signed and staunchly defended North Carolina's mean-spirited bill, further demonstrated that anti-LGBTQ positions could be politically costly. That same year, however, thirty-four states across the country saw the introduction of roughly two hundred bills meant to allow anti-LGBTQ discrimination, nearly double the number from the previous year.[30] Months after *Obergefell,* the proportion of Americans who were uncomfortable seeing same-sex couples hold hands had dropped by 20 percent from the previous year but still stood at nearly a third.[31] Nowhere was the anti-gay incarnation of this ongoing intolerance more vividly displayed than when a disturbed twenty-nine-year-old man (with possible terrorist sympathies and an uncertain sexual orientation of his own) massacred forty-nine patrons of a gay nightclub in Orlando, Florida, weeks before the one-year anniversary of the *Obergefell* decision. Those who envisioned a world where it was safe to be different still had their work cut out for them.

AWAKENING

Yet if the changes wrought by the triumph of marriage equality were incomplete, they were nevertheless profound. Even amid the rise of Donald Trump, who came to power by appealing to vocal anti-minority sentiment, marriage equality appeared deeply enough rooted to survive a full-scale reversal. With grinding persistence and a commitment to durable, incremental progress, the marriage movement had helped increase familiarity with, and approval of, LGBTQ people across the country; it spawned countless conversations about who gay people were, what marriage was for, what it meant to be normal, queer, an outlaw or an in-law; it created numerous tangible legal protections for gay people and their families; it strengthened and spread feelings of dignity and self-worth among LGBTQ people in ways few other efforts were able to achieve; and it endowed America with new and larger understandings of love, law, liberty, family, and equality.

It was not long ago that gay marriage was regarded by most of America as utterly ridiculous. It took ordinary gays and lesbians who held tenaciously to a deadly serious vision to transform that fanciful idea into a reality. "If politics is the art of the possible," said Josh Friedes, the Massachusetts marriage equality activist, "grassroots organizing is the art of making the impossible possible." Gays and lesbians brought marriage equality to America through a popular awakening that, while eventually steered by professional movement strategists, began as a people's movement of same-sex couples, accidental activists, street protestors, political organizers, straight allies, and brilliant lawyers both from inside and outside the LGBTQ movement, who gave hours and dollars, conducted research, held bake sales, marched in the streets, lobbied legislators, studied the law, filed suits, and over time came to embrace the full worth of same-sex love. The marriage movement awakened first itself and then a nation, laying brick upon brick upon brick until it created a temple—to an ideal. That ideal was not about marriage per se, but about the dignity of love, about the promise of equality, about liberation from the compulsion to be someone you weren't. When Wolfson first sat down to read the *Obergefell* decision, he noted how much it sounded like his 1983 paper, which read: "the reason samesex marriage is particularly essential to gay individuals is" because of "the importance it has as an expression of their equal worth *as they are.*" Bonauto's reflections on the ruling were characteristically understated. "I feel like I do this work because of love for so many people," she mused, "who just want to be who they are."[32]

NOTES

ACKNOWLEDGMENTS

ILLUSTRATION CREDITS

INDEX

Notes

This book is based on research of hundreds of published and unpublished documents, books and articles, audio and visual sources, court cases and legal briefs, letters and organizational memos, personal attendance at certain events and meetings, and over fifty first-hand interviews by the author. These interviews were conducted at various times over six years and could include any combination of in-person conversations, telephone calls, and email correspondences. Because of the varied nature of the interviews, and the fact that many included extensive and repeated follow-up correspondences over time, interview citations are not dated, and the word "interview" is used here to refer to any kind of on-the-record correspondence described above.

Epigraph: *Andrew Kopkind, "The Gay Moment,"* The Nation, *May 3, 1993.*

PROLOGUE

1   This book frequently uses the term "gay" to refer to those who identified as gay, lesbian, or bisexual, largely reflecting historical usage in the eras being chronicled. I have tried to broaden my nomenclature as the movement did, increasing references to bisexuality and transgender identity when referring to events that took place in the early twenty-first century, a period when the broader term "queer" also gained renewed currency to denote a conscious rejection of dominant sexual and gender identity categories. My goal has been to respect simultaneously the craft of writing for a general audience, the quest for historical clarity, and the principle of inclusion so prized by the LGBTQ community.

2   I borrow "accidental activists" from NPR's *All Things Considered,* which used it to refer to people who initially joined a political fight not to advance a cause but simply to improve their lives. Nina Totenberg, "Meet the 'Accidental Activists' of the Supreme Court's Same-Sex-Marriage Case," *All Things Considered* (NPR, transcript), Apr. 20, 2015.

1. "HOMOSEXUAL MARRIAGE?"

1   Randy Lloyd, "Let's Push Homophile Marriage," *ONE,* Jun. 1963, 5–10, http://queermusicheritage.com/jun2008one.html.

2   E. B. Saunders, "Reformer's Choice: Marriage License or Just License?" *ONE,* Aug. 1953, 10–12. Saunders's critique is not just the diatribe of a sexually rebellious gay

man but expressed a broader lament against the newly stifling norms of midcentury American views of what it meant to be a respectable adult: caring deeply about social approval, conforming to expectations, marrying and parenting while still relatively young. For social and historical context on new meanings of adult respectability, see Stephanie Coontz, *The Way We Never Were: American Families and the Nostalgia Trap* (New York: Basic Books, 1992); Steven Mintz, *The Prime of Life: A History of Modern Adulthood* (Cambridge, MA: Belknap Press of Harvard University Press, 2015).

3   George Chauncey, *Gay New York: Gender, Urban Culture, and the Making of the Gay Male World 1890–1940* (New York: Basic Books, 1994).

4   Ibid., 301–329.

5   On lesbian coffeehouses, see George Chauncey, *Why Marriage: The History Shaping Today's Debate over Gay Equality* (New York: Basic Books, 2004), 15; Lillian Faderman, *Odd Girls and Twilight Lovers: A History of Lesbian Life in Twentieth-Century America* (New York: Columbia University Press, 1991).

6   Robert O. Self, *All in the Family: The Realignment of American Democracy Since the 1960s* (New York: Hill and Wang, 2012); Chauncey, *Why Marriage*, 16–18.

7   Chauncey, *Gay New York*, 311–313, 324–325; William Eskridge, *Gaylaw: Challenging the Apartheid of the Closet* (Cambridge, MA: Harvard University Press, 1999), 46–49; Chauncey, *Why Marriage*, 5–6.

8   Nathaniel Frank, *Unfriendly Fire: How the Gay Ban Undermines the Military and Weakens America* (New York: Thomas Dunne Books, 2009), 1–9; See also George Chauncey, "'What Gay Studies Taught the Court': The Historians' Amicus Brief in *Lawrence v. Texas*," *Gay and Lesbian Quarterly* 10 (2004): 509–538; Allan Bérubé, *Coming Out Under Fire: The History of Gay Men and Women in World War II* (New York: Free Press, 1990); Charles Kaiser, *The Gay Metropolis: The Landmark History of Gay Life in America* (London: Phoenix, 1997), 27–49; Chauncey, *Why Marriage*, 18–24; Chauncey, *Gay New York*.

9   Kaiser, *Gay Metropolis*, 27–28.

10   Frank, *Unfriendly Fire*.

11   Steven Seidman, "Identity and Politics in a 'Postmodern' Gay Culture: Some Historical and Conceptual Notes," in *Fear of a Queer Planet: Queer Politics and Social Theory*, ed. Michael Warner (Minneapolis: University of Minnesota Press, 1993), 105–142.

12   Chauncey, *Why Marriage*, 20.

13   David K. Johnson, *The Lavender Scare: The Cold War Persecution of Gays and Lesbians in the Federal Government* (Chicago: University of Chicago Press, 2004).

14   Marshall Forstein, "Overview of Ethical and Research Issues in Sexual Orientation Therapy," *Journal of Gay and Lesbian Psychotherapy* 5 (2002): 169.

15   On passage of state laws, see Chauncey, *Why Marriage*, 11.

16 The law defined it as disorderly conduct for any man to "frequent or loiter about any public place soliciting men for the purpose of committing a crime against nature or other lewdness."

17 Chauncey, *Why Marriage,* 10–11.

18 Kaiser, *Gay Metropolis,* 83, 104–107; Elizabeth Lapovsky Kennedy and Madeline D. Davis, *Boots of Leather, Slippers of Gold: The History of a Lesbian Community* (New York: Penguin Books, 1993).

19 Kaiser, *Gay Metropolis;* Chauncey, *Why Marriage,* 9–10.

20 Kaiser, *Gay Metropolis,* 123; Linda Hirshman, *Victory: The Triumphant Gay Revolution* (New York: HarperCollins, 2013), 37. On the "minority" model of gay identity, see Seidman, "Identity and Politics."

21 Hirshman, *Victory,* 37–50.

22 Ibid.; Kaiser, *Gay Metropolis,* 122–124.

23 Kaiser, *Gay Metropolis,* 126, 128.

24 Ibid., 125–131; Donald Webster Cory, *The Homosexual in America* (New York: Greenberg, 1951).

25 Kaiser, *Gay Metropolis,* 138–147; Hirshman, *Victory,* 56–59, 242.

26 Phyllis Lyon, "Same-Sex Marriage: An Oral History: 'It Never Was Much of an Issue for Us,'" *Los Angeles Times,* May 26, 2009.

27 Chris Geidner, "Meet the Hero of the Marriage Equality Movement," *BuzzFeed,* Jan. 10, 2013.

28 Author interview with Edie Windsor.

29 Aaron Hicklin, "Edie Windsor and Thea Spyer: When Edie Met Thea," *Out,* Jan. 9, 2011.

30 *Edie and Thea: A Very Long Engagement,* DVD, directed by Susan Muska and Gréta Olafsdottir (2009; Philadelphia, PA: Breaking Glass Pictures, 2010); Hicklin, "Edie Windsor and Thea Spyer."

31 "Thea Spyer and Edith Windsor," *New York Times,* May 27, 2007; Ariel Levy, "The Perfect Wife: How Edith Windsor Fell in Love, Got Married, and Won a Landmark Case for Gay Marriage," *New Yorker,* Sept. 30, 2013.

32 Levy, "The Perfect Wife."

33 D. E. Mungello, "A Spirit of the 60's," *Gay and Lesbian Review Worldwide,* May 1, 2008.

34 Susan Brownmiller, "Sisterhood Is Powerful," *New York Times Magazine,* Mar. 15, 1970; Dudley Clendinen and Adam Nagourney, *Out for Good: The Struggle to Build a Gay Rights Movement in America* (New York: Simon and Schuster, 2001), 101.

35 Self, *All in the Family*.

36 Kaiser, *Gay Metropolis;* Hirshman, *Victory,* 56–59.

37 Kaiser, *Gay Metropolis,* 139–141.

38 Carlos Ball, *From the Closet to the Courtroom: Five LGBT Rights Lawsuits That Have Changed Our Nation* (Boston: Beacon Press, 2010), 14–15; Eskridge, *Gaylaw,* 91.

39 Lillian Faderman, *The Gay Revolution: The Story of the Struggle* (New York: Simon and Schuster, 2015), 138.

40 Self, *All in the Family,* 84.

41 Kaiser, *The Gay Metropolis,* 139–141.

42 Self, *All in the Family,* 85–86.

43 Timothy Stewart-Winter, *Queer Clout: Chicago and the Rise of Gay Politics* (Philadelphia: University of Pennsylvania Press, 2016).

44 On Stonewall, see Martin Duberman, *Stonewall* (New York: Plume Press, 1993); Kaiser, *Gay Metropolis,* 197–202; Clendinen and Nagourney, *Out for Good,* 11–32.

45 Kaiser, *Gay Metropolis,* 197–202.

46 Ibid.

47 Clendinen and Nagourney, *Out for Good,* 22–23; Walter T. Spencer, "Too Much My Dear," *Village Voice,* Jul. 10, 1969.

48 John D'Emilio, *The World Turned: Essays on Gay History, Politics and Culture* (Durham, NC: Duke University Press, 2002), 146–153; Clendinen and Nagourney, *Out for Good,* 11–23; Chauncey, *Why Marriage,* 31.

49 Craig A. Rimmerman, *From Identity to Politics: The Lesbian and Gay Movements in the United States* (Philadelphia: Temple University Press, 2002), 24–27; Self, *All in the Family,* 90–100, 222–225; D'Emilio, *The World Turned,* 82–85.

50 Rimmerman, *From Identity to Politics,* 24–27; Self, *All in the Family,* 90–100, 222–239; D'Emilio, *The World Turned,* 82–85; Hirshman, *Victory,* 120–123; Douglas Martin, "Arthur Evans, Leader in Gay Rights Fight, Dies at 68," *New York Times,* Sept. 14, 2011.

51 Levy, "The Perfect Wife."

52 Marriage Equality USA, "MEUSA Interview with Edie Windsor (Part 3): A Marriage Equality Legacy," YouTube video, 10:09, Jul. 24, 2014, https://youtu.be/rm0Ejm-ropM; author interview with Windsor.

53 Vito Russo, *The Celluloid Closet: Homosexuality in the Movies* (New York: Harper and Row, 1981); and see, for instance, the play *Boys in the Band,* by Mart Crowley, directed by Robert Moore, Theater Four, New York, NY, Apr. 14, 1968.

2. "WHAT WAS IMPORTANT WAS THAT WE WERE A HOUSEHOLD"

1 Dudley Clendinen and Adam Nagourney, *Out for Good: The Struggle to Build a Gay Rights Movement in America* (New York: Simon and Schuster, 2001), 199–209.

2 Craig A. Rimmerman, *From Identity to Politics: The Lesbian and Gay Movements in the United States* (Philadelphia: Temple University Press, 2002), 31–34; Robert O. Self, *All in the Family: The Realignment of American Democracy Since the 1960s* (New York: Hill and Wang, 2012), 239–241.

3 Bill Thom, "In My Own Words: Lambda Legal Founder," *Impact* (newsletter), 2008, 16; Ellen Ann Andersen, *Out of the Closets and into the Courts: Legal Opportunity Structure and Gay Rights Litigation* (Ann Arbor: University of Michigan Press, 2004), 27–58.

4 On the rise of gay male promiscuity since the mid-twentieth century, see Gabriel Rotello, *Sexual Ecology: AIDS and the Destiny of Gay Men* (New York: Plume, 1998), 50–64.

5 Josh Zeitz, "The Making of the Marriage Equality Revolution, and What It Tells Us About the Next Civil Rights Campaign," *Politico*, Apr. 28, 2015.

6 David L. Chambers, "Couples: Marriage, Civil Union, and Domestic Partnership," in *Creating Change: Sexuality, Public Policy, and Civil Rights*, ed. John D'Emilio et al. (New York: St. Martin's Press, 2000), 281–288; Michael Boucai, "Glorious Precedents: When Gay Marriage Was Radical," *Yale Journal of Law and the Humanities* 27 (2015): 1–82.

7 George Chauncey, *Why Marriage: The History Shaping Today's Debate over Gay Equality* (New York: Basic Books, 2004), 87–90; Erik Eckholm, "The Same-Sex Couple Who Got a Marriage License in 1971," *New York Times*, May 16, 2015.

8 Eckholm, "Same-Sex Couple."

9 Robert Barnes, "40 Years Later, Story of a Same-Sex Marriage in Colo. Remains Remarkable," *Washington Post*, Apr. 18, 2015; Chambers, "Couples," 282–283; Chauncey, *Why Marriage*, 91–92.

10 Garance Franke-Ruta, "The Prehistory of Gay Marriage," *The Atlantic*, Mar. 26, 2013.

11 Chambers, "Couples," 282–288; Chauncey, *Why Marriage*, 91–92.

12 "Advocates; Should Marriage Between Homosexuals Be Permitted?" May 2, 1974, WGBH Media Library and Archives, http://openvault.wgbh.org/catalog/V_57993D3 8129A433AAD10C7B04D019EF6.

13 For a discussion of same-sex marriage as radical, see Boucai, "Glorious Precedents"; Barbara J. Cox, "The Lesbian Wife: Same-Sex Marriage as an Expression of Radical and Plural Democracy," *California Western Law Review* 33 (1997).

14 Eckholm, "Same-Sex Couple."

15 Author interview with Matt Coles; Alexandra Chasin, *Selling Out: The Gay and Lesbian Movement Goes to Market* (New York: St. Martin's Press, 2000), 277.

16 On early gay rights ordinances, see Clendinen and Nagourney, *Out for Good,* 322–323; Andersen, *Out of the Closets,* 35.

17 Author interview with Coles.

18 Ibid.

19 Clendinen and Nagourney, *Out for Good,* 339.

20 Ibid., 339–349.

21 Ibid., 399–404; Robert Lindsey, "Dan White, Killer of San Francisco Mayor, a Suicide," *New York Times,* Oct. 22, 1985.

22 Clendinen and Nagourney, *Out for Good,* 291–310; William N. Eskridge Jr., "No Promo Homo: The Sedimentation of Antigay Discourse and the Channeling Effect of Judicial Review," *New York University Law Review* 75 (2000): 1351–1352.

23 Clendinen and Nagourney, *Out for Good,* 402–403.

24 Ibid., 398–403; Amin Ghaziana, *The Dividends of Dissent: How Conflict and Culture Work in Lesbian and Gay Marches on Washington* (Chicago: University of Chicago Press, 2008).

25 Eskridge, "No Promo Homo," 1352.

26 Clendinen and Nagourney, *Out for Good,* 225–226, 396–399, 429–440; Rimmerman, *From Identity to Politics,* 28–31.

27 "Legal groups" refers to advocacy organizations that represented LGBTQ people in litigation, usually accompanied by strategic public education campaigns designed to help further a case and a cause. By contrast, "political groups" refers to advocacy organizations at the national and state level that worked primarily to influence the political process—electing and lobbying officeholders and helping shape policy. The distinction is a slight oversimplification, as both types of organizations, especially in the LGBTQ movement's later years, engaged in efforts to change cultural attitudes and practices affecting LGBTQ people, whether their main focus was legal or political. Both ran educational campaigns alongside, or as inherent parts of, their legal and political work. They often worked together on overlapping terrain. Some groups, like the ACLU, had both litigation and lobbying arms. But one of the key differences that persisted for decades was that while both legal and political groups were engaged in strategies seeking incremental change, the legal groups came sooner to incorporate marriage equality as both a tool and a goal of such change, while for the political groups, other priorities more often took precedence.

28 Melissa Murray, "Paradigms Lost: How Domestic Partnership Went from Innovation to Injury," *New York University Review of Law and Social Change* 37 (2013): 291–305.

29 Judith Scherr, "Berkeley, Activists Set Milestone for Domestic Partnerships in 1984," *Inside Bay Area,* Jun. 28, 2013; author interview with Coles.

30 Cynthia G. Goldstein, San Francisco Human Rights Commission, "Two Year Report on the San Francisco Equal Benefits Ordinance," 2000; Cynthia Gorney, "Making It Official: The Law Live-Ins," *Washington Post,* Jul. 5, 1989.

31 "Board in San Francisco Backs Couples' Benefits," *New York Times,* Nov. 30, 1982, 16.

32 Wallace Turner, "Couple Law Asked for San Francisco," *New York Times,* Nov. 28, 1982, 31.

33 Scott L. Cummings and Douglas NeJaime, "Lawyering for Marriage Equality," *UCLA Law Review* 57 (2010): 1256–1257; Danielle Riendeau, "Meet the Man Who Kept the Rainbow Flag Free," ACLU blog, Jun. 22, 2012; Scherr, "Berkeley, Activists Set Milestone"; author interview with Coles; Nancy D. Polikoff, *Beyond (Straight and Gay) Marriage: Valuing All Families under the Law,* Queer Ideas / Queer Action series (Boston: Beacon Press, 2008), 50; Leland Traiman, "A Brief History of Domestic Partnerships," *Gay and Lesbian Review,* 2008, 23–24; on Berkeley, see Murray, "Paradigms Lost," 294.

34 Author interview with Coles.

35 Nancy D. Polikoff, "We Will Get What We Ask For: Why Legalizing Gay and Lesbian Marriage Will Not 'Dismantle the Legal Structure of Gender in Every Marriage,' " *Virginia Law Review* 79 (1993): 1535–1550.

36 Nancy D. Polikoff, "Equality and Justice for Lesbian and Gay Families and Relationships," *Rutgers Law Review* 60 (2009): 532.

37 Ibid., 530.

38 Andersen, *Out of the Closets,* 27–57.

39 Paula L. Ettelbrick, "Wedlock Alert: A Comment on Lesbian and Gay Family Recognition," *Journal of Law and Policy* 5 (1996): 107–166.

40 Author interview with Evan Wolfson.

41 Ibid.

42 Ibid.

43 Evan Wolfson, "Samesex Marriage and Morality: The Human Rights Vision of the Constitution," third-year paper, Harvard Law School, 1983, 17–21, 31–36.

44 Ibid., 20, 76–77.

45 Ibid., 76; emphasis in original.

3. "WE ARE CRIMINALS IN THE EYES OF THE LAW"

1 There are many examples of how the criminalization of sodomy was used to block the advance of LGBTQ equality. See, for instance, Eric Holder, "Letter from the Attorney General to Congress on Litigation Involving the Defense of Marriage Act," United States Department of Justice, February 23, 2011. In explaining the department's decision not to defend the Defense of Marriage Act, the letter recounts how federal courts justified applying the lowest level of review to gays and lesbians by pointing to the permissibility of banning consensual same-sex sodomy. See also Matt Coles, "70/50/20," in ACLU Foundation, *Annual Update of the ACLU's Nationwide Work on LGBT Rights and HIV / AIDS,* 2006, 9–11: "[Sodomy laws] become a way to keep gay people in hiding and quiet. Since same-sex sexuality was illegal, it was OK to fire gay people from government jobs, take away custody of our children, and shut down places where we congregated. There was no room for argument about whether any of that treatment was right since by coming out (or being outed, or being found in a place where gay people went) you admitted you were an unconvicted felon." See also Abby Rubenfeld, "Lessons Learned: A Reflection upon *Bowers v. Hardwick,*" *Nova Law Review* 11 (1986): 59–70 for an account of a custody case in which a lesbian's criminal status was used against her. *ONE* magazine ran a disclaimer in each issue saying that, by the nature of its subject, it "often discusses illegal sexual practices," but that was "not to be construed as an implicit approval of criminal acts."

2 Author interview with Abby Rubenfeld; Ellen Ann Andersen, *Out of the Closets and into the Courts: Legal Opportunity Structure and Gay Rights Litigation* (Ann Arbor: University of Michigan Press, 2006), 41–42; Carlos Ball, *From the Closet to the Courtroom: Five LGBT Rights Lawsuits That Have Changed Our Nation* (Boston: Beacon Press, 2010), 13–15.

3 Andersen, *Out of the Closets,* 40–42; Ball, *From the Closet,* 13–15.

4 See Carlos A. Ball, *The Right to Be Parents: LGBT Families and the Transformation of Parenthood* (New York: New York University Press, 2012), 6–7; Susan Golombok, *Modern Families: Parents and Children in New Family Forms* (Cambridge, UK: Cambridge University Press, 2015); Daniel Rivers, *Radical Relations: Lesbian Mothers, Gay Fathers, and Their Children in the United States Since World War II* (Chapel Hill: University of North Carolina Press, 2013); Nancy D. Polikoff, "This Child Does Have Two Mothers: Redefining Parenthood to Meet the Needs of Children in Lesbian-Mother and Other Nontraditional Families," *Georgetown Law Journal* 78 (1990): 465–466. On the 1989 poll, see Scott Harris, "2 Moms or 2 Dads—and a Baby," *Los Angeles Times,* Oct. 20, 1991.

5 Lawrence K. Altman, "Rare Cancer Seen in 41 Homosexuals," *New York Times,* Jul. 3, 1981.

6 Robin Herman, "A Disease's Spread Provokes Anxiety," *New York Times,* Aug. 8, 1982.

7   David Crary and Lisa Leff, "In 50 Years, There Have Been Huge Strides for Gay-Rights Movement," Associated Press, June 8, 2013; Glenn Collins, "Facing the Emotional Anguish of AIDS," *New York Times,* May 30, 1983.

8   Rex Wockner, "Ronald Reagan Remembered," *Windy City Times,* Jun. 6, 2004; Alex Ross, "Love on the March," *New Yorker,* Nov. 12, 2012; Michael Bronski, "Rewriting the Script on Reagan: Why the President Ignored AIDS," *The Forward,* Nov. 14, 2003; Lillian Faderman, *The Gay Revolution: The Story of the Struggle* (New York: Simon and Schuster, 2015), 422.

9   Andersen, *Out of the Closets,* 44.

10   Douglas Martin, "William F. Buckley Jr. Is Dead at 82," *New York Times,* Feb. 2, 2008.

11   *People v. West 12 Tenants Corp.,* 104 A.D.2d 1058 (N.Y. App. Div. 1984); *Doe v. Centinela Hospital,* 57 U.S.L.W. 2034 [C.D.Cal. 1988]; Andersen, *Out of the Closets,* 43–44.

12   Ross, "Love on the March."

13   Gabriel Rotello, *Sexual Ecology: AIDS and the Destiny of Gay Men* (New York: Plume, 1998).

14   Martin quoted in Robert O. Self, *All in the Family: The Realignment of American Democracy since the 1960s* (New York: Hill and Wang, 2012), 225.

15   Stuart Taylor Jr., "Supreme Court Hears Case on Homosexual Rights," *New York Times,* Apr. 1, 1986, A24; Al Kamen, "High Court Hears Arguments in Georgia Sodomy Law Case; Two Sides Outline a Clash of Individual and Collective Rights," *Washington Post,* Apr. 1, 1986, A6.

16   Taylor, "Supreme Court."

17   *Bowers v. Hardwick,* 478 U.S. 186 (1986). The Supreme Court cited both twenty-four and twenty-five as the number of states with sodomy bans at the time of *Bowers v. Hardwick,* but according to a detailed count by Abby Rubenfeld in 1986, the number≈was twenty-five. See Rubenfeld, "Lessons Learned: A Reflection upon *Bowers v. Hardwick.*"

18   *Bowers v. Hardwick,* 478 U.S. 186 (1986).

19   Ibid.

20   Rubenfeld, "Lessons Learned."

21   Author interview with Paula Ettelbrick.

22   Rubenfeld, "Lessons Learned."

23   Andersen, *Out of the Closets,* 44.

24   Ibid., 44; Steven A. Boutcher, "Making Lemonade: Turning Adverse Decisions into Opportunities for Mobilization," *Amici* 13 (2005): 11.

25 Elizabeth Sheyn, "The Shot Heard Around the LGBT World: *Bowers v. Hardwick* as a Mobilizing Force for the National Gay and Lesbian Task Force," *Journal of Race, Gender and Ethnicity* 4 (2009): 13–18.

26 Andersen, *Out of the Closets,* 41–42; Ball, *From the Closet,* 13–15.

27 Rubenfeld, "Lessons Learned."

28 Ibid.

29 Andersen, *Out of the Closets,* 45; Sheyn, "Shot." On how a court loss such as *Bowers* can animate activism, see Boutcher, "Making Lemonade," 11–12; see also Amin Ghaziani, *How Conflict and Culture Work in Lesbian and Gay Marches on Washington* (Chicago: University of Chicago Press, 2008).

30 David L. Chambers, "Couples: Marriage, Civil Union, and Domestic Partnership," in *Creating Change: Sexuality, Public Policy, and Civil Rights,* ed. John D'Emilio et al. (New York: St. Martin's Press, 2000), 281, 290. Chambers writes that more than a thousand couples wed. See also author interview with Robin Tyler.

31 Ball, *From the Closet,* 21–30.

32 *Braschi v. Stahl Associates Company,* 74 N.Y.2d 201, 543 N.E.2d 49 (1989).

33 Ball, *From the Closet,* 37–39.

34 Philips S. Gutis, "New York Court Defines Family to Include Homosexual Couples," *New York Times,* Jul. 7, 1989; *Braschi v. Stahl Associates Company.*

35 *Braschi v. Stahl Associates Company.*

36 Nancy D. Polikoff, "Equality and Justice for Lesbian and Gay Families and Relationships," *Rutgers Law Review* 60 (2009): 533. On Rubinstein's approach, see Ball, *From the Closet,* 39–43.

37 Ball, *Right to Be Parents,* 6–7; Nancy D. Polikoff, "This Child," 465–466.

4. "A TECTONIC SHIFT"

1 Author interview with Andrew Sullivan.

2 Andrew Sullivan, "Here Comes the Groom: A (Conservative) Case for Gay Marriage," *New Republic,* Aug. 28, 1989.

3 Ibid.

4 Ibid.; Andrew Sullivan, "The Politics of Homosexuality: A Case for a New Beginning," *New Republic,* May 10, 1993; Andrew Sullivan, *Virtually Normal: An Argument About Homosexuality* (New York: Vintage Books, 1996), 194, 222.

5 Sullivan, *Virtually Normal,* 185.

6   Ibid., 185.

7   Author interview with Richard Socarides; David W. Dunlap, "Thomas Stoddard, 48, Dies; An Advocate of Gay Rights," *New York Times,* Feb. 14, 1997.

8   Author interview with Evan Wolfson; author interview with anonymous.

9   Author interview with Alan Rothenberg; Philip S. Gutis, "Small Steps Toward Acceptance Renew Debate on Gay Marriage," *New York Times,* Nov. 5, 1989.

10   Josh Zeitz, "The Making of the Marriage Equality Revolution," *Politico,* Apr. 28, 2015.

11   Author interview with Matt Coles.

12   Evan Wolfson, "Crossing the Threshold: Equal Marriage Rights for Lesbians and Gay Men and the Intra-Community Critique," *New York University Review of Law and Social Change* 21 (1994): 567–615.

13   Author interview with Debra Chasnoff.

14   Thomas Stoddard, "Why Gay People Should Seek the Right to Marry," *Out / Look* (1989): 9–13.

15   Paula L. Ettelbrick, "Since When Is Marriage a Path to Liberation?" *Out / Look* (1989), 9, 14–17.

16   Reprinted in Nancy D. Polikoff, "Equality and Justice for Lesbian and Gay Families and Relationships," *Rutgers Law Review* 60 (2009): 529–565.

17   Mary Bonauto, "Ending Marriage Discrimination: A Work in Progress," *Suffolk University Law Review* 40 (2007).

18   Author interview with Mary Bonauto.

19   Ibid.

20   Ibid. On "no promo homo" laws in Merrimack, New Hampshire ("Prohibition of Alternative Lifestyle Instruction"), see Adele M. Stan, "House of God?" *Mother Jones,* Nov. / Dec. 1995 and Nancy Roberts Trott, "School District Anti-Gay Policy Splits N.H. Town," *Los Angeles Times,* Mar. 17, 1996; see also Janice M. Irvine, *Talk About Sex: The Battles over Sex Education in the United States* (Berkeley: University of California Press, 2004), 163. The Merrimack law, Policy 6540, was the most restrictive in the nation; its conservative Christian backers lost their majority on the board at the next election, and the new board eliminated the policy after much opposition.

21   Author interview with Bonauto.

22   Mary L. Bonauto, "Goodridge in Context," *Harvard Civil Rights-Civil Liberties Law Review* 40 (2005), 1–70; author interview with Bonauto.

23 Author interview with Ninia Baehr; author interview with Genora Dancel.

24 Author interview with Baehr; author interview with Dancel; David L. Chambers, "Couples: Marriage, Civil Unions, and Domestic Partnership," in *Creating Change: Sexuality, Public Policy, and Civil Rights,* ed. John D'Emilio et al. (New York: St. Martin's Press, 2000), 290–291.

25 Author interview with Baehr; author interview with Dancel; Chambers, "Couples," 290–291; Carol Ness, "Marriage Made in Heaven Hellishly Hard to Legalize," *SF Gate,* Apr. 27, 1995.

26 *Baehr et al. v. Miike,* 910 P. 2d 112 (Haw. 1996).

27 Evan Wolfson, *Why Marriage Matters: America, Equality, and Gay People's Right to Marry* (New York: Simon and Schuster, 2005), 29–30; Debra Barayuga, "Gay Marriage Case Plaintiff Preached Acceptance," *Star Bulletin,* Jul. 28, 2006.

28 Author interview with Baehr; author interview with Dancel.

29 Author interview with Baehr; author interview with Dancel; author interview with Nan Hunter.

30 Author interview with Dancel.

31 Author interview with Baehr; author interview with Dancel.

32 Author interview with Hunter.

33 Ibid.

34 Author interview with Baehr; author interview with Dancel; author interview with Hunter.

35 Author interview with Paula Ettelbrick.

36 Wolfson, *Why Marriage Matters,* 30–32; "25 Coolest Straight People," *Free Library,* Nov. 10, 1998, www.thefreelibrary.com/25+coolest+straight+people-a054879378.

37 Author interview with Baehr; author interview with Dancel; Carey Goldberg, "Couple Who Stirred Issue of Same-Sex Marriage Still Hopeful," *New York Times,* Jul. 28, 1996.

38 *Baehr v. Lewin,* 74 Haw. 530, 852 P. 2d 44 (1993).

39 Goldberg, "Couple Who Stirred Issue of Same-Sex Marriage Still Hopeful."

40 *Baehr v. Lewin.*

41 Ibid.

42 Jeffrey Schmalz, "The 1992 Elections: The States—the Gay Issues; Gay Areas Are Jubilant over Clinton," *New York Times,* Nov. 5, 1992; Jeffrey Schmalz, "A Delicate Bal-

ance: The Gay Vote; Gay Rights and AIDS Emerging as Divisive Issues in Campaign," *New York Times,* Aug. 20, 1992.

43   Debbie Howlett, "Gay-Rights Activists Move into the Mainstream: Crusade Now Quieter, More Focused," *USA Today,* Feb. 14, 1994. See also Urvashi Vaid, *Virtual Equality: The Mainstreaming of Gay and Lesbian Liberation* (New York: Anchor Books, 1995).

44   "Intermediate scrutiny" is sometimes used interchangeably with "heightened scrutiny," although courts have applied slightly different definitions of each.

45   *Baehr v. Lewin.*

46   Wolfson, "Crossing the Threshold."

47   Evan Wolfson, "Fighting to Win and Keep the Freedom to Marry: The Legal, Political, and Cultural Challenges Ahead," *National Journal of Sexual Orientation Law* 1, no. 2 (1995): 259–301; Wolfson, "Crossing the Threshold."

48   Wolfson, "Crossing the Threshold."

49   A 1995 memo written by Wolfson asked if valid same-sex marriages performed in Hawaii would be recognized by other states and the federal government, conferring on couples who obtained legal marriages in one state and then traveled to another all the benefits and responsibilities of marriage. The memo said, "We at Lambda believe that the correct answer to these questions is 'Yes,'" but it acknowledged that marriage equality opponents would exert great political and legal pressure to ensure a different answer. Author interview with Wolfson; author interview with Bonauto; see also Wolfson, "Fighting to Win"; Wolfson, "Crossing the Threshold"; Evan Wolfson, "The Hawaii Marriage Case Launches the US Freedom-to-Marry Movement for Equality," in *Legal Recognition of Same-Sex Partnerships: A Study of National, European and International Law,* ed. R. Windemute and M. Andenaes (Oxford: Hart Publishing, 2001), 169–176; "ABA Research Project: Massachusetts Research," Jan. 1997, in author's possession. For a helpful explanation of the role of the "full faith and credit" clause of the Constitution in the marriage debate, see Tobias Barrington Wolff, "DOMA Repeal and the Truth About Full Faith and Credit," *Huffington Post,* Sept. 20, 2011.

50   Wolfson, "Fighting to Win."

51   Chris Geidner, "Domestic Disturbance: Before DOMA, There Was Another Debate over Marriage—Within the Gay and Lesbian Community," *Metro Weekly,* May 4, 2011; Scott L. Cummings and Douglas NeJaime, "Lawyering for Marriage Equality," *UCLA Law Review* 57 (2010): 1251–1260.

52   Wolfson, "Crossing the Threshold."

5. "THE VERY FOUNDATIONS OF OUR SOCIETY ARE IN DANGER"

1   David W. Dunlap, "Fearing a Toehold for Gay Marriages, Conservatives Rush to Bar the Door," *New York Times*, Mar. 6, 1996. On thirty laws by 2000, see David L. Chambers, "Couples: Marriage, Civil Union, and Domestic Partnership," in *Creating Change: Sexuality, Public Policy, and Civil Rights*, ed. John D'Emilio et al. (New York: St. Martin's Press, 2000), 294; see also Sean Cahill, *Policy Issues Affecting Lesbian, Gay, Bisexual, and Transgender Families* (Ann Arbor: University of Michigan Press, 2006), 125. Fifteen states passed anti-gay marriage statutes by the end of 1996, with another fifteen doing so in 1997 and 1998; Hawaii and Alaska passed constitutional amendments in 1998, and Nebraska and Nevada did so in 2000.

2   John Gallagher and Chris Bull, *Perfect Enemies: The Religious Right, the Gay Movement, and the Politics of the 1990s* (New York: Crown, 1996), 150; John King, "Religious Right Raising Money over Gays-in-the-Military Fight," Associated Press, Feb. 27, 1993; Dagmar Herzog, *Sex in Crisis: The New Sexual Revolution and the Future of American Politics* (New York: Basic Books, 2008), 66–73.

3   On Senate introduction, see Senator Nickles, speaking on S4870, May 8, 1996, 104th Cong., 2nd sess., *Congressional Record* 142. See also Charles Butler, "The Defense of Marriage Act: Congress's Use of Narrative in the Debate over Same-Sex Marriage," *New York University Law Review* 73 (1998): 841. On House introduction, see "Defense of Marriage Act. 1996. H.R. 3396: Summary / Analysis," *'Lectric Law Library*, Apr. 8, 2006. The Marriage Protection Resolution was pushed by a coalition of eight conservative groups, according to Craig A. Rimmerman, *From Identity to Politics: The Lesbian and Gay Movements in the United States* (Philadelphia: Temple University Press, 2002), 75. According to Sean Cahill, *Same-Sex Marriage in the United States* (Oxford: Lexington Books, 2004), 81, three candidates signed it three days before the Iowa caucuses began. For more backstory on the creation of DOMA by right wing groups, see Robert Dreyfuss, "The Holy War on Gays," *Rolling Stone*, Mar. 18, 1999, 38–41.

4   See David S. Kemp, "The Imminent Demise of Section 2 of the Defense of Marriage Act," *Verdict / Justia.com*, Aug. 12, 2013, for a helpful explanation. See also dissenting view in U.S. Government Publishing Office, Committee of the Judiciary, Report on the Defense of Marriage Act, H.R. Rep. No. 104-664 (1996): "Whatever powers states have to reject a decision by another state to legalize same sex marriage, and to refuse to recognize such marriages within its own borders, derives directly from the Constitution and nothing Congress can do by statute either adds to or detracts from that power."

5   United States Government Printing Office, "Defense of Marriage Act," Sep. 21, 1996.

6   Defense of Marriage Act, HR 3396, 104th Cong., 2d sess., *Congressional Record*.

7 Ibid., S10068; 104 Cong. Rec. S2, 142 (daily ed. July 11, 1996), H7276, H7444.

8 104 Cong. Rec. S2, 142 (daily ed. July 11, 1996), H7443; 104 Cong. Rec. S2, 142 (daily ed. July 12, 1996), H7491, H7486.

9 U.S. Government Publishing Office, Committee of the Judiciary, Report on the Defense of Marriage Act, H.R. Rep. No. 104-664 (1996), 7, 15–16.

10 Sullivan, *Same-Sex Marriage,* 232–236.

11 Ibid.

12 See Nathaniel Frank, *Unfriendly Fire: How the Gay Ban Undermines the Military and Weakens America* (New York: Thomas Dunne Books, 2009), 54–56.

13 Defense of Marriage Act, HR 3396, 104th Cong., 2d sess. (statement of Edward M. Kennedy, Massachusetts Senator); Defense of Marriage Act, HR 3396, 104th Cong., 2d sess. (statement of Barbara Boxer, California Senator); Frank quoted in Sullivan, *Same-Sex Marriage,* 225.

14 Sullivan, *Same-Sex Marriage,* 225–226.

15 Ibid., 222–224.

16 Andrew Sullivan, "Liberation," *New Republic,* May 6, 1996.

17 Defense of Marriage Act, HR 3396, 104th Cong., 2d sess., *Congressional Record* (July 11, 1996).

18 Lou Chibbaro Jr., "Congress Expected to Vote on ENDA in '07," *Houston Voice,* Jan. 12, 2007; author interview with Wolfson; Chris Geidner, "Double Defeat," *Metro Weekly,* Sept. 14, 2011; Joseph Hanania, "The Debate Over Gay Marriages: No Unity," *Los Angeles Times,* Jun. 13, 1996; David W. Dunlap, "Some Gay Rights Advocates Question Drive to Defend Same-Sex Marriage," *New York Times,* Jun. 7, 1996.

19 Dunlap, "Some Gay Rights Advocates."

20 Katie Couric, Pat Buchanan, and Barney Frank debate on gay marriage, *Today,* NBC, Feb. 5, 2004; Paul Solman, "Why Barney Frank Took a Cautious Approach to Same-Sex Marriage," *PBS NewsHour,* December 31, 2012.

21 On calling the bill divisive, unnecessary, and "gay-baiting," see Ken Rudin, "Gay Marriage, DOMA and the Dramatic Shift in Public Opinion in One Year," NPR, Mar. 18, 2013. On the circumstances surrounding the passage of DOMA, see Chris Geidner, "Marriage Wars," *Metro Weekly,* Jul. 13, 2011. On Clinton's 1992 opposition to same-sex marriage, see Sasha Issenberg, "Hillary Clinton, First Lady, on Gay Marriage: A Case Study in Opacity," *Bloomberg,* Apr. 10, 2015.

22 Josh Gerstein, "In Clinton White House, Hillary's Staff Helped Push on Gay Rights," *Politico,* Apr. 10, 2015.

23 Defense of Marriage Act, HR 3396, 104th Cong., 2d sess., *Congressional Record.*

24 Bill Clinton, "President's Statement on DOMA," http://www.cs.cmu.edu/afs/cs/usr/scotts/ftp/wpaf2mc/clinton.html.

25 *Baehr v. Miike*, No. 91-1394, 1996 WL 694235 (Haw. Cir. Ct. December 3, 1996). The case's new name reflects a change in the director of the Hawaii Health Department, the named defendant.

26 The state's witnesses were Kyle Pruett, David Eggebeen, Richard Williams, and Thomas S. Merrill.

27 On support of Lambda and ACLU, see David Orgon Coolidge, "Same-Sex Marriage: As Hawaii Goes . . . ," *First Things,* Apr. 1997, 33–37. On Wolfson joining as cocounsel: Evan Wolfson, *Why Marriage Matters: America, Equality, and Gay People's Right to Marry* (New York: Simon and Schuster, 2005), 32.

28 The plaintiff's witnesses were Pepper Schwartz, Charlotte Patterson, David Brodzinsky, and Robert Bidwell.

29 *Baehr v. Miike,* No. 91-1394, 1996 WL 694235 (Haw. Circ. Ct. 1996).

30 Ibid.

31 Ibid; Carey Goldberg, "Hawaii Judge Ends Gay-Marriage Ban," *New York Times,* Dec. 4, 1999.

32 Lisa Keen and Suzanne Goldberg, *Strangers to the Law: Gay People on Trial* (Ann Arbor: University of Michigan Press, 1998), 3–9.

33 Ibid., 17–61; Carlos Ball, *From the Closet to the Courtroom: Five LGBT Rights Lawsuits That Have Changed Our Nation* (Boston: Beacon Press, 2010), 99–149.

34 *Romer v. Evans,* 517 U.S. 620 (1996) (emphasis in original).

35 Linda Greenhouse, "Reagan Nominates Anthony Kennedy to Supreme Court," *New York Times,* Nov. 12, 1987.

36 The Hawaii Supreme Court made that determination official in a ruling on Dec. 9, 1999: *Baehr v. Miike,* 92 Haw. 634, 994 P. 2d 566 (1999).

37 Jane Gross, "After a Ruling, Hawaii Weighs Gay Marriages," *New York Times,* Apr. 25, 1994. The *New York Times* noted on Dec. 20, 1999, that the state legislature had not exercised its authority to ban same-sex marriage following the constitutional amendment, but the amendment was interpreted to apply retroactively, thus validating the already-existing statutory language barring same-sex marriage. "Hawaii's Ban on Gay Marriage," *New York Times,* Dec. 20, 1999.

38 Robert Dreyfuss, "The Holy War on Gays," *Rolling Stone,* Mar. 18, 1999.

39 Leon Worden (television interview transcript): Leon Worden, "SCV Newsmaker of the Week: William J. 'Pete' Knight, State Senator," *The Signal,* Apr. 25, 2004, http://www.scvhistory.com/scvhistory/signal/newsmaker/sg042504.htm.

40 Ibid.

41 Ibid.

42 Jenifer Warren, "Initiative Divides a Family," *Los Angeles Times*, Nov. 24, 1999.

43 Worden, "SCV Newsmaker of the Week."

44 Ibid.

45 Richard Boudreaux, "Vatican Sees Gay Festival as an Affront," *Los Angeles Times*, Jun. 3, 2000.

46 "Clergy Ask Mormons to Drop Support for Prop. 22," *Contra Costa Times*, Jan. 6, 2000.

47 "Gay-Marriage Ban Passes Easily," *San Jose Mercury News*, Mar. 8, 2000.

48 Ibid.

49 "The 2000 Campaign: California; Those Opposed to 2 Initiatives Had Little Chance from Start," *New York Times*, Mar. 9, 2000.

50 "Conservatives Claim Vindication; Measure's Backers Laud State Ban on Gay Marriage," *San Jose Mercury News*, Mar. 9, 2000.

51 Author interview with Tom Henning; Jack Cheevers, "Beautiful Dreamers," *SF Weekly*, Dec. 23, 1997.

52 Susan Essoyan, "Hawaii's Domestic-Partner Law a Bust; Ambiguity Blamed," *Los Angeles Times*, Dec. 23, 1997.

53 Keen and Goldberg, *Strangers to the Law*; John D'Emilio, *The World Turned: Essays on Gay History, Politics and Culture* (Durham, NC: Duke University Press, 2002).

54 D'Emilio, *The World Turned*; Urvashi Vaid, *Virtual Equality: The Mainstreaming of Gay and Lesbian Liberation* (New York: Anchor Books, 1995).

55 For a fuller discussion of the role of cultural narrative in the debate over same-sex marriage in the 1990s, see Charles Butler, "The Defense of Marriage Act: Congress's Use of Narrative in the Debate over Same-Sex Marriage," *New York University Law Review* 73 (1998): 858–860.

56 Chris Geidner, "Domestic Disturbance: Before DOMA, There Was Another Debate over Marriage—Within the Gay and Lesbian Community," *Metro Weekly*, May 4, 2011.

6. "HERE COME THE BRIDES"

1 Author interview with Mary Bonauto.

2 Author interview with Evan Wolfson; author interview with Paula Ettelbrick; David W. Dunlap, "For Better or Worse, A Marital Milestone; Ithaca Officials Endorse

a Gay Union," *New York Times,* Jul. 27, 1995; David W. Dunlap, "Ithaca Denies Gay Men a Marriage License," *New York Times,* Dec. 4, 1995; *Storrs v. Holcomb,* 666 N.Y.S.2d 835, 836 (N.Y. App. Div. 1997).

3   Author interview with Beth Robinson; author interview with Bonauto; author interview with Hilary Rosen; David Garrow, "Toward a More Perfect Union," *New York Times Magazine,* May 9, 2004; Chris Geidner, "How One Lawyer Turned the Idea of Marriage Equality into Reality," *Buzzfeed,* Nov. 17, 2013.

4   Author interview with Bonauto; author interview with Robinson; Garrow, "Toward a More Perfect Union."

5   Carey Goldberg, "Vermont High Court Backs Rights of Same-Sex Couples," *New York Times,* Dec. 21, 1999.

6   Carey Goldberg, "In Vermont, Gay Couples Head for the Almost-Altar," *New York Times,* Jul. 2, 2000.

7   Ibid.

8   David Moats, *Civil Wars: A Battle for Gay Marriage* (San Diego, CA: Harcourt Books, 2004), 260.

9   Author interview with Robinson.

10   Ibid.; author interview with Bonauto.

11   Author interview with Bonauto. On GLAD's decisions, see Mary L. Bonauto, "Goodridge in Context," *Harvard Civil Rights-Civil Liberties Law Review* 40 (2005): 1–70.

12   Cosmo Macero Jr., "Lawsuit Seeks Gay Unions in Mass.," *Boston Herald,* Apr. 12, 2001.

13   *Goodridge v. Department of Public Health,* 440 Mass. 309, 798 N.E.2d 941 (2003). On how GLAD chose plaintiffs, see Bonauto, "Goodridge in Context."

14   *Goodridge v. Dept. of Public Health* (2003).

15   "Amici Curiae Brief of the Professors of the History of Marriage, Families and the Law," *Goodridge* (No. SJC-08860), Nov. 8, 2002, www.glad.org/uploads/docs/cases /goodridge-et-al-v-dept-public-health/2002-11-08-goodridge-amicus-history.pdf.

16   *Goodridge v. Dept. of Public Health* (2003).

17   Ibid. See also *Turner v. Safley,* 482 U.S. 78107 S. Ct. 2254, 96 L. Ed. 2d 64, 1987 U.S., and Evan Wolfson, *Why Marriage Matters: America, Equality, and Gay People's Right to Marry* (New York: Simon and Schuster, 2005), 8–9.

18   *Goodridge v. Department of Public Health,* 14 Mass. L Rep. 591 (Mass. Super. Ct. 2002).

19   Dale Carpenter, *Flagrant Conduct* (New York: W. W. Norton, 2013), 121–129.

20   Ibid., 123–129. Ettelbrick had said, "We didn't want to screw the whole thing up for generations to come, and took very seriously our responsibilities as lawyers to be prudent and thoughtful when messing with the constitutional rights of millions."

21 Carpenter, *Flagrant Conduct,* 130–135.

22 *Bowers v. Hardwick,* 478 U.S. 186 (1986); Carpenter, *Flagrant Conduct,* 198–200, 210–214. On the historians' brief in *Lawrence,* see *Lawrence v. Texas,* 539 U.S. 558 (2003).

23 Carpenter, *Flagrant Conduct,* 180–189.

24 Ibid., 196–197.

25 Ibid., 192–194.

26 *Lawrence v. Texas,* 539 U.S. 558 (2003).

27 Adam Liptak, "Exhibit A for a Major Shift: Justices' Gay Clerks," *New York Times,* Jun. 9, 2013; Carpenter, *Flagrant Conduct,* 212–213.

28 Author interview with Susan Sommer.

29 Sarah Kershaw, "Adversaries on Gay Rights Vow State-by-State Fight," *New York Times,* Jul. 6, 2003.

30 According to Pew, in July 2003, 38 percent were for, and 53 percent against; according to Gallup / CNN, 39 percent were for, and 55 percent against. Pew Research Center, Data Trend: Gay Marriage, www.pewresearch.org / data-trend / domestic-issues / attitudes-on -gay-marriage /; Gallup, Marriage, www.gallup.com / poll / 117328 / marriage.aspx.

31 Author interview with Kate Kendell.

32 Kershaw, "Adversaries."

33 Pam Belluck, "Same-Sex Marriage: The Overview; Marriage by Gays Gains Big Victory in Massachusetts," *New York Times,* Nov. 19, 2003.

34 For a detailed, first-person account of the successful effort to defend the *Goodridge* decision, see Marc Solomon, *Winning Marriage: The Inside Story of How Same-Sex Couples Took on the Politicians and Pundits—and Won* (Lebanon, NH: ForeEdge, 2014).

35 Author interview with Josh Friedes; author interview with Marty Rouse; Solomon, *Winning Marriage;* Mary Ziegler, "The Terms of the Debate: Litigation, Argumentative Strategies, and Coalitions in the Same-Sex Marriage Struggle," *Florida State University Law Review* 39 (2012): 467–519.

36 Author interview with Friedes; Solomon, *Winning Marriage.*

37 Author interview with Friedes; author interview with Rouse.

38 Frank Phillips, "Senate Eyes Civil Union Bill for SJC," *Boston Globe,* Dec. 11, 2003.

39 Author interview with Friedes; Solomon, *Winning Marriage,* 3–17.

40 Belluck, "Same-Sex Marriage."

41 Adam Nagourney, "Same-Sex Marriage: News Analysis; A Thorny Issue for 2004 Race," *New York Times,* Nov. 19, 2003.

42   Belluck, "Same-Sex Marriage."

43   Nagourney, "Same-Sex Marriage."

44   Belluck, "Same-Sex Marriage"; Terence Neilan, "High Court in Massachusetts Rules Gays Have Right to Marry," *New York Times,* Nov. 18, 2003.

45   Phillips, "Senate Eyes Civil Union Bill."

46   Neilan, "High Court."

47   Solomon, *Winning Marriage,* 7.

48   "Kerry Backs Mass. Amendment to Outlaw Same-Sex Marriage," *Advocate,* Feb. 27, 2004.

49   Robert Shrum, *No Excuses: Concessions of a Serial Campaigner* (New York: Simon and Schuster, 2007); Evan Thomas, "How Bush Did It (The Vets Attack)," *Newsweek,* Nov. 15, 2004, 90–94.

50   Solomon, *Winning Marriage,* 43.

51   Julie Mehegan, "Same-Sex Marriage Opponents Plot Next Course," *Lowell Sun,* May 18, 2004. On Liberty Counsel and the Supreme Court's refusal to hear, see David D. Kirkpatrick and Katie Zezima, "Supreme Court Turns Down a Same-Sex Marriage Case," *New York Times,* Nov. 30, 2004.

52   Raphael Lewis, "Romney Seeks Authority to Delay Same-Sex Marriage," *Boston Globe,* Apr. 16, 2004.

53   "Motion to Remove Justice Marshall Filed," *Boston Globe,* May 26, 2004.

54   "Excerpts from Ruling on Gay Marriage," *New York Times,* Feb. 5, 2004.

55   Author interview with Rosen; Associated Press, "Ban Sought on Same-Sex Marriage," *Cape Cod Times,* Jul. 25, 2001, http://www.capecodtimes.com/article/20010725 /NEWS01/307259977. The group later changed its name to Massachusetts Citizens for Marriage.

56   Bonauto, "Goodridge in Context."

57   James Bone, "Massachusetts Lawmakers Vote to Ban Gay Marriages," *Times* (London), Mar. 31, 2004; Rick Klein, "Gay-Marriage Ban Backed, but Uncertainty Remains," *Boston Globe,* March 12, 2004; Solomon, *Winning Marriage,* 16–41.

58   Pam Belluck, "Hundreds of Same-Sex Couples Wed in Massachusetts," *New York Times,* May 18, 2004; Alan Cooperman and Jonathan Finer, "Gay Couples Marry in Massachusetts: Hundreds Tie Knot on Day One, but Questions Remain," *Washington Post,* May 18, 2004; Tom Mooney, "Wedding Day: Across the Bay State, Same-Sex Couples Say 'I Do,'" *Providence Journal,* May 18, 2004; Charisse Jones and Fred Bayles, "First Weddings Intensify Gay-Marriage Debate," *USA Today,* May 18, 2004.

59 Belluck, "Hundreds"; Cooperman and Finer, "Gay Couples Marry"; Mooney, "Wedding Day"; Jones and Bayles, "First Weddings."

60 Quoted in Mark Follman, "Right Hook," *Salon,* May 19, 2004.

7. "POWER TO THE PEOPLE"

1 David D. Kirkpatrick, "Conservative Groups Differ on Bush Words on Marriage," *New York Times,* Jan. 22, 2004; Rose Arce, "Massachusetts Court Upholds Same-Sex Marriage," *New York Times,* Feb. 6, 2004. The article reports that "the president stopped short of endorsing a constitutional amendment that would ban marriages for gay and lesbian couples."

2 Author interview with Gavin Newsom.

3 Ibid.; Rone Tempest, "S.F.'s Hero of the Moment," *Los Angeles Times,* Feb. 16, 2004.

4 For an in-depth discussion of the decision-making process among gay lawyers around the Newsom actions, see Scott L. Cummings and Douglas NeJaime, "Lawyering for Marriage Equality," *UCLA Law Review* 57 (2010): 1274–1280.

5 Author interview with Jennifer Pizer; Cummings and NeJaime, "Lawyering," 1269–1293.

6 Author interview with Kate Kendell.

7 Peter Freiberg, "Wolfson Leaves Lambda to Focus on Freedom-to-Marry Work," *Washington Blade,* Mar. 30, 2001.

8 Author interview with Kendell.

9 Cummings and NeJaime, "Lawyering," 1277–1280.

10 Author interview with Kendell; Cummings and NeJaime, "Lawyering," 1274–1280.

11 Author interview with Kendell; Phyllis Lyon, "It Never Was Much of an Issue for Us," *Los Angeles Times,* May 26, 2009; Gavin Newsom, "There Was A Lot of Doubt . . . But I Never Regretted It," *Los Angeles Times,* May 26, 2009.

12 Associated Press, "Same-Sex Marriages Allowed in Oregon," *Topeka Capital-Journal,* Mar. 4, 2004.

13 David J. Garrow, "Toward a More Perfect Union," *New York Times,* May 9, 2004.

14 Author interview with Mary Bonauto; author interview with Susan Sommer.

15 Author interview with Evan Wolfson; Garrow, "Toward."

16 Author interview with Wolfson; Garrow, "Toward."

17 Quoting Jennifer Pizer in Cummings and NeJaime, "Lawyering," 1271–1281.

18 Garrow, "Toward."

19 Ibid.

20 Equality California, Complaint in Intervention, Superior Court of the State of California for the County of Los Angeles.

21 Cummings and NeJaime, "Lawyering," 1281–1287; Patricia A. Cain and Jean C. Love, "Six Cases in Search of a Decision: The Story of In re Marriage Cases," in *Women and the Law Stories* (New York: Thomson Reuters / Foundation Press, 2011), 337–378.

22 Elisabeth Bumiller, "Same-Sex Marriage: The President; Bush Backs Ban in Constitution on Gay Marriage," *New York Times,* Feb. 25, 2004.

23 Carlos Ball, *From the Closet to the Courtroom: Five LGBT Rights Lawsuits That Have Changed Our Nation* (Boston: Beacon Press, 2010), 121–122.

24 Stanley Kurtz, "Media Blackout," *National Review,* Sept. 8, 2003. Franklin Foer in the *Atlantic* called it "the Boston outpost of the evangelical broadcaster James Dobson's growing empire" (Dobson founded Focus on the Family); Franklin Foer, "Marriage Counselor," *Atlantic,* Mar. 2003.

25 Karen Peterson, "Man Behind the Marriage Amendment," *USA Today,* Apr.12, 2004; Kurtz, "Media Blackout." Foer, "Marriage Counselor," also suggests that getting African Americans onboard was a savvy strategic move.

26 Kurtz, "Media Blackout."

27 Associated Press, "Group Pushes Gay Marriage Ban," *CBS News,* Jul. 10, 2001.

28 Mark Oppenheimer, "The Making of Gay Marriage's Top Foe," *Salon,* Feb. 8, 2012.

29 Ibid.

30 Claudia Winkler, "Enemies of Marriage," *Weekly Standard,* Apr. 29, 1996.

31 Oppenheimer, "Making."

32 Maggie Gallagher, "Why We Need Marriage," *National Review Online,* July 14, 2003.

33 Alan Cooperman, "Opponents of Gay Marriage Divided," *Washington Post,* Nov. 29, 2003; Foer, "Marriage Counselor." According to Stanley Kurtz, the Family Research Council originally opposed the amendment as too liberal because it did not block states from offering benefits to same-sex couples. See Kurtz, "Media Blackout."

34 Dennis Prager, "San Francisco and Islamists: Fighting the Same Enemy," Townhall.com, Mar. 2, 2004, http://townhall.com/columnists/dennisprager/2004/03/02/san_francisco_and_islamists_fighting_the_same_enemy/page/full.

35 *Hannity and Colmes,* Fox News, Mar. 4, 2004.

36 This is according to two national polls, from Pew and Gallup, that found very similar levels of support. Nate Silver later aggregated nineteen polls and suggested that the Massachusetts decision had little effect on public support, but that does not seem to negate the findings of these polls, which showed falling support after June 2003. See Pew Research Center, Methodology, www.pewresearch.org /methodology/u-s-survey-research/our-survey-methodology-in-detail; Gallup, Methodology, www.gallup.com/178685/methodology-center.aspx; Nate Silver, "How Opinion on Same-Sex Marriage Is Changing, and What It Means," FiveThirtyEight .com, Mar. 26, 2013.

37 Carlos A. Ball, "The Backlash Thesis and Same-Sex Marriage: Learning from *Brown v. Board of Education* and Its Aftermath," *William and Mary Bill of Rights Journal* 14 (2006): 1511. On backlash, see also Michael Klarman, *From the Closet to the Altar: Courts, Backlash, and the Struggle for Same-Sex Marriage* (Oxford, UK: Oxford University Press, 2003); Gerald Rosenberg, *The Hollow Hope: Can Courts Bring About Social Change?,* 2nd ed. (Chicago: University of Chicago Press, 2008).

38 Ball, "Backlash Thesis," 1513–1514.

39 Marc Ambinder, "Bush Campaign Chief and Former RNC Chair Ken Mehlman: I'm Gay," *Atlantic,* Aug. 25, 2010. The article notes Mehlman's awareness that Rove was working with Republicans to put the initiatives on the ballot.

40 Marc Solomon, *Winning Marriage: The Inside Story of How Same-Sex Couples Took on the Politicians and Pundits—and Won* (Lebanon, NH: ForeEdge, 2014); Karen Testa, "More Gay Marriage Battles Loom; One Year After Mass. Court Ruling, Both Sides Dig In," *Herald Sun* (Durham, NC), Nov. 14, 2004.

41 Carolyn Lochhead, "Gay Marriage: Did Issue Help Re-Elect Bush?" *SF Gate,* Nov. 4, 2004.

42 George Chauncey, *Why Marriage: The History Shaping Today's Debate over Gay Equality* (New York: Basic Books, 2004), xiii; Solomon, *Winning Marriage,* 77–78. Solomon notes that nearly identical poll results were found in previous elections, corroborating assertions that no evidence tied the gay marriage battle to GOP victories. In a 2013 article, legal scholar Michael Klarman argues that the use of gay marriage by conservatives may, indeed, have tipped elections to Republicans, pointing out that political campaigns rely, to some extent, on rhetoric, moods, and innuendo that can be difficult to quantify, and that anti-gay sentiment was effectively deployed to these ends. See Michael J. Klarman, "How Same-Sex Marriage Came to Be," *Harvard Magazine,* Mar. / Apr. 2013. Others, including Mary Bonauto and Evan Wolfson, have argued that conservatives were using gay rights to win and keep power for years, and would have continued to do so irrespective of the efforts of gay advocates. See also Stephen Ansolabehere and Charles Stewart III, "Truth in Numbers," *Boston Review,* Feb. / Mar. 2005, 40.

43 Klarman, "How Same-Sex Marriage"; James Dao, "Same-Sex Marriage Issue Key to Some G.O.P. Races," *New York Times*, Nov. 4, 2004.

44 John M. Broder, "Groups Debate Slower Strategy on Gay Rights," *New York Times*, Dec. 9, 2004.

45 Hilary Rosen, "Paving the Middle Road of Civil Unions is Not Caving In," *Advocate*, Dec. 7, 2004, 30.

46 Broder, "Groups Debate"; Hilary Rosen, 2005 Membership Renewal, Human Rights Campaign, http://www.democraticunderground.com/discuss/duboard.php?az=view_all&address=221x2477; Sarah Wildman, "Tough Times at HRC," *Advocate*, Mar. 29, 2005, 30–37.

47 Broder, "Groups Debate."

48 On complaints against HRC regarding 2004 elections, see "HRC Is Justifying Surrender on Gay Marriage" (letter), *Socialist Worker*, Jan. 28, 2005, 8; Wildman, "Tough Times."

49 Solomon, *Winning Marriage*, 91.

50 Wildman, "Tough Times at HRC."

51 Craig Rimmerman, *From Identity to Politics: Lesbian and Gay Movements in the U.S.* (Philadelphia: Temple University Press, 2001), 33–34. Interviews of the Task Force leadership and scrutiny of documents list numerous institutional priorities, none of which include marriage (but do include "legal protections for gay and lesbian families"); Andrea Hildebran, "National State Gay Leaders Unveil New Name, New Growth, New Leadership," *GLAA*, Aug. 16, 2004, http://www.glaa.org/archive/2004/equalityfederation0816.shtml; author interview with Wolfson; author interview with Andrew Sullivan.

52 Joe Garofoli, "S.F. Foundation Supported Gay Marriage Long Before It Was Cool," *San Francisco Chronicle*, Jun. 28, 2015.

53 John Cloud, "Heroes and Icons: Evan Wolfson," *Time*, Apr. 26, 2004.

54 Molly Ball, "The Marriage Plot: Inside This Year's Epic Campaign for Gay Equality," *Atlantic*, Dec. 11, 2012.

55 Freedom to Marry, Annual Report, 2006, www.freedomtomarry.org/page/-/files/pdfs/final_2006_annual_report.pdf.

56 Civil Marriage Collaborative, "About," www.proteusfund.org/cmc/about.

57 Author interview with Andrew Lane.

58 David Callahan, "The Marriage Equality Hall of Fame: 8 Funders Who Helped Make It Happen," *Inside Philanthropy*, Oct. 7, 2014.

59 Author interview with John O'Brien.

60 Author interview with Lane.

8. "A POLITICAL AWAKENING"

1   John Cloud, "A Gay Mafia," *Time*, Nov. 10, 2008; Joshua Green, "They Won't Know What Hit Them," *The Atlantic*, Mar. 1, 2007.

2   Eric Gorski, "Benefactor's Group to Fight Effort to Ban Gay Marriage," *Denver Post*, Dec. 6, 2005.

3   Cloud, "A Gay Mafia"; Joshua Green, "They Won't Know."

4   Nancy Vogel, "Legislature OKs Gay Marriage," *Los Angeles Times*, Sept. 7, 2005; Mark Leno quoted in Scott L. Cummings and Douglas NeJaime, "Lawyering for Marriage Equality," *UCLA Law Review* 57 (2010): 1275.

5   Kevin Vance, "Why Arizona Flipped on Gay Marriage," CBS News, Dec. 2, 2008.

6   Freedom to Marry, 2006 Annual Report, www.freedomtomarry.org/page/-/files/pdfs/final_2006_annual_report.pdf.

7   In Washington, *Andersen v. King County*, 138 P. 3d 963 (2006); in New York, *Hernandez v. Robles*, 855 N.E.2d 1 (N.Y. 2006); in New Jersey, *Lewis v. Harris*, 908 A. 2d 196 (2006).

8   Chris L. Jenkins, "Ban on Same-Sex Unions Added to Va. Constitution," *Washington Post*, Nov. 8, 2006.

9   For an in-depth write-up of the In re cases, see Jean C. Love and Patricia A. Cain, *Six Cases in Search of a Decision: The Story of In re Marriage Cases*, ed. Elizabeth M. Schneider and Stephanie M. Wildman (New York: Thomson Reuters / Foundation Press, 2011), 337.

10   Gregory B. Lewis and Charles W. Gossett, "Changing Public Opinion on Same-Sex Marriage: The Case of California," *Politics and Policy* 36 (2008): 4–30.

11   C-SPAN (video of oral arguments), Mar. 4, 2008, www.c-span.org/video/?199950-1/california-samesex-marriage-cases.

12   Adam Liptak, "California Court Affirms Right to Gay Marriage," *New York Times*, May 16, 2008.

13   Ibid.

14   Maura Dolan, "Gay Marriage Ban Overturned," *Los Angeles Times*, May 17, 2008; Bob Egelko, "State's Top Court Strikes Down Marriage Ban," *SF Gate*, May 16, 2008.

15   Liptak, "California Court."

16   "Frustrated Conservatives Turn to Voters," *Inside Bay Area*, Mar. 21, 2008.

17   Liptak, "California Court."

18   "State Issues Crowd[ed] November Ballot," *Contra Costa Times*, Jun. 29, 2008.

19   The initiative proponents were listed as Dennis Hollingsworth, Gail J. Knight, Martin F. Gutierrez, Hak-Shing William Tam, and Mark A. Jansson.

20   Nancy Isles, "Marriage Licenses Were Hot In June," *Marin Independent Journal,* Jul. 11, 2008.

21   Mike Zapler, "Sex and Drugs and Animals on Ballot," *Monterey County Herald,* Jun. 30, 2008.

22   Chris Metinko, "Bay Area Same-Sex Couples Say 'I Do,'" *Contra Costa Times,* Jun. 16, 2008; Mike Swift, Mary Anne Ostrom, and Jessie Mangaliman, "Elderly Couple Who Fought for Gay Marriage Among First to Exchange Vows," *Contra Costa Times,* Jun. 16, 2008.

23   Metinko, "Bay Area"; Swift, Ostrom, and Mangaliman, "Elderly Couple."

24   Author interview with Robin Tyler; Tony Castro, "Gay Couple Will Be One of First to Marry," *San Gabriel Valley Tribune,* Jun. 14, 2008.

25   Ashley Surdin and William Booth, "California Weddings Make History," *Washington Post,* Jun. 17, 2008.

26   "Prop. 8 Facing a Fight," *San Jose Mercury News,* Jul. 18, 2008.

27   Jesse McKinley and Kirk Johnson, "Mormons Tipped Scale in Ban on Gay Marriage," *New York Times,* Nov. 14, 2008.

28   Maura Dolan, "Prop. 8 Challengers Highlight Religion's Role in Campaign," *Los Angeles Times,* Jan. 21, 2010,

29   Maloy Moore, "Tracking the Money: Final Numbers," *Los Angeles Times,* Feb. 3, 2009.

30   McKinley and Johnson, "Mormons Tipped Scale."

31   Ibid.

32   Preserving Marriage, YES On Proposition 8 (Prop 8), video, posted Oct. 16, 2008, https://youtu.be/A-jc4ujp9Ok.

33   Mike Swift, "Gay Rights Regroup After Proposition 8 Passage," *Monterey County Herald,* Nov. 9, 2008.

34   Yesonprop81025, Proposition 8 Commercial, video, posted Oct. 25, 2008, https://youtu.be/75J31N9ZzCk.

35   McKinley and Johnson, "Mormons Tipped Scale."

36   Swift, "Gay Rights Regroup."

37   Jessica Bernstein-Wax, "Police: Girl Assaulted During Proposition 8 Rally, Two Arrested," *San Jose Mercury News,* Nov. 4, 2008.

38   Swift, "Gay Rights Regroup."

39   Karen Ocamb, "DOMA-Defeater Robbie Kaplan on Prop. 8, Bill Clinton and Gay Adoption Ban (Part Two)," *Frontiers Media,* Oct. 19, 2015.

40   Cara Mia DiMassa and Jessica Garrison, "Why Gays, Blacks Are Divided on Prop. 8," *Los Angeles Times,* Nov. 8, 2008. On African American support for homosexuality and marriage equality, see Patrick J. Egan and Kenneth Sherrill, "California's Proposition 8: What Happened, and What Does the Future Hold?" National Gay and Lesbian Task Force, Jan. 2009, www.thetaskforce.org/static_html/downloads/reports/reports/pi_prop8_1_6_09.pdf; C. Nicolet Mason, "At the Crossroads: African-American Attitudes, Perceptions, and Beliefs Toward Marriage Equality," National Black Justice Coalition, http://nbjc.org/resources/at-the-crossroads-2009.pdf.

41   Ben Ehrenreich, "Anatomy of a Failed Campaign," *Advocate,* Nov. 11, 2008.

42   Jasmyne A. Cannick, "No-on-8's White Bias," *Los Angeles Times,* Nov. 8, 2008.

43   Lisa Bloom, "Prop 8 Is Simply Unconstitutional," CNN, Jan. 12, 2010.

44   Lanz Christian Bañes, "Gay Marriage Supporters Take to Lynch Canyon," *Vallejo Times Herald,* Nov. 3, 2008.

45   Rosemary Winters, "More than 600 Show Up in Salt Lake City to Rally Against Prop. 8," *Salt Lake Tribune,* Nov. 3, 2008.

46   Rex Wockner, "Thousands Protest Prop 8 in San Diego," *Wockner* (blog), Nov. 2, 2008, http://wockner.blogspot.com/2008/11/thousands-protest-prop-8-in-san-diego.html.

47   Shaya Tayefe Mohajer, "Thousands in Los Angeles Protest Gay-Marriage Ban," Associated Press, Nov. 7, 2008; Andy Towle, "Thousands Join Marriage Equality Protest at L.A. Mormon Church," *Towleroad* (blog), Nov. 6, 2008, www.towleroad.com/2008/11/thousands-join.html; John Cadiz Klemack, Patrick Healy, and Jon Lloyd, "Prop 8 Protesters March into Night," NBC, Nov. 6, 2008; "Several Gay Marriage Ban Protesters Arrested in Clashes with Police in California," Fox News, Nov. 6, 2008.

48   Jesse McKinley, "Across U.S., Big Rallies for Same-Sex Marriage," *New York Times,* Nov. 16, 2008.

49   Jeff Gammage, "Gay-Rights Rally in Phila. Part of Nationwide Protest," *Philadelphia Inquirer,* Nov. 16, 2008.

50   McKinley, "Across U.S., Big Rallies"; Rex Wockner, "The Day the Music Died for the Gay Leadership," *Wockner* (blog), Nov. 17, 2008, http://wockner.blogspot.com/2008_11_01_archive.html.

51   Towle, "Thousands Join."

52   Jesse McKinley, "Gay Marriage Ban Inspires New Wave of Activists," *New York Times,* Dec. 9, 2008.

53   Claire Cain Miller, "Gay-Rights Advocates Use Web to Organize Global Rally," *New York Times,* Nov. 11, 2008; Jeff McDonald and John Marelius, "Prop. 8 Result

Energizes Gay-Rights Supporters," *San Diego Union Tribune,* Nov. 15, 2008; McKinley, "Gay Marriage Ban."

54   Matthew Hall, "Sanders Attends Rally Against Proposition 8," *San Diego Union Tribune,* Nov. 1, 2008.

55   Wockner, "Day the Music Died."

56   Wayne Besen, "Winds of Change," *Huffington Post,* Dec. 22, 2008.

57   Frank Newport, "For First Time, Majority of Americans Favor Legal Gay Marriage" (Gallup Survey Paper), May 20, 2011.

58   Wockner, "Day the Music Died"; Besen, "Winds of Change."

59   Janet Kornblum, "Gay-Marriage Ban in California Stirs Torchbearers," *USA Today,* Nov. 14, 2008, 3A; McDonald and Marelius, "Prop. 8 Result."

60   Swift, "Gay Rights Regroup After Proposition 8 Passage."

61   Ashley Simmons, "Met In The Middle For Equality," *Socialist Worker,* Jun. 10, 2009, http://socialistworker.org/2009/06/10/met-in-the-middle-for-equality.

62   Winters, "More Than 600 Show Up In Salt Lake City To Rally Against Prop. 8."

63   Paul Liberatore, "Marin Rally Joins Outcry Over Proposition 8," *Marin Independent Journal,* Nov. 15, 2008.

64   McKinley, "Across U.S., Big Rallies For Same-Sex Marriage,"A25.

65   Liberatore, "Marin Rally Joins Outcry Over Proposition 8."

66   McKinley, "Across U.S., Big Rallies For Same-Sex Marriage," A25.

67   Rex Wockner, "San Diego Mayor Announces Daughter Is A Lesbian, Embraces Same-Sex Marriage," *Pride Source,* Sept. 27, 2007, http://www.pridesource.com/article-mobile.html?article=27168.

68   Hall, "Sanders."

69   Author interview with Ted Olson; Stephanie Mencimer, "Gay Rights Groups to Ted Olson: Thanks, but No Thanks," *Mother Jones,* May 28, 2009.

70   Jo Becker, *Forcing the Spring: Inside the Fight for Marriage Equality* (New York: Penguin Press, 2014), 3–56; Chuleenan Svetvilas, "Challenging Prop. 8: The Hidden Story: How Activists Filed a Federal Lawsuit to Overturn California's Same-Sex Marriage Ban," *California Lawyer,* Jan. 2010.

71   Svetvilas, "Challenging Prop. 8."

72   Author interview with Olson; author interview with Chad Griffin.

9. "BRICK BY BRICK"

1   "Obama Once Backed Full Gay Marriage," *Windy City Times*, Jan. 13, 2009.

2   Lucy Shackelford and Madonna Lebling, "Timeline of Obama's Gay Marriage Views," *Washington Post*, May 9, 2012.

3   "Obama in 2004: 'I Don't Think Marriage Is a Civil Right,'" Real Clear Politics, May 8, 2012.

4   For comment on MSNBC, see Shackelford and Lebling, "Timeline"; for comments in November 2008, see Chris Harris, "Barack Obama Answers Your Questions About Gay Marriage, Paying for College, More," MTV News, Nov. 1, 2008.

5   John Wildermuth, "Obama Opposes Proposed Ban on Gay Marriage," *SF Gate*, Jul. 2, 2008.

6   Andrew Sullivan, "Andrew Sullivan on Barack Obama's Gay Marriage Evolution," *Newsweek*, May 13, 2012.

7   Wildermuth, "Obama Opposes."

8   Human Rights Campaign, "2008 Presidential Questionnaire," *Politico*, May 18, 2007.

9   John Aravosis, "Rick Warren Explicitly Bans 'Unrepentant' Gays from Membership in His Church," *AMERICAblog* (blog), Dec. 19, 2008.

10   Zack Ford and Annie-Rose Strasser, "Rick Warren: I Regret Coming Out in Support of California's Anti-Gay Marriage Proposition," *Think Progress*, Nov. 28, 2012. On same-sex marriage comparisons, see BeliefnetTV Community, Beliefnet Interviews Rick Warren on Gay Marriage, video, posted December 15, 2008, https://youtu.be/RoFHg_mbBVk.

11   Justin Cole, "Continuing Media Coverage of Rick Warren Controversy," *GLAAD*, Dec. 22, 2008.

12   See Kerry Eleveld, *Don't Tell Me to Wait: How the Fight for Gay Rights Changed America and Transformed Obama's Presidency* (New York: Basic Books, 2015).

13   Jeffrey M. Jones, "Majority of Americans Continue to Oppose Gay Marriage," Gallup, May 27, 2009.

14   Nathaniel Frank, "The President's Pleasant Surprise: How LGBT Advocates Ended 'Don't Ask, Don't Tell,'" *Journal of Homosexuality* 60 (2013): 159–213.

15   Leo Shane, "SLDN: End 'Mixed Signals' on Gays in the Ranks," *Stars and Stripes*, Apr. 27, 2009.

16   Aaron Belkin, "Obama to Fire His First Gay Arabic Linguist," *Huffington Post*, Jun. 7, 2009.

17 Frank, "President's Pleasant Surprise."

18 Ibid.

19 Ben Smith and Jonathan Martin, "Gay Groups Grow Impatient with Obama," *Politico,* Jun. 4, 2009.

20 Eugene Robinson, "Time for President Obama to Stand Up for Gay Marriage," *Washington Post,* May 8, 2009; Richard Socarides, "Where's Our 'Fierce Advocate'?" *Washington Post,* May 2, 2009.

21 Jann Wenner, "Barack Obama: Ready for the Fight," *Rolling Stone,* Apr. 25, 2012.

22 Daily Dish, "The Fierce Urgency of Whenever," *Atlantic,* May 13, 2009.

23 Smith and Martin, "Gay Groups"; on views of Democrats and liberals, see Jones, "Majority."

24 For more on these topics, see Andrew Sullivan, *Virtually Normal: An Argument About Homosexuality* (New York: Vintage Books, 1996); Nathaniel Frank, *Unfriendly Fire: How the Gay Ban Undermines the Military and Weakens America* (New York: Thomas Dunne Books, 2009).

25 *Smelt v. U.S.,* No. SACV09–00286 DOC (C.D. Cal. Aug. 24, 2009).

26 John Aravosis, "Obama Defends DOMA in Federal Court. Says Banning Gay Marriage Is Good for the Federal Budget. Invokes Incest and Marrying Children," *AMERICAblog* (blog), Jun. 12, 2009.

27 Richard Socarides, "The Choice to Defend DOMA, and Its Consequences," *AMERICAblog* (blog), Jun. 14, 2009.

28 "LGBT Legal and Advocacy Groups Decry Obama Administration's Defense of DOMA," Lambda Legal press release, Jun. 12, 2009.

29 "A Bad Call on Gay Rights," *New York Times,* June 15, 2009.

30 Ibid.

31 Declan McCullagh, "Gay Rights Groups Irate After Obama Administration Lauds Defense of Marriage Act," CBS News, Jun. 12, 2009; Marc Ambinder, "Obama Admin Hearts DOMA (for Now). Do Gays Still Heart Obama?" *Atlantic,* Jun. 12, 2009; Lindsey Ellerson, "Obama Justice Department Defends Defense of Marriage Act— That Candidate Obama Opposed," ABC News, Jun. 12, 2009.

32 For a discussion of how gay advocates used the media to exert pressure on the White House during the "don't ask, don't tell" political battle, see Frank, "President's Pleasant Surprise," 159–213.

33 John Aravosis, "Obama DOJ Lies to Politico in Defending Hate Brief Against Gays," *AMERICAblog* (blog), Jun. 12, 2009.

34 Scott Wilson, "Obama Gives Some Benefits to Same-Sex Partners of Federal Workers," *Washington Post,* Jun. 17, 2009.

35 Sam Hananel, "Obama's Gay Appointees Smash Record," Associated Press, Oct. 26, 2010.

36 Ben Smith, "Gay Figures Pull Out of Biden Fundraiser," *Politico,* Jun. 16, 2009. On the earlier fund-raiser, see Smith and Martin, "Gay Groups Grow Impatient."

37 John Aravosis, "President Obama Betrays the Gay Community," *Salon,* Jun. 17, 2009.

38 This account of the decision to file the *Gill* lawsuit draws on the following sources: author interview with Mary Bonauto; author interview with Jon Davidson; author interview with James Esseks; author interview with anonymous; Mary Bonauto and James Esseks, "Marriage Equality Advocacy from the Trenches," *Columbia Journal of Gender and Law* 29, no. 1 (2015); Mary L. Bonauto, Gary D. Buseck, and Janson Wu, "New Frontiers: State Legislative Wins and Federal DOMA Challenges," in *Love Unites Us: Winning the Freedom to Marry in America,* ed. Kevin Cathcart and Leslie Gabel-Brett (New York: New Press, 2016), 183–194; Jason Pierceson, *Same-Sex Marriage in the United States: The Road to the Supreme Court and Beyond* (Lanham, MD: Rowman and Littlefield, 2014), 213.

39 Kimberly Geiger, "Same-Sex Survivor Denied Pension; Spouse of Gay Ex-Lawmaker Ineligible for Federal Death Benefit," *San Francisco Chronicle,* Oct. 20, 2006; "GLAD Files Lawsuit Challenging Denial of Critical Federal Benefits to Married Same-Sex Couples," GLAD press release, Mar. 3, 2009; Abby Goodnough and Katie Zezima, "Suit Seeks to Force Government to Extend Benefits to Same-Sex Couples," *New York Times,* Mar. 2, 2009.

40 Conor Berry, "Mass. Suing for Gay Rights," *Berkshire Eagle,* Jul. 9, 2009.

41 Abby Goodnough, "State Suit Challenges U.S. Defense of Marriage Act," *New York Times,* Jul. 9, 2009, A20.

42 *Commonwealth of Massachusetts v. U.S. Dept. of Health and Human Services,* No. 1:09-11156-JLT (U.S.D.C. for the District of Massachusetts).

43 No. 1:09-11156-JLT. Coakley's suit involved two related complaints: that the state was denied federal funding for Medicaid payments to same-sex spouses, since such spouses were ineligible in the eyes of the federal government, and that the state incurred extra Medicare tax payments—the state paid a Medicare tax based on every employee's taxable income, an amount that was raised artificially high since the federal government denied same-sex spouses the normal exemption on spousal healthcare benefits.

44 Joe Garofoli, "S.F. Foundation Supported Gay Marriage Long Before It Was Cool," *San Francisco Chronicle,* Jun. 28, 2015.

45 "Winning Marriage: What We Need to Do" (white paper), Jun. 21, 2005, https://s3.amazonaws.com/s3.documentcloud.org/documents/2108219/final-marriage-concept-paper.pdf.

46 According to one calculation by a foundation program officer, only 10–15 percent of overall funding to LGBTQ causes went toward marriage.

47 Author interview with Camilla Taylor.

48 Ibid.

49 *Varnum v. Brien,* 763 N.W.2d 862 (Iowa 2009).

50 Grant Schulte, "Iowans Dismiss Three Justices," *Des Moines Register,* Nov. 3, 2010.

51 Author interview with William Lippert.

52 Author interview with Peter Shumlin.

53 "Commission Releases Same-Sex Marriage Report," WCAX.com, Apr. 21, 2008.

54 Author interview with Shumlin.

55 Author interview with Shap Smith; author interview with William Lippert.

56 Author interview with Jeff Young.

57 Author interview with Shumlin.

58 Abby Goodnough, "Maine Governor Signs Same-Sex Marriage Bill as Opponents Plan a 'Veto,'" *New York Times,* May 7, 2009.

10. "MAKE MORE SNOWFLAKES AND THERE WILL BE AN AVALANCHE"

1 Maura Dolan, "California Supreme Court Looks Unlikely to Kill Proposition 8," *Los Angeles Times,* Mar. 6, 2009.

2 Author interview with Ted Olson; author interview with Chad Griffin.

3 Jo Becker, *Forcing the Spring: Inside the Fight for Marriage Equality* (New York: Penguin Press, 2014), 24.

4 Chris Geidner, "Video Shows a Different Story of Dustin Lance Black's Speech than Marriage Equality Book Presents," *Buzzfeed,* Apr. 22, 2014.

5 Ibid.

6 Ibid.

7 Becker, *Forcing the Spring,* 23.

8 Geidner, "Video."

9   Andrew Sullivan, "The Human Rights Campaign—the Country's Largest LGBT Lobbying Group—Has Failed," *The Stranger,* Jun. 22, 2011.

10   Ibid.

11   Geidner, "Video."

12   Jesse McKinley, "Harvey Milk's Shop, Center of a Movement, Is Now the Center of an Internal Fight," *New York Times,* Dec. 19, 2010.

13   Sullivan, "Human Rights Campaign."

14   David Boies and Theodore B. Olson, *Redeeming the Dream: The Case for Marriage Equality* (New York: Penguin Press, 2014), 47, 58, 89.

15   Becker, *Forcing the Spring,* 32.

16   Chuleenan Svetvilas, "Challenging Prop. 8: The Hidden Story: How Activists Filed a Federal Lawsuit to Overturn California's Same-Sex Marriage Ban," *California Lawyer,* Jan. 2010; Sandy Stier, "Journey Down the Aisle," *California Lawyer,* Jun. 2014.

17   Becker, *Forcing the Spring,* 29–31.

18   Ibid.; Gallup, Methodology, http://www.gallup.com/178685/methodology -center .aspx.

19   Becker, *Forcing the Spring,* 31.

20   Ibid.; Svetvilas, "Challenging Prop. 8."

21   Becker, *Forcing the Spring,* 33–34.

22   On twenty-five states, see Abby Rubenfeld, "Lessons Learned: A Reflection upon *Bowers v. Hardwick,*" *Nova Law Review* 11 (1986): 59–70.

23   *Loving v. Virginia,* 388 U.S. 1 (1967).

24   Becker, *Forcing the Spring,* 33–34.

25   Complaint for Declaratory, Injunctive, or Other Relief, *Perry v. Schwarzenegger,* 2009 WL 1490740 (N.D. Cal. May 22, 2009) (No. CV-092292VRW).

26   Jesse McKinley, *"Bush v. Gore* Foes Join to Fight Gay Marriage Ban," *New York Times,* May 28, 2009.

27   Ashby Jones, "Challenging Prop. 8 in the Federal Courts: A Bold Gambit?" *Wall Street Journal,* May 27, 2009.

28   Becker, *Forcing the Spring,* 22, 36–37.

29   Author interview with Nan Hunter; Svetvilas, "Challenging Prop. 8."

30   McKinley, *"Bush v. Gore* Foes."

31   Jones, "Challenging Prop. 8."

32 McKinley, *"Bush v. Gore* Foes."

33 Svetvilas, "Challenging Prop. 8."

34 *"Bush vs. Gore* Rivals Challenge Prop. 8 in Federal Court," *Los Angeles Times,* May 26, 2009.

35 Howard Mintz, "Trial over Proposition 8 Set to Make History," *Contra Costa Times,* Jan. 11, 2010.

36 Karl Vick, "Same-Sex Marriage Aims Higher; First Step to Supreme Court Advocates Rethink State-By-State Strategy," *Washington Post,* Jan. 11, 2010.

37 ACLU et al., "Make Change, Not Lawsuits," press release, June 2008, https://www.aclu.org/files/pdfs/lgbt/make_change_20090527.pdf.

38 Ibid.

39 Svetvilas, "Challenging Prop. 8."

40 Author interview with Kate Kendell.

41 Kenji Yoshino, *Speak Now: Marriage Equality on Trial* (New York: Crown, 2015), 69–77.

42 Shaun Knittel, "Larry Kramer Makes *Perry v. Schwarzenegger* Battle Public," *Seattle Gay News,* Jul. 10, 2009.

43 Letter from Chad H. Griffin, Board President, American Foundation for Equal Rights, to Kate Kendell, Executive Director, National Center for Lesbian Rights, Jennifer Pizer, Senior Counsel for Lambda Legal West Regional Office, and Mark Rosenbaum, Legal Director of the American Civil Liberties Union of Southern California (July 8, 2009), available at http://www.scribd.com/full/17233138?ccess_key=key-kxoafohabwd4otk776u.

44 Becker, *Forcing the Spring,* 58–59. Becker writes that Herrera suggested he could give "cover" to AFER and make the group look more reasonable by supporting San Francisco's intervention. See also Svetvilas, "Challenging Prop. 8." Svetvilas writes, "The Gibson Dunn lawyers opposed both motions to intervene, but argued that if any party were allowed, 'it should be the City alone that is permitted to join.'"

11. "WITHOUT ANY RATIONAL JUSTIFICATION"

1 Theodore Olson, "The Conservative Case for Gay Marriage," *Newsweek,* Jan. 8, 2010.

2 William Grimes, "Del Martin, Lesbian Activist, Dies at 87," *New York Times,* Aug. 28, 2008.

3 This chapter draws from Kenji Yoshino, *Speak Now: Marriage Equality on Trial* (New York: Crown, 2015).

4 Howard Mintz, "Prop. 8 Trial Day 1: Live Coverage from the Courtroom," *Contra Costa Times,* Jan. 11, 2010.

5 Transcript of Trial—Day 01 at 13–213, *Perry v. Schwarzenegger,* No. 09-CV-2292 (N.D. Cal. Jan. 11, 2010).

6 Ibid.

7 Ibid.

8 Ibid.

9 Transcript of Pre-Trial Hearing at 1–103, *Perry v. Schwarzenegger,* No. 09-CV-2292 (N.D. Cal. Oct. 14, 2009).

10 Ibid.

11 Transcript of Trial—Day 01, *Perry v. Schwarzenegger.*

12 Ibid.

13 Ibid.

14 Author interview with Mary Bonauto; Transcript of Trial—Day 01, *Perry v. Schwarzenegger;* Transcript of Trial—Day 02 at 214–457, *Perry v. Schwarzenegger,* No. 09-CV-2292 (N.D. Cal. Jan. 12, 2010).

15 Transcript of Trial—Day 02, *Perry v. Schwarzenegger;* Transcript of Trial—Day 03 at 458–669, *Perry v. Schwarzenegger,* No. 09-CV-2292 (N.D. Cal. Jan. 13, 2010).

16 Transcript of Trial—Day 06 at 1256–1479, *Perry v. Schwarzenegger,* No. 09-CV-2292 (N.D. Cal. Jan. 19, 2010); Transcript of Trial—Day 09 at 2009–2330, *Perry v. Schwarzenegger,* No. 09-CV-2292 (N.D. Cal. Jan. 22, 2010).

17 Transcript of Trial—Day 05 at 991–1255, *Perry v. Schwarzenegger,* No. 09-CV-2292 (N.D. Cal. Jan. 15, 2010).

18 Transcript of Pre-Trial Hearing, *Perry v. Schwarzenegger.*

19 Transcript of Trial—Day 05, *Perry v. Schwarzenegger.*

20 Transcript of Trial—Day 11 at 2584–2834, *Perry v. Schwarzenegger,* No. 09-CV-2292 (N.D. Cal. Jan. 26, 2010); Yoshino, *Speak Now,* 198–217.

21 Transcript of Trial—Day 11, *Perry v. Schwarzenegger.*

22 Howard Mintz, "Prop. 8 Trial Day 10: Live Coverage from the Courtroom." *San Jose Mercury News,* Jan. 25, 2010.

23 Transcript of Trial—Closing Arguments at 2953–3115, *Perry v. Schwarzenegger,* No. 09-CV-2292 (N.D. Cal. Jun. 16, 2010); Maura Dolan, "Official Prop. 8 Proponent Claims Same-Sex Marriage Can Harm Children," *Los Angeles Times,* Jan. 22, 2010.

24 *Commonwealth of Massachusetts v. U.S. Department of Health and Human Services,* 698 F. Supp. 2d 234 (2010).

25   *Gill v. Office of Personnel Management,* 699 F. Supp. 2d 374 (2010).

26   Ibid.

27   Ibid.

28   Andrew Gelman, Jeffrey Lax, and Justin Phillips, "Over Time, a Gay Marriage Groundswell," *New York Times,* Aug. 21, 2010; *Perry v. Schwarzenegger,* 704 F. Supp. 2d 921 (N.D. Cal., 2010).

12. "A RISK WELL WORTH TAKING"

1   Aaron Hicklin, "Edie Windsor and Thea Spyer: When Edie Met Thea," *Out,* Jan. 9, 2011.

2   Author interview with Edie Windsor; Chris Geidner, "Meet the Hero of the Marriage Equality Movement," *BuzzFeed,* Jan. 10, 2013.

3   Author interview with Windsor.

4   Ibid.

5   Ibid.

6   Geidner, "Meet the Hero."

7   Author interview with Windsor.

8   Ibid.; Roberta Kaplan, *Then Comes Marriage:* United States v. Windsor *and the Defeat of DOMA* (New York: W. W. Norton, 2015).

9   Lambda would file *Golinski v. Office of Personnel Management,* 824 F. Supp. 2d 968 (N.D. Cal.), in a federal court in California. GLAD would file *Pedersen et al. v. Office of Personnel Management,* 881 F. Supp. 2d 294 (2012), in a federal court in Connecticut.

10   Marriage Equality USA, "MEUSA Interview with Edie Windsor (Part 3): A Marriage Equality Legacy," video, https://youtu.be/rm0Ejm-ropM.

11   Author interview with Roberta Kaplan; author interview with James Esseks; Kaplan, *Then Comes Marriage.*

12   Author interview with Kaplan; Marriage Equality USA, "MEUSA Interview with Edie Windsor." See also Kaplan, *Then Comes Marriage.*

13   Author interview with Kaplan; Ariel Levy, "The Perfect Wife," *New Yorker,* Sept. 30, 2013. Levy writes that Kaplan identified Windsor as a perfect plaintiff to challenge DOMA. "Immediately, it was clear to me that this was the ideal case," Kaplan told Levy. The jacket of Kaplan's *Then Comes Marriage* says the same. However, Kaplan explains the apparent discrepancy in her book: she did not think her case would reach the Supreme Court before others, given how far along GLAD's *Gill* suit was, and she was committed to treating Windsor like any other client (albeit a pro bono

one); eventually it became clear that review by the U.S. Supreme Court was a real option.

14   Committee of the Judiciary, *Report on the Defense of Marriage Act, H.R. Rep. No. 104–664* (Washington, D.C.: GPO, 1996).

15   This account of how Kaplan came to represent Windsor and what the response was of movement groups draws on the following: author interview with Kaplan; author interview with Windsor; author interview with Esseks; author interview with Jon Davidson; author interview with Mary Bonauto; Kaplan, *Then Comes Marriage;* Levy, "The Perfect Wife."

16   Kerry Eleveld, *Don't Tell Me to Wait: How the Fight for Gay Rights Changed America and Transformed Obama's Presidency* (New York: Basic Books, 2015), 196–203.

17   Ibid., 202–203.

18   On meetings, author interview with Evan Wolfson; Eleveld, *Don't Tell Me to Wait,* 196–221. See also Kerry Eleveld, "What Gay Rights Activists Can Teach the Left About Winning," *Atlantic,* Sept. 26, 2011.

19   Nathaniel Frank, "The President's Pleasant Surprise: How LGBT Advocates Ended 'Don't Ask, Don't Tell,'" *Journal of Homosexuality* 60 (2013): 159–213; Eleveld, "What Gay Rights Activists"; Aaron Belkin et al., *One Year Out: An Assessment of DADT Repeal Impact on Military Readiness* (Santa Barbara, CA: Palm Center, 2012). Marc Ambinder, "Obama Won't Go to Court over Defense of Marriage Act," *National Journal,* Feb. 23, 2011. Ambinder writes that the Justice Department decision and DADT repeal show the administration no longer feared a political downside to embracing gay rights. See also Eleveld, *Don't Tell Me to Wait.* The very first pro-gay federal bill was the 2009 inclusion of sexual orientation in the federal hate crime law, but the repeal of "don't ask, don't tell" was a more difficult and more major legislative accomplishment.

20   Andrew Sullivan, "Obama's Marriage FAIL," *Daily Dish* (blog), Aug. 5, 2010, http://dish.andrewsullivan.com/category/marriage-equality/page/7.

21   Joe Sudbay, "Transcript of Q and A with the President about DADT and Same-Sex Marriage," *AMERICAblog* (blog), Oct. 27, 2010, http://americablog.com/2010/10/transcript-of-q-and-a-with-the-president-about-dadt-and-same-sex-marriage.html.

22   Marc Solomon, *Winning Marriage: The Inside Story of How Same-Sex Couples Took on the Politicians and Pundits and Won* (Lebanon, NH: ForeEdge, 2014); Eleveld, *Don't Tell Me to Wait.*

23   U.S. Department of Justice, Letter from the Attorney General to Congress on Litigation Involving the Defense of Marriage Act, Feb. 23, 2011, www.justice.gov/opa/pr/letter-attorney-general-congress-litigation-involving-defense-marriage-act.

24 Ibid.

25 Ibid.

26 Author interview with Kaplan.

27 Charlie Savage and Sheryl Gay Stolberg, "In Shift, U.S. Says Marriage Act Blocks Gay Rights," *New York Times,* Feb. 24, 2011.

28 U.S. Department of Justice, Letter from the Attorney General; and see "United States of America, Petitioner v. Edith Schlain Windsor," http://sblog.s3.amazonaws.com/wp-content/uploads/2012/10/12-307-Petition.pdf, p. 6. The now-friendly Obama administration filed a motion to dismiss Windsor's claim, "solely for purposes of ensuring that the court had Article III jurisdiction to enter judgment for or against the federal officials tasked with enforcing Section 3."

29 "Statement by House Speaker John Boehner (R-OH) Regarding the Defense of Marriage Act," Speaker.gov, Mar. 4, 2011; Felicia Sonmez and Ben Pershing, "Boehner Launches Effort to Defend Gay-Marriage Ban," *Washington Post,* Mar. 4, 2011.

30 Solomon, *Winning Marriage,* 149.

31 Ibid., 154–157.

32 Author interview with Ken Mehlman; Sasha Issenberg, "The GOP Number Crunchers Helping Gay Marriage Advocates," *Slate,* Aug. 22, 2012.

33 Marc Ambinder, "Bush Campaign Chief and Former RNC Chair Ken Mehlman: I'm Gay," *Atlantic,* Aug. 25, 2010; Sheryl Gay Stolberg, "Strategist Out of Closet and into Fray, This Time for Gay Marriage," *New York Times,* Jun. 19, 2013; Thomas Schaller, "Same Sex, Opposite Impact," *Salon,* Mar. 2, 2012.

34 Solomon, *Winning Marriage,* 185–189; Nicholas Confessore and Michael Barbaro, "Donors to GOP Are Backing Gay Marriage Push," *New York Times,* May 13, 2011.

35 Quoted in Eleveld, *Don't Tell Me to Wait,* 228.

36 Solomon, *Winning Marriage,* 165–168.

37 Ibid., 169–171.

38 Ibid., 179, 174–182; Michael Barbaro, "Cuomo Helps Groups Mobilize for Gay Marriage Bill," *New York Times,* Apr. 20, 2011.

39 Author interview with Marty Rouse; Solomon, *Winning Marriage,* 177–182, 186; Confessore and Barbaro, "Donors."

40 Solomon, *Winning Marriage,* 194–201.

41 On the Cuomo marriage equality effort, see also Eleveld, *Don't Tell Me to Wait,* 225–232. For a comparison to 2008 media coverage, see, for example, Adam Liptak, "California Court Affirms Right to Gay Marriage," *New York Times,* May 16, 2008.

42   Katherine M. Franke, "Marriage Is a Mixed Blessing," *New York Times,* Jun. 24, 2011.

13. "THE NATION IS READY FOR IT"

1   Maureen Dowd, "Why Is He Bi? (Sigh)," *New York Times,* Jun. 25, 2011.

2   Nate Silver, "Cuomo's Presidential Moment Forms Contrast with Obama," FiveThirtyEight blog, *New York Times,* Jun. 25, 2011.

3   Jo Becker, "How the President Got to 'I Do' on Same-Sex Marriage," *New York Times,* Apr. 16, 2014. Becker writes, "The campaign's internal polling revealed that the issue was a touchstone for likely Obama voters under 30. The campaign needed those voters to turn out in the record numbers they had four years earlier, and the biggest impediment was Obama's refusal to say he favored allowing gay couples to wed." See also Kerry Eleveld, *Don't Tell Me to Wait: How the Fight for Gay Rights Changed America and Transformed Obama's Presidency* (New York: Basic Books, 2015), 236–239.

4   Eleveld, *Don't Tell Me to Wait,* 235–240; Becker, "How the President Got to 'I Do.'"

5   Becker, "How the President Got to 'I Do.'"

6   Marc Solomon, *Winning Marriage: The Inside Story of How Same-Sex Couples Took on the Politicians and Pundits and Won* (Lebanon, NH: ForeEdge, 2014).

7   "'This Week' Transcript: David Plouffe and Rep. Michele Bachmann," *ABC News* (transcript), Mar. 25, 2012.

8   Eleveld, *Don't Tell Me to Wait.*

9   Becker, "How the President Got to 'I Do'"; "Biden Breaks Down Stance on Same-Sex Marriage," *Meet the Press* (transcript), May 6, 2012.

10   Becker, "How the President Got to 'I Do.'"

11   Alan Duke, "'GMA' Anchor Robin Roberts Publicly Acknowledges She's Gay," CNN, Dec. 29, 2013.

12   "Transcript: Robin Roberts ABC News Interview with President Obama," *ABC News* (transcript), May 9, 2012.

13   Scott Clement and Sandhya Somashekhar, "After President Obama's Announcement, Opposition to Gay Marriage Hits Record Low," *Washington Post,* May 23, 2012. On the North Carolina poll, see Corey Dade, "Polls Show Obama's Support for Gay Marriage Influencing Blacks," NPR, May 27, 2012. Polls, of course, vary, and Pew reported later that summer that overall views on same-sex marriage were unchanged in the polling it reviewed, but that Obama's announcement may have increased support and enthusiasm among Democrats. See "Two-Thirds of Democrats Now Support Gay Marriage," *Pew Forum,* Jul. 31, 2012.

14   Nathaniel Frank, "The President's Pleasant Surprise," *Journal of Homosexuality* 60 (2013): 159–213; Allen Bishop, "Efficacy or Justice: Overturning the Ban," *Military Review* (2010): 117–120.

15   David Axelrod, *Believer: My Forty Years in Politics* (New York: Penguin Press, 2015), 447.

16   "Transcript: Robin Roberts ABC News Interview."

17   Marc Solomon, "Developments at Let California Ring: New Partners and New Actions," www.letcaliforniaring.org/site/c.ltJTJ6MQIuE/b.5535163/k.6EF8/New _Partners_New_Actions.htm; Heather Cassell, "EQCA Raising Money for Ad Buy," *Bay Area Reporter,* Sept. 6, 2007.

18   The author is a former consultant to Movement Advancement Project.

19   Joe Garofoli, "S.F. Foundation Supported Gay Marriage Long Before It Was Cool," *San Francisco Chronicle,* Jun. 28, 2015.

20   David Lewis, "Hearts and Minds: The Untold Story of How Philanthropy and the Civil Marriage Collaborative Helped America Embrace Marriage Equality," Proteus Fund, 2015; Matt Coles et al., "Winning Marriage: The Path Forward (An Update of the 10/10/10/20 Paper)" (white paper, the National Collaborative), Mar. 25, 2010.

21   Evan Wolfson, "Freedom to Marry—Advancing the Needed Campaign, New Capacities for the Multi-Faceted Strategy" (white paper, Freedom to Marry), Aug. 19, 2009.

22   Thalia Zepatos, "The Marriage Movement's Secret Weapon: Radical Cooperation," *Huffington Post,* Jun. 26, 2015.

23   Lewis, "Hearts and Minds."

24   Office of the General Counsel, Defense of Marriage Act, Jan. 31, 1997, http://www .gao.gov/archive/1997/og97016.pdf.

25   On the use of a rights framework by marriage equality proponents in the 1990s, see Mary Ziegler, "The Terms of the Debate: Litigation, Argumentative Strategies, and Coalitions in the Same-Sex Marriage Struggle," *Florida State University Law Review* 39 (2012): 467–519.

26   Bruce Bawer, *A Place at the Table: The Gay Individual in American Society* (New York: Poseidon Press, 1993); Jonathan Rauch, *Gay Marriage: Why It Is Good for Gays, Good for Straights, and Good for America* (New York: Times Books / Henry Holt, 2004).

27   Zepatos, "Marriage Movement's Secret Weapon."

28   Author interview with Mehlman; see also Sasha Issenberg, "The GOP Number Crunchers Helping Gay Marriage Advocates," *Slate,* Aug. 22, 2012.

29   Author interview with Jennifer Green.

30   Anna Marie Cox, "The Supreme Court's Problem: How to Back America out of Anti-Gay Bigotry," *The Guardian,* Mar. 28, 2013.

31   Michael Lavers, "Will D.C. Gays Contribute to Maryland Same-Sex Marriage Campaign?" *Washington Blade,* Jul. 17, 2012; Michael Lavers, "Year in Review: Maryland Wins Marriage Equality," *Washington Blade,* Dec. 26, 2012; Scott Wilson, "Obama Gives Some Benefits to Same-Sex Partners of Federal Workers," *Washington Post,* Jun. 18, 2009; Sarah Wildman, "Tough Times at HRC," *Advocate,* Mar. 29, 2005, 30–37; Joe Boland, "Case Study: Human Rights Campaign Don't Ask, Don't Tell Repeal (Part 1)," *Fundraising Success Magazine,* Aug. 18, 2011; author interview with Marty Rouse.

32   Micah Cohen, "Gay Vote Proved a Boon for Obama," *New York Times,* Nov. 15, 2012.

33   Aaron Blake, "African Americans and Latinos Spur Gay Marriage Revolution," *Washington Post,* Nov. 12, 2012; "Gay Marriage Gains More Acceptance: Majority Continues to Favor Gays Serving Openly in Military," Pew Research, Oct. 6, 2010.

34   Lillian Faderman, *The Gay Revolution: The Story of the Struggle* (New York: Simon and Schuster, 2015), 594–601.

35   Paul D. Clement et al., "Memorandum of Law in Support of Intervenor-Defendant's Opposition to Plaintiff's Motion for Summary Judgment," Aug. 1, 2011, *Windsor v. U.S.,* 10-CV-8435 (BSJ) (JCF) (S.D.N.Y.).

36   Ibid.

37   *Windsor v. U.S.,* 10 Civ. 8435 (BSJ) (JCF) (S.D.N.Y.).

38   Roberta Kaplan to Magistrate Judge James C. Francis, July 18, 2011, re *Windsor v. U.S.,* 10 Civ. 8435 (BSJ) (JCF), https://www.aclu.org/sites/default/files/field_document /ltr_7_18_2011.pdf.

39   Filing 43, Jul. 28, 2011, *Windsor v. United States,* 10 Civ. 8435 (BSJ) (JCF) (S.D.N.Y.), http://docs.justia.com/cases/federal/district-courts/new-york/nysdce/1:2010cv08435 /370870/43.

40   *Perry v. Brown,* 671 F.3d 1052 (9th Cir. 2010); *Golinski v. U.S. Office of Personnel Management,* 824 F. Supp. 2d 968 (N.D. Cal. 2012); Lambda filed *Sevcik v. Sandoval* in April 2012; *Gill v. Office of Personnel Management,* 682 F.3d 1 (1st Cir. 2012); *Massachusetts v. U.S. Department of Health and Human Services,* 682 F.3d 1 (1st Cir. 2012).

41   Basil Katz, "Defense of Marriage Act Unconstitutional: Judge," Reuters, Jun. 5, 2012.

42   *Windsor v. United States,* 833 F. Supp. 2d 394 (S.D.N.Y. 2012); *Pedersen v. Office of Personnel Management,* 881 F. Supp. 2d 294, 333 (D. Conn. 2012).

43   *Windsor v. United States,* 699 F.3d 169 (2nd Cir. 2012). Connecticut's high court already had applied heightened scrutiny. See *Kerrigan v. Commissioner of Public Health,* 957 A.2d 407 (Conn. 2008).

44   Richard Wolf, "Supreme Court to Take Up Same-Sex Marriage," *USA Today,* Dec. 7, 2012.

45   Noah Hurowitz, "Portland Lawyer Mary Bonauto Credited as 'Mastermind' Behind Landmark Gay Rights Court Cases," *Bangor Daily News,* Mar. 30, 2013.

46   Becker, "How the President Got to 'I Do.'"

47   Joan Biskupic, "Insight: Lawyers in Gay Marriage Cases Aim Pitches at Obama," Reuters, Jan. 27, 2013.

48   Becker, "How the President Got to 'I Do.'"

49   Ibid.

50   *Brief of Dennis Hollingsworth et al. v. Kristin M. Perry et al.* No. 12-144 (9th Cir. 2013).

51   On the impact of public pressure by LGBTQ activists, see Frank, "President's Pleasant Surprise"; Eleveld, *Don't Tell Me to Wait.*

14. "LOVE SURVIVES DEATH"

1   Bill Clinton, "Bill Clinton: It's Time to Overturn DOMA," *Washington Post,* Mar. 7, 2013; Peter Baker, "Now in Defense of Gay Marriage, Bill Clinton," *New York Times,* Mar. 23, 2013.

2   For oral arguments, see Transcript of Oral Argument, *Hollingsworth v. Perry,* 133 S. Ct. 2652 (2013) (No. 12-144).

3   For oral arguments, see Transcript of Oral Argument, *United States v. Windsor,* 133 S. Ct. 2675 (2013) (No. 12-307).

4   Garance Franke-Ruta, "The Jaw-Dropping Reason Congress Drafted DOMA: 'Moral Disapproval of Homosexuality,'" *Atlantic,* Mar. 27, 2013.

5   Joseph Ax, "Octogenarian Lesbian Widow Gets Her Day in Supreme Court," Reuters, Mar. 27, 2013.

6   "Bachmann Threatens to Leave Minnesota over Marriage Equality," *Daily Current,* May 13, 2013.

7   Crosby Burns and Joshua Field, "Marriage Equality and the Supreme Court: A Guide to What Is at Stake in Upcoming Rulings," Center for American Progress, Jun. 10, 2013.

8   Philip Bump, "What Overturning Interracial Marriage Bans Might Tell Us About What Happens Next With Gay Marriage," *Washington Post,* Oct. 6, 2014.

9   Jo Becker, *Forcing the Spring: Inside the Fight for Marriage Equality* (New York: Penguin Press, 2014), 240; Jeremy W. Peters, "Olson and Boies, Legal Duo, Seek Role in 2 Cases on Gay Marriage," *New York Times,* Feb. 3, 2014; David Boies and Theodore B. Olson, *Redeeming the Dream: The Case for Marriage Equality* (New York: Penguin Press, 2014), 288–299.

10 *United States v. Windsor,* 133 S. Ct. 2675, 570 US 12, 186 L. Ed. 2d 808 (2013); *Lawrence v. Texas,* 539 U.S. 558, 123 S. Ct. 2472, 156 L. Ed. 2d 508 (2003).

11 *United States v. Windsor* (2013).

12 Ariel Levy, "The Perfect Wife," *New Yorker,* Sept. 30, 2013; author interview with Edie Windsor.

13 "DOMA Decision Rankles Some Republican Lawmakers," *NPR News* (transcript), Jun. 26, 2013.

14 *United States v. Windsor* (2013).

15 The earliest lawsuits after *Windsor* include *Whitewood v. Wolf* in Pennsylvania, brought by the ACLU on July 9; *Wright v. Smith* in Arkansas, brought privately on July 15; *Robicheaux v. Caldwell,* brought privately in Louisiana on July 16; *Bostic v. Schaefer* and *Harris v. McDonnell* in Virginia, brought privately on July 18 *(Bostic)* and by Lambda and ACLU *(Harris)* on August 1; *Obergefell v. Kasich.*

16 Richard Wolf, "Virginia Gay Couples Seek Marriage Case That Could Reach U.S. Supreme Court," *Huffington Post,* Dec. 13, 2013.

17 New Jersey Civil Union Review Commission, "The Legal, Medical, Economic, and Social Consequences of New Jersey's Civil Union Law," Dec. 10, 2008, http://www.state.nj.us/oag/dcr/downloads/CURC-Final-Report-.pdf.

18 "N.J. Gov. Christie Vetoes Gay Marriage Bill as Vowed," *USA Today,* Feb. 17, 2012.

19 *Garden State Equality v. Dow,* 82 A. 3d 336 (N.J. Super. Ct. Law Div., 2013).

20 *Garden State Equality v. Dow,* 79 A. 3d 1036 (N.J., 2013).

21 ("MEA"), Act 1 (S.B. 1), Laws 2013, 2d Sp. Sess.; Haw. Rev. Stat. §572–1 (2013).

22 "Illinois Governor Signs Same-Sex Marriage Into Law," *USA Today,* Nov. 20, 2013; Richard Socarides, "What Happened to Gay Marriage in Illinois?" *New Yorker,* Jun. 3, 2013; Monique Garcia and Clout Street, "Quinn Signs Illinois Gay Marriage Bill," *Chicago Tribune,* Nov. 11, 2013; for a thorough look at the "insider-outsider" effort to secure marriage equality in Illinois, see Kate Sosin and Tracy Baim, *The Fight for Marriage Equality in the Land of Lincoln* (Chicago: Windy City Media Group, 2014).

23 "Illinois Governor"; Sosin and Baim, *The Fight for Marriage Equality,* 205–206. On half the population, see Joanna Grossman, "Hawaii Comes Full Circle on Same-Sex Marriage," *Verdict,* Nov. 15, 2013, https://verdict.justia.com/2013/11/15/hawaii-comes-full-circle-sex-marriage.

24 *Griego v. Oliver,* 316 P. 3d 865 (2013).

25 Brooke Adams, "Meet the Man Behind Utah's Same-Sex Marriage Lawsuit," *Salt Lake Tribune,* Jan. 10, 2014; "Restore Our Humanity Founder Mark Lawrence," *Gay Salt Lake,* Jan. 16, 2014; author interview with Shannon Minter.

26   Author interview with Kate Kendell; author interview with Minter.

27   *Kitchen v. Herbert,* 961 F. Supp. 2d 1181 (2013).

28   Ibid.

29   Ibid.

30   Associated Press, "Utah Ruling Back in Court," *Politico,* Dec. 20, 2013.

31   Author interview with Al Gerhardstein.

32   *Obergefell v. Kasich,* No. 1:13-CV-501 2013 WL 3814262 (S.D. Ohio July 22, 2013) (preliminary injunction, July 22, 2013); Amanda Lee Myers, "Ohio Gay Couple's Marriage Must Be Recognized in State, Judge Rules," *Huffington Post,* Jul. 23, 2013.

33   *Obergefell v. Wymyslo,* 962 F. Supp. 2d 968 (S.D. Ohio 2013); July temporary restraining order is also at https://casetext.com/case/obergefell-v-kasich. See also Lyle Denniston, "Windsor Expanded in Ohio Ruling," *SCOTUSblog* (blog), Dec. 24, 2013.

15. "THE RESPONSIBILITY TO RIGHT FUNDAMENTAL WRONGS"

1   Katy Burns, "Gay Marriage: An American Success Story," *Concord Monitor,* Dec. 29, 2013.

2   Amanda Lee Myers, "Four Gay Couples Sue to Force Ohio's Hand on Same-Sex Marriage," *LGBTQ Nation,* Feb. 10, 2014; Susan Sommer, *"Obergefell v. Hodges*—A Leap of Love," in *Love Unites Us: Winning the Freedom to Marry in America,* ed. Kevin Cathcart and Leslie Gabel-Brett (New York: New Press, 2016), 268–281.

3   Eyder Peralta, "Federal Judge Strikes Down Oklahoma Ban on Gay Marriage," NPR, Jan. 14, 2014.

4   Ann Bowdan, "Louisville Couple Challenges State's Same-Sex Marriage Ban," WLKY (Louisville, KY), Jul. 26, 2013.

5   *Bourke v. Beshear,* 996 F. Supp. 2d 542 (2014).

6   Author interview with Dan Canon; "Same-Sex Marriage in Kentucky over the Last Two Years," Fauver Law Office, Louisville, KY, July 26, 2015, www.fauverlaw.com/News-Events/same-sex-marriage-in-Kentucky-over-the-last-two-years; Andrew Wolfson, "Couples Ask Judge to Allow Gay Marriages in Kentucky," *USA Today,* Feb. 14, 2014.

7   Michael A. Lindenberger, "Kentucky's Attorney General Explains Why He Won't Defend Gay Marriage Ban," *Time,* Mar. 4, 2014.

8   Trip Gabriel, "Kentucky Law Official Will Not Defend Ban On Same-Sex Marriage," *New York Times,* Mar. 4, 2014. This source appears to count the two California officials as one.

9   *Bourke v. Beshear* (2014); *Love v. Beshear,* 989 F. Supp. 2d 536 (2014).

10   For a helpful analysis of the powerful impact of *Windsor* on district-level decisions, see Ryan Goellner, "Obergefell, Bourke, and 'Fundamental Rights': Gradually
Bringing Same-Sex Marriage to Ohio and Kentucky" (blog), May 22, 2014, https://
uclawreview.org/2014/05/22/obergefell-bourke-and-fundamental-rights-gradually
-bringing-same-sex-marriage-to-ohio-and-kentucky/. Goellner writes that district
court judges in Ohio and Kentucky "not only utilized the constitutional momentum
generated by *Windsor* to chip away at and severely curtail those amendments prohibiting same-sex marriage, but also essentially invited the Sixth Circuit to review their
respective decisions and to reexamine its own jurisprudence on sexual orientation
in light of *Windsor."* He further writes that "Justice Kennedy's majority opinion in
Windsor featured prominently in the Kentucky district court's order, and the court
simply reproduced many passages from *Windsor,* substituting 'Kentucky' for 'United
States' to drive *Bourke* to the same conclusion as *Windsor."*

11   Bill Sizemore, "Va. Beach Lawyer in Gay Rights Case Finds His Calling,"
Virginian-Pilot, Apr. 21, 2014.

12   *Bostic v. Rainey,* 970 F. Supp. 2d 456, 484 (E.D. Va. 2014).

13   *Bostic v. Schaefer,* 760 F.3d 352 (4th Cir. 2014); Chris Geidner, "In the Fight for Marriage Equality, a Battle to See Who Will Make It Happen," *Buzzfeed,* Oct. 17, 2013.

14   By June 2015, more voters in Texas would support marriage equality than oppose
it. See Ross Ramsey, "UT / TT Poll: Texans Divided on Gay Marriage," *Texas Tribune,*
June 24, 2015.

15   *Tanco v. Haslam,* 7 F. Supp. 3d 759 (2014).

16   Author interview with Shannon Minter.

17   Roger Hagy, College of Law, University of Tennessee at Knoxville, "Inevitable,"
December 1, 2014, http://law.utk.edu/2014/12/01/inevitable; "Nashville Attorney to
Move Quickly on Gay Rights," Tennessee Bar Association, June 27, 2013, www.tba.org
/news/nashville-attorney-to-move-quickly-on-gay-rights; author interview with Abby
Rubenfeld; author interview with Minter; author interview with Kate Kendell.

18   *DeBoer v. Snyder,* 2:12-cv-10285-BAF-MJH (E.D. Mich. 2012), 1; Nina Totenberg,
"Meet the 'Accidental Activists' of the Supreme Court's Same-Sex-Marriage Case," *All
Things Considered* (NPR, transcript), Apr. 20, 2015.

19   Author interview with Dana Nessel.

20   Ibid.

21   Steve Friess, "For Lawyers, a Rocky Walk Down the Gay Marriage Aisle," *Bloomberg,* Jan. 28, 2015.

22   Author interview with Nessel; Friess, "For Lawyers." The trial order is
contained in the judge's denial of request for summary judgment, Oct. 16, 2013

(2:12-cv-10285-BAF-MJH), http://media.mlive.com/news/detroit_impact/other/Request%20for%20summary%20judgement%20denied.pdf. Article with "battle of the experts" quote in court: Gus Burns, "Read Judge Friedman's Order for Trial Before Gay-Marriage Ruling," MLive, Oct. 16, 2013.

23 Transcript of Oral Argument, *Deboer v. Snyder,* 973 F. Supp. 2d 757 (E.D. Mich. Mar. 21, 2014) (No. 12-10285).

24 Erik Eckholm, "Opponents of Same-Sex Marriage Take Bad-for-Children Argument to Court," *New York Times,* Feb. 23, 2014; Steve Friess, "The Same-Sex Marriage Trial You Don't Know About Just Came to a Close," *Buzzfeed,* Mar. 7, 2014.

25 Tresa Baldas, "State's Last Witness Says Unrepentant Homosexuals Are Going to Hell," *Detroit Free Press,* Mar. 6, 2014; Corey Williams, "Judge: Gay Marriage Trial Ruling Within 2 Weeks," *Washington Times,* Mar. 7, 2014.

26 *DeBoer v. Snyder,* 973 F. Supp. 2d 757 (E.D. Mich. 2014).

27 *Geiger v. Kitzhaber,* 994 F. Supp. 2d 1128 (2014).

28 Ibid.

29 Adam Liptak, "Sexual Orientation Is No Basis for Jury Exclusion, A Federal Appeals Court Rules," *New York Times,* Jan. 22, 2014.

30 "State's Answer and Affirmative Defenses to Amended Complaint," *Rummel v. Kitzhaber,* No. 6:13-cv-02256-MC (D. Ore. filed Feb. 20, 2014); Karen Gullo, "Oregon Attorney General Won't Defend Gay-Marriage Ban," *Bloomberg,* Feb. 20, 2014.

31 *Whitewood v. Wolf,* 992 F. Supp. 2d 410 (M.D. Pa. May 20, 2014).

32 Trip Gabriel, "Pennsylvania Governor Won't Fight Ruling That Allows Gay Marriage," *New York Times,* May 22, 2014.

33 Mark Scolforo, "Tom Corbett, Pennsylvania GOP Governor, Compares Gay Marriage to Incest," *Huffington Post,* Oct. 4, 2013.

34 *Whitewood v. Wolf* (2014).

35 Campbell Robertson, "Federal Judge, Bucking Trend, Affirms Ban on Same-Sex Marriages in Louisiana," *New York Times,* Sept. 4, 2014. The twenty-one wins included those in district and circuit level courts. Wolfson told the *Washington Post* that gay advocates have won "nearly all of the 40 state and federal marriage cases this year"; see Cheryl Wetzstein, "Federal Judge In Louisiana Breaks Gay Marriage Winning Streak," *Washington Post,* Sept. 3, 2014.

36 Chris Geidner, "How One Lawyer Turned the Idea of Marriage Equality into Reality," *Buzzfeed,* Nov. 17, 2013; *Kitchen v. Herbert,* 755 F.3d 1193 (10th Cir. 2014).

37 *Kitchen v. Herbert* (2014); *Bishop v. Smith,* 760 F.3d 1070 (10th Cir. 2014).

38 *Bostic v. Schaefer* (2014); Robert Barnes and Jenna Portnoy, "Appeals Court Upholds Decision Overturning Virginia's Same-Sex Marriage Ban," *Washington Post,* Jul. 28, 2014; Michael K. Lavers, "Court Allows LGBT Groups to Join Va. Marriage Lawsuit," *Washington Blade,* Mar. 10, 2014; Adam Serwer, "Divided Panel Hears Virginia Case for—and Against—Gay Marriage," MSNBC, May 13, 2014.

39 Lawrence Hurley, "U.S. Supreme Court Puts Hold on Gay Marriage in Virginia," Reuters, Aug. 20, 2014.

40 *Wolf v. Walker,* 986 F. Supp. 2d 982, 1028 (W.D. Wis. 2014).

41 Adam Liptak, "Supreme Court Delivers Tacit Win to Gay Marriage," *New York Times,* Oct. 6, 2014.

42 David Crary, "Ginsburg Questions 1973 Abortion Ruling's Timing," Associated Press, Feb. 10, 2012; Jeffrey Toobin, "Heavyweight: How Ruth Bader Ginsburg Has Moved the Supreme Court," *New Yorker,* Mar. 11, 2013.

43 Liptak, "Supreme Court Delivers Tacit Win."

44 Chris Geidner, "Cert. Denied, Stays Denied, Marriage Equality Advanced: How the Supreme Court Used Nonprecedential Orders to Diminish the Drama of the Marriage Equality Decision," *Ohio State Law Journal Furthermore* 76 (2015): 161–172.

45 *DeBoer v. Snyder,* 772 F.3d 388 (6th Cir. 2014).

46 On fifty rulings, see "MOMENTUM IN KY: Circuit Judge in Kentucky Rules in Favor of Freedom to Marry" (blog), Apr. 17, 2015, www.freedomtomarry.org/blog /entry/momentum-in-ky-circuit-judge-in-kentucky-rules-in-favor-of-freedom-to-.

16. "IT IS SO ORDERED"

1 Chris Johnson, "ACLU Opposes DOMA Lawyer's Intervention in Marriage Case," *Washington Blade,* May 5, 2014. ACLU joined the *Obergefell* case in April 2014. Kaplan also sought to intervene in the *Kitchen v. Herbert* case in Utah.

2 Michael K. Lavers, "AFER Paid Law Firms More than $6.4 Million in Prop 8 Case," *Washington Blade,* Mar. 20, 2014; Michelangelo Signorile, "Five (or So) Questions I Put to Superlawyer Ted Olson About Gay Marriage and Prop 8," *Huffington Post,* June 23, 2014; Jeremy W. Peters, "Olson and Boies, Legal Duo, Seek Role in 2 Cases on Gay Marriage," *New York Times,* Feb. 3, 2014; author interview with Kate Kendell.

3 Peters, "Olson and Boies, Legal Duo"; author interview with Kendell.

4 Author interview with Jon Davidson.

5 Jacob Ryan, "Stanford Law Attorney, ACLU Join Kentucky Plaintiffs' Team in Same-Sex Marriage Case," WKMS.org, Dec. 24, 2014.

6   Steve Friess, "For Lawyers, a Rocky Walk down the Gay Marriage Aisle," *Bloomberg Politics,* Jan. 28, 2015.

7   Author interview with Dan Canon.

8   This account of how the oralists were chosen to argue before the Supreme Court is taken from interviews with the following, as well as interviews with anonymous sources who shared their recollections of the deliberations: Mary Bonauto, Dan Canon, Jon Davidson, James Esseks, Al Gerhardstein, Kate Kendell, Shannon Minter, Dana Nessel and Abby Rubenfeld. It also draws from the following sources: Marcia Coyle and Tony Mauro, "Lawyers Strategize over Who Will Argue Marriage Cases at Supreme Court," *Fulton County Daily Report,* Jan. 29, 2015; Marcia Coyle and Tony Mauro, "Marriage-Rights Advocates at Odds Over Who Will Argue Cases," *National Law Journal,* Mar. 26, 2015; Joan Biskupic, "U.S. Gay Rights Advocates Near Decision on Top Lawyers for Landmark Case," Reuters, Mar. 30, 2015; Chris Geidner, "Marriage Advocates Set for Supreme Court Arguments on April 28," *Buzzfeed,* Mar. 31, 2015; David G. Savage, "Democratic National Convention Live Updates: Bill Clinton Speaking After His Wife Was Nominated," *Los Angeles Times,* Jul. 26, 2016.

9   For oral arguments, see Transcript of Oral Argument, *Obergefell v. Hodges,* 135 S. Ct. 2584 (2015) (No. 14-556); Ruthann Robson, "Guide to the Amicus Briefs in *Obergefell v. Hodges*: The Same-Sex Marriage Cases," *Constitutional Law Prof Blog* (blog), Apr. 16, 2015, http://lawprofessors.typepad.com/conlaw/2015/04/guide-to-amicus-briefs-in -obergefell-v-hodges-the-same-sex-marriage-cases.html.

10   *Obergefell v. Hodges,* 2015 WL 213646 (U.S. April 28, 2015) (transcript of oral arguments).

11   The historian John Boswell posited in *Christianity, Social Tolerance, and Homosexuality* (Chicago: University of Chicago Press, 1981) that same-sex unions have enjoyed the same social and sometimes legal recognition as marriages in various cultures throughout history. His arguments faced heavy criticism, and most scholars today view his book as overstating the extent to which same-sex couples could actually marry in premodern cultures. However, given that marriage as a legal status was often far less formal in earlier cultures, the evidence Boswell marshaled for historic examples of same-sex marriages is suggestive enough that it should give pause to the declarations by the justices that the twenty-first century was the first ever to allow them.

12   Whether lack of familiarity or outright animus spurred legislatures to ban gay marriage, the effect was the same, and the laws were, in the view of many scholars, equally unconstitutional. Kenji Yoshino of New York University has argued that, based on Supreme Court precedent, "even when state institutions are not *created* with discriminatory intent, they can be *maintained* with such intent in a manner that renders them constitutionally invalid." See Kenji Yoshino, "Justices' Questions, Answered," *Slate,* Apr. 24, 2015.

13   *Obergefell v. Hodges,* 135 S. Ct. 2071 (2015).

14   On Kennedy's judicial philosophy, see Frank Colucci, *Justice Kennedy's Jurisprudence: The Full and Necessary Meaning of Liberty* (Lawrence: University Press of Kansas, 2009).

EPILOGUE

1   Author interview with Mary Bonauto.

2   Ibid.

3   Richard Wolf and Brad Heath, "Supreme Court Gives Big Boost to Same-Sex Marriage," *USA Today,* Jun. 27, 2013.

4   Baldwin quote is in Kristen H. Carroll, "Tammy Baldwin, Our Voice of the Future," *Huffington Post,* Nov. 7, 2012.

5   Roberta Kaplan, *Then Comes Marriage:* United States v. Windsor *and the Defeat of DOMA* (New York: W. W. Norton, 2015), 322.

6   Marriage Equality USA. "MEUSA Interview with Edie Windsor (Part 3): A Marriage Equality Legacy," YouTube video, 10:09, Jul. 24, 2014, https://youtu.be/rmoEjm-ropM.

7   Nancy Polikoff and Katherine Franke were among the most respected scholars to maintain a steadfast critique of marriage. See Nancy D. Polikoff and Michael Bronski, *Beyond (Straight and Gay) Marriage: Valuing All Families Under the Law* (Boston: Beacon Press, 2009); Katherine Franke, *Wedlocked: The Perils of Marriage Equality,* Sexual Cultures series (New York: New York University Press, 2015); for an example of a feminist marriage critic who later reconciled her critique with marriage equality, see Barbara Cox, "Marriage Equality Is Both Feminist and Progressive," *Richmond Journal of Law and the Public Interest* 707 (2014): 707–738.

8   *Obergefell v. Hodges,* 135 S. Ct. 2071 (2015).

9   Author interview with Paula Ettelbrick.

10   Author interview with Matt Coles.

11   Kathy Belge, "Kate Kendell—Lesbian Activist," About.com, http://lesbianlife.about.com/od/activistspoliticians/a/KateKendell.htm.

12   On the fastest-changing social issue, see Pew Research Center, "Growing Support for Gay Marriage: Changed Minds and Changing Demographics," Mar. 20, 2013. On 61 percent support for marriage equality, see Gallup, "Marriage," www.gallup.com/poll/117328/marriage.aspx. Results, of course, vary across polls, and Pew put the figure at 55 percent; see "Changing Attitudes on Gay Marriage," Pew Research Center, May 12, 2016. On between 11 and 23 percent support for marriage, see Michael Klarman, *From the Closet to the Altar: Courts, Backlash, and the Struggle for Same-Sex Marriage* (Oxford: Oxford University Press, 2003), 45; On 60 percent moral

acceptability, see "Birth Control, Divorce Top List of Morally Acceptable Issues," Gallup, Jun. 8, 2016, www.gallup.com/poll/192404/birth-control-divorce-top-list-morally-acceptable-issues.aspx; on 21 percent moral acceptability, see John Balzar, "The Times Poll: American Views of Gays: Disapproval, Sympathy," *Los Angeles Times,* Dec. 20, 1985. The 21 percent figure was largely unchanged since 1973.

13 It also sheds light on a long-standing debate over whether court rulings and policy changes create parallel changes in attitudes and beliefs or instead prompt backlashes against the change. It is of course true that the long fight over marriage equality saw several instances of backlash, such as federal and state defense-of-marriage legislation, as well as efforts to amend state constitutions between 1998 and 2012. Yet the Williams research together with the relatively fast pace of marriage equality legalization, as well as the increase between 1993 and 2016 in public approval of both gay marriage and of gays and lesbians generally, offer more evidence that the LGBTQ movement's eventual embrace of marriage as a priority was an effective way to familiarize Americans with gay people and reduce anti-gay animus. See Nate Silver, "Change Doesn't Usually Come This Fast," *Fivethirtyeight.com,* Jun. 26, 2015; Andrew Flores and Scott Barclay, "Backlash, Consensus, Legitimacy, or Polarization," *Political Research Quarterly* 69 (2016): 43–56; Andrew Flores and Scott Barclay, "Trends In Public Support for Same-Sex Couples by States" (white paper), Williams Institute, UCLA, Apr. 2015, http://williamsinstitute.law.ucla.edu/wp-content/uploads/Trends-in-Public-Support-for-Same-Sex-Marriage-2004–2014.pdf.

14 Robert Andersen and Tina Fetner, "Cohort Differences in Tolerance of Homosexuality," *Public Opinion Quarterly* 72 (2008): 311–330; Pew Research Center, "Growing Support for Gay Marriage"; Nate Silver, "How Opinion on Same-Sex Marriage Is Changing, and What It Means," *FiveThirtyEight* (blog), *New York Times,* Mar. 26, 2013; Silver, "Change Doesn't Usually Come."

15 Pew Research Center, "Growing Support for Gay Marriage."

16 David Ferguson, "Ruth Bader Ginsburg Tips Her Hand: Same-Sex Marriage Is Coming, So Get Used to It," *Raw Story,* Feb. 12, 2015; Joseph Ax, "Octogenarian Lesbian Widow Gets Her Day In Supreme Court," Reuters, Mar. 27, 2013.

17 Marc Solomon, *Winning Marriage: The Inside Story of How Same-Sex Couples Took on the Politicians and Pundits—and Won* (Lebanon, NH: ForeEdge, 2014), 139–146.

18 Gay, Lesbian, Bisexual and Transgender News Network, "Change of Heart: Prop 8 Defense Attorney Planning Lesbian Step-Daughter's Wedding," San Diego Lesbian and Gay News, Apr. 17, 2014, http://sdgln.com/news/2014/04/17/change-heart-prop-8-defense-attorney-planning-lesbian-step-daughters-wedding.

19 Sasha Issenberg, "With These Words," *New Yorker,* July 27, 2012.

20 Chris Kirk and Hanna Rosin, "Does Gay Marriage Destroy Marriage?" *Slate,* May 23, 2012.

21 Darren Samuelsohn, "Biden: Gay Activists 'Freeing the Soul of the American People,'" *Politico,* Aug. 26, 2012; Associated Press, "Biden: Businesses Should Do More on LGBT Rights," YouTube video, 2:47, Jan. 20, 2016, https://youtu.be/2BjyDt9_g3A.

22 "Transcript: Michelle Obama's Convention Speech," NPR, Sept. 4, 2012.

23 See, for instance, Cox, "Marriage Equality."

24 See, for instance, Sharon Otterman, "A Complex Case Tests New York State's Expanded Definition of Parenthood," *New York Times,* Oct. 18, 2016; Douglas Ne-Jaime, "Marriage Equality and the New Parenthood," *Harvard Law Review* 129 (2016): 1187–1266.

25 E. J. Graff, "Retying the Knot," *The Nation,* Jun. 24, 1996.

26 Nate Schweber, "Evan Wolfson and Cheng He," *New York Times,* Oct. 21, 2011.

27 Andrew Sullivan, "Andrew Sullivan: Why Gay Marriage Is Good for America," *Newsweek,* Jul. 18, 2011.

28 "United States Government says L.A. Gay Couple's 1975 Marriage is Valid," *The Pride LA,* Jun. 7, 2016.

29 Chris Johnson, "One Year After Marriage Ruling, Pockets of Defiance Remain," *Washington Blade,* Jun. 22, 2016.

30 Ashley Fantz, "Mississippi Measures Have Companions Elsewhere in U.S.," CNN, Apr. 7, 2016.

31 GLAAD, "Accelerating Acceptance" (report), 2016, http://www.glaad.org/files/2016_GLAAD_Accelerating_Acceptance.pdf.

32 Author interview with Josh Friedes; Eddie Rosenstein, *The Freedom to Marry,* directed by Eddie Rosenstein (Brooklyn, NY: Eyepop Productions, 2016).

Acknowledgments

Just as the marriage equality movement stands on the shoulders of the countless social change advocates who came before it, the act of writing about such a movement, particularly one whose history is so recent, is only possible by incurring enormous intellectual debts. I owe thanks, first of all, to the scholars, journalists, and other writers whose sharp analysis, dogged reporting, and humane and often courageous chronicling of the lives of LGBTQ Americans helped the world to truly see those who were too long ignored or misunderstood. Specific credits appear in the book's notes, but a few names deserve special recognition for the quality, volume, or impact of work they produced that helped me tell this story: George Chauncey, John D'Emilio, Kerry Eleveld, Chris Geidner, E. J. Graff, Charles Kaiser, Marc Solomon, Rex Wockner, and Kenji Yoshino.

Several scholars, legal experts, movement strategists, and generally sharp thinkers read versions or sections of the manuscript or thought through vital substantive issues with me, offering invaluable input that was, in some cases, shared across many hours of fruitful conversation: Emily Bazelon, Aaron Belkin, Marie-Amelie George, Andrew Lane, Anna Lvovsky, Douglas NeJaime, and Amy Widman. Special thanks are due to my uncle, Bill Rosenblum, for reading the manuscript so thoroughly and giving me so many helpful suggestions. My intrepid research assistant, Ali Talan, saved me from missing many a deadline with quick turnarounds on research briefs and lengthy legal citations that I dreaded looking up myself. David Lobenstine, a friend, advisor, and terrific editor, was instrumental in helping me figure out what I was actually trying to say in the book's early chapters. I also thank June Thomas and the editors and readers of *Slate* for the opportunity to sound out some of the main themes and ideas in this book.

At Harvard University Press, my editor, Thomas LeBien, ably steered the book to completion and always knew how to coax me to improve my writing without forcing me to start from square one. I thank Brian Distelberg for helping conceive of the project and for his thoughtful early guidance on the manuscript. I am also grateful to Sue Warga and Kim Giambattisto, whose rigorous copyediting improved the manuscript immeasurably.

On the home front, my parents, John and Elaine Frank, not only offered years of enthusiasm for my work and support of a thousand kinds, but instilled in me an intellectual curiosity that has been essential for doing that work and has, I hope, helped infuse it with the empathy and humanity that good history requires. Their marriage has shown me, indelibly, what it truly means to belong. And on that note: how do I even begin to thank my husband, Dominick Mach? A tireless cheerleader in his unique way, he constantly intoned "Back to work!" while somehow not seeming like he was just trying to have the TV room to himself. He once actually tied me to my desk chair to force me to focus on my work. Through it all, he has shown me, first-hand and in the best way possible, what it really means to be a husband—indeed, why all of this matters.

My greatest debt is to the subjects of this remarkable story. It seems fruitless to thank millions of people at once, but every American who came out made things easier for those who followed, helping gay, lesbian, bisexual, transgender, and queer people step closer to justice. My final thanks go, specifically, to the movement leaders, activists, and other participants who spent time speaking with me, fielded repeated queries about historical, legal, and political matters, and trusted me to bear witness to their efforts to build a world where people could live freely, love freely, and be who they are.

ILLUSTRATION CREDITS

Index

Abercrombie, Neil, 109, 304

The Abolition of Marriage (Gallagher), 162

Abortion, 45, 103, 165, 177, 180, 194, 332

Adams, John, 81

Adams, Richard, 41, 365, 366

Ad-Hoc Task Force to Challenge Sodomy Laws, 60–61

Advocate (newspaper), 41, 83, 166–167, 168

African Americans, 18, 22, 28–29, 161, 259, 269, 273, 284; support for Proposition 8, 182–183, 194

AIDS: discrimination against people with, 62–64; gay activism and, 59, 64–66, 360; gays and lesbians uniting to combat, 249–250; relationship recognition and, 75

AIDS Coalition to Unleash Power (ACT UP), 66, 72, 97

AIDS Memorial Quilt, 65–66

AIDS Project LA, 65

Alabama: federal court striking down gay marriage ban in, 343; resistance to *Obergefell v. Hodges,* 366–367

Alaska: marriage lawsuit in, 126–127; state amendment prohibiting same-sex marriage, 118

Alesi, Jim, 266

Alito, Samuel, 303, 345–346, 348

Allen, Arenda Wright, 318, 330

Allen, Douglas, 325–326

Alliance for Marriage (AFM), 161

Allred, Gloria, 158

Altman, Brad, 179

Amendment 2 (Colorado), 115–118, 170

AMERICAblog, 197, 200, 257

American Bar Association, 101, 135

American Civil Liberties Union (ACLU), 376n27; attitude to marriage equality, 98; *Baker v. Nelson* and, 41; *Bostic* case and, 318, 337, 338; *Braschi v. Stahl* and, 74; challenge to marriage discrimination in Pennsylvania, 303; challenge to marriage laws in Hawaii and, 92–93; challenge to sodomy bans, 60, 67–68; declining to defend gay people, 27;

discrimination against AIDS patients and, 64; Kaplan and, 252; lawsuit challenging Proposition 8 and, 226–227, 228, 231–232; *Obergefell v. Hodges* and, 335; response to suits against Newsom marriages, 158; *Windsor* case and, 254–255; work with Task Force and Lambda, 38

American Family Association, 104

American Foundation for Equal Rights (AFER), 263, 293, 318, 335; *Perry v. Schwarzenegger* and, 224–232, 248

American Psychiatric Association (APA), 17, 19, 37

American Psychological Association, 135

American Values, 163

Amicus briefs: *DeBoer v. Snyder,* 323; *Hollingsworth v. Perry,* 290, 291–293; *Lawrence v. Texas,* 135; *Obergefell v. Hodges,* 342; *Windsor* case, 272, 289–290

Analyst Institute, 282

Anti-discrimination ordinances, towns and cities, 37, 46

Anti-gay discrimination: criminalization of gay life and, 19; gay visibility and, 52; history of, 240; overt homosexuality and, 15

Anti-gay ideology, 15

Anti-gay initiatives on state ballots, 164–165

Anti-gay stereotypes, 48

Aravosis, John, 197–198, 200, 201–202, 257

Arcus Foundation, 171

Arizona: 2012 ballot contest, 283; defeat of constitutional amendment, 174

Arkansas, striking down gay marriage ban in, 328

Arkes, Hadley, 161

Arlington Group, 163

Arthur, John, 309–310, 311, 317, 332

Assimilation, 2–3, 6, 21, 28, 45, 59, 80, 82, 85, 87, 130, 365

Atlantic Monthly (magazine), 198

Avery, Sean, 266

Axelrod, David, 257, 274

Index

Index